# Masters of Illusion

THE WORLD BANK
AND THE POVERTY
OF NATIONS

## Catherine Caufield

PAN BOOKS

First published 1996 by Henry Holt and Company, Inc

First published in the UK 1997 by Macmillan

This edition published 1998 by Pan Books
an imprint of Macmillan Publishers Ltd
25 Eccleston Place, London SW1W 9NF
and Basingstoke

Associated companies throughout the world

ISBN 0 330 35321 7

9 8 7 6 5 4 3 2 1

A CIP catalogue record for this book is available
from the British Library.

Printed and bound in Great Britain by
Mackays of Chatham PLC, Chatham, Kent

THIS BOOK IS FOR CLC,
WHO WEARS HER COURAGE LIGHTLY

# Acknowledgments

I would like to express my thanks to the scores of Bank employees and consultants who helped me write this book. They were generous with their time, their insights, and their trust, and I have tried to reflect the idealism and dedication that I found in many of them. Unfortunately, I cannot thank them publicly because the Bank has always made it clear that, in the words of its current president, "externally voiced criticism of the Bank is an indication of a desire to find alternative employment." I have therefore named in the book only those Bank staffers who spoke to me in interviews arranged by the Bank's press office. This office is increasingly geared to what its internal memos call "news management" rather than to answering unscripted questions. Nonetheless its staff, notably Bill Brannigan, Shantal Persaud, and Tim Cullen, did their best to respond to my often recondite queries, and I thank them.

The many groups that monitor the Bank, lobby for its reform, and offer alternative visions of development in action have no need—and certainly no desire—for anonymity. Thus I can express my gratitude for the help given me by Livia de Tomasi of Ação Educativa; Cindy Buhl, Chad Dobson, Martha Hall, and Kay Treakle of the Bank Information Center; Nancy Alexander of Bread for the World; Anil Agarwal and Dan Nelson of the Center for Science and Environment in New Delhi; Paul Craig Roberts of the Center for Strategic and International Studies; Sonia Wright of Centro Luiz Freire; Jessica Woodroffe of Christian Aid; Doug and Steve Hellinger of the Development Group for Alternative Policies; Korinna Horta, Bruce Rich, and Stephen Schwartzman of the Environmental Defense Fund; Brent Blackwelder, Andrea Durbin, and Marijke Torfs of Friends of the Earth; Manisha Aryal and Kanak Mani Dixit of *Himal*; Ashish Kothari and Shekhar Singh of the Indian Institute of Public Administration; Owen Lammers, Juliette Majot, Patrick McCully, Glenn Switkes, Lori Udall, and Petra Yee of International Rivers network; Smitu Kothari of Lokayan; Shripad Dharmadhikary, Medha Patkar, and Himanshu Thakker of the Narmada Bachao Andalan; Lucy Mutumba Múyoyeta of Oxfam; David Hubbel and Grainné Ryder of the Project for Ecological Recovery; Patricia Adams and John Thibodeau of Probe International; and Madhu Kohli and Kavaljit Singh of the Public Interest Research Group.

Many individuals also kindly responded to my requests for interviews and provided me with valuable insights, information, and advice. Among them are Jayanta Bandyopadhyay, Hugh Brody, Patrick Coady, Clifford Cobb, Judy Coburn, Rajendra Dahal, Ajaya Dixit, Mohiuddin Farooque, Marilia Fonseca, Mary Fricker, Donald Gamble, Dipak Gyawali, Marc Herold, Michael Hudson, Benjamin King, Miloon Kothari, Arun Kumar, Nick Ludlow, Farhad Mazhar, Raymond Mikesell, Bradford Morse, Deepak Nayyar, Bikash Pandey, Vijay Paranjype, Stephen Pizzo, Allan Potkin, Sanjeev Pradash, Atiq Rahman, Bittu Sahgal, Jonathan Sanford, Thayer Scudder, Ali Sharif, Tasneem Siddiqui, Melanie Tannen, and Richard Webb.

I owe an even greater debt to those kind souls who offered me not only information but also hospitality during my travels. Sunil Roy and his family took me into their home. Balraj Maheshwari and Father Joseph of the Raj Pipla Social Services Society gave me a place to stay and accompanied me to parts of the Narmada Valley that the Indian authorities preferred I not visit; Grainné Ryder traveled with me through Thailand, helping me unravel the story of the Yanhee Dam; Imran Khan, Ahyam Nandoskar, and Rizwam Sheik of Bombay's National Unity Society helped me discover the many faces of Bombay's Dharavi, the world's largest slum—and a far richer place than that phrase suggests. Majibul Huq Dulu and Florence Durandin not only showed me the beautiful, besieged countryside of Bangladesh, but also turned their home into an infirmary for me.

Though their efforts were in vain, E. O. Wilson, W. S. Merwin, Diane Johnson, and Peter Matthiessen did their best to convince the Guggenheim Committee that this book was worthy of support, and I thank them very much for their encouragement. Donald Ross of the Joint Library of the

World Bank and the International Monetary Fund and Charles Ziegler of
the World Bank Archives were both very helpful. I am also very grateful to
the dedicated interviewers who have captured much of the Bank's history
on tape, especially to Robert Oliver. Jim Mokhiber scoured the Bank's
library for me when I could not be in Washington. I especially want to
thank Kerry Lauerman, who took a great weight off my shoulders by finding many of the documents, reports, and books I needed—some of them in
very strange places—and by wrestling various bits of computerized data to
the ground for me. I also thank Gill Coleridge and Joy Harris for their
mothering; Marian Wood for her enthusiasm; and Richard Kirschman for
his wholly inappropriate suggestion that I call the book *Piggybank*. I am
also grateful to Joe Kane and Peter Matthiessen for their comments on
early drafts and even more for the good humor with which they laid their
own work aside for a spot of gossip. My fellow members of the Society for
the Organization of Complex Materials, Whitney Chadwick, Mark Dowie,
Stephen Pizzo, and David Weir, gave me invaluable insights into the higher
uses of index cards and Post-it notes. Mark Dowie was not only a great
telephone pal throughout the writing of this book, he also found us our
new home and was, with Wendy Schwartz, a wonderfully welcoming
neighbor. Finally, I thank Phil Williams for, in addition to so much else, his
mastery of the art of constructive criticism.

One thing I deeply regretted in writing this book was that I could not
bring to public attention all that I witnessed during my research. Many
people went to great lengths to enable me to study various World Bank
projects—taking me to them, providing me with documents about them,
and introducing me to those affected by them. I will always remember with
deep admiration Nasiruddin Ahmed of the Indravati People's Movement
Committee, who, with his wonderful family, took me into his home and
then spent days escorting me around the Upper Indravati Valley so that I
could see for myself the devastating effects of the Bank-financed dam going
up there. Likewise, Avdesh Kumar and Madhu Kohli, who generously took
me into the nooks and crannies of India's Singrauli region, home to a huge
dam, five coal-fired power plants, and twelve massive open-pit coal mines.
These developments have displaced 300,000 people, many of whom have
been forced from their homes two, three, and even four times in succession.
Singrauli's air, water, and soil are grossly polluted and the area is full of
shantytowns populated by farming families no longer able to make a living
from the land and unemployed laborers brought into the region for short-
term construction jobs. The World Bank has been a major source of financing for Singrauli for twenty years and it is now lending another $1.2 billion

for the construction of six more enormous power plants in the region. Though I learned much from studying these and other Bank-financed development disasters—and though I feel a great debt to those victims who steeled themselves to tell me their stories—I could not include them all in this book if it was to be more than a catalogue of tragedies. However, I thank and will always remember gratefully all those who exposed their sufferings to a stranger who could do nothing for them.

When I began writing this book I asked the Bank to supply me with the names of the completed projects of which it was most proud. As I travelled, I wanted to be able to visit these as well as the many that had been brought to my attention by critics. I repeated my request on several occasions, always receiving the assurance that a list would be sent to me soon. The list, however, never materialized. Finally, only a few days before leaving on my first overseas research trip, to South Asia, I telephoned, once more, the Bank's press department and explained that I did not want to visit the Bank's largest client, India, without having the names of some successful projects. "Yes, yes, I'm sorry it's taken so long," said the official with whom I had been dealing. "I'll get back to you before you go." And, indeed, the day before I left, he called to say that the only name he had been able to pry out of the Bank's operational staff was the South Bassein Offshore Gas Development Project. No one in India to whom I spoke had heard of this project. When I returned, I discovered that its original name, and the one still in use in India, is the Bombay High Offshore Development Project. It is a large gas field in the Arabian Sea for which the Bank has made three loans, totalling $772 million. Through back channels, I obtained the Bank's report on the third phase of the project, which is described as having "greatly contributed to the economic development of India." Being offshore, it did not cause any resettlement problems, though it did take twice as long to complete as planned, and the Bank ultimately had to cancel more than a third of the loan "due to misprocurement."

# Contents

# MASTERS OF ILLUSION

# Prologue

It's not what you think of as a bank, the World Bank. It will take your money—and if you're a taxpayer in almost any country in the world, it already has. But don't go to its Washington, D.C., headquarters to make a withdrawal or apply for a loan because the World Bank lends only to governments. In fact it lends only to governments that can't borrow money elsewhere. It is the banker of last resort, offering loans to countries that are such poor credit risks that they cannot obtain capital on reasonable terms from private investors. Since 1946, the World Bank has lent more than a third of a trillion dollars to such countries.

The Bank's business is Third World development, an activity that might be described as the art—for it is certainly not a science—of improving life in the countries of Asia, Africa, and Latin America. What exactly constitutes improvement and how to achieve it have been matters of dispute for more than fifty years. But whatever development is, the World Bank is its leader.

The Bank is the biggest single lender to the Third World: It holds more than 11 percent of its long-term foreign debt, public and private. But the Bank does much more than lend money; to a great degree it also decides how its loans will be spent. It proposes, designs, and oversees the implementation of the projects it funds. It requires its borrowers to adopt the economic and other domestic policies it considers conducive to successful development. Moreover, it has enormous influence over the decisions of other funders to support or abandon a project—or a country.

The Bank is also the dominant influence in the so-called development community, which includes smaller regional development banks, other aid agencies, public and private, and academic economists and planners. The deference the Bank is accorded owes much to its vast experience of making loans and much also to the size of those loans.

The Bank works hard to keep its leadership position: It spends a great deal of money promulgating its development philosophy through its publications, through seminars and conferences, and through its own training institute for recipients of its loans. As a result, its view of development prevails both in discussion and in action. As Gustav Ranis, professor of international economics at Yale University, has written, "Other lenders, public and private, may carp, resent, at times criticize, and occasionally even deviate from Bank positions . . . but there is little question that the Bank dominates the scene in virtually every dimension."

That the Bank—created to fill a postwar need—has survived more than half a century of dramatic global economic and political changes is due largely to its ability to redefine itself. Among the personas it has adopted are those of a capitalist tool, a friend of big government, an international mediator, a force for industrialization, a voice for social justice, a hard-nosed financial institution, a coordinator of the global economy, a social services agency, and an advocate of private entrepreneurship.

These identities have in common the Bank's assertion that all would, in one way or another, improve the lot of the poor. Over the years, giving help to the poor has become an increasingly important aspect of the Bank's idea of itself. Poverty alleviation, at first seen merely as a desirable side effect of the Bank's lending, is now the central object of its existence.

Certainly the Bank, through its massive projects and its even more massive influence on government policies, has a great impact on poor people. But the Bank depends on and affects many other groups besides the poor. These include the international financial markets that have lent it hundreds of billions of dollars; the taxpayers who have guaranteed the repayment of those hundreds of billions; the rich-country politicians who engineer those guarantees; the poor-country governments whose continued borrowings are its reason for existing; the contractors and consultants who earn billions every year working on the projects it funds; the private banks with which it competes and cooperates; the international corporations that do business with its borrowers; the developing-country bureaucrats who work with it and who, if they are lucky, go to work for it; and last but not least, the ten thousand employees whose generous salaries it pays.

How the Bank serves these varied constituencies—how it, as the acknowledged leader in the field, practices development—is the subject of this book.

# One

They hadn't believed it at first, that the government was going to build a dam across the Narmada River. Obviously those surveyors and engineers hadn't seen the river in the monsoon, huge and powerful, surging through the canyons and across the plains. But the people of Gadher knew the power of the river. They had lived beside it, with it, for centuries. And even if it were possible to control such a force of nature, would anyone really dare to impound the most holy river in India? Shiva himself had named it Narmada, the "ever-delightful." As the old people say, you wash away all your sins by bathing seven times in the Yamuna or three times in the Saraswati or once in the Ganges, but the mere sight of the Narmada has the same effect!

Well, in the last few years they had seen the dam rising, and now they believed. There would be a dam, and the village of Gadher—along with hundreds of others like it—would be submerged. They had to move, and soon. It wouldn't be easy to find good land, especially with so many others looking at the same time, so it was fortunate that the government was helping them. The Land Purchase Committee had already found some land it thought the people of Gadher would like. With some trepidation, a group of men from the village went with the committee to look it over.

What they saw was a pleasant surprise. The soil was rich, there was water nearby, and the previous owners had planted lots of banana trees.

There was no forest, unfortunately—so it would be hard to find bamboo for building, fiber for rope, herbs for medicine, or fodder for the goats. And it was so flat! With no hills to hide behind, how would one find the privacy needed to perform the most basic functions? No, it certainly wasn't home. But then, home—Gadher—would soon be deep under water.

They were fortunate, they knew, to be offered a fertile plot. Nonetheless, it was strange buying land—not something they'd ever done. They were *adivasi,* the original dwellers. They lived and farmed where their parents and grandparents before them had lived and farmed. They had little money—hadn't had much need for it up to now—but the government had promised to pay them for the land they lost. They would get half in cash, and the government would use the rest to pay for their new land. Or so they understood. Actually, the government would only make a down payment on the land; they would have to pay the balance—in twenty interest-free annual installments—from what they could earn by selling their crops.

The officials who had brought them here were anxious to make a deal. They explained that the government would build a school and health clinic here, and put in roads, electricity, and a water pump. And because the men from Gadher liked what they saw, they agreed to sign the papers—well, not sign, because they couldn't read or write—but affix their thumbprints. They did so, and the officials congratulated them and said they were landowners now, and asked them how soon they could move. The men went back to Gadher to tell their families, and a few weeks later they were ready to go. There were about seventy of them, more than a tenth of the village—sad to quit their lifelong home, but hopeful, too. They understood that by forsaking the beloved land of their fathers they were ensuring a better future for their children.

Moving day came. The people loaded their belongings onto the government trucks and climbed aboard. After the convoy had traveled for an hour or so, the trucks stopped and the men jumped down, eager to show their families their new home. The first things they noticed were the corrugated tin huts, all close together in rows. With the hot sun beating on them, they weren't inviting, but they were only a temporary measure, to be replaced with wooden houses before too long. It was the land that mattered, and, as they looked around, it was the land that stunned them. There were no banana trees, there was no water; it was a wasteland! They walked around, confused, trying to orient themselves. They turned to the officials: This isn't the land you showed us. Oh, yes, came the reply. This is your land. Here are the deeds you signed.

No, no, no. It wasn't right. The villagers shook their heads. This is not it.

The officials looked at one another. Then one spoke in soothing tones. You're upset because you expected to see roads and schools—everything already in place. But you must understand, all that will take some time.

No, said the men. We were shown rich land; this land is useless. It is not what you offered us.

The man in charge sighed. Look here, he said. Just give it a chance. See if you can make it work. If you really aren't satisfied in a year or so, then we'll find you some new land.

What could they do? They stayed.

———

That was in 1990. The people of Gadher stayed at the Timbi resettlement site for two years, struggling to make the saline soil produce. By the time I got there, in April 1993, they had abandoned the place and moved back home. The dam was already half finished and in a few months, when the summer rains came and the river backed up behind it, Gadher would be flooded. Nevertheless, the people had returned to Gadher because they couldn't feed themselves at Timbi and they had no place else to go. It was hard to tell that there had ever been a settlement at Timbi. The people had taken everything with them, including the sheets of tin under which they had lived for two years. The only evidence of their stay was a few blackened firestones, scattered among the weeds. Because the government had never supplied any of the amenities it had promised, there were no roads, no electric poles, no school or clinic, no well or handpump to mark the site of what had once been—not a village, exactly; more a refugee camp.

The people in a neighboring hamlet had seen the Gadher refugees come and go. "Oh yes," one old man said, "those poor families. When they arrived, we told them the land was no good, but by then the sale was complete." Someone else added, "If we had known that the land was going to be sold, we would have warned the buyers. The big landlords who had owned all this land had been trying to sell it for a long time, but no one around here would have it. It's full of salt, no good at all." The owners, however, had finally gotten lucky: the Land Purchase Committee agreed to act as their broker, to sell the land for them. But even with thousands of villagers desperate for land, the committee had had to resort to fraud to unload it.

There is, in the heart of India, a sacred pool surrounded by temples and shrines. From this pool rises India's holiest river, the Narmada. Since ancient times, pilgrims have come here to be blessed by the river as it begins its 800-mile journey westward through the hills, forests, and plains of three states to the Arabian Sea. Some go on to make the *parikrama,* the ritual circumambulation of the river, from its source to its mouth and back. This trip, from temple to temple along the riverbank, traditionally takes three years, three months, and three days to complete. Nonbelievers too have been drawn here. Rudyard Kipling set his *Jungle Book* in these forests.

India began thinking about damming the Narmada, its fifth-longest river, in 1946. The official Narmada Valley Development Plan now calls for 30 major, 135 medium, and 3,000 small dams to be built on the Narmada and its tributaries over the next 50 years. The centerpiece of the scheme is to be the Sardar Sarovar Dam, stretching 4,000 feet across the river and rising to the height of a 45-story building. When its associated canals, irrigation works, and power transmission lines are taken into account, Sardar Sarovar is the biggest water development project in India, and probably in the world. The multibillion-dollar venture is intended to irrigate nearly 4.8 million acres (2 million hectares) of farmland and bring drinking water to 30 million people. It will also take the land of at least 320,000 people, many of whom are the indigenous or tribal people known in India as *adivasi.*

My first guide to the Narmada Valley was M. P. Shah, public relations officer for the local dam resettlement agency. He informed me that I could not visit Gadher. It, along with most of the other places I wanted to see, was off limits to journalists because of the danger from outside provocateurs opposed to the dam. Only two days earlier some local social workers had been stoned and their cameras stolen, he told me. In any case, I would be wasting my time, he added, because Gadher "is already vacated." The story I had heard, about the people of Timbi having returned to Gadher, was "false information," put out by opponents of the dam. No one, Shah said, had abandoned their resettlement site for their old village. I expressed a willingness to brave the stones of the antidam forces, but Mr. Shah was adamant. Gadher was too dangerous and too far away. Poor Mr. Shah—I was clearly not the first journalist who had pestered him with what he regarded as impertinent questions. He had recently been seconded to this job from the complaints division of the tax collector's office and I had the feeling that he would be applying to be transferred back soon. His exasperation was contagious, and I decided that it would be no hardship to wait to see Gadher until I was on my own.

———

Gadher, home to five hundred families, is one of the largest of the several hundred villages to be submerged by the dam. For centuries, the people of Gadher have lived peacefully as subsistence farmers, cattle and goat herders, and gatherers from the river and forest. It was, at least until the shadow of the dam fell across it, a thriving village, though poor by Western standards. Its thirteen hamlets are scattered across low hills, surrounded by forest, fields, and grazing land, and bordered by the river. There are no paved roads; oxcarts, bicycles, and a few motor scooters are the only transport. The houses, mostly wooden with thatched or tiled roofs, are spread out so that each family has room for a vegetable plot and a few animals.

Our car kicked up a dust storm on the dry dirt road as we turned into the village. A young woman balancing a brass water pot on her head hurried out of our way. I was, as always in Indian villages, dazzled to see such heavy work being done so gracefully by such a slender creature. Her gold and red sari was probably synthetic, not silk, and it may have been the only one she owned, but in elegance of dress and bearing, she and the other women of this dusty village cast the women of New York or Paris into the shade.

As soon as we stopped, a crowd gathered, curious to discover our business—and to investigate our car, some sort of jeep. Outsiders—city people—are rare here, and the villagers are understandably wary of strangers. Fortunately, I was with Balraj Maheshwari, a lawyer who is well known locally. Mr. Maheshwari works with the Rajpipla Social Services Society, a local organization founded in 1975 by a Catholic priest and dedicated to helping the poor of the region. Once he vouched for my good intentions, people were eager to tell their stories. Within a few minutes, two young men appeared carrying a beautifully carved daybed draped with a woven rug. They placed it under the shade of a large fig tree and motioned me to sit down. Mr. Maheshwari, an old man of the village named Ramsin Pijiyu, and a few of the more daring children joined me on the couch. The other men arranged themselves around us, while the women and children peered from behind the fence of a neighboring house, turning away to giggle each time I smiled at them.

Several villagers expressed pleasure at having a chance to speak to an outsider. "When others come to get information, they go only to Kevadia [the dam headquarters]," said Ramsin Pijiyu. "Then government officers come and take one or two persons from here to tell the visitors that every-thing is fine. Sometimes we have to pretend that we are from a different village, or that we are resettled someplace. You are the first from abroad to come here. It is good because we can tell you how we are." A cynic from the back of the crowd called out, "But if they find out someone from abroad has been here, they'll be patrolling in project trucks tomorrow."

By April of 1993, when I visited Gadher, most of its residents had been moved out of the village—split up among thirty-one different resettlement sites. But roughly a third of them had returned to Gadher because of intol-erable conditions in the resettlement colonies, ranging from barren land to polluted drinking water and outbreaks of cholera. The returnees—and the fifty or so families that had never left the village—were under pressure to move before the summer monsoon began. But they were wary: Twice lately, officials had taken groups from Gadher to see potential resettlement sites and each time they had discovered that the land they were shown was not the land they were to move to. "We've been cheated once, so we look very carefully now," said a middle-aged man named Kanti Bhoga who had recently returned from Timbi. "If good land is given and we could cultivate the land and our life is happy, then we should go. But without good land—if they want to cheat us only—then how can we go?"

It's not only the quality of the land they have been offered that con-cerns the people of Gadher. What they have tasted of the refugee existence has deeply discouraged them. They have discovered that in leaving their land, they are leaving behind a way of living. "Life in the other place was very congested—all the houses side by side," Mr. Pijiyu explained. "If we have a choice between the two, we will choose this. All the traditions, all the social life that we know and enjoy are here. If we move a hundred kilometers away, the traditions will be different. So, will ours survive? That worries us. At the other place when someone died, we were not allowed to burn the body in the open in the natural way. We had to bury it on our land. That was a very bad experience. Here we can get everything free: Water is free; wood and other things from the forest are free. It means that our livelihood is very easy and we are not in trouble. But if we go else-where, we will have to buy everything—water, forest produce, everything. So it's not good to leave our homeland. Whether this dam is good for someone else or not, we don't know, but for us it's very bad."

———

Work on Sardar Sarovar began in 1961. On April 5 of that year India's first prime minister, Jawaharlal Nehru, flew to the remote dam site to lay the foundation stone. The helipad on which he landed was built—as were the dam's offices and the guest quarters for visiting dignitaries—on land obtained by the forcible eviction of at least eight hundred families. As it turned out, the villagers had been forced from their homes somewhat prematurely: Construction was stopped for twenty years by an argument over how the costs and benefits of the project would be divided among the three states through which the river flows—Gujarat, Madhya Pradesh, and Maharastra.

In 1969 the government appointed a tribunal to settle the quarrel. After ten years of testimony and debate, the tribunal awarded most of the project's irrigation and drinking water to Gujarat, the driest of the three states. The tribunal also ruled, however, that Sardar Sarovar is not viable on its own. It requires three more reservoirs upstream so that the massive amounts of water that flow through the river during the monsoon season can be stored and released later in the year. Known collectively as the Narmada Sagar Projects, these three upstream reservoirs will displace another 200,000 people and cost another $1.6 billion. But because planners say this additional storage capacity is essential if Sardar Sarovar is ever to recoup its cost, the tribunal stipulated that the Narmada Sagar dams should "be completed at the same time as, or prior to the [Sardar Sarovar] dam." All four dams, said the tribunal, "should be viewed as a technically and economically interdependent project."

The World Bank had long been interested in helping to finance Sardar Sarovar, but it could do little while the tribunal was still debating the matter. Once the tribunal ruled, however, the Bank was swift to act. Bank staffers, working closely with Indian officials, spent several years reworking the project, trying to maximize its financial and technical viability and minimize its negative side effects. Once the project plans were finalized, four delegations of Bank staffers and consultants—missions, in Bank parlance—visited India to appraise the technical and economic aspects of the project. They did not, however, consider social or environmental issues, an omission that worried the Bank's tiny environmental office.

There was cause to worry. India's resettlement record is disturbing, to say the least. A conservative estimate of the number of Indians forced from their homes by large dams since Independence is 11 million, another 4 million having been displaced by mines, industrial developments, and wildlife sanctuaries. Some authorities put the figure at 20 million or more. Three-quarters of these people were not "rehabilitated"—bureaucratese for returned to their previous standard of living. As a result, millions of poor but self-sufficient peasants have ended up as beggars in the slums of the nearest big city.

The Bank too has had many bitter experiences with resettlement. According to its own experts, Bank-funded development projects across the world have displaced millions of people, pushing many into destitution. In 1980, belatedly recognizing the harm it had done, the Bank announced that all new projects must "ensure that, after a reasonable transition period, the displaced people regain at least their previous standard of living." Two years later, the Bank looked specifically at the impact of displacement on the world's tribal peoples. It found that "tribal people are more likely to be harmed than helped by development projects" and stated that "the Bank will not assist development projects that knowingly encroach on traditional territories being used or occupied by tribal people, unless adequate safeguards are provided." The Bank also said it "would not be prepared to assist with a project if it appears that the project sponsors had forcibly 'cleared' the area of tribal people beforehand." Thus, by the time the Narmada loan was under consideration, the Bank had already adopted policies and standards designed to prevent forcible relocation and to ensure that displaced persons, especially tribal people, would be protected from the negative side effects of development.

India has no national laws governing resettlement, but the tribunal had imposed resettlement standards on the Narmada project. Ousted landowners were to receive not merely financial compensation but "land for land"—at least 4.8 acres (2 hectares) of irrigated land per farming family—and each son eighteen years old or older was to be given his own land. In addition, though the tribunal's ruling ignored the plight of the many thousands of tribal farmers who have no legal title to their traditional lands, India is a signatory to a 1957 United Nations convention that recognizes the rights of tribal people to their traditional land and requires governments to provide displaced tribal people with "lands of quality at least equal to that of the land previously occupied." But these enlightened pledges were worthless, because India—with the Bank's knowledge—violated them from the beginning.

After 1961, when the first six villages were razed to make way for the helipad and dam offices, construction stopped for twenty years. Then in 1981, five more villages were destroyed to make room for the holding tanks for the main irrigation canal. Jai Prakash Associates, the contractor building the tanks, was also given the task of clearing the land of people. Construction workers and company officials pressured the villagers to affix their thumbprints to deeds of sale, or to blank sheets of paper to be filled in later. Some relinquished their land this way; others refused. The homes of those who resisted were demolished. When some villagers appealed to the Gujarat High Court for a stay against forcible removal, the contractors stepped up the pace of demolition so that the stay, when granted, was useless. A few of the four thousand oustees were paid for their property according to a formula that a World Bank–sponsored study says "invariably undervalues land." Three-quarters, however, received no compensation at all. Years later, the Bank reported that many of them "could be seen camping in extreme poverty at the edge of what remained of their lands."

Aware of this sorry history, the Bank's environmental office sent Thayer Scudder, a Cal Tech socioeconomist well known for his studies of the impact of large engineering projects on poor people, to investigate the current resettlement plan for the Narmada dam. Scudder found that there *was* no resettlement plan and that the government had not even begun to collect the information needed to make a plan. No one even knew how many people the dam would displace. After Scudder reported that no resettlement plan existed, the Bank dropped its insistence that India submit a resettlement plan as a condition of receiving the loan.

All Bank loans must be approved by its board of directors, which bases its decisions on the formal Staff Appraisal Report (SAR) prepared for each proposed loan. The report for Sardar Sarovar acknowledged that the project had already harmed thousands of people, but it offered assurances that India would correct those wrongs and treat all future oustees fairly and in accordance with Bank policies on resettlement. It did not mention that India's Ministry of Environment had refused to approve the dam on the grounds that more information was needed about its environmental and social impact. On March 7, 1985, the board of directors of the World Bank unanimously agreed to lend India $450 million for the Sardar Sarovar dam. The loan agreement gave India until December to come up with plans for resettlement and for dealing with the dam's environmental problems.

---

In 1985, a thirty-year-old social worker from Bombay named Medha Patkar arrived in the Narmada Valley to conduct a study of some of the villages that were due to be submerged. Soon, however, she put her professional work aside and made it her mission to help people being displaced by the dam get the land and compensation to which they were entitled. At that moment the future of Sardar Sarovar was rewritten.

With her master's degree in social work and her urban upbringing, Medha Patkar is an unlikely candidate for the revered leader of tens of thousands of tribal people and peasant farmers, though that is what she has become. She is, however, from a family of activists: Her father, a trade unionist, fought against the British for Indian Independence; her mother works with a women's organization. Medha is a small woman—she stands just five feet tall and weighs only ninety pounds. Blessed with an almost photographic memory for facts and figures, she is a formidable debater and strategist. As a public speaker she is passionate without being melodramatic.

Wearing canvas sneakers and a faded sari, Medha Patkar traveled thousands of miles up and down the Narmada Valley. She learned the languages of the tribal people, ate their food, and lived their spartan life. In village after village, she exhorted people to organize and demand just treatment. She wasn't the only—or even the first—person to try and help those the dam would harm. But it was Medha whom the crowds trusted; she whom they came to hear.

After several years of agitating for better treatment of oustees, Medha Patkar concluded that the government had neither the land nor the will to resettle people properly. Others were coming to the same conclusion. In August of 1988, a number of local groups that had been working to secure better resettlement decided to oppose the dam outright—on economic and technical as well as social grounds. Thousands of villagers rallied to the call for nonviolent mass protests. A year of strikes and rallies followed. In response, the Indian government imposed the Official Secrets Act on the region around the dam—a move that effectively banned gatherings of more than five people. Several hundred people were arrested for violating that ban.

In 1989, local opponents of the dam joined with national groups to form a national organization, the Narmada Bachao Andolan (Save the Narmada Movement). The Andolan staged huge protests all around India, using the Gandhian tools of mass rallies and nonviolent civil disobedience. In September 1989, 60,000 people representing 250 organizations came to a remote part of Madhya Pradesh to rally against "destructive development." The following January, 5,000 men and women marched on the Narmada Valley Development Authority offices, forcing them to close. In March, 10,000 protesters blocked the highway from Bombay to Agra for two days, and in May 2,000 people staged a sit-in outside the prime minister's house in Delhi.

The most significant, though not the biggest, demonstration against Sardar Sarovar began on Christmas Day, 1990. In what came to be known as the Long March, three thousand oustees and supporters set out to walk down the valley to the dam site. After a week of walking, the protesters reached the Gujarat border but were barred by police from going farther. Medha Patkar and six others then embarked on a hunger strike, demanding that the government suspend work on the dam and hold an independent review of the entire project. Two of the hunger strikers were hospitalized, but the government refused to budge. After twenty-two days, the remaining hunger strikers broke their fast. The Long March did not stop the dam, but it made Narmada a national issue and Medha Patkar a national heroine. It is a role she disowns, pointing to the many others who have devoted their lives for the past several years to the antidam movement.

By the time of the Long March, Murlidhar Devidas Amte, affectionately known as Baba Amte, had joined the fight against the dam. A seventy-six-year-old social worker whose work with leprosy patients has earned him the admiration of the country, Baba Amte decided to devote his last years to saving the holy river. He moved to the small village of Chhoti Kasrawad on the bank of the Narmada and vowed to stay with the village and drown if the dam were built. Gradually the dam was accumulating a roster of distinguished opponents, men and women the government could not dismiss as manipulated peasants, opponents of progress, or dupes of subversive forces.

The year 1990 was an especially bad one for the project. Shortly after Baba Amte threw his considerable moral weight into the fight against the dam, B. D. Sharma, the government's commissioner of scheduled castes and tribes, appealed publicly to the president of India to suspend the project. "The execution of Sardar Sarovar, like many other projects, is not in keeping with the provisions of the law and the law itself is violative of the Constitutional safefuards provided for the tribal people, as also of human rights," he said. "The people are determined not to move out from their homes in the Valley and prefer a watery grave than disorganization and destitution in an unknown world which has been the story of all displaced so far."

Also in 1990, India's Department of Environment and Forests declared that the conditional approval it had given Sardar Sarovar in 1987 "must be deemed to have lapsed," since the "studies, surveys and action plans" due in 1989 had not been produced. And last but not least, the World Bank reported in 1990 that 40 percent of the 105 legal covenants attached to its loan agreement with India had been fulfilled only partially or not at all. This finding had little impact, however, because it was kept hidden from the public and the Bank's directors.

Since Independence, India—with considerable help from the World Bank—has built more than 1,500 large dams, structures that Nehru extolled as the temples of modern India. India is now one of the most dammed nations on earth—and many more dams and irrigation projects are planned or underway. So far most have been failures. Seventy percent of the large irrigation projects started since Independence are still incomplete. Referring to this state of affairs, Prime Minister Rajiv Gandhi said in 1986, "We can safely say that almost no benefit has come to the people from these projects. For sixteen years we have poured money out. The people have got nothing back, no irrigation, no water, no increase in production, no help in their daily life."

I saw an example of this not far from the abandoned Timbi resettlement site. Next to the road was an empty canal, intended to carry water for the Karjan Dam (another Bank project). That dam was completed by 1989, but the canal—indeed the entire irrigation system—has never functioned. The cement lining was badly cracked—in places it was nonexistent—and weeds sprouted from the fissures. The underlayer was made not of the requisite concrete, but of rough sand and rocks. As we stood looking down at this shoddy piece of workmanship, a passerby on a motorbike dismounted and joined us. He was a local man and seemed amused by our interest in the canal. "They're relining it—for the second or third time," he remarked. "But the material is weak; it's not what they promised." Balraj Maheshwari, the lawyer from the Rajpipla Social Services Society, who had been shaking his head silently, said, "This project is meant only for the rich people to collect money from abroad and to put it in their pockets. The bigger the project they don't execute, the more money goes into their pockets. That is the politics." As Father Joseph, the Catholic priest from south India who founded Rajpipla Social Services Society, expressed it to me, "The profits of a dam are running long before the water runs."

A 1987 study by the Gujarat State Legislature found wide discrepancies between the amount of land that planners said would be watered by irrigation projects and the amount that actually was. Panam Dam, in northern Gujarat State, for example, was expected to deliver water to 118,490 acres, but in fact irrigated less than half that area. Damanganga Dam, also in Gujarat, was to irrigate 135,900 acres of land; in fact only 1,336 acres were ever actually irrigated. Both these dams were funded by the World Bank. The reasons for the shortfalls are many. Planners overestimate the amount of water required by or available to the system; contractors carry out substandard work; and, in the Bank's own words, "most irrigation schemes have been poorly operated and maintained." Frequently the first farmers along an irrigation network commandeer most of the water, leaving only a trickle for those downstream. A 1991 World Bank review of its Indian irrigation projects found that "economic viability [has] been poor all along for most projects." These problems led the Bank to conclude that India should spend the next ten years improving the performance of existing irrigation systems rather than building new ones.

But new schemes, like Sardar Sarovar, continue to be started—if not finished. On the one hand it seems that such schemes proceed against all logic and reason. On the other, their progress is entirely rational in view of the opportunities they present for their backers to enrich themselves at the public's expense. With a large project like Sardar Sarovar, engineers and bureaucrats can look forward to kickbacks from those whose land they overvalue for compensation purposes or purchase at inflated prices to resell to oustees, as well as from contractors who increase their profit margins by using shoddy materials or simply not doing the work at all.

Big projects enable politicians to acquire power by exercising patronage and money by taking bribes. Thus it often happens that the ruling party supports such activities, while the opposition rails against them. *The Times of India* cites one such example: the fundamentalist Hindu Bharatiya Janata Party in Madhya Pradesh. "When in power, they have supported [Sardar Sarovar]," noted the paper. "But when out of it, they have opposed it."

Some argue that the Narmada dam must be built precisely because India's record of irrigation projects is so poor. "Most existing irrigation schemes are not operational," Amar Gargesh, the project's press officer, told me. "That's why we need this one." Gargesh also maintains that Sardar Sarovar should not be subject to a conventional cost-benefit analysis. "It's not fair to evaluate it like a commercial project," he said. "With our droughts we need this project." Both the Indian government and the World Bank say that Sardar Sarovar is a good investment, but their calculations are based on many assumptions—such as those about sedimentation rates, the availability of water, and the impact on the environment—that their own experts say are wildly overoptimistic. By the government's own admission, half the country's large dams haven't come close to their projected economic rates of return. "All their claims for Sardar Sarovar are based on one assertion only," says Girish Patel, a Harvard-trained Gujarati lawyer who has studied the project closely: " 'Forget the past; in the future it will happen differently.' But we say that you cannot forget the past. You can improve on it slightly, but you cannot go from 40 percent efficiency to 100 percent in one jump."

Perhaps the strongest economic argument against Sardar Sarovar is that the three Narmada Sagar dams, which the tribunal said were essential to its success, are not being built. R. C. Singh Deo, Madhya Pradesh's former Irrigation Minister, says that "it is impossible for Madhya Pradesh to complete Narmada Sagar. . . . It has had to beg from the Central Government to pay its share in the Sardar Sarovar project." The World Bank has admitted that there is no guarantee that the upstream projects will be built. Without them, however, Sardar Sarovar will irrigate 30 percent less land and provide 25 percent less power than projected. That alone makes Sardar Sarovar a money-losing investment.

---

BACKBONE OF WESTERN INDIAN ECONOMY

THE ONLY REMEDY AGAINST RECURRING DROUGHT

A  PLANNED  ECOLOGICAL  HARMONY  AMONGST  MEN,  WATER  AND  VEGETATION

A RAY OF HOPE TO THIRTY MILLION IN WESTERN INDIA

Billboards extolling, in Hindi and English, the good things Sardar Sarovar will do for India line the road leading to the dam site. But though the signs assert that the people of India will benefit greatly from the project, they don't say precisely how. Is Sardar Sarovar primarily an irrigation project, a drinking-water supply project, or a power project?

Until recently, promoters pointed to irrigation as the chief rationale for the project. The project brochures, which are many and glossy, are enthusiastic about the benefits to farmers. One, called "You Be the Judge," declares that "Sardar Sarovar will mean richer farmers . . . Sardar Sarovar will mean increase in agricultural produce . . . Sardar Sarovar will mean eternal smiles on millions of faces." Actually, however, most of the land to be irrigated by the project already has access to water, and most of the region's poor, dry, and tribal areas will receive no irrigation water. Even if the planned irrigation system is completed, it would deliver water to only 28 percent of Gujarat's drought-prone districts and 11 percent of its tribal lands.

There is disagreement in the Bank as to what the real purpose of the dam is. Officially it is an irrigation project with a power component, but some say it only makes sense as a power project, with irrigation added on to make it politically palatable. One staffer who has analyzed the project for the Bank says, "The hydro benefits from that project are of tremendous benefit to India and to millions of Indians, but it turns out that the irrigation part doesn't really pay. The Bank thinks of it as an irrigation project, but it's a hydro project." Another Bank employee who has worked on the project confirmed this view: "Providing hydro power for industry wouldn't be popular, so irrigation was added. But the irrigation is money-losing—in fact, they discovered they could boost the rate of return by reducing the amount of land to be irrigated."

At the heart of these issues is the matter of the dam's height. The tribunal considered limiting the dam to a height of 436 feet, which would have been enough to provide the desired amount of irrigation water. But a higher dam would produce more hydro power—and hydro is the only benefit Madhya Pradesh, the state with the most people to be displaced by the project, will get from it. The tribunal, therefore, opted for a 455-foot-high dam. The extra 19 feet will produce 10 percent more electricity. But it also increases by 50 percent the amount of farmland to be submerged and by 70 percent the number of people to be displaced in Madhya Pradesh by the reservoir.

Originally only urban centers were to get drinking water, but, as criticism of the project mounted, officials expanded the drinking-water program to include villages. Planners now say that by the year 2025, some 8,000 villages will have water piped directly to them, and "You Be the Judge" promises that "Sardar Sarovar will mean no drinking water problem in all villages." In this drought-plagued region, an adequate supply of drinking water would be an enormous boon. Amar Gargesh emphasized this aspect of the project when I spoke to him in his office in Gujarat's capital, Gandhinagar. The government office blocks that dominate the town are arranged around a massive statue of Gujarat's most famous son, Gandhi, sitting cross-legged at his spinning wheel. From my position by the window, I gazed out on the Mahatma as Mr. Gargesh spoke of Gujarat's desperate need for water. "You have to see the problems these people have with water to appreciate them," he said. "In some places the groundwater is so depleted that the wells are empty. People spend all day collecting a single bucketful. With Sardar Sarovar, not a single village will be left without drinking water. That's official."

If true, this would be a powerful argument in favor of the dam. But a brief investigation into these promises reveals that there is little behind them. The list of villages to be serviced was assembled so hastily that it includes several hundred that India's census says exist only as names on out-of-date maps. A Bank report points out that, although the number of people the authorities say will receive drinking water from the project has increased by more than 25 percent since 1991, there has been "no corresponding increase" in the amount of water allocated to domestic purposes in the project plan. Although project officials count the supply of drinking water to thousands of villages among the benefits of the project, they do not count the hundreds of millions of dollars such an undertaking would require among its costs. The project has no funds budgeted for village water supply. Nonetheless the promoters of the dam continue to insist that it will bring water to millions. "It's cruel," says Girish Patel, the lawyer who has represented in court the villagers forced out by the dam. "The people in those areas are just waiting for water, when the project officials know it's not going there."

Neither the Bank nor the Indian government ever claimed that the Sardar Sarovar project was entirely benign. In the Bank's words, "The argument in favor of the Sardar Sarovar Project is that the benefits are so large that they substantially outweigh the costs of the immediate human and environmental disruption." There is nothing sinister about setting costs against benefits. We do it every day when choosing what to eat, how late to stay up, and whether or not to take the risk of, say, smoking or driving a car. But there is a dilemma when one person or group gets the benefits of a given activity, while another pays the costs. This is the case with Sardar Sarovar. As S. C. Varma, the chairman of the Narmada Valley Development Authority, put it, "The family getting displaced . . . undergoes hardship and distress and faces an uncertain future so that others may live in happiness and be economically better off."

In some cases, taking from one group and giving to another makes sense. A society may decide, for example, to assist its neediest citizens at the expense of its wealthiest ones, in order to ensure a minimum standard of living. Many countries do this to a certain extent through taxation or social welfare schemes. But large irrigation projects tend to do the reverse: to take from the poor and give to the rich. The Ukai irrigation project, just south of Sardar Sarovar, is a striking illustration of how this happens.

Ukai is the largest functioning irrigation project in Gujarat. Built with World Bank funds, its dam and irrigation works displaced 70,000 people, mostly tribals. The farmers of the area had previously grown their own food, mostly millet, barley, and corn. With irrigation it became possible to grow more "demanding" but saleable crops, such as sugar cane and wheat. Most small farmers could not afford the fertilizers and pesticides that such intensive, irrigated agriculture requires, but the largest and wealthiest landowners were able to take advantage of the possibilities of irrigation and in doing so increased their earnings considerably. As a result, the value of all the irrigable land in the area rose—as did taxes and the price of even basic farm supplies—and the small farmers found that they could no longer afford to keep farming in the old way.

Most small farmers eventually sold out to wealthier men who could capitalize on the new conditions. Vast sugar cane plantations now dominate the area. Balraj Maheshwari, the lawyer who took me to Gadher, knows the Ukai area well. "I could show you prosperous landowners who were turned into laborers, step by step," he told me. "Their children went to Baroda University. Now they're living in the slums of Baroda." Some have joined the 100,000 wretched souls who work on the big cane estates from May to October every year, living in miserable conditions and sleeping in the street. Girish Patel, who has represented the cane workers in their legal appeals for better working conditions, calls them "migrant slaves."

"The saying is 'Unless we have a cake we cannot share it. So let us produce a cake,'" says Father Joseph. "But the sharing never comes. As the cake is produced, about ten to fifteen percent of the population gobbles it up." Where once the Ukai region was more or less uniformly poor, now it is divided into a dominant class of rich sugar cane magnates and a subclass of near-destitute sugar cane workers. "We are not enamored of the old way and it is not our objective to see people living in the same circumstances as in the past," says Girish Patel. "But these circumstances are worse."

---

By 1988, it was already difficult for surveyors, researchers, or anyone connected with the project to work in the Narmada Valley. Local hostility to the dam was so intense that large areas of the submergence zone were effectively off limits to project authorities and Bank officials. On several occasions, Bank officials canceled or cut short their trips to the valley on the advice of the Indian government, which warned that they were in danger of being physically attacked if they entered the submergence zone. Though many villages were militantly uncooperative, one consultant asserts that India exaggerated the dangers in order to keep researchers out of the area.

Construction proceeded, however, and as the dam grew higher and the time for flooding drew nearer, pressure mounted for villagers to leave the submergence zone. Many were willing to leave, if only they had someplace to go. Nearly everyone had heard some discouraging tale from friends or relations who had already moved. In 1989 about a hundred people left Gadher for a place called Amroli. They were told they would get houses, a school, a dispensary, and free electricity. Because the land was not irrigated, the government also promised to sink a well on each five-acre plot.

After three years, however, the people still had no houses—and no land on which they could build their own houses. They had no electricity, no school, no dispensary, and no source of water fit for humans or animals.

When a World Bank team visited Amroli in 1992, they found fewer than forty people still living there; the rest had returned to Gadher. A number of men complained that the land they received was not the land they had been shown—just as in the case of Timbi. Moreover, many people had fallen ill since coming to Amroli. One women told the visitors, "This place is like a crematorium. Our children suffer from vomiting, diarrhoea, and dehydration." Indian officials discount such reports. "There has been talk of malaria. There has been talk of dysentery. But it has not become a problem," Amar Gargesh assured me. "No one is resettled where there is no good drinking water. But it may become contaminated later—that we cannot help."

News of such disasters—along with the Andolan's insistence that by refusing to move, the people could defeat the dam—convinced tens of thousands of people in the reservoir area to defy orders to leave their homes. Many, including Patkar, took a vow to drown as the waters rose about them rather than leave the threatened villages. Clashes between villagers and the police sent to evacuate them became increasingly common. On several occasions government agents used bulldozers to destroy homes in villages about to be flooded. Villagers accused the police of harassment and brutality, and police charged that Andolan members were inciting violence.

In 1992, the human rights group Asia Watch sent a team to the Narmada Valley. The team confirmed reports of government mistreatment and concluded that "these abuses appear to be part of an increasingly repressive campaign to prevent the groups from organizing support for protests in villages affected by the dam and disseminating information about the social and environmental consequences of the dam."

As resistance was spreading across the valley, the Andolan's supporters in Europe, Japan, Australia, the United States, and Canada were pressuring the Bank directly and through their parliamentary and congressional representatives. The international campaign, coordinated by Lori Udall of the Washington-based Environmental Defense Fund, turned Sardar Sarovar into a worldwide symbol of all that is wrong with the development industry, big dams, and the World Bank.

In 1989, the campaign brought Medha Patkar and other key figures in the Narmada struggle to Washington, D.C., to testify before a special House hearing on the World Bank's role in the project. In 1990, the campaign organized a major symposium in Tokyo attended by members of the Diet as well as academics and journalists, which led the Japanese government to take the unprecedented step of canceling its $200 million financial and technical support of the project (having first, according to one Bank staffer, taken the precaution of designing the dam to take only Japanese turbines). The campaign also sent several Andolan activists on a speaking tour of Europe, bringing the issue to the attention of European Parliamentarians and the European members of the Bank's board of directors. And it lobbied hard for an independent review of the project.

The furor over Sardar Sarovar was doing nothing to improve the Bank's reputation as a champion of the poor, or its chances for future financial support from Japan, the United States, or its European members. In 1989, the Bank, under pressure from outside, reluctantly asked Thayer Scudder to look once again at the resettlement situation. His findings, as presented in a report by the Bank's India country department, indicated that resettlement was finally progressing well, especially in Gujarat, where all major problems had been resolved and resettlement targets would soon be met. In reality, Scudder had reported nothing of the sort. He had found the situation highly unsatisfactory and recommended that the Bank stop the loan until the major resettlement problems were resolved. When Scudder's own report was leaked, it became apparent that the Bank's management was so wedded to Narmada that it would ignore or distort the advice of its own experts if that advice was unwelcome.

Within the Bank, the Narmada project was being pushed by the India Country Department, whose director is known in Bank jargon as "head of India." The India Department finds it difficult to say no to India. A staffer who works closely with the department explains why: "The India Department has one job—to lend money to India. Of course every country department pushes its own country, but for years, during the Cold War, India held a special position as the largest nonaligned democracy. The donor community treated it with kid gloves for years—and the India Department still thinks that way."

India has long been the Bank's most important client. For nearly forty years, says one long time Bank official, "India was the Jewel in the Crown of the World Bank. . . . The reputation of the Bank tended to be measured in terms of what it could do for India." Over the years, the Bank has lent India $40 billion, nearly twice as much as it has lent any other country. As greater and greater sums of money passed between them, the Bank succeeded in putting its imprint on India, but India's imprint on the Bank is just as deep. The fact that India owes the Bank so much money only serves to increase its power in the institution. As Bank officials are fond of observing—on condition of anonymity—if you owe a bank $100,000, you worry; if you owe it $100 million, the bank worries.

The India Department apart, concern about the handling of the Narmada project was growing within the Bank. It was nothing new for the Environment Department to complain about a particular project, but suddenly it had allies in the legal and agricultural divisions. The debate was a gentlemanly one, no open quarrels or threats of resignation, but by 1991 it had spread so far throughout the Bank that it was impossible to keep it private. Internal memos were promptly leaked, and journalists and activists had no trouble getting damaging quotes from anonymous Bank officials. Moreover, the executive directors—the twenty-four-member board whose job it is to oversee the Bank's management—were being fiercely lobbied by environmental groups on the practical and moral shortcomings of the project. Some directors were beginning to question the official version of events. "It was really becoming an embarrassment to the Bank, and there were tremendous tensions between the executive directors and the senior management," remembers one close observer.

Even Barber Conable, the Bank's president and thus its top manager, wasn't sure where the truth lay. There was simply too much conflicting evidence. Opponents and supporters of the project agreed on only one thing—that Sardar Sarovar was far from the worst of the Bank's projects. "India has two or three hundred other big projects—some financed by the Bank—with worse resettlement problems. Sardar Sarovar is probably the best, certainly one of the best," remarked one staffer, echoing the words of many people I spoke to on all sides of the issue. The spotlight was on Sardar Sarovar not because it was the most egregious example of destructive development but because of the remarkable alliance of determined villagers, local activists, and international groups that fought it.

In 1991, Conable agreed to commission an independent review of the project's social and resettlement problems. Conable, a Republican congressman for twenty years before moving to the Bank, asked his former colleague, Bradford Morse, to lead the review team. Morse had spent six terms as a Republican congressman before becoming head of the United Nations Development Program. His deputy was to be Thomas Berger, a distinguished Canadian jurist, a man admired for his even-handed reviews of several controversial projects. It was an unprecedented step for the Bank—and a much more radical one than Conable realized at the time.

The Bank had never asked—nor indeed allowed—outsiders to critique an entire project. It often hires consultants, but they have limited remits, typically spending only a few days at the project site, a few weeks on an assignment. Their reports are edited by Bank staff and circulated privately. This was all the Bank wanted from Morse. As one participant in the negotiations said, "The Bank had in mind a couple of weeks in India and a typewritten document, stapled at the corner."

But Morse, after consultations with Berger, who was experienced in conducting independent reviews, and with critics of the dam who warned him about the pitfalls of doing business with the Bank, laid down tough conditions for accepting the commission. He demanded access to all relevant documents, total freedom from the Bank, and complete control of a million-dollar budget. He also insisted that the team retain copyright in its report and publish it independently. The Bank was taken aback, but Morse prevailed on all points. He and Berger selected two other full-time team members: Hugh Brody, a British anthropologist, and Donald Gamble, a Canadian environmental engineer.

In September 1991, the team embarked on nine months of research in India and Washington, sorting through old reports and speaking with politicians, bureaucrats, scientists, environmentalists, and the oustees themselves. Unlike normal Bank missions, the Morse team—whose appointment had been welcomed by the dam's opponents—was able to enter the "refusenik" villages as well as the resettlement sites. Its members also spoke privately to many people in the Bank and examined old project papers. "People in the India Department would talk about how their hands were tied by politics, by India's special status," reported one team member, who added, "I was amazed at what I saw of how the Bank works. I thought I had understood the Bank and I was a great admirer. I felt that they were setting a precedent in many of their environmental issues, and some of the social issues. On paper it's terrific. In practice, it's another story."

The review team found that there had been no environmental impact assessment of the project and that neither India nor the Bank had considered the effect such a huge project would have on people living downstream. This despite the fact that the Bank's own experts had warned that the dam would result in increased salinity in the lower reaches of the river, destroying one of India's most lucrative fishing grounds, that it was likely to silt twice as fast as was being assumed, and that the project would be able to deliver only half as much irrigation water as had been stated. The team also discovered that only a few months earlier a Bank consultant had described parts of the project as "death traps," as "ideal breeding sites" for malarial mosquitoes, and had said it was "taking malaria to the doorsteps of the villagers." "People have died," concluded the team, "yet the Bank's status reports simply say that the preventive measures required by the formal [loan] agreements seven years ago are 'not yet due.' "

With regard to the key question—resettlement—the team found that India still had neither a comprehensive resettlement plan nor the data on which to base one. Each time India had missed a deadline for submitting a resettlement plan, the Bank had simply set a new one. A succession of deadlines, in December 1985, December 1988, March 1989, and June 1989, had all slipped quietly away, unmet. In June 1990, the Bank changed its tack and began to request only partial plans. Those too failed to materialize. The review concluded that "there developed an eagerness on the part of the Bank and India to get on with the job. Both, it seems, were prepared to ease, or even disregard, Bank policy and India's regulations and procedures dealing with resettlement and environmental protection in the hope of achieving the much-needed benefits."

Most disturbingly, the review team found that virtually all the flaws and problems it discovered in the project had already been reported to the Bank by staff technicians and consultants, and simply ignored by those higher up the chain of command. "All this information was in the Bank's files. Morse told [Lewis] Preston [Conable's successor as president] they could have saved a lot of money by just looking in their own files," said a member of the review. "This will happen again, only next time it'll be worse—and if the Bank doesn't realize that, they're dreaming in technicolor. The Bank thinks its problem is in India. It isn't in India, it's in Washington, D.C."

In June 1992 the team published its findings in a 385-page paperback book. It fell on the Bank like a hammer blow. "There wasn't a soul in the [India] department that had any idea what an impact the Morse Report was going to have," one insider told me. "It was like watching a ship hit an iceberg in slow motion. The Bank thought they could ride roughshod right over it. They were unconcerned up until the day it arrived." The report's detailed description of the project and of the Bank's part in it was devastating. The review team had been asked to suggest ways of improving the project. Instead it said that the Bank should "step back from the Project and consider [it] afresh."

Ten weeks after receiving Morse's report, the Bank made its response. In a document called "Narmada: Next Steps," the Bank assured its directors that since the completion of the Morse Report, the Indian Government had adopted "a comprehensive set of actions in line with the recommendations of the Bank mission" and had demonstrated its "seriousness of pur-

pose . . . by several important discussions." There was therefore no
reason to "step back" from Sardar Sarovar as Morse had recommended.
The document angered many who had expected the Bank to use the Morse
Report as an excuse to withdraw or suspend funding for the project. One
long-serving staffer said at the time, "If Narmada is not suspended, it's the
death knell for the environment in the Bank. If they can't suspend this one
on environmental grounds, they'll never suspend anything."

Shortly after "Narmada: Next Steps" was published, more than 250
environmental, human rights, and grass-roots development groups signed a
full-page open letter to Lewis Preston in the *Financial Times* under the
headline "The World Bank Must Withdraw from Sardar Sarovar Immediately." Failure to do so, the letter said, "will confirm that the Bank is
beyond reform" and will lead to a campaign to cut off funding to the Bank.

When the members of the review team saw "Narmada: Next Steps,"
they too were furious. Though Morse was in the hospital suffering from a
bout with emphysema, he and Berger held a telephone conference call with
Joseph Wood, the vice president responsible for the India Department, and
several executive directors. Morse told the directors that the document
ignored or misrepresented his report's main findings. Berger and Morse
also put their charges in writing in a letter to Lewis Preston. Citing numerous examples of misrepresentation, they concluded: "The Bank may reject
our finding that its incremental strategy has failed. . . . The Bank may
decide that overriding political and economic considerations are so compelling that its Operational Directives are irrelevant when decisions have to be
made about the Sardar Sarovar Project. But it should not seek to reshape
our report to support such decisions." The letter was also sent to each
executive director, despite Preston's last-minute plea to the bedridden
Morse not to do so.

On October 23, 1992, ten days after Morse and Berger sent the letter,
the board met to consider the future of Sardar Sarovar. Several directors
from industrial countries—notably those from the United States, Canada,
Japan, Germany, Australia, and the Scandinavian countries—called for a
suspension of disbursements. But the rest sided with the developing countries, and the board voted to give India five more months, until April 1,
1993, to comply with the terms of the loan. Patrick Coady, the U.S. executive director, sternly warned his fellow directors that voting to continue the
loan was a "signal that no matter how egregious the situation, no matter
how flawed the project, no matter how many policies have been violated,
and no matter how clear the remedies prescribed, the Bank will go forward
on its own terms."

On March 31, 1993, the day before the Bank's deadline was to expire, the government of India asked the Bank to cancel the Sardar Sarovar loan. This was a face-saving maneuver, agreed ahead of time with the Bank, which otherwise would have had to cancel the loan the following day on the grounds of noncompliance. Medha Patkar hailed the cancellation as a giant step toward victory: "The exit of the World Bank from Sardar Sarovar has given a great boost to the Andolan and our supporters and has shown that the dam is not a fait accompli." Supporters of the project also claimed to be pleased, describing the move as evidence of India's unwillingness to be dictated to by foreigners. "The government felt the Bank was encroaching on the sovereignty of India. We needed to put our foot down," said Amar Gargesh.

The immediate financial impact was only moderate, because India had already received all of the Bank's $250 million low-interest loan and $30 million of the $200 million the Bank had lent on normal terms. India's move also killed another $440 million worth of loans for the project that had been in negotiation, but soon after the Sardar Sarovar loan was canceled, the Bank announced eight new loans, totaling $2.3 billion, for India.

The Bank would like to put Narmada behind it, but that may be impossible. "Just because India has said 'We don't want any more World Bank money' doesn't mean the Bank's responsibility ends," argues Smitu Kothari, one of the founders of the Andolan. "They legitimized this dam for years, financially and politically. They made it possible." The Bank's Legal Department agrees. In an internal memo, the Bank's General Counsel expressed concern that the directors had been given the impression that the Bank is no longer involved with the Sardar Sarovar project. "This is not the case," it said. The government of India is still "legally obligated towards the Bank to carry out its obligations under the loan agreement."

Though the Narmada Valley Development Authority is determined to complete the project, the loss of Bank financing may have doomed it. The authority is nearly out of money; it faces huge debt service payments on its outstanding loans; and it has not been able to raise any more funds, public or private, from abroad. In any case, construction of the project has been halted since January 1995 by a ruling of the Indian Supreme Court. Each monsoon season, however, the half-built dam floods nearby villages. Despite police efforts to cordon off the submergence zone, every year scores of people who have taken the "drowning pledge" manage to enter those villages and barricade themselves in the low-lying houses. So far, the dam's interrupted construction and the monsoon rains have combined to flood most areas only to chest height. A higher dam or heavier rains will change that.

A year after the loan's cancellation, Lewis Preston reflected on the lessons of Narmada. It was, he acknowledged, a public relations disaster. "The Bank has paid the highest price for not recognizing the importance of the environment," he said. "That mistake, I think, has, in terms of the criticisms of the Bank, eroded some of the support that the Bank is entitled to." Otherwise, however, he found little to be concerned about. "The Narmada project is not one to be ashamed of, in terms of what it will eventually do for the people of India. . . . It will help two million people and that is significant in anybody's language."

# Two

## GOING WILD ON BORROWING

The boat train arrived at the Gare du Nord at noon on Friday, March 11, 1932, bringing to an end the week-long journey from New York. Among the disembarking passengers was a middle-aged Swedish gentleman who passed anonymously through the waiting crowd. Though millions knew Ivar Kreuger's name, his face was not familiar. He was a retiring man and had taken great pains to keep his photograph out of the paper. Kreuger was one of the world's wealthiest men: He controlled the world's richest gold mine; was part owner of Europe's biggest iron producer; owned banks in Paris, Amsterdam, Berlin, and Warsaw; had valuable holdings in telephones, cinema, newspapers, real estate, and timber; and possessed a near-global monopoly on that humble but essential item, the match. Kreuger's fame was based not on his wealth, however, but on what he had done with it. Since the end of World War I, he had advanced hundreds of millions of dollars to cash-starved governments. He had rescued France and Germany from the threat of bankruptcy and had taken over the entire national debt of several lesser countries. At that moment, Ivar Kreuger was arguably the most powerful financier in the world.

Until 1927, Kreuger had been a successful but obscure businessman. He owed his extraordinary debut on the world stage to France's financial woes. After the war, France had borrowed millions from J. P. Morgan and Company, the world's leading banking firm, at 8 percent interest. Unable to support this huge debt, French President Raymond Poincaré searched for a lender willing to undercut Morgan—to lend at a lower rate of interest. He found no one. Then suddenly, Kreuger—who had previously made smaller loans to Peru, Greece, and Poland—stepped in, offering $75 million at just over 5 percent.

It was a sensational entrance into international finance and it made the quiet Kreuger a household name—at least within the House of Morgan, which he had so badly upstaged. France awarded Kreuger the Legion of Honor, and he went on to lend large sums to Ecuador, Yugoslavia, Hungary, Turkey, and many other governments. In 1929 he lent Germany $125 million for payment of its war reparations.

Kreuger began lending to governments as a way to use the excess cash from his businesses, but soon he was lending money he had raised by selling his companies' bonds. He financed the loan to France, for example, largely by selling $50 million worth of International Match bonds. Paying dividends of from 25 to 30 percent, Kreuger's companies were famous as good investments, and his bonds were popular, both with knowledgeable investors and those who emulated them. Among his purchasers were the Chase National Bank; Bankers Trust; Harvard, Yale, and the Groton School; the Baptist, Episcopal, and Presbyterian churches; the estate of Henry Cabot Lodge; and Boston's Cardinal William O'Connell. By 1932 Kreuger had sold nearly a quarter of a billion dollars' worth of bonds in the United States alone.

Kreuger owed his ability to raise such enormous sums to the vogue for foreign bonds that swept the United States after World War I. Lending was new to Americans. Until the war, America had been a borrowing nation, relying heavily on money from abroad to finance its growing infrastructure. Foreign investors—primarily British, but also German, French, and Dutch—lent billions to American businesses and state governments, which used the money to build the country's canals and railroads and to create its major mining, oil, electricity, steel, real estate, and liquor companies. Not all the investments were successful, or honest. In the mid-nineteenth century, the states of Maryland, Pennsylvania, Mississippi, and Louisiana, among others, defaulted on their foreign debts. In Anthony Sampson's words, many London bankers saw the United States "as a very unreliable developing country, with a black record of embezzlement, fraudulent prospectuses, and default."

Among the many victims of these defaults was Sydney Smith, an English clergyman and literary figure known for his sharp wit. Writing in the London *Morning Post*, Smith expressed astonishment that citizens of the defaulting states had the nerve to socialize in England. "How such a man can set himself down at an English table without feeling that he owes two or three pounds to every man in company, I am at a loss to conceive: he has no more right to eat with honest men than a leper has to eat with clean men."

World War I changed America's standing in the international financial community. The United States was virtually the only industrialized nation to emerge from the war with its manufacturing base intact—the only nation with money to invest abroad. Now the rest of the world needed money to rebuild, and American investors—large and small—were able and eager to supply it. Between 1914 and 1930, more than $17 billion worth of foreign bonds was floated in the United States. These bonds were issued by national governments, by provinces and cities, and by just about every other enterprise imaginable, from mortgage companies to steamship lines, from chain stores to religious institutions.

Foreign bonds became popular because they carried high interest rates and they were energetically promoted by the banks that sold them at what a 1933 Senate report called "outrageously high profits." They were so profitable, in fact, that representatives of elite investment firms like J. P. Morgan and Kuhn, Loeb & Company searched the world for business, "competing on almost a violent scale," as Morgan partner Thomas Lamont put it. Governments found it hard to resist what Lamont described as "a horde of American bankers sitting on their doorsteps offering them money."

Lamont was not exaggerating: At one period there were twenty-nine representatives of American securities houses trying to drum up business in Colombia alone. The result, the American commercial attaché in Bogota reported, was that "Colombia is going wild on borrowing. She has started too many railroads and too many highways, and she has not any idea where she is going to get all the money [to repay the loans]." Nor were national governments the only objects of the bankers' attentions. Thirty-six firms competed to lend money to the city of Budapest and there is a contemporary account of "a Bavarian hamlet, discovered by American agents to be in need of about $125,000, [which] was urged and finally persuaded to borrow three million dollars in the American market."

In this frenzied atmosphere, few bankers were inclined to look too closely at the creditworthiness of would-be borrowers. In 1927 and 1928, for example, a syndicate of the top American firms floated $100 million worth of Peruvian government bonds, though one advisor had warned them that "the government treasury is flat on its back and gasping for breath" and another had reported that "the way things were going the loans would be in default within five years." The president of the Reserve Bank of Peru even came to New York to caution the syndicate that the country could not afford such large loans and to plead with them to offer less. They refused. All the bonds were sold, and the syndicate made a profit of $5.5 million, of which half a million went as a "commission" to Juan Leguia, the son of the country's dictator. Five years later—as predicted—Peru defaulted on those bonds. In another case, the Argentine province of Mendoza managed to borrow $6 million in the United States, although it was already in default on its existing foreign debts.

These were far from isolated incidents, but ordinary bond buyers knew nothing about them. They were in no position to appraise the soundness of a foreign government, much less of a particular bond issue. They simply trusted the respected firms that sold the bonds. In 1927, a survey by J. P. Morgan & Company found that 85 percent of the people who bought foreign bonds were small investors—"schoolteachers, army officers, country doctors, stenographers, clerks"—whose chief reason for investing in overseas securities was "the fact that [they] had confidence in the banker[s] who offered [them] the investment."

A cursory examination of the uses to which the bond money was put would have revealed that many loans were unlikely ever to be repaid. Some were simply wasted on the standard items with which rulers traditionally indulge themselves—presidential palaces, personal railway cars, polo ponies. Others were used to buy the loyalty of the people—rich and poor. Brazil, for example, borrowed $300 million to keep coffee prices artificially high, a practice that benefited only a small elite. The support of the urban masses was sought through the construction of municipal swimming pools—a good deed, but one not likely to produce the foreign exchange needed to repay its underwriters.

Some public works schemes were no more than employment projects aimed at defusing social unrest. This was the case with a road from Lima to Callao that was built right alongside an existing road linking the two cities. Another Peruvian road-building project, noted Lawrence Dennis, drew "hundreds of thousands of Indians from the mountains, where they were living quietly and happily in a primitive state . . . into the cities to work at 75 cents or a dollar a day. Then, when the work ceased, it threw that floating population on the cities, without resources to return to their native places and resume their former modes of life." As Dennis, an official in the U.S. embassy in Lima, remarked, "You only needed to get off the boat and take one look around [to realize] that the expenditures in Peru would not produce income."

Even ostensibly productive investments were often ill conceived. Colombia borrowed $150 million to build a railway tunnel through a mountain to link the valleys on either side, ignoring two important facts: The valleys each had an outlet to the sea and were already connected by sea transport, and local authorities were also building a road over the 9,000-foot high mountain. In any case, the tunnel proved impossibly expensive and was abandoned, half completed. The chief beneficiaries of many public works were the construction companies that built them.

As their debts mounted, governments began taking out new loans in order to pay off old ones. Bolivia, for example, borrowed $21 million and spent two-thirds of it paying off public debts and most of the rest on arms and military roads. By 1935, 38 percent of the foreign bonds held by Americans were in default.

Irresponsible bond salesmen weren't the only ones to blame. The United States was pursuing policies that made it difficult or even impossible for America's borrowers to repay their debts. In the words of the historian and economist Herbert Feis, "We sought and rejoiced in the expansion of our foreign trade. But we refused to face the fact that it lacked a healthy balance; and that it was being sustained by loans that would in the end be too great a burden upon foreign debtors. We maintained high tariffs. We tenaciously claimed repayment of war debts which prejudiced prospects of solvency of the private investment we were encouraging." Under such conditions, said Feis, outright defaults and long-term moratoria—postponements of repayment—were inevitable.

It was not the big financiers and international investment banks who suffered most from the defaults, but ordinary people who had followed their advice. The big banks that issued the bonds had protected themselves well. They took their commissions up front and unloaded most of the bonds on thousands of small "correspondent" banks who sold them on to individual investors. When the bond market collapsed, half the banks holding defaulted foreign bonds were rural banks, the institutional equivalent of the small investor. The defaults "contributed to the failure of numberless small country banks" during the Great Depression, according to one historian of the period.

———

In this setting, Kreuger stood out. Unlike the investment bankers, he was not a financial juggler, but a producer of goods, a contributor to the wealth of nations. *The Economist* praised him as "no mere gambler on a gigantic scale in the world's bourses, no mere 'promoter' in quest of personal profit

. . . [but] a man of great constructive intelligence and wide vision." As *Fortune* magazine put it, "At a time when credits had dried up and Europe was starving for money," Kreuger appeared out of nowhere like a knight in shining armor, with hundreds of millions of dollars to lend.

Borrowers, of course, welcomed Kreuger. So did the many investors who had money to invest but had lost faith in the existing bond market. Kreuger offered solid investments. In the first place he did not sell the bonds of foreign governments; he sold the bonds of his highly rated American and European companies and used the money from those sales to buy the foreign bonds himself. Secondly, Kreuger was selective in his lending. He had little to do with South America, a continent in which every country except Argentina was in default by the end of 1933. Finally, he secured his loans by demanding that the borrowing country grant him a match monopoly. The royalties he owed the state from his match company were his collateral for the money the state owed him. Kreuger's genius was to have devised a way of getting rich that earned him the support of governments, the awe of his fellow financiers, and the gratitude of his investors.

With the world in the midst of the Depression, however, even Kreuger was not immune to financial worries. He had come to Paris that Friday in 1932 to raise funds that he had been unable to obtain in New York. From the station he went first to meet with his accountants and then with the head of the Scandinavian Credit Bank, of which he was a part owner. In the evening he went back to his apartment on the avenue Victor-Emmanuel III, escorted by Krister Littorin, vice president of Swedish Match. The two men reviewed the day's events and confirmed tomorrow's appointments. Then Littorin left. Soon afterward, Kreuger also went out. He returned shortly, carrying a small package. The concierge greeted him as he passed, but—as she afterward recalled—he seemed distracted and didn't give his usual reply.

The next morning, Saturday, Kreuger sat at his desk and wrote three letters. He had an appointment at eleven, but instead of leaving the flat, he went into his bedroom, unwrapped the Browning automatic he had purchased the previous evening, drew the blinds, and lay down, fully dressed, on the unmade bed. He opened his waistcoat, snapped a cartridge into the revolver, pointed the gun at his heart, and drew the trigger.

It was several hours before Littorin and Kreuger's housekeeper discovered his body. When they did, their first concern was to forestall an international economic panic. News of Kreuger's death was likely to destabilize, temporarily at least, not only his own concerns, but also the many others with which his were linked. His business associates in New York, Paris, and Sweden were informed of the suicide, but the Paris police kept the news quiet until the New York Stock Exchange had ended its Saturday trading. When the Swedish government learned that its wealthiest citizen had killed himself, Parliament went into an emergency session at midnight. Fearing chaos when the news broke, it ordered the nation's stock exchanges closed and granted Kreuger's business empire a moratorium on its debts. On Sunday, when the suicide was finally made public, flags in Stockholm flew at half-mast.

The news of Kreuger's death stunned and saddened the financial and diplomatic world. It became known that he had been in ill health and that the management of his vast financial empire had become an insupportable strain. Virtually everyone sympathized with the personal despondency that must have pushed Kreuger to his desperate deed, and this blemish on a brilliant career was widely regretted. *The Times* of London paid him homage in its editorial columns: "The man who was driven on Saturday to this last act was no common adventurer caught up and cornered at last by the self-defeating ingenuity of his devices. . . . A man of ambition but no vanity, Mr. Kreuger seems to have had no weakness of the kind that brings weaker timber to wreck. . . . Least of all does personal suspicion light upon him in his last day."

There are inquiries after any death, and the suicide of a powerful millionaire invites special scrutiny. The Swedish government appointed a six-man Investigating Commission to look into Kreuger's affairs. Three days after his funeral, the commission announced that things were "worse than had been feared." This disturbing statement caused observers to recall certain earlier incidents that, in retrospect, took on an ominous cast. In 1929, for example, Mahlers Bank in Holland had severed relations with Kreuger because he had failed to provide them with all the information they required. Two years after that, in a public lecture, an eminent Danish economist had said of Sweden, "The ship of that country carries too dangerous a cargo: I speak of Mr. Ivar Kreuger." And of course, there was Percy Rockefeller's famous comment after visiting Kreuger's Swedish headquarters in 1925: "It seemed almost too good to be true."

Only a few days after the commission's disclosure, Kreuger's bankers made their own terse announcement: "Gross frauds have been perpetrated by Mr. Kreuger." Among the maze of his companies and holding companies, it had been discovered, were scores of fictitious businesses, each rich with imaginary assets held by imaginary banks.

The blind faith that had been shown by Kreuger's bankers was stunning. The investigating accountants said of Kreuger's financial reports that "the manipulations were so childish that anyone with but a rudimentary knowledge of bookkeeping could see the books were falsified." It turned out, however, that none of Kreuger's bankers *had* seen his books. His reputation was so solid and his plausibility so great that virtually the entire financial community worldwide took the same view as the head of the Chase National Bank's executive committee, who explained that Chase had never bothered to check up on Kreuger because "we had no doubt as to everything being all right."

To take one particularly striking example, Kreuger had put up $150 million worth of Italian bonds (received, he explained to his bankers, in return for a secret loan to the Italian government) as security for several different loans, including one from the Bank of Sweden. He was able to do this because his lenders didn't actually require him to deposit the bonds with them. After his death, the bonds were found in Stockholm and claimed by the Swedish government. Eager to beat other creditors to the punch, the Swedish minister of justice himself took the bonds to Rome to redeem them. Mussolini received the minister, examined the bonds, and pronounced them forgeries—and not especially good ones. Not only had they been printed in Stockholm, but Kreuger had left clear signs of pencil tracing and misspelled several Italian words, including the names of the officials who had supposedly signed the bonds.

Thus within a month of his death, the man the *New Statesman* had called "a very Puritan of finance" was revealed as a bankrupt, a forger, and a swindler on a colossal scale, a man who had robbed investors of at least $750 million. The consequences of his perfidy were wide-ranging. Politicians and businessmen in several countries, including Germany, Poland, Spain, and Italy, were found to have collaborated with Kreuger, mostly by taking bribes in return for loans. The prime minister of Sweden, for example, was forced to resign when it came out that Kreuger had given substantial gifts to his party shortly before being granted a multi-million-dollar credit by the National Bank. This single loan seriously depleted Sweden's foreign exchange reserves and led to the country's abandonment of the gold standard.

Among Kreuger's innocent investors were many prominent men, scores of whom were ruined when his bonds went into default. But what the rich called ruin was often merely inconvenience, as when Prince Carl, brother of the king of Sweden, was forced to move to more modest quarters. Kreuger's real victims were the hundreds of thousands of ordinary people who had entrusted him with most or all of their savings. According to Max Winkler, vice president of Moody's Investor Services, Kreuger's bonds were held "by innumerable widows and orphans." "Within a week the suicides were coming in," said *Fortune* magazine—among them were a municipal clerk who slit his wrists, an office worker who killed himself in one of Stockholm's public gardens, a German lumberman, and a baker.

The collapse of the Kreuger empire dealt a fatal blow to the trade in foreign bonds, weakened as it already was by the defaults of Bolivia, Chile, Colombia, Peru, Hungary, Greece, Bulgaria, and Austria. Suddenly people's eyes were opened to the risks of lending money to sovereign nations. In the past, American investors had derived a sense of security from the government's willingness, as a last resort, to use military action to protect the interests of its financiers. U.S. troops were even then defending U.S. economic interests in Haiti and Nicaragua, and had only recently left the Dominican Republic. But those incursions had been ordered at a time when foreign investment was still an elite activity. The U.S. government was not eager to extend its occupation of foreign countries for the sake of small investors—however numerous they were. The new philosophy was "Let the buyer beware." Some states tried to protect the public with laws banning the sales of foreign securities, but such laws were hardly necessary in the 1930s. Foreign investment had lost its allure. There was a depression on. What money they had, Americans kept to themselves. The United States was no longer the world's banker.

# Three

The withdrawal of American investors from the world market deepened the global depression of the 1930s. In an effort to maintain their share of the shrinking world market, country after country tried to undercut their competitors with policies that succeeded chiefly in provoking damaging retaliatory measures. These dueling currency devaluations and trade barriers only pulled the world deeper into the vortex. It became clear that no industrial nation could isolate itself from the global economy.

Though World War II interrupted this downward spiral, it did not eliminate its causes. There was widespread fear that peace would bring a return to ruinous trade battles, which have a history of leading to battles of another sort. Thus the Allies—in particular the United States and Britain—were convinced that their future security depended as much on reforming international trade as on winning the war. Even at the height of the fighting, this problem occupied them.

The first serious proposal for a new postwar economic order was put forward by an American economist named Harry Dexter White. In 1934, White left a teaching career at Harvard to join the Treasury Department, where he moved quickly up the ranks of the civil service. By 1941, he was director of the Division of Monetary Research and chief economic advisor to Treasury Secretary Henry Morganthau. Though his name has a pluto-cratic ring to it, White was in fact the child of Lithuanian immigrants who ran a hardware shop in Boston.

In the late summer of 1941, White surprised his Treasury colleagues with a two-pronged plan that called for the establishment of a "stabilization fund" that could keep world exchange rates in equilibrium, and "a bank for reconstruction and development" to invest in war-damaged and poor countries. White's scheme had no official standing. He had developed it on his own initiative, working at home during his off-hours, and its opening words were a modest "I believe . . ." Morganthau, however, was impressed by White's ideas, and on December 14—one week after the attack on Pearl Harbor and America's entrance into the war—asked him to draw up a more formal paper for President Roosevelt to consider.

White's stabilization fund was an attempt to address a well-recognized problem: the barrier to international trade posed by differing national currencies. The need for a "world bank" was less well understood, but to White, no less pressing. He reasoned that though the United States would emerge from the war with a reasonably robust economy, it would suffer from a lack of healthy trading partners. It would therefore be necessary to reconstruct Europe and to bring the countries of Africa, Asia, and Latin America up to world market standards, a feat that would require massive investments. Americans would have money to invest, but after the experience of the 1920s and 1930s they would be reluctant to do so. White's bank would foster needed investments by guaranteeing to cover any defaults on loans of which it approved.

In White's eyes, the bank and the fund needed one another. The fund would help create a stable climate for international trade by harmonizing its members' monetary policies, and the bank would enable its members to improve their capacity to trade. It was clear, said one contemporary observer, that "the two things, monetary reconstruction and the reconstruction of trade, were quite inseparable." Together they would contribute to a worldwide prosperity that was the best possible guarantee of peace. Morganthau and Roosevelt liked White's proposal, and in July 1942 the Americans sent the British government a copy.

There was one person in Britain above all others whose opinion of his plan White was eager to hear. That was John Maynard Keynes, the preeminent economist of the age, who was then serving as an advisor to the British Treasury. Keynes, White knew, believed strongly that prosperity was essential to peace. Attending the Paris Peace Conference at the end of World War I as a representative of the British government, Keynes had been so appalled by the onerous war reparations being imposed on Germany that he resigned his position in protest. He predicted that the vengeful conditions forced on Germany by the Allies would drive that country into chaos—with disastrous consequences for the rest of Europe. World War II proved him right.

Unbeknownst to White, Keynes too had a plan, a near-utopian design for global economic cooperation through an international currency union. Keynes's proposed union was more powerful, more radical than the fund White had envisioned. The union was to be the central bank for the nations of the world, accepting deposits, extending credit, and charging interest. It would also issue its own currency. This "new-fangled international monetary unit" was to be called the bancor—or possibly the unitas, the dolphin, the bezant, or the daric. Keynes was ambitious for the union; he hoped it "might become the pivot of the future economic government of the world."

In the fall of 1943, American and British officials met in Washington to discuss the Keynes and White plans. The Americans felt that Keynes's plan went too far. They disapproved in particular of his proposal to charge interest not only on overdrafts but on trade surpluses as well. It was Keynes's thesis that imbalances in trade were the responsibility of both the debtor and the creditor nations. He maintained that countries with a long-term surplus of foreign currency contribute just as much to international disequilibrium as do those that cannot repay their trading partners. The Americans, then the world's major creditors, saw this as heresy, though U.S. officials today take very much the same line with trading partners, such as Japan, who have a long-term surplus of dollars.

The negotiators finally merged the two plans into a proposal—one with more of White than of Keynes in it—for "a permanent institution for international monetary cooperation" to be known as the International Monetary Fund. Next they were to take up the proposal for a world bank. The British insisted that these discussions be held in strict secrecy, because they felt that the public would not accept two major new financial institutions. News of the bank proposal appeared in the press, however, and the discussions were promptly ended.

In 1944 President Roosevelt invited the Allies to a conference at the Mount Washington Hotel, near the resort of Bretton Woods in New Hampshire's White Mountains, to consider the proposed International Monetary Fund. In mid-June, shortly after D-Day, the Queen Mary left England with a cargo of British and European-exile economists and civil servants bound for the conference. White's plan for a world bank, which had never really been seriously discussed outside the Treasury Department, was not on the agenda, but a draft of the bank idea surfaced aboard the Queen Mary during the crossing and generated a great deal of interest. Keynes, who had been disappointed at the watering down of his currency union idea, took up the bank proposal with enthusiasm and became its leading spokesman. It was not surprising that the idea of making loans to governments should appeal to Keynes. His influential critique of classical economics was based on the notion that the way to end recessions was for government to stimulate the economy, through deficit spending if necessary. By the time the *Queen Mary* docked, the European contingent, under Keynes's leadership, had completed a "Boat Draft," rounding out White's proposal, and added the bank proposal to the Bretton Woods program.

In the peace and quiet of rural New England, more than four hundred delegates from forty-four Allied countries spent the first three weeks of July devising a new shape for the postwar international economy. The atmosphere was not entirely democratic, as this excerpt from a memo by Keynes to the British Treasury indicates: "Twenty-one countries have been invited which clearly have nothing to contribute and will merely encumber the ground. . . . It is the most monstrous monkey-house assembled for years." It was not all work, either, at least not for the twenty delegates who registered for dancing lessons with Arthur Murray instructor Mignon MacLean, or for those who took time to explore the nearby forests and seashore, hotel bars, and movie theaters.

Surprisingly, the bank proved to be far less controversial than the Fund, though the Fund had been debated for the previous several years and the bank not at all. In a remarkably short time the conference drafted the charter and bylaws for what came to be called the International Bank for Reconstruction and Development, the IBRD, or World Bank, for short. One of the delegates reported that "if one measured the time spent during those [twenty-one] . . . days of work at the Bretton Woods Conference, the Bank probably didn't take more than a day and a half."

The conference also passed a resolution urging the creation of a third agency, the International Trade Organization, whose role it would be to oversee trade relations. Both White and Keynes regarded such a body as an essential element in the hoped-for new economic order. A charter was drafted, but despite extensive negotiations, the proposal fell into limbo, where it remained for most of the next five decades until emerging, in 1995, as the newly formed World Trade Organization.

As for the World Bank, it was agreed that it would be open only to countries that first joined the Fund, and that each member would pledge a sum of money proportionate to its national income. The Bank would start life with nearly $10 billion. Each member would put up 2 percent of its subscription in gold or dollars and 18 percent in its national currency. The other 80 percent would be called in only if it was needed to cover a default.

The World Bank was not intended to compete with private banks. The original idea was that it would guarantee loans made by private lenders, but most private lenders were still reluctant to lend overseas, even with the Bank's guarantee, and the Bank soon found that it could offer loans itself at lower rates of interest than private lenders wanted to charge. It would make such loans, however, only when foreign exchange was not available on reasonable terms from private lenders. Thus it would deal in high-risk loans, but it would minimize the risks by ensuring that its loans were used, in Keynes's words, "only for proper purposes and in proper ways, after due enquiries by experts and technicians, so that there will be safeguards against squandering and waste and extravagance which were not present with many of the ill-fated loans made between the wars." Reducing its risk would enable the Bank to charge lower interest rates, which would in turn reduce the likelihood of default.

A key aspect of the Bank's operations was that it would lend only foreign exchange and it would insist on being repaid in the currencies it lent. Therefore the projects it funded would have to earn foreign exchange. The Bank was empowered to lend both to governments and to private businesses, but in either case it insisted that the loan be guaranteed by the government in question. As a result, the Bank had few private borrowers.

The Bank was to be governed by its members, which were to have votes in proportion to their financial contribution. The United States' $3.2 billion earned it 35 percent of the votes; Britain, the next largest contributor, had 14 percent, and Panama, the smallest member, had .002 percent. The Bank would be controlled by a board of governors made up of one representative from each member nation, usually a country's treasury minister or the governor of its central bank. This board, however, would meet only a few times a year. The day-to-day responsibility for the Bank was vested in an executive board to be composed of twelve full-time executive directors—one each from the top five shareholders and seven more elected by the remaining members. It was agreed that the Bank's headquarters would be in the United States and that English would be its official language.

A public debate on the proposed Fund and Bank took place over the next year, as each member country considered whether to ratify the Bretton Woods agreement. Fiscal conservatives, who detested the interventionist ethos of Keynesian economics, warned bitterly that the new institutions would place an intolerable burden of lending on the United States and of debt on the borrowing countries. One right-wing American critic, John F. Neylan, called Keynes a "brilliant exponent of the project of substituting economic imperialism for political imperialism with London and other European capitals as the seats of Empire" and warned that "the Bretton Woods agreement does not contemplate a new world order based upon freedom and expanding development of all the human race. It is a document which seeks to create an economic strait-jacket for the benefit of a continent which for centuries has drained the treasure of the rest of the earth to finance its wars and to support it in intervals of peace."

The biggest stumbling block to congressional approval of the Bretton Woods agreement was the opposition of Republican Senator Robert Taft of Ohio, the formidable son of the twenty-seventh president. He could not, he announced, allow "American money [to be placed] in a fund to be dispensed by an international board in which we have only a minority interest." Taft was brilliant, eloquent, and in the words of one political journalist, "thoroughly respected even by those of his colleagues who disagree with him most." He criticized the Bank on economic, political, and even sociological grounds, warning that the poor nations of the world would become dependant on "a largesse which cannot and will not continue" and that "a nation that comes to rely on gifts and loans from others is too likely to postpone the essential tough measures necessary for its own salvation."

The American people, it is fair to say, were apathetic about the prospective Bank. A survey showed that fewer than a quarter of the population associated the phrase "Bretton Woods" with world affairs. Among those who did, however, some worried "that the United States will be a 'sucker' nation, playing 'Santa Claus' to the world." To whip up popular support, the administration embarked on a highly organized propaganda effort. Morganthau hired a New York public relations whiz named Randolph Feltus, who started out by enlisting every influential organization imaginable—from the League of Women Voters to the Council on Foreign Relations—to sell the idea. It was, wrote a scholar of the period, "one of the most elaborate and sophisticated campaigns ever conducted by a government agency in support of legislation."

The American Federation of Retailers mailed 1.8 million letters, urging its members to demand approval of the Bretton Woods agreement. The Congress of Industrial Organizations announced that approval of Bretton Woods would create 5 million new jobs in foreign trade. The League of Women Voters put more than 100,000 flyers and pamphlets in doctors' offices, beauty salons, and grocery stores. One explained to schoolchildren what would happen if the Bretton Woods agreement was not approved. The United States would adopt high tariffs and refuse to engage in foreign trade, making other countries poorer and poorer, and soon "madder and madder" until "everybody began rattling their GUNS."

The campaign was successful in getting support for the Bretton Woods agreement, if not in explaining it. As Senator Sheridan Downey of California said, "I do not imagine or claim that one citizen out of a hundred in our world community possesses accurate or detailed knowledge of the provisions of the Bretton Woods proposal. . . . But to millions it has come, nevertheless, to represent a symbol of our sincerity, our determination, to make good on our promises and pledges of a better postwar world."

Though a majority of the Senate came to support the Bretton Woods agreement, the opposition, still led energetically by Taft, posed a serious threat to American membership because a treaty requires the approval of two-thirds of the Senate. To circumvent this condition, the Treasury Department rewrote the Bretton Woods treaty as a multilateral executive agreement, a form that requires the approval of only simple majorities in both houses of Congress.

Congress passed the Bretton Woods Agreements Act and President Truman signed it into law on July 31, 1945. Many more nations had to ratify the accord, however, before the Bank and the Fund would officially come into being. The deadline for ratification was December 31, 1945, but by November 14 only the United States, South Africa, and Venezuela had signed on. The Soviet Union decided not to join, but at the last minute twenty-six other countries followed the U.S. lead. On December 27, at a signing ceremony in the State Department, the Bank and the Fund formally came into being.

———

Late in the autumn of 1944, Peter Lieftinck, a Dutch economist imprisoned at the Nazi concentration camp at Buchenwald, saw a guard drop a newspaper. He picked it up, and

> hid it under my jacket, my prisoner's jacket, and I went back to my barracks and opened the paper. It was a small, local paper, and I found in that paper a little paragraph about a conference at Bretton Woods by the enemies where they had decided to establish after the war a World Bank and an International Monetary Fund. . . . I wrote to Geneva to request such information on that Bretton Woods conference as they could obtain. Three months

later I received a Red Cross package in camp. Imagine almost starving—really starving—and receiving a package of something! I opened the package: no food, no cigarettes, but papers, documents: the minutes and the conclusions of the Bretton Woods conference. . . . I started studying those papers. I started lecturing to my coprisoners. Then in June '45, I came back to Holland and was invited to join the first postwar cabinet as a minister. . . . [Soon] it became clear that I knew more about Bretton Woods than anybody in all of Holland.

As finance minister, Lieftinck was, ex-officio, Holland's governor of the World Bank. In that capacity, he attended the inaugural meeting of the board of governors in Savannah, Georgia, in March of 1946. The United States was keen to impress its foreign partners with the depth of American support for the Bank. As Lieftinck and the other governors stepped off the train that brought them from Washington, they were amazed to find that "the whole population of the town of Savannah had come to welcome us, and the streets were lined with people and children with little flags."

At Savannah, the governors dealt with a number of unresolved issues on which the British, led by Keynes, and the Americans strongly disagreed. At the heart of them all was the question of whether the Bank would be free of all political interference, as Keynes thought essential. Though it was a foregone conclusion that the Bank's main office would be in the United States, which was, after all, its major shareholder and the country from which most of its funds would be raised, Keynes felt strongly that the Bank should operate from New York, the nation's financial capital, not Washington, its political one. The U.S. government, however, wanted the Bank in Washington, and its view prevailed. The Bank moved into 1818 H Street, a State Department building just two blocks from the White House.

There was also the matter of salaries. The American view was that salaries had to be set quite high in order to persuade Wall Street that the Bank was a serious institution. Its partners, however, considered the pay rates the United States proposed grossly inflated. Again, as the most powerful member, the United States carried the day. The Bank's president's salary was set at $30,000 a year, and its executive directors' at $17,000. By comparison, U.S. cabinet members were earning $15,000 a year and British MPs less than $4,000. Keynes condemned Bank salaries as "scandalous."

The third major battle was inconclusive. Keynes thought that the executive directors should act mainly as liaisons between the Bank and its member states, and that the Bank itself should be run by its staff, who would be expert economists and engineers. He feared that the directors would put the interests of their own governments before those of the Bank. The United States, on the other hand, wanted an active, full-time board, through which the U.S. executive director could vigorously promote American interests. The issue was not resolved, but Keynes took the granting of large salaries to the directors to be a bad omen, portending a meddlesome board.

Savannah was a sad disappointment to the British. As one student of the Bank's early days put it, "The British returned from Savannah feeling that the Fund and the Bank were little more than schemes of the United States to gain control of world trade. They had opposed the selection of Washington as the site for the Bank and the payment of large salaries to the officers and executive directors and they had been overruled by the United States on both issues." Keynes had argued so bitterly at Savannah with U.S. Treasury Secretary Fred Vinson and was so distressed by the course on which the Bank seemed to be set that his friends blamed the meeting for the heart attack he suffered on the train back to Washington, and for a second, a month later, which killed him at the age of sixty-three.

Keynes's partner in the creation of the World Bank, Harry Dexter White, came to a sad end a few years later. After the war, Whittaker Chambers, the Communist spy turned informer, accused him of being the leader of a spy ring in the Treasury and of having passed information to the Russians and the Chinese Communists. Though a grand jury refused to indict White, his career was destroyed by the allegations. At his own request he appeared before the Committee on Un-American Activities on August 13, 1948 to defend himself. There, to the applause of spectators, he vigorously denied the charges. He returned to his home in New Hampshire, weakened by the stress of the experience. Three days later he was felled by a fatal heart attack.

---

Today only a hermit could be unaware that hundreds of millions of people around the world live in poverty, but we were not always so well informed. It was not until 1935 that there was a worldwide review of the extent of hunger and malnutrition, published by the League of Nations. Five years later, the British economist Colin Clark published his classic study *Conditions of Economic Progress,* which first laid out the gulf between the living standards in rich and poor countries in hard statistical terms. The American people first had their attention drawn to world poverty as a political issue by Harry Truman in his 1949 inaugural speech. Truman proposed the first peacetime foreign aid plan in history: The United States, he declared, must undertake "a bold new program . . . for the improvement and growth of underdeveloped areas." Appealing to altruism and to fear, he told Americans that "more than half the people of the world are living in conditions approaching misery" and warned that these unhappy people were easy prey for communism, "the false philosophy which has made such headway throughout the world, misleading many peoples and adding to their sorrows and their difficulties."

In referring to some countries as underdeveloped, Truman implied that there is an order to societal development, that all societies move in the same direction, along a single path. The farther along this path they have gone, the closer they are to realizing their full potential. A few countries are out in front, others are moving up rapidly, but most lag far behind. In this, Truman echoed, no doubt unconsciously, Karl Marx, who wrote in the preface to *Das Kapital*, "The industrially more developed country presents to the less developed country a picture of the latter's future." Truman's refinement on Marx was the notion that it is the duty of the front-runners, especially the United States as leader of the pack, to help those countries that trail behind.

Truman was presenting a new, seemingly more benevolent view of the human condition than that which had held sway in earlier days. The colonial powers did not think that the rest of the world could or should aspire to a Western way of life. True, most felt they had a duty to introduce some aspects of their own civilization to their domains—Christianity, modern standards of hygiene, and at least enough law and order to ensure the safety of colonial administrators and businessmen. But the overriding aim of the colonial powers with respect to their colonies—and one for which they offered no apology—was to secure from them a good supply of raw materials. They were traders first, missionaries second: The two roles were distinct.

Truman and the newly hatched company of development specialists took a different line. To them, trade and civilization were inseparable. Trade brings prosperity; prosperity brings peace and a whole host of other good things, from longevity to literacy to creative freedom to democracy. By "mak[ing] available to peace-loving people the benefits of our store of technical knowledge" and "foster[ing] capital investment," Truman explained, we would "help them realize their aspirations for a better life."

As the Depression and World War II demonstrated, we live on a small planet where no country can isolate itself. The financial burden imposed on Germany after the previous war led to domestic political upheavals that ultimately drew virtually every country, no matter how stable or self-reliant, into a global conflict. More than anything else, the public case for the International Monetary Fund and the World Bank rested on the argument that they were essential to the establishment of global prosperity, without which the world would again sink into war. A 1945 United Nations pamphlet promoting the Fund and Bank paraphrased a famous remark of President Lincoln's to make the point: "We may say that a world half prosperous and half starving cannot long preserve peace, and that prosperity must be achieved for all unless insecurity is to spread to all."

———

In deference to its position as the largest shareholder in both the Fund and the Bank, the United States has, by tradition, always chosen the leaders of both institutions. It had at one time been expected that Keynes would be appointed to run the World Bank and White to run the International Monetary Fund. This would give the leadership of one organization to a European and the other to an American, a division that suited the major powers. Keynes's premature death and rumors of White's Communist sympathies ended that plan. Instead, Camille Gutt, formerly the finance minster of Belgium, was appointed to the IMF's top post. This established the tradition, continued ever since, that the Fund is headed by a European and the World Bank by an American.

It proved surprisingly difficult, however, to find an American willing to be president of the World Bank. In May 1946, when it opened its doors for business, it still had no leader. The problem was that the financial world was highly skeptical about the new institution and no financier of stature was willing to risk his reputation on the infant institution. It was widely assumed that the Bank's operations would be dictated by political pressures rather than by sound financial considerations.

"People thought that the Bank was headed for failure, that in a few years it would probably exhaust all its money and become bankrupt," said Luis Machado, who at that time represented Mexico and several other Latin American countries on the Bank's executive board. As the Bank's own authorized history put it, "To most U.S. investors the Bank was, at the outset, just another device for channeling hard-earned U.S. savings into the pockets of foreigners of doubtful probity." President Truman offered the post to—and was refused by—a succession of influential financiers. No one, it seemed, wanted to be head of an institution whose prospects were as dim as the World Bank's.

Nor did anyone want to buy its bonds. "We could not sell one bond anywhere," said Machado. "Our only market was the United States, and we found out that the business community . . . actually was against the Bank." While the search for a president went on, the Bank's executive board tried to win the confidence of Wall Street. It soon discovered that it faced not only skepticism, but legal barriers. The federal government had rescinded its prewar ban on the sale of foreign securities, but many states still had their own restrictions on the sale of foreign bonds. Several even imposed new bans specifically aimed at the World Bank. In 1946, for example, Wisconsin prohibited the sale of Bank bonds because, in the words of one state banking official, they were guaranteed by governments whose pledges weren't "worth a whoop in hell."

"We had to start converting every one of those states to the idea of allowing the World Bank bonds to be sold—and that was an excruciating job," said Machado. The U.S. director, an energetic and strong-willed State Department economist named Emilio Collado, led the campaign to make the sale of Bank bonds legal. "And did we have opposition! In New York State we almost didn't make it. I got it in New Jersey over the opposition of the Prudential and they were mad as hell. Maybe I shouldn't put this in the record, but this went on. . . . I did all sorts of strange things that I never in my life thought I would have to do."

In June 1946, President Truman finally found a leader for the World Bank. He named Eugene Meyer, publisher of The Washington Post, as Bank president. The seventy-year-old Meyer was a former investment banker with a long record of public service, but his appointment came out of the blue. According to Collado, what happened was that "President Truman one day was having lunch with Gene Meyer and said, 'How would you like to be president of the World Bank?' And Gene said, 'Yes.' He wasn't told of any of the conditions. He didn't even know there was an international board. . . . This is something the President did on the spur of the moment and without consulting anybody and—well, I would just say that there was a certain degree of desperation."

Meyer soon discovered that the World Bank did indeed have an international board—one that did not intend to turn control of the Bank over to him. The twelve-man board included several formidable figures, men such as Pierre Mendès-France, the future prime minister of France, and Sir James Grigg, Britain's secretary of state for war during World War II, who were accustomed to delegating, not relinquishing, power. The dominant member of the board was the American director, Emilio Collado. Both Collado and Meyer owed their jobs to the U.S. government, but Collado's loyalty was to the United States, while Meyer's had to be to the World

Bank. The United States was anxious for funds to flow—and flow quickly—to its wartime allies and potential new friends, so Collado pressed the Bank to begin lending immediately. Meyer, on the other hand, was convinced that the Bank would fail unless it acquired a reputation for prudence and sound management. He insisted that the Bank proceed cautiously in order to win the confidence of Wall Street—and to comply with the conditions laid down in the Bank's charter, its Articles of Agreement.

These conditions—the most important of which are that the Bank can lend only for "specific projects" and for "productive purposes"—make lending a slow process. The Bank must thoroughly scrutinize every project in advance to ensure that it will earn back its investment. Often the Bank insists that projects be redesigned to produce a better rate of return. Once a loan is approved, funds are disbursed gradually as the project proceeds under Bank monitoring.

The Truman administration argued that these conditions should be relaxed for the advanced economies of Europe. First, because those countries urgently needed money to pay for the imported materials required to rebuild their physical infrastructure. And second, because they had the expertise and experience to spend their borrowings intelligently without close supervision from the Bank. Meyer understood this argument but believed nonetheless that making large, quick-disbursing, relatively unsupervised loans—even to such worthy borrowers—would do nothing for the Bank's reputation as a reliable financial institution. Shortly after he took office, France and Denmark both applied for general-purpose loans, but Meyer held out against the pressure to approve them.

Chile was the first developing country to apply for a loan. In September 1946 it asked for $40 million. The request was accompanied by a book, beautifully bound in black morocco leather, explaining how the money was to be spent. Bank officials who studied the book called it vague, "more of an idea about a project [than] a project sufficiently prepared." Like the earlier requests from Europe, Chile's loan application triggered a quarrel between Meyer and his board. Collado was enthusiastic. He wanted the loan approved at once. This would finally put the Bank in business and give support to a country toward which the United States was favorably inclined. Chile, Collado stoutly declared, "was good for $40 million."

Meyer, on the other hand, was struck by the number of questions the application raised. What exactly was the money intended for? Was private funding available for that purpose? Would the investments be productive? Was Chile really "good for" the money? The question of Chile's creditworthiness was made more worrisome by the fact that the country was still in default on almost $300 million in bonds issued between 1885 and 1930. Meyer insisted that the Bank would make no loans to countries in default on earlier bonds until they negotiated a repayment schedule with their creditors. Throughout his tenure, Meyer refused to approve the loan. Meyer's tenure, however, proved to be short. Frustrated by his failure to get control of the organization he headed, Meyer surprised his colleagues by suddenly resigning in early December, after only six months on the job.

Once again the post was shopped around to a number of prominent men, including Secretary of the Navy James Forrestal and John J. McCloy, a Wall Street lawyer and former assistant secretary of war. But the aura of failure that hung about the Bank had only been strengthened by Meyer's abrupt resignation, and there were no takers. This second leaderless period so soon after the first demoralized the Bank's staff and worried the U.S. government. In desperation, the administration approached McCloy a second time. Finally, after demanding and receiving assurances that he, not the board, would run the Bank, McCloy agreed to take the job. He insisted that a friend of his, a vice president of Chase National (later Chase Manhattan) Bank named Eugene Black, be installed as the American executive director in place of the troublesome Collado. McCloy also brought in another old friend, Robert Garner, the former treasurer of Guaranty Trust, to be vice president. McCloy, Black, and Garner worked together closely at the Bank, and for a time even lived together—in a Washington house owned by a fourth pal, Nelson Rockefeller.

When McCloy took over in March 1947, a Swiss newspaper summed up the Bank's achievements in its first year as "zero." *The New York Times* characterized it as "split by dissension, sadly lacking in prestige, and [having] not lent one dime." McCloy was under pressure to get the Bank working before it became a laughingstock. Despite Collado's and Meyer's vigorous efforts to win over Wall Street, the Bank was still regarded with suspicion by financiers. "When we came down [to Washington]," Garner recalled, "there wasn't a Wall Street man who would touch the bonds with a ten-foot pole." But because McCloy, Black, and Garner were Wall Street men themselves, their presence at the Bank's helm heartened the financial community. The three were, in fact, so closely linked to Wall Street that, in the words of the economist and historian Robert Oliver, they "gave the Bank the reputation for being more concerned with protecting the interests of their former clients in New York—purchasers and underwriters of the Bank's bonds—than with actively pursuing the development of their new clients—the less developed countries of the world." That was just the image McCloy wanted to establish. In speech after speech, he made the point that he was not operating a charity for foreigners. The Bank would be good for American business, he promised; it would "create markets for U.S. trade . . . [and] stop Communism."

This was what Wall Street wanted to hear. Within four months of his arrival, McCloy felt he had enough support among his former colleagues to announce the first sale of World Bank bonds. At 10 A.M. on July 15, 1947, as he and Emil Schram, president of the New York Stock Exchange, looked on, the bidding began. By noon the $250 million offering was oversubscribed and Bank officials repaired to a celebratory lunch hosted by the Stock Exchange. The triumph was gratifying, though not entirely surprising: The Bank had planned its first excursion into the market with care. Reluctant to put itself completely in the hands of Wall Street, it had courted dealers all over the country, offering a guaranteed commission more than twice the normal rate. By "bending over backwards to accommodate [small] dealers indiscriminately," as The New York Times put it, the Bank outflanked Wall Street and created a momentum that eventually pulled in even the big institutional investors.

The successful sale was all the more welcome because the Bank was already almost out of cash. Two months before, McCloy had made the Bank's first loan—$250 million to France. He held back the loan until the French government gave evidence of its economic soundness by ridding the cabinet of Communists. That first loan was swiftly followed by three more: to Denmark, Holland, and Luxembourg. The Bank had only about $700 million in U.S. dollars and gold; the rest of its capital was in currencies that were unacceptable in international commerce. Thus, these four loans, together totaling $497 million, nearly depleted its lendable capital.

It was now clear that the Bank could not lend on the scale required to put Europe back on its feet. Even before the Bank had made a single loan, the Truman administration had allocated several billions of dollars to European reconstruction and was on the verge of announcing the Marshall Plan, a $12 billion program of American aid for Western Europe. The Marshall Plan dwarfed the World Bank and made its reconstruction role obsolete, a turn of events the Bank accepted with aplomb. McCloy calmly described the Bank as a rowboat compared to the Marshall Plan's Queen Elizabeth. The Bank continued to lend money to Europe and Japan during the 1950s and 1960s—but only for specific projects or programs, not for general reconstruction work. Despite its formal name, the International Bank for Reconstruction and Development was not to be the vehicle for the reconstruction of Europe. It would concentrate instead on the development of Africa, Asia, and Latin America.

There was an obstacle, however, to beginning this work. McCloy, like Meyer before him, refused to lend money to any country until it made good its existing foreign debts. This stance, recalled Garner, occasioned "a very strong attack by some of our directors, by some of the press, [and] by others, that this was an improper role and that we were Wall Street bill collectors." Nonetheless, McCloy held strong—and eventually prevailed. The Bank made its first development loan to Chile—$13.5 million for a dam—on March 25, 1948, the day after Chile reached a settlement with its foreign creditors. Thus the Bank began its development work.

Development, however, did not much appeal to McCloy. His biographers describe him as having "little understanding of or interest in the Third World." In 1949, having served only two years of his five-year term as president, he left the Bank for a more prestigious post, that of U.S. high commissioner in Germany.

# Four

When McCloy resigned as president, rumor had it that Eugene Black, who was then the U.S. executive director, would be named to succeed him. Black, traveling in Europe, heard the gossip, but he had no intention of prolonging his stay in Washington. He had come to the Bank only out of loyalty to McCloy and was eager to return to New York and his work at Chase Manhattan. "I sent back word," Black later said, "that under no conditions did I want my name to be put up. . . . I made various suggestions of other people. I did everything on earth to prevent my taking the job. I didn't want it. I wanted to make a career in the Chase Bank."

It wasn't to be, however. "The pressure was put on me and the pressure was put on the Chase Bank to release me, and [in May 1949] I finally took it," recalled Black. Like his predecessor, Black was a reluctant president, but unlike McCloy, he soon warmed to the job. "I became very interested in what I was doing and I found there was more inner satisfaction in doing this than there was in making money. That's why I stuck it out. . . . [My years at the Bank have] been among the most interesting years of my life, the happiest years of my life." They were also, in retrospect, the happiest years of the Bank's life. During Black's thirteen-year reign, the Bank enjoyed a public respect and an inner steadiness that have eluded it ever since.

Black's Southern upbringing, the charm and courteousness for which he was known, endeared him to the board and staff. He was friendly and approachable, and the staff liked his chatting with them in the elevator, playing baseball at staff picnics, and handing out the awards at the Bank bowling league's annual dinner. He courted and consulted the directors so assiduously—the staff called them his "concubines"—that they did not seem to mind that they exercised no more power during his reign than they had during his predecessor's.

In Black the Bank finally had more than a transient leader. Meyer had served just six months; McCloy, two years. Each put his stamp on the infant Bank, but it was under Black, the longest-serving president the Bank has ever had, that the institution reached its maturity. McCloy had regarded the Bank as a stopgap institution. He believed it would "go out of business in due course because the long-term capital needed for development would eventually be provided directly by private investors." Black felt the same way when he took office but he soon changed his mind. "When the Bank first started," he told an interviewer in 1961, "[it] was looked on as a sort of bridge between war and peace. When peace came along, pretty soon the different foreign governments would be able to borrow their money in the private market, and there wouldn't be a need to use the Bank. Well, we didn't realize how long the bridge was going to be."

It was, in the beginning, a very lightly traveled bridge. The Bank had expected to be besieged with requests for money from eager developing countries, but in its first eighteen months of operation it received only three loan applications from developing nations—Chile, Iran, and Mexico. Eventually, Bank officials took to touring the developing world trying to drum up business. As board member Luis Machado put it, the Bank had "to convince the countries we represented [that] they should borrow money from us."

When the applications began at last to come in, another problem arose. They were impossibly vague. Colombia asked for $78 million without giving any clear indication of how it planned to spend the money. Its application mentioned railroads, highways, power plants, ports, and other artifacts of industrialization, but offered no details about specific projects or about their relative urgency or financial soundness. Poland's request for several hundred million dollars had no accompanying documentation. Black complained publicly about "the lack of well-prepared and well-planned projects ready for immediate execution."

Not that there was a shortage of requests for the kind of loan that had given foreign lending a bad name; Robert Garner described an interview with Cuban President Carlos Prio Socarras in the early 1950s.

One of the things he wanted was a tunnel under Havana Harbor. It was commonly reputed that the people in the know had bought up the real estate on the other side of the harbor, and if a tunnel was put under there, it would be a great boost to real estate.

I said, "Mr. President, that's perfectly absurd. New York had to carry things back and forth across the Hudson River for a great many years before they ever felt they could afford a tunnel, and you can do the same thing."

"Well," he said, "Mr. Garner, you may be right, but it's like a diamond on the hand, it's something that just shines—it just appeals to me."

Garner rejected the request with a preemptory "Well, it doesn't appeal to me."

The Bank's Articles of Agreement state that "except in special circumstances", its loans must "be for the purpose of specific projects of reconstruction or development." This restriction was imposed in an effort to avoid the unexamined and unwise investments made during the lending frenzy of the 1920s and early 1930s. But McCloy had flouted this requirement in the first four loans he made—to France, Denmark, Holland, and Luxembourg. All four countries received "general purpose" loans, untied to any specific projects, on the grounds that they were quite capable of spending the money they borrowed wisely without close scrutiny from the Bank.

There were many in the Bank who believed that, whatever the Articles of Agreement said, the Bank should continue making general-purpose loans. They argued that trying to bring nations into the twentieth century project by project was too time-consuming. The economist Paul Rosenstein-Rodan and others argued that the Bank should make large, quick-disbursing loans in return for a country's agreeing to adopt efficient economic policies. The loans might be used to build roads and bridges, or they might be used to pay off other foreign debts; the only important thing was that the borrowers should embrace certain agreed-on reforms—the use of modern accounting techniques, for example, or the streamlining of various bureaucratic procedures.

Potential borrowers also felt that the Bank's insistence on lending only for thoroughly scrutinized projects was too restrictive. Borrowers naturally want as few restraints as possible placed on the use of the money they borrow. In 1949, the UN General Assembly—spurred by its Third World members—urged the Bank to make general-purpose loans "not only in special circumstances but generally." But Eugene Black was not an advocate of general-purpose loans. He rejected the UN's plea with the withering observation that a loan for general purposes "really means a loan for a purpose or purposes unknown."

Despite his project-oriented approach to lending, Black agreed with Rosenstein-Rodan that developing countries need efficient policies and competent bureaucracies as much as they do modern infrastructure, and under his direction the Bank did not hesitate to use its influence to push for reform in these arenas. "We have made no secret of the fact," he declared, "that we sometimes refuse to lend to countries which are pursuing unsound policies." Almost every Bank loan was conditional on the adoption of one or more pertinent reforms. Loans for power stations, for example, often required the borrowers to stop subsidizing electricity, because the Bank felt that such subsidies made it harder for borrowers to earn back the money to repay the loan and encouraged wasteful use of energy. By linking project loans to reform, the Bank felt it could keep a close eye on its money *and* have a broader influence on its borrowers.

Black did make a few general-purpose loans—program loans, in Bank jargon—but most were to industrialized countries like Australia, Italy, and Norway. The only developing country to receive a program loan during Black's reign was oil-rich Iran, to which the Bank made a $75 million "general development loan" in 1957.

———

Though Black believed that funding projects was the Bank's proper task, he wanted to avoid a piecemeal approach. He thought that borrowers should draw up comprehensive plans for their development. In 1949, after a certain amount of prodding by Vice President Garner, Colombia became the first country to ask the Bank to help it draw up such a plan. The Bank entered enthusiastically upon the task. It asked Lauchlin Currie, an economist and former advisor to Presidents Roosevelt and Truman, to assemble a group of specialists in finance, transportation, health, industry, and agriculture to study the prospects for development in Colombia.

Currie's fourteen-man team was a mixture of Bank staffers, U.S. government employees, and independent consultants, all but two of them American citizens. They descended on Bogota that summer. Some stayed in Colombia only a few weeks; others almost four months. The result of their labors was the first comprehensive analysis of the Colombian economy, a 642-page report outlining a five-year, $2.5 billion (equivalent to $20 billion in 1993) program of public investment in agriculture, industry, transportation, health, housing, education, and reform of public administration and fiscal policy.

The Bank organized the Currie mission; it contributed staff to it; it put up half the money for it; and it reviewed and revised its report. But Bank officials wanted the Currie report to be seen as a Colombian document. Publicly, they depicted the Currie mission as a group of independent experts in whose findings the Bank was merely very interested.

At the Bank's urging, the Colombian government set up a bipartisan committee of prominent citizens to study the report and advise on its implementation. Currie called the committee a "device used to translate a foreign report into a national program." The six-man Committee on Economic Development, as it was called, was aided in its deliberations by Currie himself and by several other Bank technicians. After nearly a year of study the committee endorsed the Currie report and most of the projects it proposed.

The Currie mission identified an abundance of sound development projects in Colombia, but the Bank doubted that the country had the expertise and the political will to execute them. It therefore offered to help the Colombian government establish a National Planning Council to oversee its new development program. Colombia agreed and—at the Bank's suggestion—hired Currie and the American economist Albert Hirschman as advisors to the council. The Bank was now the driving force behind the decisions Colombia was making about its long-term development. As the government considered what to invest in, said Currie, "In the background was always the expectation of bountiful loans to come if Bank approval was obtained."

The Currie mission was so successful in finding fundable projects that Colombia became one of the Bank's biggest clients. Between 1950 and 1963, the Bank lent Colombia more than $300 million, more money per capita than any of its other borrowers. This was a mixed blessing, as each project brought with it several new "missions." As David Lilienthal, former chairman of the Tennessee Valley Authority and an advisor to the Bank in its formative years, noted in 1961, the steady stream of foreigners looking for investment opportunities for the Bank was not universally appreciated. "The criticism one hears from the most responsible sources in Colombia is summed up this way: *too many Bank missions.* A census of the 'missions' from the Bank during recent years makes one ill. One after another they come trekking to Colombia. I wonder if any country has been so examined and measured and 'missioned.' "

More than two-thirds of the Bank's loans to Colombia went to autonomous public agencies, such as the National Highway Foundation, TELECOM, and the Cauca Valley Corporation (modeled on the Tennessee Valley Authority) rather than to the central government. The Bank helped establish most of these agencies, even to the extent of drafting the legislation under which they operated, legislation that generally gave them a great degree of freedom from government scrutiny and control. They were staffed with technocrats, many of whom had served a spell at the Bank, not run-of-the-mill political appointees. The Bank believed that the technical expertise of these agencies and their relative independence from partisan politics would make them more efficient than the central government in executing development projects.

The Colombian experience was considered such a success that the Bank sent similar missions to two dozen other countries, including Turkey, Nicaragua, Cuba, Iraq, Jamaica, Libya, and Uganda. These and other borrowers were encouraged to follow—and generally did follow—Colombia's example in creating a national planning authority and quasi-independent agencies for every aspect of the economy, from roads to agriculture to mining. In fact, by the early 1970s, more than half of all its loans went to autonomous agencies it had helped to establish in scores of countries.

Some Bank staffers believed that the Bank was becoming too involved in the design and selection of projects that it would later be asked to evaluate and fund. Such people were in the minority, however. Then, as now, the Bank had confidence in its own impartiality. In Eugene Black's words, "The World Bank is the only place that anybody can go to get money where there's no selfish motive. . . . I've said to a number of governments: 'You can dislike us all you want to and you may disagree with us all you want to, but it's the only place you can go. There's no motive in back of what we do. The only motive we've got is to help you. Now you won't agree with us a lot of times. . . . But you can't claim we've got any ulterior motive.' "

———

The Bank was founded on a disdain for—and even a fear of—local knowledge and opinion. Its founder, John Maynard Keynes, had remarkably little faith in the acumen of the common man. "It is most dangerous," he wrote, "that the people should, under normal conditions, be in a position to put into effect their transient will and their uncertain judgment on every question of policy that occurs." Eugene Black kept this attitude alive at the top, warning that most people in developing countries would not want to "abandon old habits and attitudes and work in favor of new ones. . . .

The apostles of a new life . . . are the minority, typically those whose close contact with Western education, Western political thought, and Western material living standards has led them to want greater opportunities to practice their knowledge, greater outlets for their ambition, and a better material lot for their countrymen."

It was an article of faith to Bank staffers that only highly educated specialists had the skills and the knowledge needed to guide developing countries into the future. The trial-and-error method, the common wisdom that had worked for centuries in the backwaters of Africa and Asia, would not suffice in the postwar world. By translating complex and messy real-life problems into numerical terms that could be broken down and analyzed, the Bank's Washington experts could formulate solutions to problems in countries they hardly knew.

"We in the Bank had an extraordinary arrogance in those days," Albert Waterston, a Bank economist, recalled thirty years later. "Many of the [developing] countries are small, whereas we were coming from Washington, which we thought of as the center of civilization, and we had money, and that made us brilliant! The worst thing about this was that the people with whom we dealt in these countries actually accepted much of what we said, or at least kept quiet because they distrusted themselves. . . . Who wanted to give up that kind of power? Of course, I didn't know what I was talking about half of the time, but it was a wonderful feeling."

In 1952 the Bank sent Albert Hirschman to Colombia to devise "an ambitious economic development plan that would spell out investment, domestic saving and foreign aid targets for the Colombian economy over the next few years." Though Hirschman had never set foot in Colombia, the Bank assured him that "the new programming technique" now made his task "quite simple . . . even without close study of local surround-ings." Hirschman, who was new to the Bank—and to development—wa dismayed at the Bank's apparent contempt for Colombians, and at Colom bians' calm acceptance of the insult. He later described the prevailing at tude: "The task was supposedly crucial for Colombia's development, no Colombian was to be found who had any inkling of how to go about it. That knowledge was held only by a few foreign experts who had had the new growth economics revealed to them. It all seemed to be an affront to the Colombians . . . who were, initially at least, treating the foreign advisors as a new brand of magician."

The Bank's expert-oriented approach to development had its critics even then. Perhaps the most prominent was David Lilienthal, who believed in "the almost unlimited latent capacity of the average man." Lilienthal argued that local people should be involved in the selection and execution of development projects. This, he said, is the only way to create truly indigenous institutions that can carry on the work of development. If ordinary people are incapable of helping to plan and implement projects, then those projects, he said, are wrong for the area and likely to fail in any case.

Much modern infrastructure is indeed the province of experts. It cannot be designed, built, maintained, or, in many cases, operated by the ordinary people it is intended to help. Nonetheless giant infrastructure projects are what the Bank was designed to finance. It lends the foreign currencies that are needed to pay for imported equipment and expertise. It lends the huge sums needed to finance these huge undertakings. Its demand for profitability in its projects is answered by well-designed dams, ports, and railroads that can produce measurable economic benefits in a few years. And modern infrastructure is essential to the industrialization the Bank sees as the key to economic growth.

With its mandate to invest in infrastructure, the Bank came to believe that a modern infrastructure is the foundation on which all economic development must rest. Its *Annual Report* for 1951 stated that "an adequate supply of power, communications and transportation facilities is a precondition for the . . . industrialization and diversification of the underdeveloped countries." Other development agencies had different mandates and thus different ideas about the best way to proceed. The UN Food and Agriculture Organization, for example, maintained that improving agricultural efficiency was the key to improving living standards for developing countries. The UN Educational, Scientific and Cultural Organization was just as certain that investment in education was the most important thing. The World Health Organization declared that investments in health were the most productive.

The World Bank, however, was the only agency that could back its theories with hard cash. While the Bank was financing a multitude of infrastructure projects, its rivals had little money for the agriculture, education, and health programs they espoused. With cash available for infrastructure, the infrastructure-based theory of development was soon dominant in development circles. As the World Bank's official history acknowledges, "It was the availability of financing for such undertakings that stimulated philosophizing about the vital role of economic infrastructure in the development process, rather than the reverse." Much of the philosophizing was done by the Bank's own think tank and "staff college," the Economic Development Institute.

The EDI, established in 1956 with funding from the Ford and Rockefeller foundations, teaches people from developing countries how to create and carry out programs in line with the Bank's theories of development. It has its own teaching and research staff, and it also gives scholarships for graduate work outside the Bank. The idea behind EDI, according to Sir Alexander Cairncross, its first director, was that "if people came into association with the Bank through studying here, they would carry with them ideas that were more congenial to the Bank when they went back to their own country." Over the years, many EDI alumni have achieved positions of prominence at home, forming what one Bank official affectionately termed "the EDI mafia."

Not everyone, however, agreed with the Bank's emphasis on large-scale physical infrastructure. The pioneering development economist Colin Clark categorized as "a disastrous error" the notion that "the creation of industrial employment would automatically enrich the country." This belief, he told a World Bank seminar in 1984, combined with the egotism characteristic of political leaders, gave "some truth [to] the lampoon that the real needs of a developing country are a steel works, an airline, a six-lane highway, and an invitation for the president to address the Washington Press Club. One consequence of such follies is that the world is now hopelessly overcapacitated with both steel works and airlines, and it will take a long time to absorb the surplus."

Worship of technology—and of the experts who held the key to it—was not confined to the World Bank during this period. World War II had brought the ultimate technology, the atomic bomb. One response to the awful power of the bomb, one way to look hopefully instead of fearfully to the future, was to emphasize technology's other side, its life-giving aspect. Politicians, writers, and speech makers jumped to tout the redemptive powers of technology: It would end hunger, create an inexhaustible supply of cheap energy, free men and women from drudgery, make war obsolete, and turn backward agrarian countries into thriving industrial economies. The Bank's enthusiasm for technology—for heroic feats of engineering and construction—was part of the spirit of the age.

The Bank realized, of course, that social progress is also important to developing countries. In its 1949 annual report it warned that levels of education, nutrition, and housing must improve if its borrowers were to be able to make good use of the expensive power, communications, and transportation facilities they were building. Nonetheless, such programs were not the Bank's business; they were not productive in strict financial terms, nor did they require foreign currency. One internal Bank memo recorded a discussion in which "Mr. A. agreed with Mr. D. that pure water had many valuable side effects, but [pointed out that] one could not measure their contribution to production." In 1952 the Bank rejected Colombia's request that it finance the foreign costs of a water treatment plant on the grounds that it was a "social," not an "economic" project.

Lauchlin Currie's 1950 report on Colombia had recommended investment in a broad range of programs, social as well as industrial. Though he knew the Bank would not finance the social components, he hoped that it would give its imprimateur to the overall program. Initially the Bank seemed to back Currie's integrated approach. But, as he later recalled, "One fateful day, [Vice President Robert] Garner suddenly realized where I was leading him, and he drew back, saying, 'Damn it, Lauch. We can't go messing around with education and health. We're a *bank*!' Rarely can the collapse of a Grand Design be so pinpointed in one remark. . . . I felt that the Bank had missed an opportunity to establish a precedent of linking nonbankable with bankable projects in an overall country program."

The Bank's preference for infrastructure projects had a profound influence on its clients. Countries tended to proceed on those projects the Bank was willing to finance and to postpone those it wasn't. Because the Bank was interested in building railways and highways, for example, more than 50 percent of Colombia's public spending during the late 1950s was for transportation, whereas education received only a few percent. "As a result," one independent study concluded, "the Colombian government may well have spent too much on transportation projects in the 1950s and 1960s."

The Bank not only restricted its own investments to industrial infrastructure; it also discouraged developing countries from undertaking social projects with their own money. In 1955, when Colombia proposed to build a waterworks with a French loan, Garner told the country's president that if it borrowed the French money, "The Bank would have to withdraw as banker to Colombia." David Lilienthal, who was present, recorded the meeting in his diary.

Said the President: "Without health, nothing is good. People must have water to have good health. Everywhere I go in Colombia they ask me for water, water plants."

Garner was in a lecturing mood, trying to explain that, unless people could afford things, they should spend their money in increasing their productivity, then in time they could afford things that made life better. "First you need to have more pie," he said, "and then there will be more pie to divide."

By the late 1950s, the Bank faced a new problem: a shortage of suitable clients. Demand for its loans had not flagged, but the Bank was in an awkward position: It could lend only to countries that could not obtain private financing, but could repay their loans. "We cannot and will not lend more than borrowing countries can afford to repay," Black declared. One consequence of this policy was that, as the writer James Morris noted, "The bank is running out of clients. Many poor countries are 'exhausting their creditworthiness'—which means that they are too heavily in debt to get another loan. . . . In short, the World Bank has almost priced itself out of the market, not by the cost of its money, but by the altitude of its standards."

All the Bank's members are members also of the United Nations, where debate is freer than it is in the Bank's boardroom. The developing countries, therefore, turned the UN General Assembly into a forum for their resentment at what they regarded as the arrogance of the Bank's management and its grudging approach to lending. In 1949, the UN's Subcommission on Economic Development suggested that the United Nations consider establishing a new agency that would make money available to countries that did not qualify for World Bank loans.

Neither the Bank nor the United States nor its allies in the developed world were in favor of a new international aid agency, but the clamor for it would not die. Throughout the 1950s, the developing countries "showed extraordinary ingenuity in keeping the issue alive," according to the Bank's official history. In 1952 the General Assembly endorsed the idea of a Special UN Fund for Economic Development (SUNFED).

Technically, the Bank is a specialized agency of the United Nations, but it prides itself in holding its parent body at arm's length. The UN has no control over the Bank's budget or operations, and the 1947 agreement under which it became a UN agency explicitly states that "the Bank is, and is required to function as, an independent organization." The Bank's authorized historians say it "regard[ed] the UN and its subsidiaries as busybody empire-builders or do-gooders, blind to the realities of international finance, bent on jeopardizing the Bank's standing on Wall Street, agitating for more development finance than could be used productively, and sending out survey missions that should have been organized by the Bank and would have been better if they had been." It was not only the UN that aroused the Bank's hostility; its attitude toward all "competing official lending institutions . . . was negative."

Thus, although the Bank had deep reservations about the wisdom of lending money to uncreditworthy nations, it was even more worried by the prospect of a rival agency stepping in to do so. That prospect became more likely as the SUNFED idea ground its way through the tortuous UN committee process. The Bank fought the idea as long as possible, but in 1958 Eugene Black accepted the inevitable and proposed that the Bank establish an affiliate, the International Development Association (IDA), to provide money to poor countries on easy terms. Black later admitted that IDA, which was formally established in 1960, "was really an idea to offset the urge for SUNFED." "IDA," says the authorized history of the Bank's first twenty-five years, "had to be invented to keep the Bank preeminent, or at least eminent, in the growing complex of multilateral agencies attempting to facilitate international development." It also, as the Bank soon realized, saved the IBRD by taking over its most uncreditworthy clients.

IDA and the IBRD are really only labels that the Bank attaches to two different types of financing. The two share office, staff, and management; they differ only in the nature of their lending and the source of their funds. IDA's money is donated by its member governments, not raised on the bond market, as is the IBRD's. Normally IDA's funds are replenished every three years through new pledges by member governments. Thus IDA dramatically reduced the Bank's financial—and political—autonomy.

IDA loans, called credits, are for countries with poor creditworthiness and a per capita income below a certain level—in 1995 there were sixty-three IDA countries and sixty-two IBRD countries. In addition, there are a few so-called "blend" countries that are eligible for loans from both IBRD and IDA—in 1995 there were fifteen "blend" countries. IDA loans are nominally interest-free, though borrowers are charged an annual "administrative fee" of .75 percent. Borrowers have a grace period of ten years before they must begin to repay IDA loans and another thirty-five to forty years to complete repayment. The IBRD, by contrast, charges interest on its loans at a near-market rate that is adjusted semiannually. In early 1996, the rate was 6.98 percent. Its loans have only a five-year grace period and must be repaid within fifteen or twenty years. The IBRD also charges a .75 percent "commitment fee" on undisbursed loan balances. Annually since 1990, however, the Bank has waived .50 percent of that charge. Even the reduced fee, however, brings in around $120 million a year to the Bank.

IDA was not the first offshoot of the Bank. As early as 1948 the triumvirate of McCloy, Black, and Robert Garner wanted to extend the Bank's powers so that it could make loans to private enterprises without the need for government guarantees. Nelson Rockefeller, Truman's advisor on international development, picked up the idea and recommended to the U.S. government that the Bank create a subsidiary international finance corporation with an initial capital of $400 million.

Many people, inside the Bank and out, questioned the wisdom of lending money to private businesses that cannot attract private financing. They feared that the extra risk would make it harder to sell Bank bonds. The United Nations, on the other hand, was enthusiastic, though it didn't necessarily agree that the new organization should be part of the World Bank. Several UN agencies pushed their own variations of the idea. Bank officials, however, were determined that if there was to be a new agency, it should belong to the World Bank, not be a rival.

The issue was finally resolved in 1956, when the Bank created the International Finance Corporation (IFC), assigning it the task of furthering economic development by lending to and investing in private companies. Like the IBRD, it must limit its activities to "cases in which sufficient private capital is not available on reasonable terms." Unlike the IBRD, it does not require, indeed is forbidden to obtain, government guarantees that it will be repaid. The IFC is "an entity separate and distinct from the Bank."* It has its own chief executive and its own staff. However, its board of directors is composed of the same individuals who are on the boards of IBRD and IDA and it is chaired by the president of the World Bank (who also chooses the IFC's chief executive).

The IFC raises funds in two ways: by borrowing on the bond market and by borrowing from IBRD. Its bonds are backed not merely by the promises of its members to make good any shortfalls, but by reserves of U.S. dollars and gold already contributed by its members. IFC started life with 31 member governments and paid-in capital of $80 million.

Despite lingering reservations about the soundness and usefulness of the IFC, the United States contributed $35 million, becoming its chief subscriber. U.S. support was largely due to the realization that the United Nations was not going to let the idea of a private development agency die. According to the Bank's historians, the UN schemes "were so repugnant to conservative secretaries of the U.S. Treasury that, by comparison, the no-

---

* A brief note on nomenclature: When IBRD was the only branch of the World Bank, the two names were used interchangeably. The simple phrase "the World Bank" now refers to both IBRD and IDA (though none of the other branches), and anyone wishing to speak of just one must specify which. The phrase "the World Bank Group" refers to IBRD, IDA, and IFC, along with two smaller agencies, the Multilateral Investment Guarantee Agency (MIGA), which since 1988 has offered private investors in developing countries insurance against loss due to political upheaval, and the International Centre for Settlement of Investment Disputes, founded in 1966 to arbitrate disputes between governments and private investors.

tion of an IFC [as part of the Bank] came in time to seem to them positively attractive."

The IFC got off to a slow start. In 1963 it lent or invested $18 million, less than 3 percent of the World Bank's lending that year. Twenty years later, though the IFC's annual financing had grown to $425 million, it was still responsible for less than 3 percent of the Bank's annual lending.

---

Even as the Bank defended itself against the United Nations' attempts to expand, it was itself encroaching on what might be considered UN territory—the arena of international diplomacy. Its first foray came in 1951, when it unsuccessfully attempted to resolve a dispute between Britain and Iran over the distribution of profits from the Anglo-Iranian Oil Company.

Of more consequence was its subsequent intervention in a quarrel between India and Pakistan. In 1951, in an article in *Collier's* magazine, David Lilienthal suggested that tensions between the two countries, which were nearly at war over Kashmir, might be relaxed if they could "concentrate on other important issues where cooperation was possible." He proposed that they work out an arrangement for sharing the waters of the Indus Basin rivers, which had been cut in two in 1947 when the countries were divided at Independence. Black took up Lilienthal's suggestion and prodded the two countries into beginning discussions under its sponsorship.

It was declared that the Bank was in a position to exert considerable influence on the negotiations. Not only was it a major lender to both parties but it had also created—and was chair of—the consortiums of all the agencies and governments that provided aid to the two countries. This gave the Bank a near veto over the flow of foreign funds to India and Pakistan and ensured that neither would receive large amounts of aid, especially for water projects, until they settled their argument. Over the succeeding years, the Bank formed such consortiums for many other of its clients, and its chairmanship of them did much to ensure its position as the predominant development institution in the world.

On September 19, 1960, after nine years of negotiations, India and Pakistan signed the Indus Waters Treaty, and the donor countries formally established—and contributed $640 million to—an Indus Basin Development Fund to be administered by the Bank. The agreement gave India rights to the three easternmost rivers and Pakistan rights to the three westernmost. Because almost all existing dams were on the rivers allotted to India, the agreement also included a pledge to finance a dam-building program in Pakistan. The Indus negotiations were protracted and difficult, but they added a feather to the Bank's cap. They set it up as an international mediator, a reservoir of diplomatic as well as financial expertise to rival and perhaps outdo the United Nations. James Morris was not alone in imagining that the Bank would one day overshadow its nominal parent. "I find it difficult to believe," he wrote, "that . . . the United Nations will ever mature into a world government: it lacks the fiber, the discipline, the command, the strong hand. In 1818 H Street, though, it is not hard to envisage the nucleus of a properly international civil service, dedicated not just to the dispersal of money but to the development of the world's welfare in the fullest sense."

# Five

Eugene Black's thirteen-and-a-half-year reign ended in January 1963. He had inherited a tottering organization that had been prematurely abandoned by both its former presidents and had made only seventeen loans. The institution he bequeathed to his successor had made 370 loans worth more than $7 billion, had never suffered a default, and had a balance sheet that was the envy of its commercial counterparts. In Black's last year, the Bank's net income was $83 million. "The Bank was piling up profits at almost an indecent rate," notes *The World Bank Since Bretton Woods*, the authorized history of the Bank's first twenty-five years, written by Edward Mason and Richard Asher.

Black also won for the Bank the respect of Wall Street and of money markets all around the world. His Bank was financially sound. It hired the best economists and engineers. It did not have the taint of corruption and mismanagement that attached to other international agencies. In 1952, the president of Mexico paid tribute to the Bank's cautious approach to lending, calling it "a guarantee that the loans the Bank allows will never prove to be a heavy charge for the peoples that receive them." The Bank was also admired for the nobility of its mission: helping the world's neediest nations. Magazines carried admiring articles about its work with titles such as "Power from the Andes," "Free-World Growth and Progress," and "Vitamins for Growth."

With Black at the helm, the Bank changed the physical face of the developing world. Among the hundreds of schemes it financed were railways in the Ivory Coast, Yugoslavia, Rhodesia, and Brazil; telephone systems in Ethiopia, Costa Rica, and El Salvador; irrigation projects in Sudan, Mexico, Peru, and Thailand; highways in Burundi, South Africa, Iran, Haiti, and Guatemala; ports in Nigeria, Ecuador, Burma, and Israel; pulp and paper mills in Pakistan and Chile; power plants in Swaziland, South Africa, Mauritius, and Uganda; gas pipelines in Pakistan; cattle ranches in Uruguay and Chile; grain silos in Turkey, Panama, and Nicaragua; coal mines in India; an iron mine in Mauritania; a manganese mine in Gabon; a steel mill in Colombia; an airline in India; a potash factory in Israel; a meat-processing plant in Chile; and a cement works in Peru.

Under Black's leadership the Bank was more than a mere lender. It became a diplomat, acting as a middleman in disputes between nations. It became a force in academia, shaping the newly emerging field of development theory. It became the unofficial planning agency for the Third World, coordinating the lending of other aid donors. It became an international phenomenon. According to his speechwriter, Nathaniel McKitterick, "Black made a point, a brilliant point, of always having a special deal going. . . . He intuitively, not intellectually, always identified himself with something big and interesting and public. . . . Everyone knew the Bank's purpose: Black was acting it out in a grand way."

In short, by the time Black left, the World Bank was the most respected, most profitable, and most influential development lender in the world. The Bank's mission, however, was not to amass profits or popularity, but to promote the development of its borrowers. And, as its authorized history succinctly put it, "By development is meant to the Bank Group an increase in GNP [Gross National Product]." (GNP is the value of all the goods and services a country produces in a year. A related index, Gross Domestic Product, omits income from foreign operations.) The Bank's plan was to increase GNP "by fostering more rapid growth of medium- and large-scale manufacturing and commercialized agriculture."

Thanks in large part to the Bank's huge investments in the basic infrastructure of production, the developing world's gross national product increased between 1960 and 1967 by an average rate of 4.8 percent a year, faster than that of the United States or Europe—though still short of the Bank's target of 5.5 percent. The Bank was confident that, as the newly created wealth trickled down through all layers of the economy, standards of living would rise, transforming unstable regimes and needy nations into peaceful neighbors and prosperous trading partners.

Though the way was clear, the task was immense, and during Black's reign, the Bank shed the idea that its job was a temporary one and discovered that there was a permanent need for its services. As one economist involved with the Bank since Bretton Woods put it, "Relatively poor countries will always be with us and the World Bank is under no compulsion to work itself out of a job."

Everything depended on the Bank—and its borrowers—making wise, profitable investments. The Bank took great care to ensure the quality of the projects it financed. It closely appraised the financial viability of projects it was asked to fund, and rejected or redesigned those that did not meet its standards. Though it started with virtually no technical expertise, it built up that side of its operations and began to scrutinize each stage of each project, from design through implementation.

Curiously, however, the Bank did not study its completed projects to see whether they lived up to expectations. In 1964, an internal study recommended that the Bank review completed projects to determine "whether the economic results of projects are in line with those forecast during appraisal, and if not, why not?" Even this modest proposal, which made no reference to the broader social and environmental effects of Bank investments, was largely ignored for another eight years, however. Not until 1972, twenty-five years after it began lending, did the Bank start to evaluate completed projects. As a result, it did not know whether its projects succeeded or failed. To this day, the Bank has only examined nine of the projects it financed with the 370 loans it had made by end of 1962.

———

Black, though a banker, was also a literary man, a serious student of Shakespeare. He combined his literary interests and his ambitions for the Bank by asking a favorite writer, James Morris, to write a book about the World Bank, pledging his full cooperation. Morris accepted Black's offer and the resulting book, *The Road to Huddersfield*, was published in 1963. Morris captured the Bank at the height of its infatuation with infrastructure, and it is clear that, despite his many thoughtful reservations about modernization and the loss of what he calls "the old pastoral ways," he was impressed by the daring and the scale of the Bank's projects. He writes of emerging at the top of a forested mountain in Thailand and gazing down on the new Yanhee dam: "Gleaming there and humming, Yanhee stands like a very talisman of change, a miraculous intrusion, as though its engineers have flown down from Mars itself and brought their anvils with them."

In Colombia the Bank financed a railway alongside the Magdalena River, a scheme that, Morris notes, "was not unanimously acclaimed. . . . To this day many sensible men in Colombia consider the project an error of judgment, and maintain the old Magdalena [riverboat] service to be perfectly good enough." But it was impossible not to be awed by the achievement of building a railroad through 400 miles of virgin rainforest—rough country beset with bandits, guerrillas, and uncharted technical challenges. "Whether or not it succeeds in all its objectives," wrote Morris, "it is to my mind . . . one of the most exciting things to see in all the Americas."

Of the World Bank–financed Kariba Dam on the border between Northern and Southern Rhodesia (now Zambia and Zimbabwe), Morris wrote: "There are some engineering works that can . . . themselves transform the destinies of a nation: in one cutting of the tape, one press of the generating button. . . . [One] such monumental project is Kariba, the tremendous Zambezi dam that can multiply the potential of the Rhodesias, if politics do not switch its turbines off and drain away its kilowatts."

These three are among the twenty-one largest development projects funded during the Black years, in what might now be called the golden period of World Bank infrastructure lending. The list comprises seven dams, five railways, three highways; three loans for iron and steel production, and one each for a thermal power plant, an oil pipeline, and improvements to the Suez Canal. Together these twenty-one projects represent an investment of $1.9 billion, more than a third of the Bank's development lending during Black's term in office. They are worth examining in some detail.

———

Dam building is the world's most popular form of development. Black devoted $2 billion—more than a quarter of his lending—to dams. The popularity of dams stems from their dual functions. They regulate water and they exalt the rulers who build them. The steel and turbines of a single dam declare far more spectacularly that a country has entered the modern age than do any number of one-room schools or village water pumps. There are many dams in the World Bank's history: dams for hydroelectricity; dams for flood control; dams for irrigation; and, most often, dams for all these things at once.

Black's Bank built dams in Ghana, Zambia, India, the Philippines, Ceylon, Thailand, Yugoslavia, Brazil, Chile, Colombia, Costa Rica, Ecuador, El Salvador, Honduras, Mexico, Nicaragua, Panama, Peru, Uruguay, Venezuela, Iran, Iraq, Lebanon, Syria, and Turkey—not to mention in the already industrialized countries of Japan, Austria, Finland, Iceland, Italy, Norway, and Australia. His successor, George Woods, extended the dam building to Ethiopia, Malawi, Nigeria, Sudan, Malaysia, Singapore, and Argentina. By 1968, the Bank had financed more than ninety dams in thirty-nine countries. Woods's successors, too, kept the faith. By 1994, the Bank had invested $28 billion—nearly 10 percent of its total lending—in more than six hundred dams in ninety-three countries. Seven of the 21 largest projects during the Black years were dams.

In 1957 the World Bank announced that it would lend Thailand $66 million to dam the Ping River, which flows through the country's agricultural heartland. The Yanhee Dam, the Bank said, would "bring an end to the increasingly acute shortage of electricity which Thailand has been experiencing for several years, . . . make possible the control of floods, and . . . increase agricultural production by . . . $15 million a year" by providing irrigation water to more than 2 million acres. It was a massive undertaking. The 500-foot-high Yanhee was the tallest dam in all of Southeast Asia, and one of the tallest in the world. In honor of the fact that the Yanhee was Thailand's first hydroelectric dam, the Thai monarch, King Bhumipol, allowed its name to be changed to his own. In doing so, he cast a royal cloak of protection over the dam, because criticism of anything named after the sovereign is a serious crime in Thailand.

In *The Road to Huddersfield,* published the year before the dam began operating, Morris hailed the Bhumipol as "a new prodigy of Asia," but he was equally taken with the ancient and prosperous riverside villages he visited. "Nowhere are there signs of want. The houses are charmingly and substantially built of teak, and the little shops are full of good things," he wrote. "If there is anyplace in the world where the old pastoral ways can still keep a people happy, it is in these rich rice lands of Siam."

There was a sadness in Morris's description of the pastoral life, for he knew that the dam would destroy it for thousands of people. Bhumipol's reservoir put 300 square kilometers of teak forest and riverine farmland under water. Lert Decha-In, one of the twenty thousand displaced villagers, was in his early twenties when the authorities ordered his family to move. "They said that as we are a developing country electricity is very important. They beseeched us to think of the benefits for our country. They said we must sacrifice for all." The best that can be said for the Bhumipol resettlement arrangements is that they were typical of their day: With little warning, families were ripped from the villages in which they had lived and farmed for generations; given meager amounts of cash as compensation for the loss of their homes and crops; moved to poorly prepared sites lacking schools, drinking water, and sanitation facilities; assigned small plots of land of dubious fertility; and forgotten.

Many oustees were totally demoralized by their eviction and subsequent treatment, but Lert Decha-In kept pushing the government to keep its pledges. His success, though modest, endeared him to the people of his village, to whom he became Paw (Father) Lert. Largely due to his efforts, Goh Ta, a resettlement village of about a hundred families, has a health clinic, a school that goes to up grade nine, and, since 1992, electricity. But Goh Ta's chief problem persists: Though it is only 9 kilometers from the reservoir, it has no water for agriculture. For years officials have been promising to drill a well deep into the rocky land or find some other way to enable the people to water their crops, but these promises are unkept.

Unable to make a living by farming, most adults from this and the other displacement villages spend much of the year in Bangkok, more than 300 miles away, earning money to send back home. Paw Lert's wife has stayed behind to take care of her nieces and nephews as well as her own three children. Sitting on a beautifully carved teak bench, a remnant from her family's old home, she explains that her brothers and sisters return to the village only for festivals. Of their life in Bangkok they tell her little, except that "they hardly eat anything, because their pay is so low and they must save it to send back here." She has not been to Bangkok and is not eager to go. "Nobody wants to go to Bangkok," she declares, "but they must, to keep the village alive." Her brothers and sisters, she says, work in factories where they earn 80 to 115 baht, the equivalent of $3 to $4.50, a day. I wonder to myself if she knows that unskilled workers may find it easier to get a job in Bangkok's sex industry than in a factory.

Whatever damage it did to the ousted villagers, Bhumipol did provide the electricity Thailand needed so desperately in the mid-1960s. In 1966 it alone produced more than half the country's energy. But now Thailand's energy needs are met by huge thermal plants, each able to produce many times more energy than a hydro dam. The country's dams serve only as backup, providing extra power at periods of peak demand.

Bhumipol's second task is to irrigate the farms of the Chao Phraya Basin, Thailand's major farming belt. Traditionally, farmers here grow one crop of rice a year, in the rainy season. With water from the Bhumipol, they would, it was hoped, be able to grow two or even three crops a year. It was not easy to convince Thai farmers to change the way they farm. Like farmers all over the world, they are a conservative group. Irrigated farming involves not only new techniques and longer hours, but also investment in equipment, irrigation facilities, and fertilizers. Gradually, however, with the encouragement of the Royal Department of Irrigation, the Chao Phraya farmers changed their old ways. By 1979, more than 1.4 million acres in the Basin, 60 percent of the maximum possible, were planted with a second, irrigated crop. The same year, however, a government-commissioned study warned that there was not enough water in the system to support so much irrigated agriculture. In 1980 the government announced that there was only enough water to irrigate half a million acres of the Basin. The same farmers who had been pushed to invest heavily in irrigated rice were suddenly told to abandon that crop.

The problem is not so much lack of water as conflict over its use. The Electricity Generating Authority of Thailand (EGAT) operates the Bhumipol and most of the country's other dams. EGAT cannot allow the water in the reservoir to fall below the level required to turn the turbines. Thus, EGAT is willing to release water during the rainy season, knowing that the reservoir will soon be refilled, but it is reluctant to do so in the dry season, when farmers need water most. In its efforts to meet the demand that it has stimulated, the Thai Government built a second dam, depleting the natural flow of the river so much that saltwater from the Bay of Thailand has intruded far upstream, killing fish and contaminating farmland.

Nonetheless, large areas of the Chao Phraya Basin now receive no irrigation water at all in the dry season, or receive it only in alternate years. In 1993, the Agriculture Ministry ordered the area devoted to dry-season rice in the Basin reduced to 400,000 acres. The government's answer to the growing demand for water is to build more dams. It faces opposition, however, not only from environmentalists who object to further interference with the country's rivers, but, increasingly, from the people whom the dams would displace.

Paw Lert became part of that opposition. In 1990, having learned of a plan to dam the Yom River in the north of the country, he met with people from that region and told them of his own experiences with the Bhumipol. "For us, it's a dam of tears," he said. "We don't have water to drink, nor rice to eat. And we can't eat teardrops."

The dam in question, Kaeng Sua Ten Dam, would flood fifteen villages and a large part of the Mae Yom National Park, including 38 square kilometers of Thailand's last teak forest. It is needed to divert water into the reservoir of an earlier Bank-funded dam, the Sirikit, which has been drying up. Paw Lert's words inspired local people to resist the dam, which was being considered for funding by the World Bank, and encouraged Thailand's growing antidam movement. In May 1992 Lert Decha-In was assassinated by an unknown gunman.

In 1994, a World Bank mission appraising the Kaeng Sua Ten was surrounded by five thousand angry villagers who told them to leave the area. "There is no need for any more studies, because we oppose the project," said one of the protesters. When several consultants returned two days later, they were dragged from their car and beaten. No new missions have been sent.

---

The Kariba Dam, on the Zambezi River, which forms the border between Zambia and Zimbabwe (then Southern Rhodesia), was the first great dam in Africa. It was higher than St. Paul's Cathedral; it had the largest reservoir in the world; and it was built with $80 million from the World Bank, the largest loan the Bank had ever made. But the Kariba was more than an engineering feat; it was evidence that even the wildest parts of Africa were being brought into the modern world. The purpose of the dam was strictly industrial—providing power to the area's two huge copper companies. There were no plans for rural electrification or irrigation for local communities.

Kariba, which was completed in 1963, displaced fifty thousand people. They were not told that they would have to leave until the reservoir was beginning to fill. When the African National Congress took up their cause—accusing the government of not offering adequate compensation and not providing water at the resettlement sites—it was banned from the area. The government maintained that it had not given local people warning of the move "because they would have been unable to comprehend the problem." Rebellions broke out in some resettlement sites. Several officials were attacked with spears, and at least eight Africans were killed and many were wounded by gunfire. Outside the country the plight of the human oustees was unknown, but the international media gave much attention to the dramatic and heart-warming events of Operation Noah, the rescue mission for animals caught in the reservoir's rising waters.

In 1964, Zambia gained independence and a white racist government was elected to power in Southern Rhodesia, which the following year declared its independence from Britain. Though Zambia had shared in the cost of building the dam, Rhodesia had sole control of its operation. The Kariba dam was an important political tool for the outlaw regime, which used the threat of cutting off power to restrain Zambia from taking actions of which it disapproved. Kariba's cheap electricity also helped Rhodesia to withstand the economic blockade the United Nations had imposed on it.

In 1967, a Bank-financed study of Kariba found that from a financial point of view, "the completed project turned out to be even more attractive than it appeared originally." The Bank later acknowledged, however, that it "has not itself carried out any studies on the Kariba Dam to evaluate its environment effects." Such studies were not common practice at the time the project was approved, it explained, adding that the dam's "proponents believed at the time that the project's anticipated benefits to [what was then] Northern and Southern Rhodesia would far outweigh its potential adverse effects."

Thayer Scudder, a Cal Tech socioeconomist and frequent Bank consultant, has studied the Kariba oustees for nearly thirty years. In a 1993 interview he said that in 1963, five years after being moved, many were "beginning to get back on their feet." During the next decade, the living standard for the majority rose every year. Since then, however, things have gotten worse, due to the collapsing fertility of the poor farmland they were given and the antagonism of the people on whose land they were settled. "The majority—and their children—are now definitely worse off than if they had not moved," said Scudder, adding that the dam has also been "disastrous" for farming and fisheries well over 1,000 kilometers downstream.

———

The day after the Indus Waters Treaty was signed, the Bank lent Pakistan $90 million to build a dam on the Mangla River. The Mangla dam was one of several envisioned in the treaty, but the political pressure to resolve the dispute between India and Pakistan was so intense that the Bank did not have time to conduct more than a superficial study of any of them. Thus, when it made the loan for Mangla, the Bank had next to no information about the cost of the project or about its technical aspects. As James Morris explained, "When the treaty was being negotiated, nobody knew within many millions of dollars how much cash would be needed. The available data was meager in the extreme. . . . When the treaty was signed, all that was known about it was contained in one small booklet."

When construction of the Mangla dam actually began, the cost overruns were staggering. The dam and its associated irrigation canals cost $1.2 billion, much more than envisioned for the entire Indus Basin Plan. "We had to go back to the contributing governments for additional funds," recalled Simon Aldewereld, the head of the Bank's project division. The technical study of the dam was also rushed through. The division of the waters agreed by the negotiators made it necessary to build canals and irrigation channels perpendicular to the slope of the land. This impedes drainage, speeds siltation, and creates a plethora of breeding grounds for disease-bearing insects. As a consequence, the Mangla has had a number of serious unforeseen negative effects on Pakistan's economy and ecology. Among these are the salinization—and consequent drop in productivity— of large tracts of agricultural land; the reduced flow of fresh water to the river's estuary, which once sustained a major coastal fishery; and a shortened life for many of the system's reservoirs and irrigation canals.

There have been social costs also. The dam displaced ninety thousand people, and though the Bank firmly believes that "the people were better off in their new locations," former Bank Vice President Willi Wapenhans admits that "when they came back and saw the water levels rise above the mosques and villages you had riots." Nonetheless, the Mangla was completed ahead of schedule and is now crucial to the economy of Pakistan. Along with its sister dam, the Tarbela on the Indus River, it provides 50 percent of the country's irrigation water and 40 percent of its electricity.

———

In 1915, Great Britain, the colonial ruler of Ghana (then the Gold Coast), considered building a dam on the Volta River to produce the electricity needed to process Ghana's large bauxite deposits into aluminum. The idea languished until after World War II, when aluminum was once again in short supply. In 1953 the British set up a "preparatory commission" to study the dam. The commission's head, Sir Robert Jackson, saw the Akosombo Dam as the key to the modernization of Ghana. Jackson's wife, Barbara Ward, then foreign editor of *The Economist,* was an advisor to Eugene Black, as she later was to his successors, George Woods and Robert McNamara. Black's speechwriter called Ward, who died in 1981, "the Queen of Development to all World Bank presidents so long as she lived," and McNamara once said, "She influenced me more than anyone in my life."

Kwame Nkrumah was elected prime minister at independence in 1957 and declared himself president for life in 1960. Nkrumah was passionately in favor of the dam: Like Jackson he saw it as his country's passport to industrialization. "Newer nations such as ours . . . must have electricity in abundance before they can expect any large-scale industrial advance," he said. "That, basically, is the justification for the Volta River Project."

Another attraction was the sheer scale of the project. The 8,500-square-kilometer reservoir would be the largest man-made lake in the world. Such a massive undertaking would signal the birth of an aggressive, enterprising new nation. "It will be a feather in Ghana's cap as an independent country to have such a gigantic project," said one Ghanaian legislator.

By 1957, however, the world aluminum shortage was over and the British had lost interest in Akosombo. Nkrumah, who was still determined to build the dam, turned to the United States and found President Eisenhower eager to demonstrate his goodwill toward Africa's first newly independent country and to keep Nkrumah from the embraces of his Communist suitors. The United States agreed to help pay for a study of the project by the Henry J. Kaiser Company, part of the Kaiser Aluminum empire.

The Kaiser consultants recommended building the dam, but not the auxiliary developments that Jackson and Nkrumah had wanted—the railways, irrigation systems, and ports. They also considered a smaller, less expensive dam, but found that unsuitable because it "would be relatively economical only for the general public supply of electricity, [and would not provide] the very large block of low cost power" needed for an alumina smelter.

The United States pushed the World Bank to fund the dam. In 1957, the Bank sent a three-man mission to Ghana. The mission was unenthusiastic about the dam. It found that "the sheer size of the project is itself a problem" because the dam was so expensive it would make other investments impossible for Ghana. Moreover, the mission warned, the fact that dam would produce more power than the country could consume would put Ghana at the mercy of Kaiser or whatever large consumer might agree to buy its massive output. The mission concluded that "the project would not necessarily bring outstanding benefits to Ghana." However, the Bank kept the project alive, and in 1960 sent out a second mission, which was as lukewarm about the dam as its predecessor. That mission report stated flatly that "the Volta Project is not very attractive." Nevertheless, in 1961 the Bank lent Ghana $47 million for the dam.

Black told David Lilienthal privately that "when the [United States] State Department learned that Nkrumah was going to Moscow, they said we had to get the World Bank Ghana loan all buttoned up before he went. . . . They wouldn't wait on the Bank's finishing its study." Construction of the dam began as soon as the Bank approved the loan. But there was no plan for dealing with the eighty thousand villagers, mostly subsistence farmers and fishermen, whom the dam displaced. Resettlement was left until the last moment—the rising waters helped convince unwilling villagers to leave. Each family was promised twelve acres of land, though the government announced that it could not afford to replace the markets, hospitals, roads, and other public amenities the villagers had enjoyed in their old homes. Some displaced families were given one-room concrete sheds; the rest fended for themselves.

Because there was not enough land for the oustees to practice their traditional form of agriculture, the government decided to promote more intensive, Western methods of farming. Farmers were assigned specific crops, and the government promised to supply seeds and tools, though these never materialized. When widespread starvation threatened, the United Nations had to intervene, providing emergency food relief to the resettlement sites for six years. By 1968, two years after the dam was completed, two-thirds of the oustees had abandoned the resettlement sites. Most sought a better life in Ghana's cities.

In addition, the changed river flow altered the balance between fresh and saltwater in the estuary, causing serious harm downstream. A thriving freshwater clam industry that had employed two thousand women was severely damaged. The estuarine clam and sport fisheries were destroyed. Aquatic weeds invaded the region, preventing river transport and providing breeding grounds for the snails that spread the often-fatal illness schistosomiasis. This, in turn, drove tourists away from the area's white sand beaches.

The sacrifices of the oustees and the downstream population, though far greater than anticipated, were made for the sake of the nation as a whole. But Akosombo never made the contribution to Ghana's economy that its supporters hoped it would. The reservoir, which put 4 percent of the country under water, created new breeding grounds for infectious diseases. In central Ghana, the rate of infection with schistosomiasis grew from 5 percent to 80 percent within a few years of the filling of the reservoir.

River blindness, a disease transmitted by a fly that breeds at the edges of reservoirs, is another problem the dam caused. By 1980, 100,000 people in the region were afflicted with river blindness, and 70 percent of them were completely blind. According to a Bank study, "Massive dosing of the river with DDT, and later, dieldrin, gave only temporary relief to the people residing within five miles" of the reservoir. Fear of river blindness caused the abandonment of 40 percent of the land area of northeastern Ghana. In the early 1980s, the newly built Kpong Dam, downstream of Akosombo, flooded some of the breeding grounds of the river-blindness fly, thus easing the problem in certain areas.

In his determination to build the dam, Nkrumah needed Kaiser far more than Kaiser needed Akosombo. Thus Kaiser, operating as the Volta Aluminum Company (Valco for short), was able to negotiate a thirty-year contract for as much electricity as it wanted at a below-price cost. There was no discount for Ghana's householders and industries, however. They paid many times more than Kaiser. Valco was also exempted from import duty, export taxes, and company taxes.

These arrangements worried many within the Bank. Simon Aldewereld told David Lilienthal, "I have always had serious reservations about the Volta River scheme. The engineering and construction are good, but the only economic justification would be very low cost power for a large load; Kaiser said they would build an aluminum plant if the rates were low enough. But the rates the people of Ghana have to pay are twenty times as great as the aluminum rate, and the people of the country won't accept or understand that, not for long."

The high cost of the dam and of the electricity it produced fueled public anger at Nkrumah, who was overthrown in 1966, the year the dam was completed. In 1985, Ghana renegotiated its contract with Valco. Though the price charged for electricity was quadrupled, it remains only a fraction of the price that individual consumers and small businesses must pay. Valco is still by far the largest consumer of the dam's power. In fact, it takes 45 percent of all Ghana's hydroelectricity.

In order to reduce its vulnerability to the Ghanaian government, which, it feared, would nationalize its operations, Kaiser decided at the outset to spread the production of its finished product, aluminum, over three countries. It built the Akosombo-fueled alumina smelter in Ghana— with the help of a $96 million loan from the U.S. government. But, rather than supply the smelter from Ghana's rich reserves of bauxite, it imports bauxite from its own mines in Jamaica. And instead of building an aluminum-processing plant in Ghana, it sends the alumina from the smelter to its own plants in the United States to be turned into finished aluminum. Thus Ghana, for all its bauxite reserves, its hydropower, and its smelter, must import all the aluminum it uses.

None of Ghana's early plans for other dam-related developments, such as irrigation and lake transportation, have been implemented. A 1963 U.S. government study found that irrigation would be at least as profitable a use of the Volta's water as power production, but Kaiser's engineers, wanting to avoid future debates over water allocation, had deliberately designed a dam that could not be used for irrigation. They also designed one of the most inefficient dams on earth. In a recent survey of the forty biggest dams in the world, Akosombo was ranked thirty-seventh in terms of electricity produced per acre of land flooded.

C. K. Annan, former head of the Ghana Water Supply Industry, calls the dam "a short-sighted and prodigiously narrow-minded project." He and others argue that a series of smaller dams would have been cheaper, caused less social and environmental upheaval, kept the river open to navigation, and generated power even in the droughts that have recently brought Akosombo power production to a near halt.

————

The Bank's loan for the building of the Dez Dam, a massive power and irrigation project in the Iranian desert, was granted only reluctantly. Iran first approached the Bank to help fund the project in 1957. It had already contracted with the Development and Resources Corporation, a private American firm headed by David Lilienthal, to design and build the dam. The Bank, however, judged Dez too big and too expensive, believing that a smaller irrigation project would be more economical.

The Shah, however, had his heart set on the Dez, as did Lilienthal. In a meeting at the Shah's summer palace in late 1957, Lilienthal drew tears from his listeners as he described the place chosen for the dam. "The canyon and site are so remarkable and so suited to the storing of water . . . that I felt there was something here that went beyond engineering. Without being unduly mystical about it, I said, I could not explain this combination of extraordinarily fortunate circumstances except that Fate had a hand in it all; that God must have intended that a dam be built in that great gorge." Lilienthal went on to tell the Shah that "this heroic structure has not only a technical and an economic but also a symbolic meaning. It will be a symbol of the way in which an ancient nation is moving into the future."

Lilienthal tried to sway Black by arguing that if the World Bank wouldn't help Iran, the country would fund the dam themselves or turn to Moscow for funding. Black replied, "It isn't our business to make loans to prevent the spread of communism." Not only did the Bank have serious reservations about Dez, it also believed that Iran was pursuing unsound fiscal policies, a point with which Lilienthal agreed. Black did not want to make a large loan to Iran because he did not think that Iran would agree to make any of the fiscal reforms he believed were necessary. "The trouble with Iran," Black told Lilienthal, "is they are so darned rich. You can't handle countries that have money the way you can those that don't have it."

In early 1960, however, the Bank suddenly changed its mind and lent Iran $42 million for the Dez dam and an irrigation scheme that was somewhat smaller than originally planned. A Bank study noted that the decision was made "in spite of the doubts . . . as to the economic justification of the project." The report attributed the Bank's change of mind to "the fact that the Bank's freedom of choice had been considerably reduced by the investment already made by Iran of about $15 million in the dam and generating equipment." In other words, because the Shah was determined to go ahead with the Dez project, the Bank decided that, whatever its concerns about the project, it was better to be part of the action than to sit on the sidelines.

———

At the time it was built, the Furnas dam on Brazil's Rio Grande was the largest ever built in Latin America. The Bank made the Furnas loan in 1958, during a period when it had been refusing to finance projects in Brazil on the grounds that the government was pursuing an inflationary economic course. The Bank was persuaded to make an exception for the Furnas project by the Canadian-owned São Paulo Light Company, which bought stock in the state-owned company that would operate the dam and worked out an agreement to buy all the power it produced. Some Brazilians objected to the government's borrowing money to build a dam that would provide all its power to one private, foreign-owned company: One deputy in the Brazilian Congress called the Furnas dam a "crime against the nation."

The last of the seven dams in the top twenty-one projects funded by Black is Colombia's Colegio Dam, which was completed in 1967 and provides power to Bogotá. Colegio cost 45 percent more than expected. Although the Bank has never studied its investment in Colegio or most of the other projects it financed during its first two decades, a 1972 internal report declared that "despite the large cost overruns, the large majority of the generating plants financed [in Colombia] by the Bank appear still to have been economically optimal."

———

Eight of Black's top twenty-one projects were railroads or roads. In 1959 the Bank lent Iran $72 million for the import of equipment needed to build 1,600 miles of roads. Two years later, India received $60 million and Argentina $48.5 million, also for the import of road-building equipment. Information on these and the Bank's other early road-building programs is sketchy, though Simon Aldewereld concluded that the Bank's financing of India's highways was less than successful. "For various reasons, one of them possibly the reluctance on the part of the Indian authorities to retain consultants," he said, "the completion of some of the trunk highways was severely delayed, with the result that substantial economic benefits were lost."

By contrast, according to Aldewereld, "The Bank considered its lending to the Indian Railways as very successful." The Bank lent India nearly $450 million to modernize the country's railroads, its biggest investment by far during the Black years. Its second-biggest investment was $150 million financing for a railway system in South Africa to assist the movement of industrial freight and "the expansion of gold mining operations in the Orange Free State." The Bank also made large loans to Pakistan and Mexico for the construction and maintenance of their national rail systems.

The Atlantic Railroad through Colombia's then-untouched rainforest was the "most important single transport investment financed by the Bank in Colombia" during Black's reign. Hailed by James Morris as "one of the most spectacularly interesting projects of our time," it was also one of the worst planned. A foreign engineering firm declared the proposed route excellent on the basis of a single aerial survey. "It is the only route of easy construction . . . and a line with easy curvature and flat grades can be secured without excessive grading cost," its report declared. In fact, as locals and travelers to the region had known for centuries, the land was swampy and subject to frequent flooding.

One consequence of the inadequate survey work was that the 400-mile-long railway took eight years to complete instead of the originally estimated five years, and cost not $58 million, but $98 million. The delays in construction meant that inflation reduced the value of the contracts that had been awarded; in response many contractors simply "reduced the quality of their work," reported one independent study of the project. Moreover, even before the railway was complete, the swath of land cleared for it opened the Magdalena Valley, which had previously been protected by its inaccessibility, to a wave of unplanned colonization. The assault of the settlers on the wild forests of the valley took a heavy toll on both—and on the Indians who had long lived in isolation there.

In 1959, with the railroad still under construction, David Lilienthal spoke with Lauchlin Currie, who had settled in Colombia, become a Colombian citizen, and was having second thoughts about the railroad he had once promoted. "I got the impression," Lilienthal wrote, "that if he had to do it over again, with greater knowledge of the realities, he would have omitted the railroad in place of more highways—and I think I would too. With improved access, squatters are pouring into the Valley by the thousands, burning the hillsides to make little farms, dynamiting the fish in the streams, cutting down trees, etc. Nothing being done about it. Nothing in the Currie Plan specifically foreshadowed this consequence."

In 1974, the Bank looked back at the Atlantic Railroad and didn't like what it saw. It called its construction "a most painful and lengthy process"; it blamed the railway, and the subsequent colonization, for what it called "a widespread misuse of the region's natural resources"; and it concluded that "even under the most favorable assumptions" investment in the railway was not justified. This is not surprising in view of the fact that while the Bank was helping Colombia build a railroad, it was simultaneously investing in a national highway network that largely duplicated the railroad and whose many hidden public subsidies made it more attractive to consumers. The railroad also had to compete with the established transport system of the Magdalena River, to which it ran parallel. The investment in the Atlantic Railroad, the Bank concluded, "has had dubious results." But the highway scheme was, if anything, even more discouraging. It took ten years to build instead of three, and the final cost, leaving aside inflation, was more than three times the original estimate. The entire episode was uncannily reminiscent of the bad old days of uncontrolled foreign lending before the war, when Colombia had borrowed millions abroad to link two valleys by railway and road simultaneously.

———

Under Black, the major recipients of World Bank industrial loans were two privately owned iron and steel companies in India and one in Mauritania. The Tata Iron and Steel Company received $107.5 million, and the Indian Iron and Steel Company received three loans totaling $71 million. All the loans were for the expansion of production and were guaranteed by the Indian government. The first loan—to the Indian Iron and Steel Company—for $31.5 million was made on the recommendation of a mission led by George Woods, then chairman of the First Boston Corporation. The contract for the work to be carried out under the loan was awarded to Kaiser Engineering. Woods had a longtime interest in Kaiser. Until 1963, when he succeeded Black as president of the World Bank, he sat on the board of Kaiser's parent company and when he left the Bank he joined the board of the Kaiser Foundation. According to Woods's authorized biographer, Robert Oliver, throughout his career "Kaiser interests took more of Woods' time than any other one enterprise."

The Bank's $66 million loan to finance the development of Maurita-nia's rich iron ore deposits made that small country the fifth-largest recipi-ent of Bank funds per capita during the Bank's first quarter-century. The loan was made to a consortium known as MIFERMA, which included the state-owned steel companies of Britain and Italy. Richard Westebbe, who led a Bank mission to Mauritania in 1967, called MIFERMA a "foreign enclave, developed with foreign capital and staffed at the higher levels almost entirely by Europeans." Though the project was intended, Westebbe said, "to bring the age of industrialization to Mauritania . . . in fact, its influence on the economy in terms of income, employment, and technologi-cal change has been slight, while it has not lived up to expectations in providing revenues to the state budget."

There are three other loans in the top twenty-one, about which there is little information available. In 1959 the Bank lent $56.5 million to the Suez Canal Authority, a loan guaranteed by the government of Egypt. The money was used to deepen and widen the canal to accommodate new, larger oil tankers. In the same month, the Bank lent $50 million to a joint venture between France's largest oil company and the French government for the building of an oil pipeline through the Sahara. And in 1962 it lent $95 million to finance a thermal power plant to provide Buenos Aires with electricity. The loan went to a government-owned utility, on condition that it "be returned to private ownership . . . as rapidly as market conditions will allow." This finally occurred in 1992.

———

These twenty-one loans account for one-third of the money the Bank lent to the Third World during Black's tenure. In those thirteen years, the Bank also made several hundred smaller development loans, as well as numerous loans to industrial countries. But these twenty-one projects were the Bank's major investments, its showpieces. Despite their size and importance, the Bank did not study any of them once they were completed. Thus it did not see—or learn from—many of its own mistakes. Instead, it financed their replication around the world. Now, years later, it is clear that during the Bank's glory years many of its most important projects did more harm than good.

# Six

FOR GOD'S SAKE, LISTEN

George Woods, the prominent New York investment banker who was Eugene Black's successor, did not enjoy Black's happy relationship with his board and his staff. Woods was a self-made man, perceptive and intelligent, but he could be extremely abrasive. He was democratic in his rudeness, however, as willing to offend board members and government officials as his own subordinates. In the words of Julian Grenfell, a member of the British House of Lords who served as Woods's speechwriter, he "treated the Board as though it was always his quarter in the telephone when he was addressing them." Woods's disregard for diplomacy upset many people. At his first meeting with the African finance ministers, for example, he sat quietly as each expressed his views on the Bank. Then, to everyone's shock, instead of beginning his response with "Your Excellencies," he burst out with, "I've listened to what you guys have had to say. Now you listen to me."

Woods had other qualities, however, that served the Bank well. While still a private citizen, he had undertaken several delicate missions for the Bank, including settling the claims arising from Egypt's expropriation of the Suez Canal Company in 1956. Thus he entered office with a better understanding of the Bank and of the Third World than any of his predecessors had had. Though he served only one five-year term, Woods dramatically changed the Bank at a crucial moment in its history.

Soon after taking office, Woods discovered that Black's Bank, "the most solvent and profitable of international organizations," as *The New York Times* put it, was facing some very serious problems. In the first place, twenty years of development had left the Third World dangerously in debt to foreign lenders. By 1965 poor countries were taking in about $14 billion annually in export sales and in aid donations from rich countries, but half of that was going right back in the form of debt service payments. Their gross domestic products were increasing by 4.8 percent a year, but their foreign debts were growing three times that fast. Such heavy debts, warned the Bank's experts, "constitute a serious obstacle to substantial amounts of further borrowing."

"The fact is," explained Simon Aldewereld, the head of the Bank's project division, "that the debt service, the interest, and the principle payments on development loans we made during these past twenty years of the World Bank are more than many, perhaps most, of the countries we have made the loans to can carry. . . . This means that we simply made a major misjudgment—a mistake—when we assumed that conventional banking terms and conditions could be applied to such countries—India, Pakistan, countries in Africa."

George Woods asked a high-level international commission headed by former Canadian prime minister Lester Pearson to study, among other matters, the debt burdens of developing countries. In its report, *Partners in Development,* issued in 1969, the Pearson Commission called the increase in debt over the previous fifteen years "explosive." It discovered that developing countries were using a huge proportion of their foreign loans simply to pay the interest due on earlier foreign loans; in South Asia the figure was 40 percent and in Latin America, 87 percent. The commission warned that if borrowing continued at existing levels, by 1977 South Asia would be spending all its foreign loans to service its outstanding debts; Africa's annual debt service payments would be 120 percent of its new borrowings; and Latin America's would be 130 percent.

For the third time in its short history, the Bank was faced with a shortage of suitable borrowers. This is a serious problem for an institution whose mission is to make loans. In the Bank's earliest days, few developing countries wanted to borrow money from it, and even fewer knew how to go about it. The Bank remedied this by actively soliciting business from developing countries and helping them design appropriate projects. By the late 1950s, another shortage loomed, this one due to the fact that the Bank's poorer clients had exhausted their creditworthiness and could not afford to take on new loans. The solution to this crisis had been the establishment of the International Development Association (IDA) to make loans on concessionary terms to countries that could not afford to borrow on the Bank's usual terms. IDA enabled the Bank to go on lending to its poorest clients, but the developing world was accumulating foreign debt at such a pace that by the mid-1960s, the Bank was once again running out of creditworthy borrowers.

To a lot of people, the fact that so many countries were deeply, dangerously in debt merely indicated that they should borrow more. *The New York Times,* for example, had welcomed Woods's appointment to the Bank with an editorial calling on him to step up its lending: "Though the bank is rich in prestige and accomplishments, its work is not done. The fact is that the developing nations are burdened with foreign debt and their development will be stunted if they cannot get an increasing amount of funds."

The growing debt burden of his major borrowers was not the only problem Woods had to face. There was also the dawning realization that the Bank's—indeed the whole world's—efforts at development had fallen far short of expectations. Since the war, the GDPs of developing countries had grown at a good pace, almost 5 percent per year. Population increases, it was true, meant that per capita growth was only about half that. But the real problem was that the gap between the world's rich and its poor was not narrowing, but widening.

In 1968, the rich countries were richer compared to the developing countries than they had been in 1947. In 1947 average per capita income in the United States was $1,600; in other industrialized countries it averaged about $650. In most of the countries of Africa, Asia, and Latin America, it was less than $100. By 1966, average per capita income had risen to $3,650 in the United States and $2,000 in Western Europe; but only to $120 in the 40 poorest developing countries. Leaving out the United States—with its superhigh incomes—the gap between rich and poor countries had widened from 6.5:1, to 16:1.

Even more disheartening, rich and poor were further apart in the developing world than they were in the industrialized world. In the United States, for example, the per capita income of the richest segment of the population was five times greater than that of the poorest. In many developing countries, however, the rich were not five times richer than the poor, but fifteen or thirty times richer. Thus two decades of development had left the poor of the developing world poorer in relation to the industrialized world—and to their own countrymen.

Woods became president at a time when scores of colonial territories, especially in Africa, were gaining their independence and joining the Bank. Between 1954 and 1964, the Bank's membership jumped from 56 nations to 102. Many were poor and uncreditworthy by the Bank's standards, but Woods wanted to lend to them and was frustrated by what he saw as the Bank's straitlaced notions of who was fit to borrow and what was a suitable project. "I never saw a more rigid institution," he complained to David Lilienthal. "Creditworthy—that's the word they use. That means saying *No*."

When Senior Vice President Burke Knapp boasted at a board meeting that the Bank had never had a default, Woods interrupted him, saying, "Burke, I'm not sure that is anything to be proud of. . . . Do you really think that a development finance agency ought to measure its success by the lack of defaults? We shouldn't be that concerned with whether a country is able to service a loan. We should be more concerned with what good it is doing for the country." On another occasion Woods reprimanded a senior official who expressed doubt about the advisability of making a loan for a huge hydroelectric project in Argentina. To Woods's inquiry about whether the project should be funded, the official replied, "Well, Mr. Woods, the rate of return is only about 6 percent." "Little people only think in terms of rates of return," snapped Woods.

Instead of granting or withholding loans according to a country's creditworthiness or the profitability of its projects, Woods believed the Bank should demand of its borrowers that they adopt and stick to an overall economic policy of which it approved. Under Woods the Bank became more involved in the broad economic life of its borrowers and the Bank's economic staff grew from twenty to more than two hundred. "This is more and more what we find ourselves talking about with our member countries—fundamental policies to govern their day-to-day economic decisions," he said. The Bank did not hesitate to use its financial muscle to pressure its clients to follow its economic prescriptions.

Woods also wanted to expand the range of activities for which the Bank could lend. He was frustrated by what he saw as its narrow and restrictive focus on infrastructure. It was clear to him that building up a country's industrial infrastructure could take it only so far, and that there were many other aspects to development. Investments in health, education, and sanitation were also essential—and Woods wanted the Bank to fund such investments.

In the past, however, the Bank had shunned such enterprises because they were unlikely to earn enough foreign exchange to repay their cost. Woods's predecessors had directed far less than 1 percent of the Bank's lending to education and water-supply projects—and lent none at all for health and nutrition. Woods succeeded in taking the Bank into the realms of "social lending," albeit in a modest way. Of the 290 loans the Bank made during Woods's tenure, only 19 were for education and 10 for water supply and sewage, and even these were to a great extent for bricks and mortar, for pipe laying and school construction. But though it was small, the seed of social lending that Woods planted eventually grew into a mighty tree.

———

The move into social lending helped Woods in his other effort: the quest to increase the Bank's lending, which was chiefly held back by the Bank's standards of "creditworthiness." Woods's new stable of economists argued that by expanding its range of investments, the Bank would actually increase its clients' capacity to borrow.

Bank officials accepted that there was a limit on the amount of foreign currency any developing country could usefully employ or "absorb." As a country developed, its "absorptive capacity" would grow, but development was partly a result of internal investments in education, health, sanitation, vocational training, so-called social investments that did not depend on imports and thus did not require expensive foreign loans. However, once the Bank had decided to make social as well as infrastructure investments, there was hardly a limit to the degree to which it could further the development process. It no longer had to wait for a borrower to make the social investments that would lift its absorptive capacity to the next level before the Bank could make another round of infrastructure loans. Instead, as its official history puts it, the Bank came "to realize that creditworthiness was essentially a function of growth and that absorptive capacity increased with absorption." In other words, borrowing enables countries to grow, and growth enables them to borrow more. Thus, by expanding the range of projects it financed, the Bank also expanded the creditworthiness of its clients.

This theory enabled the Bank to ignore the warnings of its own experts that heavy indebtedness was "a serious obstacle to substantial amounts of further borrowing." Its 1965 annual report acknowledged that many of its clients had problems servicing their debts, but added that "none of these, however, should be taken to mean that developing countries cannot afford, and hence should avoid, any increases in debt service obligations." Woods believed that the Bank's clients needed much more money and he intended to lend it to them.

It fell to the Bank's chief economist, Irving Friedman, to determine exactly how much more borrowing the Bank's clients could "absorb." To do so, he later recalled, he went "to each loan officer and ask[ed] him to list from experience what investment projects he personally knew of that were being held back which in his opinion were worthy of being financed and yet were not being financed because of lack of foreign exchange." On the basis of this survey, Friedman decided that developing countries could make good use of $4 billion per year. He and Woods decided that half the $4 billion should be in the forms of grants or "soft" loans and that the Bank's concessionary arm, IDA, should provide half of that—$1 billion a year. To make that possible, Woods asked the Bank's rich members to quadruple their contributions to IDA. "There is no future in the World Bank Group," he warned, "unless IDA becomes more important than conventional lending."

Though the response to request for more money for IDA was tepid, Woods did dramatically increase the Bank's rate of lending. In his five years in office, the Bank made nearly $6 billion worth of loans, compared with $7 billion over the previous fifteen years. It also encouraged private banks to step up their lending to the Third World. The 1965 annual report told of the Bank's "strenuous efforts to encourage and enlarge the flow of private capital into the less developed countries. There is no doubt that this flow can be expected to increase."

Despite this ever-increasing flow, however, many developing countries found it harder than ever to service their debts. Throughout the mid-1960s, the Bank continually emphasized the need to "lighten the [debt] service burden" of these countries. But the Bank felt that this was a task for other lenders, not itself, and it should be achieved not by cutting back on lending, but by rescheduling existing loans—that is, stretching out the loan period so that debtors had lower monthly payments. Between 1957 and 1969, international creditors, often with the Bank acting as mediator, carried out twenty-one reschedulings, notably for Argentina, Turkey, Ghana, Indonesia, Brazil, and India.

But rescheduling could help only countries that were suffering from a short-term trade imbalance, not those that were over their heads in debt. For the most heavily indebted countries, the Bank prescribed—more borrowing. Ceylon (now Sri Lanka), Ghana, India, and Pakistan were among the countries that the Bank described as so in debt "that they are likely to encounter serious and protracted debt service difficulties unless large amounts of external assistance are available to them."

The need to get large amounts of money quickly to desperate countries called for a new type of loan. Project loans would not be of much help to countries in such desperate straits because they are disbursed gradually, over the months or years it takes to complete a project—and because most are too small to make a significant dent in a country's total foreign debt. Heavily indebted countries trying to stave off default need very large, quick-disbursing loans, often called balance-of-payment loans. The Bank's founders had been anxious to prevent the Bank from making such loans, which is why its Articles of Agreement restrict it to project lending.

Nevertheless, the Bank was eager to make such loans, particularly to India, its major borrower, which was suffering through a prolonged balance-of-payments crisis. To get around the Articles of Agreement, Irving Friedman, who "had become quite convinced that the Bank ought to do more in the way of balance-of-payments financing," suggested that the Bank create a new facility armed with the power to make such loans. This was a radical suggestion: This facility would have violated the spirit, and probably the letter, of the Bank's charter and would have alarmed the Bank's friends on Wall Street. Luckily, as Julian Grenfell explained, a much simpler solution was found:

> In the end, it wasn't necessary to create a new facility, because when we got into the business of making large loans to facilitate India's imports we simply called them "industrial import loans." . . . It was Woods who took the decision himself. Why can't we just make them a loan? Make a list of things they are going to import. . . . As far as he was concerned, it was a project, [but] it was [actually] balance of payments support; it had the same effect as a balance-of-payments loan.

Between 1964 and 1976, the Bank made India eleven of these balance-of-payments loans disguised as "industrial import loans," for a total of nearly $1.5 billion.

John Maynard Keynes had anticipated the Bank's current predicament, warning that an institution like the World Bank could expect to be repaid only as long as it financed repayment of past loans by the commitment of new ones. This is assuredly not the official view of the Bank, which maintains that every one of its borrowers has a solemn obligation to repay its loans, whether or not more loans are forthcoming. In practice, however, it is generally assumed within the Bank that an endless supply of new loans *will* be forthcoming—an assumption that improves the credit rating of the Bank's borrowers.

According to Benjamin King, an economist who served more than thirty years in the Bank, "The hard line definition of creditworthiness" is reflected in the question: "Do we expect this country to pay back the loans that we've made, if we never make another loan?" However, King adds, there is another question, which is, " 'Do we expect this country to pay off these loans, provided that they are going to get more capital from us in the future?' That's a somewhat softer line. No one would expect poorer countries to stop getting loans in the foreseeable future."

----

Shortly after taking office President Kennedy proclaimed the 1960s as the Decade of Development. Kennedy portrayed aid as a magnanimous response to human suffering rather than as a device for preventing world communism—and thus helped generate a worldwide enthusiasm for development. This altruistic fervor was short-lived, however. As the intractibility of the problems facing the developing world became apparent, enthusiasm turned rapidly to disappointment and cynicism. By the mid-1960s, the rich nations had begun to feel that, in Woods's words, more aid "would simply send good money after bad." Instead of increasing the proportion of GNP they gave to development, they reduced it. Woods devoted his last months in office to efforts to overcome this disillusionment and to inject political leaders and the public in general with a sense of urgency and hope about development.

He began by acknowledging that "waste, inefficiency and even dishonesty have all too often deflected resources from development," giving rise to a widespread feeling of "discouragement and skepticism about the general effectiveness of aid." Nevertheless, he warned the rich nations that if they gave up on development, they would "leave the great majority of our fellow men hungry, restless and reduced to a sort of delinquent despair." Woods's urgings fell mainly on deaf ears, however. The Bank's rich members gave IDA less than half the $1 billion he had sought for it.

Woods's energetic fund-raising efforts were overshadowed by his deep concern that development—no matter how well funded—was not working out as intended. He knew that during the past two decades, during which the Bank had lent billions of dollars to the Third World, the gulf between the rich and the poor had widened, and many countries had been burdened with impossible debts. Six months before he left office, Woods used the occasion of an address to the Swedish Bankers' Association to call for a reassessment of the Bank's work—and of the development process in general. His speech betrayed a deep unease about the future of the developing world and about what one of his vice presidents called "the inadequacy of the Bank's efforts." According to Julian Grenfell, "The Stockholm speech was saying, 'Look, I am leaving the Bank. This is my last major public pronouncement. . . . This development decade has run out of steam. The money that is going in is simply not doing the job. . . . For God's sake, listen."

———

Robert Strange McNamara, a man described by Senator Barry Goldwater as "an IBM machine with legs," was Woods's successor. McNamara was only fifty-one when he reached the World Bank in June 1968, but he had already held a succession of important jobs in which his failures had been as spectacular as his successes. As president of the Ford Motor Company, he modernized the U.S. automobile industry—and gave the world the Edsel. As U.S. secretary of defense, he streamlined the Pentagon bureaucracy—and helped divide the nation over Vietnam. McNamara had entered the public consciousness in the late 1940s as one of the supersmart "whiz kids," a new breed of businessmen determined to replace the old-fashioned seat-of-the-pants style of management with rational, orderly, modern systems analysis.

McNamara himself says he does not know if he resigned from the Defense Department or was fired, but Eugene Black told Nathaniel McKitterick, who had been his speechwriter at the Bank, that in 1967 Lyndon Johnson called him in and said, "I think Bob is going to jump out the window like Forrestal [secretary of defense from 1947 to 1949, who left office prematurely and committed suicide shortly thereafter]. Can we get him over to the World Bank?" George Woods was already lobbying for McNamara to succeed him, having been impressed by a speech to the American Society of Newspaper Editors in which McNamara had argued that the best guarantee of international security was a decent standard of living for all people. McNamara's appointment was announced in late 1967; he took office in April 1968.

Though eager to return to New York, Woods prolonged his tenure at the Bank so that McNamara could wind up affairs at the Defense Department. When McNamara did move to the Bank, Woods arranged to stay on for a few weeks in order to help him make the transition. McNamara, amply endowed with self-confidence, felt no need of advice from the older man, however. He ignored Woods, who spent his last days at the Bank ignominiously sitting in his temporary office and talking on the phone to his New York stockbroker.

McNamara was an aloof and rigid man more comfortable with numbers than with people, but he was also a man of deep feeling whose boyhood ambition had been "to help the largest number of people." He was determined to forestall the disastrous future of which George Woods had warned if the development effort continued on its stumbling, failing course. He would use his management and analytical skills to put both the Bank and the developing world on the right path.

He was a big man with big ambitions, and he expanded the Bank job to fit them. He wanted to do much more than merely provide the developing world with foreign capital. "Our ultimate goal," he said, "is to help . . . create a political, social and economic environment in which individual men and women can more freely develop their own highest potential." McNamara is often credited with turning the Bank into an instrument of social change, though it was Woods who first took the Bank into social development.

McNamara's unique contribution was the missionary zeal, the quasi-religious fervor he brought to his task. Whereas previous World Bank presidents had characterized development as essential to international stability, McNamara cast it as an ethical issue, declaring that "the rich and the powerful have a moral obligation to assist the poor and the weak." He also believed that poor people were more likely than the well off to turn to communism, as so many had in Vietnam. Perhaps it is true, as many have speculated, that McNamara's crusade against poverty was rooted in his anguish over the debacle in Vietnam and in a desire to atone for his part in it. But he was also moved by his famous determination to solve difficult problems and his lifelong yearning to do good. Like a conscientious pastor, he spent a considerable amount of time visiting his flock, the poor of the world. By all accounts, he enjoyed his encounters with the peasants and slum dwellers he met while inspecting Bank projects. But like most missionaries, McNamara believed that he was there to teach, not to learn.

During his first days at the Bank, McNamara "gorged himself on statistics," poring over figures on Bank lending and world poverty, according to William Clark, a British journalist who was his closest aide. He had trouble adjusting to the scale of the Bank's operations. As secretary of defense, he had presided over an annual budget of more than $70 billion and he was shocked to discover that the Bank was lending less than a billion dollars a year. "He kept talking in billions," Burke Knapp told McNamara's biographer, Deborah Shapley, "and then he would correct himself and say 'I meant millions.'"

At the end of the first week, McNamara called his senior managers together. He announced that, given the magnitude of the developing world's problems, the Bank should be lending much more. The assembled officials tried to explain to their new boss that the Bank's ability to lend was limited by the number of sound projects and creditworthy borrowers among its members and by its need to assure Wall Street that its investments were secure. McNamara cut them off, ending the meeting with a demand for a list of every project the Bank would consider funding if money were no object. The officials, reported Clark, "filed out in a state of shock."

Staffers spent the following weeks frantically "bringing out of bottom drawers proposals that had been rejected for lack of funds, working out new proposals for countries that had previously been considered as having had their full share, and even proposing some projects for countries previously rated too backward to be able to cope with Bank-style development." McNamara added together the cost of all these proposals and announced that the Bank would lend $11.6 billion over the next five years, more than it had during its first twenty years. The Bank's treasurer resigned in protest, warning that it would be impossible to raise the sum of money required without endangering the Bank's financial credibility. In the next three months, however, the Bank raised a record sum, proving perhaps that Wall Street was less interested in the quality or quantity of the Bank's lending than in the fact that its bonds were guaranteed by the richest nations on earth.

At his first meeting with the board of governors (the formal ruling body, made up of representatives from every member country, which has delegated day-to-day oversight of the Bank to the board of executive directors), McNamara said flatly that the old ways of development were not working. The previous two decades had failed to produce the expected "trickle-down" effect. "It is already clear beyond contradiction that . . . the income gap between the developing and the less developed countries has increased, is increasing and ought to be diminished," he said.

McNamara believed, however, that he could fine tune the system to ensure that the wealth being created would settle more evenly throughout the economy. He would do this primarily by investing more in basic social services aimed at the poor. "Redistribution with growth" became the Bank's new slogan. What Woods had begun in lending for social programs, McNamara greatly intensified. Under him, the Bank lent more money than ever before for nutrition and education and made its first family planning loans. McNamara also pushed the Bank deeper into the countryside, where the bulk of the poor live, putting a great deal of money into rural development, especially into agriculture.

It took only a few years, however, for McNamara to decide that more dramatic changes were needed. By 1971, according to a close aide, he was "convinced that growth was not trickling down." Despite the changes he had made, the Bank was still helping the rich at the expense of the poor. He acknowledged, for example, that richer farmers "have received disproportionate shares of irrigation water, fertilizers, seeds, and credit" from the Bank. His chief economist, Hollis Chenery, declared that the previous decade of rapid growth "has been of little or no benefit to perhaps a third of the population." Yet McNamara was convinced that "more equitable income distribution is absolutely imperative if the development process is to proceed in any meaningful manner."

McNamara spoke passionately about the nearly 800 million people who had to survive on 30 cents a day. He termed this group, which constituted 40 percent of the population of the developing world, the "absolute poor"—defining absolute poverty as "a condition of life so degraded by disease, illiteracy, malnutrition, and squalor as to deny its victims basic human necessities." Mere economic growth, he asserted, would not end this destitution, not if—as in the past—it was "highjacked by the privileged." It was worse than pointless, he warned, to "concentrate on the modern sector in the hope that its high rate of growth would filter down to the rural poor." Under that approach "disparities in income will simply widen."

The answer, he decided, was a frontal assault on poverty, a concentrated effort to see that the basic needs of the people were met. McNamara's new direction was not universally popular in the Bank. Many wanted the Bank to stick to its mandate of providing "finance for productive purposes." In the words of sociologist Sheldon Annis, who has served as a consultant to the Bank on poverty issues, "Many Bank old-liners saw poverty alleviation as a sop."

McNamara forged ahead nonetheless. He lectured developing countries on the need to make a decent life possible for all their citizens, though "it be at the cost of some reduction in the pace of advance in certain narrow and highly privileged sectors whose benefits accrue to the few." He even suggested that "reasonable redistribution of land, currently held in excessively large blocks, would be desirable." But McNamara was not proposing that the Bank take on this revolutionary task. The Bank, he said, would put its "primary emphasis not on the redistribution of income and wealth—as necessary as they may be in many of our member countries—but rather on increasing the productivity of the poor, thereby providing for a more equitable sharing of the benefits of growth." In other words, the Bank would not seek prosperity for the poor at the expense of the rich.

Many economists argued that wealth is more fruitful when it is amassed by a few who can invest their surplus in productive enterprises than when it is divided into insignificant individual shares. But McNamara, backed up by *his* economists, insisted that there was no conflict between a more equal distribution of income and economic growth. Developing countries could have prosperity *and* social equity if they followed a two-pronged approach. They must keep investing in industrialization and they must also invest in agriculture and basic social services so as to increase the productivity of the poor. Because all this investment would require more foreign currency than could be obtained through aid or loans, developing countries would also have to dramatically increase their exports.

McNamara also changed the Bank's position on lending to state-owned enterprises. The Bank was founded by capitalist powers who believed in the primacy of the private sector. Though most of its loans had been made to governments, they were for roads, ports, hydroelectric dams, and other essential aspects of the national infrastructure, which even the most adamant capitalists of the time agreed were the province of governments, not the private sector. But the Bank took a different view of industry: It "refused to lend to manufacturing enterprises in the public sector on the ground that they were unlikely to be managed efficiently." The few publicly controlled industrial projects it did finance "were designed to be turned over to private control at a specified stage."

McNamara, however, abandoned that hard line. For one thing, many of the Bank's newer members had socialist governments that were committed to public control of their emerging industrial sectors, and McNamara sympathized with their stated concern for a more equitable distribution of wealth. In addition, from the Bank's point of view, public borrowers have several advantages over private ones: They can absorb more money than can individual private enterprises; it is easier to keep tabs on a few massive government projects than on a welter of small independent projects; and investments in private businesses, no matter how successful, can have only an indirect effect on the poor, whereas it seemed to many of McNamara's senior officials that it was possible to reach the poor directly through governments. Thus, under McNamara, the Bank began to fund not just public utilities, but manufacturing and mining firms and even state-controlled agricultural enterprises.

―――――

To ensure that his overall target of doubling the Bank's lending was achieved, McNamara set annual lending targets for each country. And he expected them to be met. According to Warren Baum, then associate director of the projects department, McNamara "generated tremendous pressure within the institution to reach lending targets; . . . he felt it was a personal embarrassment to the institution if he said we were going to make 182 lending operations and we only did 176." And Benjamin King recalls that "success was measured by whether you kept to your lending targets or not."

In his zeal to step up lending, McNamara ignored many of the restrictions in the Articles of Agreement. "There is little doubt that several of the constraints so much emphasized in earlier years are now treated much more casually," reported a 1977 study by the Carnegie Endowment for International Peace and the International Legal Center in New York, giving the following examples: "Competition with private enterprise is not considered any more as an obstacle to a project's approval. . . . 'Program lending' for development 'projects' involving entire sectors of the economy has become more common. The Bank is now more often willing to lend funds to cover a project's local costs and it does not limit itself as much as it used to to foreign exchange costs only."

Staffers often complained that the pressure to lend resulted in poorly prepared and poorly executed projects. "There was tension as to how much time you could spend on appraising and supervising projects," according to Baum. Those hoping for advancement could not afford to look too closely at a project's problems, says King: "The brownie points were earned for finishing your project. Certainly no brownie points were earned for engaging in a policy discussion which might hold up a loan."

In 1978, a Bank staff association report found that "the assembly-line approach to project preparation has increasingly become the mode of operation at the bank. A growing number of staff members . . . are discouraged and disoriented by what seems to be an overriding concern with forms and procedures, not with substance." The increasing emphasis on what the Bank called "new style loans" meant that projects were getting harder to evaluate. "With a lot of this stuff," said one staffer, "it's very hard to say the project works or it doesn't work. The more we move into the social realm, the harder it gets to have any kind of a yardstick."

After undertaking in 1988, a review of the Bank's lending to Zambia, King concluded that during the McNamara period (1968–1981) "The main object was to go out and make loans. And many of the projects just folded." A 1989 evaluation of the Bank's lending to Senegal under McNamara concluded that the loans were "based less on intimate knowledge of and experience with Senegal than on internal Bank pressure to produce and to carry out a lending program for a politically attractive country in high-priority Africa."

The rush to meet targets reached a point of near absurdity toward the end of the Bank's fiscal year (which runs from July 1 to June 30). Staffers would scramble so desperately to boost their annual lending figures that, as one Bank officer told Forbes magazine, "We're like a Soviet factory. The push is to maximize lending. . . . In May and June the pressures to lend are enormous and a lot of people spend sleepless nights wondering how they can unload projects [on the board]." McNamara's supporters attributed such complaints to troublemaking old-timers who, in William Clark's words, "found themselves being hustled out of their customary rather leisurely perfectionism."

During McNamara's tenure, 40 percent of all IBRD loans were pushed through in the last two months of the fiscal year, a pattern that continues to this day. This flood makes it impossible for the directors to exercise any meaningful oversight of the Bank's lending. Not that the board was much inclined to exercise its independent judgment in any case; under McNamara it kept its unblemished record of never refusing a loan, trusting in management to submit only those worthy of approval.

A common complaint among the staff is that the Bank's lending targets—which still exist—drastically reduce its power in its negotiations with clients. Borrowers are well aware of the targets that have been set for them—and know that careers depend on those targets being met. Benjamin King explained it this way: "If you're a loan officer and you go down to Brazil and say, 'You know, if you don't fulfill these conditions you may not get the loan.' They'll say, 'That's fine, buddy'—or whatever the Brazilian equivalent of buddy is—'you can just take the next plane back to Washington because we know you're going to make that loan to us. Otherwise you're out of a job.' "

Senior managers conceded that the Bank was putting fewer conditions on its loans but said the difference was insignificant. In 1980, Munir Benjenk, vice president for external relations, told one reporter, "In the old days, if we got 99 percent, we'd hold out for 100 percent. We're asking now, how much harm is done is you took 80 percent?" But other officials maintained that the true rate of erosion in the Bank's bargaining power was more like from 50 percent to 35 percent.

Whatever the terms of the final loan agreement, borrowers soon learned that they risked little in violating those terms, says Benjamin King. "When a loan was being considered for a particular country and it had been very lax, to say the least, in fulfilling its obligations under the previous loan agreements, the Bank always turned soft and instead of saying, 'We're not going to make this loan until you live up to your side of the bargain,' they said, 'Well, you know, you can't expect Syria'—which was one of the worst offenders—'to adhere to these agreements. We must keep on lending.' "

By keeping on lending, the Bank hoped to ensure that its clients would keep on repaying. It also believed that, given enough investment, the Third World would experience a growth in export earnings that would enable it to repay its debts and escape the vicious circle in which it was trapped. But things were not working out as planned. Between 1968 and 1973, the Bank doubled its lending, but at the end of that period McNamara told the Bank's board of governors that the expansion had to continue. "Far from relaxing the momentum of our operations over the next five years, [we] must increase it." He asked them not to be concerned about the developing world's enormous and fast-growing indebtedness. The *size* of the debt, he explained, is not the problem. The problem is "the fact that debt, and debt payments, are growing faster than the revenues required to service them."

———

Under McNamara the Bank was a repository for statistics of every kind. It compiled them, analyzed them, and used them to produce innumerable reports. It came to think of itself as "the foremost world center for authoritative studies of key development issues." McNamara was above all a numbers man. His numerical obsession was so well known that when he was appointed to the Bank, *The New York Times* cautioned that "development goes far beyond a mastery of techniques and introduction of systems analysis." McNamara himself recognized the dangers of an overreliance on statistics. In asking Irving Friedman to stay on as his chief economist, he said, "You know I have a weakness for numbers. Please protect me from my weakness for numbers."

His "statistical approach to reality" upset many in the Bank, who believed that it blocked out the complexities of the real world. Some senior managers mockingly coined a private slogan: "What can't be counted, doesn't count." His insistence on being told exactly how many poor people each project would help drove Bank staff to invent numbers to satisfy him. In 1978, the Bank's Staff Association issued a report decrying "management's obsessive concern for details and statistics." David Lilienthal described McNamara at the Bank as having "surrounded himself with fancy mathematical economists as he surrounded himself with 'analysts' in the Defense Department; the bitter fruit of that reliance is too well known: the bloody Vietnam debacle."

McNamara was insatiable for facts only until he made up his mind. At that point, he did not wish to be presented with opposing information. "People who antagonize him or contradict him in a meeting never have a chance to see him," said one Bank official. Not many people dared to stand up to McNamara; he was a powerful and intimidating man who, according to more than one colleague, "ruled the place through fear." He also kept the board on a tight leash, intimidating it by the force of his personality and his mastery of statistics.

Mahbub ul Haq, who came to the Bank in 1970 after serving as the chief economist of Pakistan's Planning Commission, became one of McNamara's favorites, one of the few who were allowed to contradict and challenge him. But even ul Haq acknowledged that McNamara "browbeat people intellectually. He never really invited comments. He had made up his mind and . . . he would feel uncomfortable if dissenting voices were raised." Moreover, when, as was often the case, he was sure he was right, McNamara was not above massaging the numbers to strengthen his argument. He "was very good at manipulating statistics," said another staffer, "not with ill intent, but in an excess of advocacy."

McNamara took the Bank's annual lending from less than $1 billion in 1968 to more than $12 billion in 1981. In thirteen years, he lent more than $77 billion. To keep pace with the increased lending, he doubled the size of the staff in a year, and tripled it in three. He presided over a significant increase in the wealth of the developing world and learned that wealth was not enough.

"We have come to see our planet as 'spaceship earth,'" he said. "But what we must not forget is that one-quarter of the passengers on that ship have luxurious first-class accommodations and the remaining three-quarters are traveling in steerage. That does not make for a happy ship." Wealth creation, he warned, was only part of the solution; poverty—at least absolute poverty—must also be ended. "However important an increase in GNP may be as a necessary condition of development, it is not a sufficient condition. . . . If we achieve the 'quantity' goals, and neglect the 'quality' goals of development, we will have failed. It is as simple as that. We will have failed."

# Seven

## McNAMARA'S GHOSTS

McNamara's passionate rhetoric created the impression that the Bank was now concentrating on fighting poverty, but his statistics show otherwise. Most of the $77 billion worth of loans made during his reign supported industrialization through traditional infrastructure projects: highways, dams, gas pipelines, ports, cargo-handling facilities, and the like. Less than 10 percent went to education, health, family planning, water supply, and other programs that might help the poor directly. In that category, too, most of the funds were spent on construction and the import of high-tech equipment, not on the provision of services.

Under McNamara, loans for agriculture became the fastest-growing segment of Bank lending. By the end of his reign, one-third of the Bank's financing was for agriculture. However, although farming is the chief livelihood of the poor in developing countries, most of McNamara's agriculture loans were not targeted at poor farmers, but at wealthy ones, the fortunate 2 percent of landowners who control three-quarters of the developing world's farmland. The Bank promoted Western-style, capital-intensive agriculture, the kind that requires more land and more access to credit than most small farmers have.

If the Bank was only interested in increased production, it would have done better to concentrate on helping small and subsistence farmers, since many studies have shown that they make more efficient use of extra resources than do larger landowners. But it was also anxious that its agricultural investments should earn foreign exchange by producing surplus crops for export, or at least that they should save foreign exchange by reducing the need for imports. Large landowners produce to sell, whereas smaller farmers are more likely to concentrate on producing food to eat or to trade locally. The Bank's 1975 report, *Assault on Poverty,* concluded that "lending only to those [farmers] with investment opportunities sufficient to produce a significant marketable surplus is perhaps the best way to reduce the level of default."

It was awkward for the Bank to ask for more food exports from countries whose people often didn't have enough to eat. But the so-called Green Revolution of the 1960s and 1970s seemed to solve that problem by promising such leaps in production that poor countries could feed themselves *and* sell overseas. The Bank threw itself energetically into financing the auxiliary infrastructure of modern farming—pesticide factories, meat-packing plants, marketing boards, and crop-processing facilities. It invested billions of dollars—more than a billion in India alone—in factories that make fertilizer and pesticides, including substances such as DDT and BHC that are banned or severely restricted in Europe and the United States. One researcher estimated that pesticides accounted for 10 percent of the Bank's agricultural loans. The Bank also established farm credit programs for individual farmers, but the credit was made available in amounts too large for small-scale farmers to hope to repay. In most cases, Bank credits could be used only for advanced machinery, livestock, seeds, fertilizers, and other goods chosen by the Bank or its technical advisors. Often credit approval was conditional on the farmer's adopting new techniques, switching to particular crops, buying insurance, and selling to a specified buyer who would deduct the loan repayments from the farmer's earnings.

The Bank admits that more than half its rural credit funds supported large and medium-sized farming operations, but even this is most certainly an understatement because the Bank's idea of a small farm includes many that, by the standards of the Third World, are medium or large. The Bank typically counts anyone with holdings of 12 acres (5 hectares) or less as a small farmer, although only the top 20 percent of Third World farmers have more than 12 acres. For one loan, to Guatemala, the Bank defined small farmers as those with less than 112 acres—a category that includes 97 percent of the country's farmers. In two World Bank rural credit programs in the Philippines, almost every penny went to farmers with more than 7.2 acres (3 hectares), even though three-quarters of the farmers in the targeted areas had less land than that.

The Bank downplayed the degree to which it was helping the rich get richer, preferring to highlight its work with the poor. Nonetheless, it acted consciously, out of a conviction that the best way to create new wealth is to invest in the wealthy, not the poor. In 1970, when the board was considering livestock loans for two Latin American countries, one board member objected to the loans on the grounds that they "were made to comparatively affluent farmers, while the vast majority of cultivators in these countries, who were certainly not affluent, were neglected." As reported in its authorized history, a director from Latin America retorted that he was surprised "to see it suggested that the Bank should be concerned with redistributing income; he had understood that the purpose of the Bank was to promote economic development, in which case it was appropriate to finance those who were capable of assisting such development." Both loans were approved.

The Bank's willingness to lend to those least in need is also partly explained by institutional ambition; it did not want to drive eager borrowers into the arms of rival lenders. In 1969 the Bank was debating whether to lend India and Pakistan large sums of money to buy imported tractors. One side argued against the loans on the grounds that "they served the interests mainly of large, well-to-do farmers and would tend to replace techniques of production that were decidedly more labor-intensive, thus creating undesirable employment effects." The opposing side conceded this, but countered that mechanization was "inevitable" and that if the Bank didn't lend India the money, someone else would. The Bank made the loans.

Major corporations, as well as wealthy individuals, received help from the Bank through agriculture loans. In 1978, Zaire received a $9 million low-interest World Bank loan intended to revive its flagging palm oil industry. The Bank's appraisal report stated that "three companies would benefit from the project"—two Belgian firms and a subsidiary of Unilever, the giant British-based multinational. The government's interest in the project, a Bank official familiar with it told me, was largely explained by its proximity to President Mobutu's home region. "It's an illusion to think that this was an example of the Bank working with the private sector," said another staffer. "In fact, it was the Bank helping private monopolies that collude with the government."

The loan was classified as agricultural because the companies were to use much of it to import bulldozers and other land-clearing machinery so that they could replant their palm oil plantations. They were to use the rest to upgrade their oil mills and to build housing, schools, dispensaries, and stores for plantation laborers. The project was supposed to result in 3,500 additional jobs for plantation workers. But even before the loan was made, a Bank report warned that it was unlikely that those jobs would be filled unless there was a dramatic "improvement of both social conditions on the plantations and the earnings of the workers," whose "real wages have gone down by as much as 75 percent since 1960." The Bank's analysis of the project stated that "in some places the local population would probably be better off if it grows its own cash crops . . . since this generates a higher cash income than the companies are able to provide."

Though the plantations were planted as planned, the project was a failure. Its economic rate of return was not 16 percent, as the Bank had predicted, but 5 percent. The Bank's forecasts of world palm oil prices were grossly overoptimistic; the lower prices caused one of the two Belgian companies to drop out early in the project and drove the other to bankruptcy. The worker housing was not completed, and the companies built only one of the twenty-five schools, stores, and dispensaries that had been planned. The Bank concluded that the project was a success in one regard: It "contributed substantially to policy formulation" by making it clear "that artisanal (small-scale) palm oil production . . . has a better future than plantation production."

---

During McNamara's time the Bank also lent heavily to ranchers; in 1975, one-third of all its agricultural loans were for livestock operations. Those loans, the Bank's official historians concluded, "have benefitted directly and primarily the relatively well-to-do ranchers in Latin America." This was predictable because ranching is a rich man's pursuit. It is extremely land-intensive—especially on cleared rainforest soils, where the rule of thumb is that a single cow requires 10 or more acres of grazing land. To justify its preferential treatment of large ranchers, the Bank invoked the trickle-down theory, arguing that "the tax revenues generated from these ranches are expected to help the government provide rural services to other needy areas."

Unfortunately, the Bank's own analyses of its cattle loans indicate not only that they chiefly helped the biggest ranches, but also that the biggest ranches were the least efficient producers. In many cases, big landowners used the Bank's money not to modernize, intensify, or otherwise improve production, but to consolidate control of their holdings in anticipation of efforts to assign idle land to landless farmers. "A cynic could claim," noted an internal review, "that all the Bank has been doing is to help large farmers take evasive action by putting in a minimum of infrastructure to pass legal tests of utilization."

The Bank's lending did not merely help large farmers; it harmed smaller ones. A review of its programs in Colombia found that "the availability of credit, supporting services and new technology . . . has tended to favor the larger farmers and inadvertently work to the disadvantage of the small farmer." In 1975, the Bank acknowledged that some of its agricultural credit programs "may have undermined the position of the smaller farmers. For example, in Colombia, Ethiopia, and Pakistan, the new technology financed by loans contributed to the displacement of tenants."

---

Irrigation was at the heart of the Bank's efforts to increase agricultural productivity. In 1989, the Bank evaluated fourteen representative irrigation projects conducted in the McNamara years. All fourteen projects were designed to raise food production and to earn or save foreign exchange. But only three of the fourteen achieved the crop production levels predicted by Bank staff.

One reason for the low productivity is that every project was plagued with technical problems. In half, the area under irrigation had shrunk within a decade of completion. "The reasons," the evaluators noted, "included water shortages, flooding, soil waterlogging or salinization, incomplete construction of irrigation networks, and the use of inadequate topographic maps at the preparation and construction stage." The chances of most of these projects recovering their cost is slim, according to the Bank, because poor construction, maintenance, and project design mean that "only a few projects will reach the term of their expected useful life." Ten of the fourteen also had "some degree of adverse impact on the environment." When Bank evaluators visited Mexico's Sinaloa project five years after it was completed, 26,000 acres—17 percent of the project area—could no longer be farmed because it was so waterlogged and saline.

In half the projects, "Large farmers were found to have captured the bulk of the benefits." Nonetheless, in all but one project, average family income rose, though always by less than predicted. The higher incomes, however, were often cancelled out by higher expenses. In several projects women had to abandon their own subsistence plots because their labor was needed in the newly irrigated, more intensively cultivated family rice fields. "Unfortunately, for most families the incomes from rice production were not high enough to make up for the decline in subsistence production," a Bank study found. The same study also found that "increased demands on family labor for farming worked against efforts to improve children's literacy and education."

In presenting the projects to the board for approval, Bank staff predicted that all fourteen would have an economic rate of return higher than 10 percent; in five, they said, the ERR would be greater than 20 percent. In actuality, only six projects reached 10 percent and several had negative rates of return.

India was the Bank's star pupil in terms of increased agricultural production. Bank officials were truly elated by its remarkable turnaround between 1967, when it was the world's second largest cereal importer, and 1979, when it produced enough food to feed its population. That "India can feed itself," said a Bank spokesman, ". . . is a tribute to sensible government policies . . . as well as assistance from development agencies such as the World Bank." But though India can now feed itself, it does not do so. Most of the Green Revolution's extra production is exported, not consumed by the country's malnourished millions. In testimony to a committee of the Canadian Parliament in 1992, Smitu Kothari, director of the New Delhi–based independent research center Lokayan ("Voice of the People"), said, "In terms of aggregate numbers the country has become self-sufficient in its food production. There has been an increase in cash crop production, no doubt about it. There has been an increase in the food piles and food stocks of the country, no doubt about it. [But] there has been a decline in the production of pulses, which is the basic protein for a large number of people living in the rural areas. There has been a decline in crops grown for local consumption."

Between 1971 and 1981, while India's exports of rice, fish, beef, fruits, vegetables, and grains more than quadrupled, government surveys found more than 85 percent of Indian children under five suffering from some degree of malnutrition. This undernourishment does not end as these children grow older; millions of adults in India live, according to the director of the Delhi-based Centre for the Study of Developing Countries, in "a state of destitution, semi-starvation and chronic malnutrition, a long period of physical and psychological stunting and slow death." Whatever short-term boost there is to India's economic status from the exporting of food needed by its people will be negated many times over by the limitations resulting from a substantial proportion of its population suffering such permanent impairment.

In a paper published by the World Bank to celebrate its fiftieth anniversary, two independent scientists, Uma Lele and Balu Bumb, credit the Green Revolution with having increased food production, but warn that its benefits have not spread to the poor. "Clearly, much remains to be done to make sure that South Asia's 300 million poor do not have to go to bed hungry, lacking employment and income to buy the increased food supplied by the Green Revolution." Lele and Bumb also list the problems caused by the policies and institutions introduced to propel the Green Revolution: "excessive use of chemicals, the peaking in yields, increased salinization, silting of dams, waterlogging, interregional disparities, and mounting agricultural subsidies."

In recent years, the institutions that promoted the Green Revolution most vigorously have concluded that many of the farming techniques they induced Third World farmers to adopt have in fact been counterproductive. One of the most prominent of these is the Consultative Group for International Agricultural Research (CGIAR), which is housed at and partly financed by the World Bank. "In the last two years CGIAR has changed its focus," its chairman, World Bank Vice President Visvanathan Rajagopalan, said in 1993. "The research over the last four or five years has shown that continuous application of fertilizers and pesticides does not lead to a continuous increase in yield. In fact, some decline has been noted."

Teams of advisors from CGIAR and its sister organizations are now fanning out across the Third World in an effort to convince farmers not to use the pesticides they previously pushed. Pesticides are expensive, many are a hazard to the health of those who use them, and, say researchers, they do more harm than good to crop production by eliminating scores of "good" insects as well as the "bad" ones they target. "For most circumstances," says Ken Fisher, deputy director of CGIAR's International Rice Research Institute, "there's no reason to apply the insecticide to their fields."

———

Though most of the Bank's resources were dedicated to promoting industrialized agriculture, McNamara did not forget the smallholders, the 40 percent of farmers who are squeezed onto 1 percent of the developing world's land. Subsistence agriculture is the main livelihood in most developing countries; whether as landowners, tenants, sharecroppers, squatters, or daily laborers, most people get their food by growing it, not buying it.

The Bank's plan was to help subsistence farmers by increasing their productivity. More specifically, it wanted to take them out of the subsistence economy and bring them into the international money-based economy. The Bank's obligations to its bond holders dictated this strategy. If its loans were to repaid, it would not do for subsistence farmers merely to grow more food, sharing or trading their extra production with their families and neighbors. Rather, they must *sell* what they produce. Only by "produc[ing] a marketable surplus," the Bank pronounced, do small farmers "contribute to the development process," as measured by a growing GNP. The Bank saw rural development, therefore, as "concerned with the modernization and monetization of rural society, and with its transition from traditional isolation to integration with the national economy." It described its agricultural programs as "instruments to draw farmers from subsistence to commercial agriculture."

The Bank is philosophically opposed to subsidies, which it deems incompatible with a free marketplace. It finds them useful, however, in encouraging subsistence farmers to make the transition to commercial cropping. Farmers are naturally more likely to risk experimenting with new crops and techniques when they are provided with subsidized equipment, seeds, and chemical inputs and guaranteed high prices for the crops they produce. Eventually the subsidies and price supports are removed, often at the insistence of the Bank. When that happens, farmers get less for their crops and pay more for their supplies, but by then they are bound to the cash economy by their new needs, their new possessions, and the debts they incurred in acquiring them.

Even hefty subsidies, however, were not enough to convert all farmers to the Bank's way of thinking. Many farmers, though interested in increasing their production, did not *want* to switch from the relative security of subsistence living to the much more risky venture of commercial farming. In a 1976 report on Papua New Guinea, the Bank noted that farmers were reluctant to change to cash-cropping because their traditional farming methods gave them an easy and reliable way of feeding themselves and their families, whereas the modern techniques that could produce surplus food were more time consuming, required expensive chemicals and equipment, and involved greater risk of failure.

In the face of this resistance, the Bank did not waver. It stuck to its American-inspired formula for increased food production and made no real effort to adapt its advice to local circumstances. Among the aspects of local life it ignored were that women farmers produce much of the food in developing countries, that much land is communally owned and worked, that traditional leaders may control food prices and distribution, and that there are many complex systems of profit-sharing, wealth accumulation, and trading that conflict with standard Western ideas of marketing and profit maximization. Rather than adjusting its program to take account of these realities, the Bank, which was in fact largely unaware of their existence, simply insisted that farmers change their ways of thinking and acting. In the case of Papua New Guinea, for example, it concluded that the only hope for increasing food production was for the country's farmers to become hooked on goods they could not make for themselves and thereby be compelled to turn to cash-cropping.

> A characteristic of PNG's [Papua New Guinea's] subsistence agriculture is its relative richness: over much of the country nature's bounty produces enough to eat with relatively little expenditure of effort. . . . Until enough subsistence farmers have their traditional life styles changed by the growth of new consumption wants, this labor constraint may make it difficult to introduce new crops.

In many cases the Bank's efforts to reach small farmers were frustrated by more powerful farmers who highjacked the Bank's programs for their own benefit. The Bangladesh tubewell project is a case in point. In 1970, the Bank gave Bangladesh (then East Pakistan) a $14 million low-interest loan for the installation of 3,000 deep tubewells. At that time 60 percent of Bangladesh's farmers owned less than 1 acre of land and it was these small farmers the project was aimed at. The wells provided irrigation, thus extending the regular planting season and allowing farmers to grow an extra crop of rice in the dry season. Each tubewell was operated by a farmers' cooperative. The typical cooperative had forty-three members, with an average of 2 acres apiece. That was just the sort of farmer the Bank had aimed to help.

But a study done for the Swedish government's International Development Authority found that the 2-acre average did not accurately reflect the character of the group.

> The applications show that a small group of big farmers took the initiative of applying for the deep tubewell. Then realizing they had to form a cooperative, they included whatever people they could get hold of in the area. In many cases, small farmers are not aware of the fact that they have been included in the scheme.

Control of the tubewells was mainly in the hands of the largest landowners. They were the chairmen or managers of the cooperatives or had physical custody of the tubewells by virtue of owning the land on which they were installed. Two American researchers, Betsey Hartmann and James Boyce, who lived for a year in one of the tubewell villages, corroborated the Swedish findings. "The tubewell in our village," they wrote, "was considered the personal property of one man: Nafis, the biggest landlord of the area. The irrigation group, of which Nafis was supposedly the manager, was in fact no more than a few signatures he had collected on a scrap of paper." Nafis, they noted, had obtained the $12,000 tubewell by spending a mere $300 on bribes to various local officials. In the end, because the World Bank's $14 million is a loan (albeit a very low-interest one), not a grant, the people of Bangladesh will pay for Nafis's $12,000 tubewell.

Nafis leased part of his land to sharecroppers (farmers who paid their rent in kind). After the well was installed, he raised their rent from one-half to two-thirds their harvest. "After all", he told Hartmann and Boyce, "I bought the well," referring to the bribes he paid. In addition, since he owned only 30 acres and his tubewell could irrigate up to 60, Nafis intended to charge his neighbors for the use of the tubewell, though few could afford to pay the prices he asked. If, as is probable, he spent his profits from the tubewell buying more land, the project will have succeeded chiefly in making the rich richer and the poor landless. When Hartmann and Boyce told one of the project's foreign consultants about their findings, he expressed no surprise. "I no longer ask who is getting the well. I know what the answer will be and I don't want to hear it. One hundred percent of these wells are going to the big boys."

———

The poorest of the poor in rural areas are not smallholders but those with no land at all. One-third of farmers in developing countries are in this category; they are squatters, sharecroppers, or day laborers. If it is to keep its pledge to help the poor, the Bank must reach beyond landowners, rich or poor, to the tens of millions of landless. This is its greatest challenge.

Land reform, the Bank says, "may well be a necessary condition" for development. At the very least, "egalitarian distribution of land increases the effectiveness of other policies aimed at reducing poverty." But the Bank will not fund land-reform projects. Indeed, as it has acknowledged, many of its own programs and policies have worsened the problem of landlessness.

The Bank cannot undertake land reform because, as McNamara put it, such an act would "affect the power base of the traditional elite groups in the developing society." The Bank is emphatic in its belief that tangling with that segment of the population would be counterproductive: "Avoiding opposition from powerful and influential sections of the rural community is essential if the Bank's program is not to be subverted from within." Thus, for example, during a 1981 meeting of Peru's aid donors, the Bank praised Peru for ending its land-reform program, an action it termed "an important measure to instill investor confidence." The Bank prefers measures that are, as it says, "likely to be more popular."

Its solution to landlessness has been to open "new land" by cutting down forests, draining wetlands, and building roads to previously isolated areas. During the McNamara years, the Bank became the largest international investor in land-colonization projects. Between 1968 and 1981, it financed scores of colonization schemes in which millions of people were settled on tens of millions of acres of newly cleared land.

These massive programs were to a large degree experimental. Though the Bank was the acknowledged leader in development lending, it had no experience of working with the landless poor, having devoted itself almost exclusively to promoting economic growth. "We have to admit," McNamara said in 1971, "that in this whole area we are still feeling our way." Two years later, he repeated the caution: "Neither we at the Bank, nor anyone else, have very clear answers . . . nor can we be fully precise about the costs. . . . We will have to improvise and experiment. And if some of the experiments fail, we will have to learn from them and start anew." The experiments, in which the fate of whole communities, and even nations, hung in the balance, were conducted on a scale unprecedented in history. Among them are several now famous for the economic, ecological, and social damage they have wrought.

In 1974, the Bank lent Nepal $6 million for a project that involved logging 45,000 acres of pristine lowland tropical forest, exporting the timber, and settling about 50,000 refugees from the country's deforested hills on the newly cleared land. Almost as soon as the project got underway, however, the Nepalese government, in the Bank's words, "began to reconsider its resettlement strategy and to embark on a conservationist course after becoming aware of the rapid depletion of the country's forestry resources." Nepal banned most hardwood exports and withdrew support for the project.

In the face of the government's resistance, the Bank had briefly considered canceling the loan, but it decided that the project had to go ahead so that there would be a place to settle the large number of refugees from other deforested areas of the country: "Without [the project], there is likely to occur not only disorderly settlement, but also serious damage to the environment." In the face of governmental opposition and criticism from environmentalists, the Bank kept the project alive for six more years.

Finally, in 1982, the Bank succumbed. It canceled the undisbursed portion of the loan—more than $3 million. Though only 40 percent of the target area had been logged by then, the environment had been seriously damaged. In the Bank's words: "Areas were completely clearfelled regardless of the slope of the land, posing erosion hazards . . . and creating a future shortage of firewood." The project was also an economic disaster. The Bank had predicted that its economic rate of return would be 42 percent; it turned out to be only 7 percent. The only bright spot for the Bank was that the project caused so much damage that it created an opportunity for a follow-up loan. Even before the original project was canceled, the Bank was planning a follow-up to reforest the area deforested by the first. The second loan—for $18 million—was approved eight months after the cancellation of the first.

Many of the Bank's resettlement projects were connected with irrigation schemes. In 1977 the Bank agreed to lend Kenya $40 million for the Bura Irrigation Project. The idea was to irrigate 16,000 acres along the Tana River, in the semiarid eastern part of the country, and bring in 5,000 families to grow cotton and other crops for export. Within nine years, the project's costs had quadrupled, the irrigation works had failed, and 20 percent of the settlers had abandoned the area. Those who remained were seriously indebted, had a high incidence of malaria and malnutrition, and had a death rate several times greater than the rest of the country. This was not a good return on an investment of more than $20,000 per family.

By the mid-1980s, things were so bad at the Bura site that even the project managers avoided the place, insisting instead on running the program from offices in Nairobi. A 1985 Bank review blamed most of the project's problems on a poorly prepared feasibility study by the British engineers Sir Murdoch MacDonald & Partners, though the Bank should have seen the feasibility study before it approved the loan. By the early 1990s, the Bura project was eating up half of Kenya's entire rural development budget.

The most ambitious resettlement project the Bank has ever been involved in—the most ambitious in history, in fact—is Indonesia's Transmigration program. In 1950, then President Sukarno announced a plan to relieve population pressure in the fertile inner islands of the Indonesian archipelago, chiefly Bali and Java (where 1 percent of the landowners have one-third of the land), by moving 140 million people from there to the nation's unpopulated, rainforest-covered outer islands by 1985.

The massive scheme was also motivated by the government's desire to establish control over the long-rebellious inhabitants of the outer islands, a diverse group whose cultures, languages, and religions are distinct from those of Indonesia's Javan rulers. "Javanization" of the outer islands became even more important in 1963, when Indonesia annexed Irian Jaya, the western half of the island of New Guinea, over the objections of the indigenous people.

The Transmigration project, as it was called, was impractical on several counts: It ignored the fact that soils on the outer islands were far from fertile, that the islands were well populated by tribal people who lived by hunting, fishing, and light farming, and that large-scale land clearing would be devastating to their livelihoods and to the soils, the water supply, and the wildlife of the islands. Luckily, economic and logistical problems prevented the government from achieving more than a tiny fraction of its goal. By 1974, fewer than 700,000 people had been resettled.

In 1976, however, the World Bank stepped in. The Bank's interest in this dubious enterprise, an official involved in the Transmigration loans said, stemmed from the fact that "McNamara wanted to work with Suharto, and this was Suharto's pet project." According to McNamara's biographer, Deborah Shapley, "McNamara knew that Suharto's resettlement program was politically inspired and entailed some brutality, but the role McNamara had carved out of a partnership, of making the Bank 'of' the Third World—and his everlasting zest for action—propelled him to buy in to the program. To influence it, he hoped."

Over the following decade the Bank lent the Indonesian government more than $1 billion for Transmigration. As soon as Transmigration received the Bank's imprimatur, other agencies and governments added their millions to the pot, and the project speeded up. By 1990, about 7 million people had moved to the outer islands, half within the Transmigration program, the other half, drawn by government propaganda, on their own.

Neither the target islands nor the government's Transmigration agency were able to cope with this massive invasion. Because the best areas had long ago been settled, the colonists were put in swamps and pristine rainforests. To meet the program's needs for land, forests were bulldozed and burned. The widespread deforestation caused soil erosion on such a scale that some reservoirs silted up within years of being built. Settlers, who had left established villages behind, did not find the houses, schools, health clinics, roads, and electricity they had been promised. The tribal people who hunted and fished these lands for centuries can no longer feed themselves because the forests are gone and the rivers are polluted.

Many settlers, unable to make the low-fertility soils respond to the farming techniques they learned on the volcanic soils of Java, turned to slash-and-burn agriculture, further damaging the forests, soils, and rivers of the islands. Others drifted to burgeoning urban centers, sprawling cities where pollution, joblessness, and crime are growing problems. Of those who stayed, half had incomes below what Indonesia defines as the poverty line; 20 percent were below the subsistence line.

The Bank continues to lend large amounts for Transmigration. Since the late 1980s, however, its loans have been not for new Transmigration sites but for the "consolidation" of existing sites. A Bank official involved in Transmigration explained what the Bank means by consolidation: "It doesn't mean undoing the damage you did. It means ignoring it. You can continue doing what you were doing before, but get away without new environmental assessments."

Instead of detailing the Bank's many other failed colonization projects, it might be instructive to look at its greatest successes. The projects carried out by Malaysia's Federal Land Development Authority (FELDA) are generally regarded as the most successful Bank-financed colonization schemes. Between 1968 and 1981, the Bank lent FELDA $288 million for seven such programs, which involved the resettlement of hundreds of thousands of people. The largest of these was the Jengka Triangle Land Settlement, for which the Bank lent $52 million, about one-third of the scheme's total cost. Between 1968 and 1980, FELDA cleared 100,000 acres of swamp and forest land northeast of Kuala Lumpur, planted it with rubber and palm oil trees, and gave each of 9,200 landless families 10 acres of trees, a one-room house, and a small vegetable plot. FELDA provided the necessary infrastructure: palm oil mills, roads, and schools. Each family also received a guaranteed monthly salary for the first few years.

Each family has twenty years to reimburse FELDA for the salary it has received and the cost of its plot, along with the cost of any other goods or services provided by the agency, such as fertilizers, technical advice, processing, and marketing. The settlers do this by selling their rubber or palm oil harvest to FELDA, which sets its rates in line with world commodity prices. FELDA pays the settlers a set amount and applies the balance of their earnings to the reduction of their debt. If the harvest proceeds do not cover the agreed income, the debt is increased. Once the loan is repaid, the settlers receive some form of title to the land, though not necessarily outright private ownership.

A 1985 Bank review lauded the Jengka scheme as an "efficient but costly, settlement system [which has resulted in] a significant improvement of settlers' incomes." Settler families earn approximately twice as much as they did before they joined the scheme, even after their debt repayments are deducted. A survey of the settlers found that 85 percent are satisfied with their new situation. The aspect of the project that pleased them most was better schooling for their children, followed by improved housing, a guaranteed minimum income, and the prospect of owning land once they paid off their debt to FELDA. They most disliked the lack of roads, the shortage of clean water, and the state of the environment.

The review did, however, note numerous problems with the project. Before it was cleared, the Jengka Triangle area was an official nature reserve, "largely undisturbed forest and swamp land." The clearing of these extremely diverse lowland rainforests sent numerous rare species, including the Sumatran rhino, further into decline. The freshwater fish population has also dwindled as a result of deforestation. It is impossible to be more specific about the project's environmental effects because there has been no environmental monitoring. The Bank's appraisal report stated that the forest was unpopulated. When several hundred indigenous tribal people were later found to live in the forest, they were moved out.

One reason for FELDA's success is the "striking degree of planning and control of settlers' day-to-day lives." This oversight is expensive, however, and has "resulted in stifling the settlers' sense of initiative and self-management." Settlers put a high value on security; surveys show that 51 percent want their children to be civil servants. The Bank also criticizes the way the program deals with women. Although women share in the agricultural work, only men can obtain loans and land titles. Women receive technical assistance only by special arrangement.

Though the program was intended for Malaysia's landless population, less than three-quarters of the settlers were actually landless farmers; the rest were tradesmen, fishermen, and even civil servants. The Bank says that FELDA, whose programs "are the most expensive rainfed settlement projects in the Bank's portfolio," may be paying too high a price for its successes. For the Jengka Projects the agency spent $15,000 ($24,000 in 1993 dollars) to resettle each family. With income targets "which have generally been considered to be above the limits normally calling for Bank assistance," FELDA projects "absorb scarce resources which could be better used for helping the remaining poor."

In 1985, the Bank asked Thayer Scudder, the resettlement specialist who teaches at CalTech, to review twenty-seven of its resettlement projects. All were carried out during McNamara's time at the Bank, though two were approved before he took office. Scudder's unpublished report found "major inadequacies" in the Bank's appraisal report for 70 percent of the projects, which may explain why in 75 percent of the cases the Bank overestimated the economic rate of return.

Data about the environmental effects of the projects Scudder examined was not always available, but in three-quarters of the cases for which it was, he found that major ecological damage had occurred or was likely to have occurred in the project area. Neither severe ecological damage, however, or other major problems ever caused the Bank to cancel or stop a loan. On the positive side, Scudder found that in half the projects the average income "probably exceeds average rural income," though income in all projects was still below the national average.

Scudder reached a similar conclusion. It found that there is "a lack of understanding within the Bank about the nature, potential and implications of land settlement." Three years later, in 1988, another Bank study reached a similar conclusion. It found that half of the sixty-four area development and settlement projects approved between 1974 and 1979 had failed.

————

When the Bank began its work, developing countries were overwhelmingly rural. Poverty was located in the countryside, because that's where the people were. One consequence of development, however, has been a dramatic shift from the country to the city. By the year 2000 it is expected that more than half the population of the developing world will be crammed into its cities—many driven there after Bank-financed projects drove them from their traditional homes. The problems to which this population shift has given rise are truly staggering. In Madras, in southern India, for example, half the population lives in shantytowns with no water supply, no sanitation, no streets, and no electricity.

The Bank did little in its first thirty years to address the problem of urban poverty. At the 1975 annual meeting, after seven years in office, McNamara signaled his determination to change that. Speaking with the passion he always brought to the topic of human suffering, he said: "Even the most hardened and unsentimental observer from the developed world is shocked by the squalid slums and ramshackle shantytowns that ring the periphery of every major city. . . . It is the image that is seared into the memory of every visitor." On a more hardheaded note, he also warned that urban poverty threatened the peace of the better-off: "Historically, violence and civil upheaval are more common in cities than in the countryside. Frustrations that fester among the urban poor are readily exploited by political extremists. If cities do not begin to deal more constructively with poverty, poverty may well begin to deal more destructively with cities."

McNamara ordered a review of the urban poverty problem and of the Bank's past efforts to combat it. It concluded that there were about 190 million people living in "absolute poverty" in Third World cities, less than a third as many as were estimated to be living in the countryside, but still a huge number—and a rapidly growing one. The report was critical of the Bank's earlier urban programs. Only one-third had "provided clear evidence of [generating] substantial unskilled employment." Less than a quarter "could be said to have favorable impacts for the urban poor in improving their relative access to urban services." In general, the Bank's urban loans had "concentrat[ed] on large infrastructure and industrial projects providing little evidence of direct benefits to the poor or of direct increases in the capacity of the cities to absorb the target populations."

In the typical urban renewal project of the mid-1970s, poor families were evicted en masse and their makeshift hovels replaced with buildings they could not afford to live in. In 1978, for example, the average government-built house in Nigeria cost a staggering $40,000. The rent charged for such structures put them far beyond the reach of the poor. McNamara attacked this approach in his 1975 speech: "There is one thing worse than living in a slum or squatter settlement—and this is having one's slum or settlement bulldozed away." The Bank proposed a new method. In city centers, instead of slum clearance there would be slum upgrading, in which roads would be paved, footpaths built, and sewers installed with as little disturbance as possible to existing dwellings.

When it was a case of building brand-new settlements—usually on the outskirts of cities, where land was available—the government and the Bank would provide building sites and services such as clean water, sewers, and transportation. The poor would build their own homes, with the help of loans and their own savings. When this was tried in Madras, the poor managed to scrape together two-thirds of the cost of construction by selling "previously unproductive assets, such as jewelry."

Initially, most Third World governments disliked this low-key approach. They resented the suggestion that their citizens should be satisfied with less than those of Europe and the United States, and they were not enthralled by the prospect of pumping hundreds of millions of dollars into the housing sector and still ending up with something that looked very much like a slum. Eventually, however, the Bank succeeded in convincing most borrowers that insisting on expensive Western-style housing was unrealistic and would not improve the lot of the urban poor.

Essential to the Bank's approach, in both slum upgrading and new urban settlements (so-called sites and services projects), was that the poor should have security of tenure. One reason the Bank considers this so important is that it believes housing projects should be as self-financing as possible. Residents are more likely to be willing to pay rents, maintenance, user fees, and taxes if they have tenure.

The Bank now regards its urban shelter work with some satisfaction. "By and large our housing projects have been successful and beneficial," one generally skeptical Bank official told me. In general they have exceptionally high rates of return. In 1979, the average rate of return was almost 50 percent, according to one Bank study. Nonetheless, the Bank has rarely been able to meet its dual goal of serving poor people and making its projects pay for themselves. Very often, in fact, the poor have been priced out of Bank projects. One reason is the Bank's tendency to be overoptimistic in its projection of what poor people can afford to spend to build, rent, or maintain a house. Frequently only better-off households are able to take advantage of Bank programs. Really poor families, the ones the Bank is actually targeting, often do not have the collateral needed to obtain even a Bank-subsidized housing loan.

In the Tanzania "sites and services" project, for example, the Bank funded a housing bank, which was to lend the Bank's money to poor families so that they could buy the materials needed to build a house. In fact, wrote one independent reviewer, the housing bank "provid[ed] loans only to clients who could guarantee repayment and only at interest. The result was that loans were restricted to wage and salaried workers, the dominant petty bourgeoisie, and excluded entirely the majority of low-income families." Because so many potential borrowers were eliminated by the housing bank's stringent standards, there were not enough takers for all the loans available. Therefore the government opened the subsidised loan program to wealthier families. In addition, it gave permission for a quarter of all the plots to be given to individuals "regardless of income" so long as they could afford to build a house there.

Even slum upgrading projects designed to avoid displacing the poor may force people from their homes. Once a neighborhood is upgraded, for example, some families may not be able to afford the higher user fees, rents, or taxes on their improved property. Or, if maintenance of newly-installed roads and sewers is inadequate, as it often is, residents may be unwilling to pay such charges. This was the case in several East African projects: "Problems developed after the start-up period, as the necessary follow-up services, such as maintenance and social services, were not provided as promised. Households became disillusioned and increasingly reluctant to pay."

Families whose homes are reclaimed by the government for nonpayment of fees or taxes are left homeless and worse off than before, having sunk all they had into building or improving their home. Often a family that cannot pay its rent or taxes decides to sell its home or plot or land, an act made easier by its acquisition of legal title. Sometimes such sales are illegal, but they take place nevertheless. A Bank study of the Tanzanian "sites and services" project concluded that "many of the plots have been unofficially transferred to more affluent individuals."

In the mid-1970s, a slum in central Jakarta received a typical World Bank "upgrade": a footpath was paved and sewage was diverted into a canal. These small improvements increased the market value of the homes; the government raised property taxes by 15 percent; and by 1977, according to The Wall Street Journal, "The poor were selling out to richer people and moving to illegal settlements on Jakarta's fringe. The poor are selling both to avoid the property taxes and to make some money."

There is no formula for dealing with urban poverty. The Bank describes itself as "learning by doing." In the urban field much more than in others, it has responded to its failures. Nonetheless, it is still confronted on all sides by baffling and contradictory pressures—to the gratification, it would seem, of some observers. One independent review of the Tanzanian housing project remarked that the Bank had set building standards so high that the true poor could not afford to participate and the better-off benefited disproportionately. In the second phase of the project, the Bank acknowledged these problems and responded by making the project smaller and lowering construction standards. The result, the reviewer noted with gloomy satisfaction, was overcrowding and "a rapid deterioration of project housing stock," making residents less willing to continue their payments and threatening the project's financial viability.

Even if the Bank someday discovers the secret to successful urban housing programs, the most worrisome question about its urban housing work will remain. Is construction of domestic housing a legitimate use of the

Bank's money? To pose the question from the borrower's point of view: Does it make sense to borrow money from abroad to build houses at home? "Why should Mexico borrow dollars to build houses? You don't need dollars to build housing in Mexico," says one of the Bank's urban housing specialists. "The Mexicans have our housing loans. But they don't use the money to build houses. They use it to repay other debts. So, how will they repay us? The bet, when you go into debt, is that you are someday going to increase your productivity. Is housing the kind of investment that enables you to increase your productivity?"

Some in the Bank argue that converting fetid slums into decent neighborhoods will necessarily improve productivity, but there is little hard evidence of a direct link between the two. There is, in fact, says the same Bank housing official, "zero data on whether housing makes people more productive. It does create construction jobs, but these are short-term." This is a delicate issue for the Bank, one that raises a question the Bank would like to ignore: Does it make sense for a country to borrow money from abroad in order to fund its efforts to improve housing, education, health, or population control? Will such investments, however desirable, produce enough money—and, in particular, enough foreign currency—to repay their cost?

---

In 1981, Mahbub ul Haq, McNamara's right-hand man in the war on poverty, returned to Pakistan, deploring the fact that the Bank had failed to reach those most in need of help. The bottom 20 percent of the population, he said, "has remained largely outside the scope of our projects." Indeed, McNamara succeeded chiefly in helping neither the rural nor the urban poor, but in advancing industrialization in developing countries. Bank reviews of nearly four hundred projects approved during his tenure rated 40 percent of the agriculture and rural development projects unsatisfactory. The Bank was happier with its urban projects, rating two-thirds as satisfactory. But by the end of McNamara's tenure, such projects accounted for only 4 percent of the Bank's annual lending. It was on energy, transport, and industry that the Bank concentrated its spending. And it was in those sectors, where the Bank deemed 80 percent of its projects satisfactory, that it achieved, by its own standards, its greatest successes.

# Eight

## ALL HOLD HANDS
## AND JUMP

**M**cNamara did not restrict himself to increasing the Bank's lending. He took every opportunity to encourage others to lend more also. He rhapsodized to private lenders about the opportunities developing countries presented and dismissed fears that they were over their heads in debt. The Bank's 1971 annual report assured investors that "the size of a country's external debt represents not so much the size of its 'problem' as the extent to which foreign nations have been willing to assist by extending it credit. There is nothing intrinsically threatening, therefore, in a rapid rate of growth of external debt, and . . . many developing countries could now make effective use of additional external capital." In 1977, McNamara declared that the Bank was "even more confident today than we were a year ago that the debt problem is indeed manageable." Five years later, there was "an even greater need to ensure that Bank lending helps to stimulate external flows of capital to developing countries."

Private banks had begun to recover their confidence about lending to developing countries in the early 1960s. Within a decade, they had supplanted the World Bank as suppliers of foreign capital to the Third World. Two factors spurred this dramatic expansion of private investment overseas: the efforts of the U.S. government to prevent it, and a financial tool devised by Chinese Communists.

In 1949, the Communist party assumed control of China and of its foreign assets, which included some dollar accounts in U.S. banks. Then, even more than now, the dollar was the currency of international trade. Fearing that the United States would freeze its American accounts, the Communist government came up with an ingenious way of keeping its dollars safe. It transferred them to a Paris bank, which agreed to leave them as dollars. The bank the Chinese chose was the Russian-owned Banque Commerciale pour L'Europe du Nord, whose cable address, Eurobank, gave rise to the term "Eurodollar" for dollars held outside the United States. The Russian government soon followed the Chinese example, shifting their dollars to the Banque Commerciale and another Russian-owned bank in London.

A few capitalists became aware of the Chinese maneuver. They saw the advantages of keeping dollars outside the United States, where they were not subject to tough American banking laws that, among other things, controlled interest rates, and they opened Eurodollar accounts of their own. These Eurodollars functioned as an unofficial universal currency, greatly simplifying international financial deals. Perhaps fearing government crackdowns, however, bankers kept the new device to themselves. According to financial writer Paul Einzig, there was "a remarkable conspiracy of silence" about the Eurodollar. "I stumbled on its existence by sheer accident in October 1959, and when I embarked on an enquiry about it in London banking circles several bankers emphatically asked me not to write about the new practice."

By 1960, however, the secret was out, and the Eurodollar market was booming. U.S. banks entered the Eurodollar market in a big way in the early 1960s in order to evade new domestic restrictions on foreign lending. In 1960, only eight American banks had branches abroad; by 1972, 107 did. In 1973 Eurodollar accounts were the major source of money to developing countries. Some expert observers worried aloud that many banks were taking unjustifiable risks with their foreign lending. In 1969, the journal *Banking,* published by the American Bankers Association, noted that "many poor nations have already incurred debts past the possibility of repayment." A few months later, it cautioned that "international loans, even if made on 'businesslike' terms, have a way of getting lost unless they are repaid out of the proceeds of additional loans." In 1972, *The Wall Street Journal* ran a front-page story on the reckless lending by the American banks "that have flocked to Europe since the mid-60s to feast on the trade in Eurodollars. . . . Their medium-term loans are often made without collateral; maturities are stretching out into what would have seemed like futuristic mists only four years ago; and the grace periods before borrowers must begin repayment have likewise lengthened, all compounding the risks."

The competition to lend was so fierce, said one American banker in London, that banks "have been giving loans to second- and third-rate borrowers at rates that don't even begin to compensate for the risks." But a fierce optimism permeated the banking community throughout the 1970s and early '80s, one that ignored warnings and sought solace in fine distinctions. The credit manager of the London branch of Dallas's First National Bank, for example, assured *The Wall Street Journal* that "credit quality is disturbing, but not alarming."

In 1974, the foreign loan business got another boost. The fabulous fortunes created by the oil price rise of the previous winter began flowing into the Eurodollar market. Banks competed wildly for the business of the new oil billionaires, offering Olympian rates of interest. To pay these rates, banks had to invest their huge deposits lucratively—and loans to the Third World were among the most rewarding investments available. Developing countries seemed to have a boundless appetite for borrowing, and their poor creditworthiness justified the imposition of high interest rates and administrative fees. Loans to developing countries were so profitable that in 1977 the nine biggest U.S. banks, which, taken together, had only 8 percent of their assets in such loans, derived at least half their earnings from them.

Foreign lending presented banks with a peculiar problem. Past experience indicated that they should watch closely over their loans. It was, after all, the misuse of borrowed funds that had led to the World Bank's being established with the mandate to make loans "for productive purposes" only. It was difficult, however, for banks to get reliable information about would-be foreign borrowers and the uses to which their loans would be put. They did not have the resources to conduct their own in-depth analysis of each borrower and each proposed investment.

For this reason, banks followed the example of the World Bank and insisted on a government guarantee for all foreign loans, whether to public or private entities. That way they only had to evaluate a few dozen governments, rather than tens of thousands of individual borrowers and projects. Of course, evaluating the creditworthiness of sovereign nations is hardly a simple task. It calls for an understanding of scores of languages, familiarity with many different political and economic systems, and a network of reliable informants in governments and industries around the world—all attributes in short supply among Western bankers, especially American bankers. Fortunately there was a tool—developed at the World Bank—that was reputed to make all this unnecessary.

The tool was "country risk analysis," and it had been developed by Irving Friedman while he was George Woods's chief economic advisor at the World Bank. In 1974, Friedman joined Citibank and introduced country risk analysis to private banking. Friedman's technique was to sift through masses of information, both political and financial, to determine how much a government should be allowed to borrow. He cautioned his fellow bankers not to be guided only by "quantitative indicators" but to "rely on in-depth knowledge of the country, preferably based on firsthand experience." Having virtually no firsthand experience, however, most bankers ignored this instruction. Instead, deskbound, they carried out their own, quite inadequate, risk analyses. Comforted by the thought that their methods had the imprimatur of the World Bank, they were emboldened to lend ever more massive amounts of money abroad.

Citibank was the most aggressive lender to the Third World during the 1970s and early 1980s. Its chairman, Walter Wriston, was an indefatigable cheerleader for overseas lending. He was especially enthusiastic about loans to governments, and famously declared that a government could never go bankrupt. Wriston was correct in the sense that the legal state of bankruptcy is not open to sovereign governments. Nonetheless, governments have repudiated their foreign debts with remarkable frequency over the years. In fact, the first foreign loan in history—by two Florentine banks to Edward I of England in the late thirteenth century—ended in default. Less than fifty years after his grandfather received the loan, Edward III disavowed it, causing the collapse of the Bardi and Peruzzi banks. The spiritual father of the World Bank, John Maynard Keynes, noted that repudiation is a natural reaction to an intolerable debt burden: "The active and working elements in no community, ancient or modern, will consent to hand over to the bond-holding class more than a certain proportion of the fruits of their work."

If he was aware of the past or of Keynes's warning, Wriston did not let them intimidate him. By 1982 Citibank's loans to just five of its Latin American clients amounted to twice its net corporate assets. However, Citibank—and the other major banks—found ways to spread their risks without spreading their profits. As the big bond houses had in the 1920s, they began inviting smaller, regional banks to join them in loan syndicates. The lead bank charged a substantial "up front" fee on the whole amount of the loan, while sharing the risk with its junior partners, who largely relied on the majors for information. As Chase Manhattan's syndications expert later explained, "Many of the participating banks had no firm understanding of whom they were lending to; very few performed any type of credit analysis." "It was the easiest money going," one banking expert told the journalist Anthony Sampson. "You took 1 percent on the turn for signing a cheque for a few million dollars."

In this way the big banks drew many smaller banks into foreign lending. By 1983, nearly 1,500 small American banks had entered the overseas loan market. A few set up an office in London or Berlin, but most settled for sending a loan officer abroad several times a year to meet with potential clients. Each bank had its own tiny international department to evaluate loans, but there were not enough experienced international bankers to staff these departments. Most were manned by raw amateurs. In 1986, one such, Samuel Gwynne, wrote a book called *Selling Money,* in which he related his experience as one of three analysts in the international division of the credit department of the venerable Cleveland Trust Company.

Gwynne entered the banking world in the late 1970s at the age of twenty-four, armed with a bachelor's degree in history, a master's degree in creative writing, and two years' experience teaching French in a private school. His two fellow analysts shared "one undergraduate economics degree, one Russian degree, and three months of banking experience." After a month-long credit class, Gwynne, though he spoke no Spanish, was appointed the credit analyst for Latin America—charged with analyzing million-dollar loans. The bank's other Latin American experts were "one 32-year-old vice-president with a halting fluency in Spanish and Portuguese [and] two 30-year-old assistant vice-presidents, with a total of eight years' banking experience between them." The shortage of experience and resources was not regarded as important because Cleveland Trust, like the rest of the small banks, relied on the majors to provide them with information and analysis.

The pressure to get in on the syndication action was intense, especially for the smaller banks, which found the excitement of doing deals with the big boys almost irresistible. "When I first signed a loan agreement for twenty million dollars for a country I hardly knew anything about, I thought, 'We must be crazy,'" one American banker stationed in London confessed to Sampson. "There's no greater fun than to know that everyone wants to talk to you at cocktail parties and to be part of the world of big BMWs and parties at Annabel's. When an ambassador rings you up to suggest you join a loan, you want to be part of it: the Americans are specially vulnerable to flattery. Syndication depends on only about a hundred people in London and you soon get to know them all. Everyone feels that they're in it together. They hate to be left out."

The high interest rates, the exorbitant signing fees, the excitement of international deals—all these things made foreign lending attractive, but at bottom the lending boom rested on bankers' confidence that they were acting on sound information and advice. The trouble is, they weren't. Their primary source of information was the World Bank, whose data came from member governments, not all of which provided reliable figures. In 1971 the Bank warned that "some of the largest debtor countries themselves have no accurate idea of the total extent of their debt." It went on to admit that its own external debt figures were probably understatements. One example of how unreliable official statistics could be was Venezuela's declaration, in September 1982, that its foreign debt was $18 billion. Two months later, the government discovered another $17 billion in unreported short-term loans, and by February of 1983, the official estimate had risen to $43 billion.

In Gwynne's words, most loan officers were "a virtual compendium of bad or questionable information, meticulously gathered and studiously analyzed." There was not much learning from experience, either. In the fast-moving world of international banking, chances were good that a loan officer or credit analyst would be in a new job at a new bank long before the loans he or she worked on began to go bad. Quite possibly the person who made the loan would never find out that it had failed. To paraphrase Oscar Wilde's characterization of fox hunting, the lending boom of the 1970s and early '80s was the uninformed in pursuit of the uncreditworthy.

---

In many ways the lending frenzy of the 1970s was a replay of the one fifty years earlier that had given birth to the World Bank. In the 1920s, lenders had paid so little attention to the uses to which their money was put that the Bank's founders specified it could lend only "for productive purposes." But half a century later, with the Bank cheering them on, lenders were being just as cavalier about how their money was used.

This looseness made it easy for wealthy individuals in developing countries to commandeer huge amounts of borrowed money and send it to safe havens in the United States, Europe, and Japan. In theory, this is impossible; every country jealously guards its foreign currency, keeping it in its central bank and releasing it only to pay for essential imports. A Bolivian businessman, for instance, who needs dollars in order to buy a piece of American machinery, must take proof of his intended purchase to his country's central bank (or an authorized private bank), which would then sell him the dollars he requires. If he sells goods abroad, he must bring the dollars or yen in which he was paid to the central bank and exchange them for bolivianos. But as the supply of dollars burgeoned in central banks around the world, so did the temptation—and the opportunity—for individuals to amass them.

One of Samuel Gwynne's clients explained a typical way around the system. "If you had connections, you told the central bank that you wanted the dollars to import goods; the connections made sure that no one ever checked to see if you had imported anything; then you used the dollars to buy a permanent, offshore investment in dollars." This procedure involves paying for dollars with local currency, but there are cheaper ways of acquiring hard currency. Writing in *The New Republic* in 1986, James Henry described some of the more popular forms of graft that flourish around foreign-funded projects: "phony intermediary companies that recontract with foreign suppliers on public projects and take a hefty spread; importers who get permits to purchase foreign exchange for imports that either never get bought or are wildly over-invoiced; developers who get public loans for projects that don't exist; local 'consultants' who are paid by U.S. suppliers in New York dollar accounts; and so on."

Graft grew hand in hand with foreign borrowing. By 1982 Zaire had accumulated a foreign debt of $5 billion, and its president, Mobutu Sese Seko, had accumulated a personal fortune of at least $4 billion, which, according to a number of sources, including a former prime minister, he had stashed away in banks and property throughout Europe. (In 1989 Mobutu, who sometimes claims to be the seventh-richest man in the world, declared he had only $50 million in his European bank accounts and asked piteously, "What is that, after twenty-two years as head of state of such a big country?") Though Mobutu's graft—and that of his favored subordinates—was on an exceptional scale, Zaire is not a singular case. According to an investigation by the U.S. National Security Agency, Mexico's President Miguel de la Madrid deposited at least $162 million in a Swiss bank in 1983 alone.

The amount of money that left the Third World during the lending boom is staggering. The World Bank estimates that between 1976 and 1984, capital flight from Latin America equaled the increase in the continent's external debt. As a study by Morgan Guaranty Trust Company noted, "This was no coincidence." Morgan also estimated (conservatively, it said) that in a single year, 1985, capital flight from just eighteen developing countries amounted to $198 billion. Mexico alone lost at least $35 billion between 1974 and 1982. Bought or stolen, these dollars were invested in everything from condominiums to car dealerships, nightclubs to jewelry, venture capital funds to drug rings. A new specialty, "international private banking," arose to accommodate this lucrative and growing market. All the major banks offered this service, which emphasized secrecy and ingenious ways of moving money across borders and sheltering it from taxes. Morgan Guaranty reported that in September 1985 American banks had $31 billion in such accounts, and banks in other countries had an equal amount.

The Morgan study found that 70 percent of borrowings by the big ten Latin American debtor countries between 1983 and 1985 financed capital flight. And "flight capital" in turn financed loans to developing countries to replace the dollars that had been illicitly siphoned away. Indeed, according to James Henry, "The banks' real role has been to take funds that Third World elites have stolen from their governments and to loan them back, earning a nice spread each way." One international consultant calls capital flight "cooperation among the world's powerful for exploitation of the world's weak." If the wealthy of the developing world had invested their millions and billions in their own countries instead of depleting their countries' foreign exchange reserves and smuggling their dollars into the United States and Europe, those countries would not have had to borrow so heavily and so expensively. "The problem," remarked one member of the U.S. Federal Reserve Board, "is not that Latin Americans don't have assets. They do. The problem is, they're all in Miami."

There is a well-known joke, or lament, to the effect that when a small borrower can't keep up his payments, he is in trouble, but when a big borrower is in the same position, his bank is in trouble. For a lender, acknowledging a default has many unpleasant aspects. For one thing, the bank must record the loss on its books, exposing itself to the scorn of Wall Street and the anger of its shareholders. For another, default is believed to be contagious: If one customer gets away with it, who knows how many others will try the same trick? Thus, banks regard almost any price as worth paying if it will deter an outright default. If an important client is having trouble making payments, his bank may agree to ease his repayment schedule or to lend him what he needs to keep his payments up. Even when a client actually stops making payments, the word "default" can be avoided. Instead of being in default, debts are described as in nonaccrual, in nonpayment, or in arrears; or they are said to be in the process of being restructured, reprofiled, or worked out.

International bankers had numerous opportunities to use these expressions during the 1970s. By the middle of the decade, many developing countries had borrowed so much that they could not keep up their payments. Partly to prevent defaults, banks went on lending to these borrowers. Half of all the money lent to Latin America in 1976 went to service old loans, according to the Inter-American Development Bank, a regional version of the World Bank. The following year, the figure was up to 65 percent. In the short term, there was every reason to keep lending. Not only were the banks staving off default for their customers, they were also making a good income, because their refusal to countenance the possibility of default did not prevent them from seeing the need to raise interest rates for these less creditworthy clients.

It is doubtful, nonetheless, that banks would have risked throwing good money after bad had they not believed that the World Bank, the IMF, and the industrial nations would rescue them if large-scale international defaults did loom. David Levine, the executive director of the Chase Manhattan Bank, put it this way in 1974: "On the one hand, a purely technical analysis of the current financial position [of lending to the developing world] would suggest that defaults are inevitable; yet on the other hand, many experts feel this is not likely to happen. The World Bank and the IMF and the governments of major industrialized nations, they argue, would step in rather than watch any default seriously disrupt the entire Euromarket apparatus with possible secondary damage to their own domestic banking systems."

The financial press warned that banks were putting themselves in jeopardy. The external debts of the developing countries increased from less than $100 billion in 1972 to more than $600 billion in 1981. But, as *Euromoney* magazine noted, "The scare headlines about the size of these debts, and the general dearth of credit information . . . [have] had little or no effect on the willingness of the banks to keep on lending." Nor did the IMF and the World Bank consider it their job to discourage excessive lending. Both institutions stepped up their lending and encouraged private banks to do the same, even—indeed especially—to nations they knew to be on the verge of default.

The idea was to get developing countries the money they needed to stay solvent, not to act as the guardian of the banking industry. As Citibank's Irving Friedman explained to a reporter in 1977, "The Fund can't be giving danger signals, warning bells to all these private institutions. Because if you're worried about a country, what you're trying to do is help the country eliminate the problem. You're not trying to advertise the problem. Because if the Fund did advertise it, it would be responsible for a self-fulfilling prophecy." The Bank took the same view. As economist Richard Feinberg has pointed out, it "did not want to discourage their clients or their foreign lenders—and judgments of 'not creditworthy' also would have raised inconvenient doubts about the Bank's own lending program."

The first major crack in the system appeared in June 1976, when Zaire stopped making payments on its more than $700 million debt to private banks. The banks refused Zaire's request that they reschedule its debt payments, fearing that this would set a precedent for their other overextended customers. Citibank's Irving Friedman took on the task of averting an outright default on behalf of the nearly one hundred banks that had outstanding loans to Zaire. He persuaded his fellow bankers to pledge the country another $250 million so that Zaire could keep up its repayments. Citibank's vice chairman, Al Costanzo, was exuberant about Friedman's success, telling a reporter, "If we can do it for Zaire, we can do it for anybody." Only killjoys dwelt on the fact that this $250 million "booster loan" was unlikely to do much more than get Zaire further into debt, since the full amount would be returned at once to the banks to cover Zaire's overdue loan payments.

In any case, Friedman's quarter-billion-dollar loan never materialized because Zaire broke a pledge to adopt economic reforms and to keep up payments on another $800 million it owed to other governments, to the World Bank, and to the International Monetary Fund. At the insistence of the IMF, Erwin Blumenthal, a retired Bundesbank official, was put in charge of Zaire's central bank in 1978, but after a year, he reported that there is "no (repeat: no) prospect for Zaire's creditors to get their money back in any foreseeable future." After several more rounds of negotiations and broken promises, the banks quietly wrote off their Zairean loans.

A few months after Zaire's collapse, it became apparent that Peru was also in a perilous state. Its foreign debt was $4.4 billion, more than four times what it had been eight years earlier. This time the bankers decided to act *before* the situation reached crisis point. Once again Friedman took the lead, pushing the government to cut public spending, raise taxes, and devalue its currency. The inducement the banks offered for adopting this IMF-style "stabilization program" was a new infusion of cash, $386 million. But the thought of foreign bankers attempting to dictate government policy infuriated the Peruvian public and provided the country's politicians with a superb opportunity for demagoguery. The nation's outraged sovereignty was unleashed in hostile editorials, blustering speeches in Parliament, and riots in the streets of Lima. Peru's bellicose reaction to their proposal convinced the world's bankers that they did not have the clout to impose terms on a sovereign nation, even a deeply indebted one. During this time the World Bank continued lending to Peru, giving it nearly a quarter of a billion dollars in new loans in 1976 and 1977 alone.

With the bankers having failed to move Peru, the International Monetary Fund stepped in. It was a lot harder to ignore. Because Peru was itself a member, the Fund was not a mere intruder in its internal affairs. And because nearly every other lending country in the world was also a member, Peru could not appeal elsewhere for help. Finally, in late 1978, Peru had no choice but to come to terms with the Fund. It agreed to adopt the standard IMF economic austerity program in return for a loan of $200 million. At least as important to Peru as the money was that the IMF's seal of approval would encourage private bankers to restart their lending. As Chase Manhattan's David Levine had predicted, the world's governments had stepped in and used their taxpayers' money rather than allow a major default to destabilize the private banking industry. To ensure that the Fund had the resources to undertake such missions in other teetering countries, its members contributed another $10 billion.

The breakdowns in Zaire and Peru were followed by crises in Turkey in 1978, Iran in 1979, and Poland in 1981. All borrowed freely right up to the moment of collapse. But rather than seeing a pattern in this series of disasters, the banking industry attributed each one to a unique set of conditions. Never was it a simple case of overborrowing; instead it was the consequence of some combination of corruption, incompetence, and revolution—circumstances, apparently, that lenders could not be expected to anticipate. Instead of pulling back, the commercial banks and the World Bank redoubled their efforts to lend to developing countries, particularly to those most heavily in debt. Loans to non-oil-producing developing countries tripled in less than five years, from late 1977 to mid-1982.

In his book *The Money Lenders*, Anthony Sampson brilliantly describes anxious bankers seeking to make deals with foreign governments at the World Bank's 1980 annual meeting, an event that had become the state fair of foreign lending. They were "lingering awkwardly by the elevators, dawdling by the news-stand, and then suddenly walking—almost running—too fast for dignity. . . . As they pursue their prey down the escalators, up the elevators, along the upstairs corridors into the suites, they cannot conceal their anxiety to do business. For these men who look as if they might have been trained to say No from their childhood are actually trying to sell loans. 'I've got good news for you,' I heard one eager contact man telling a group of American bankers: 'I think they'll be able to take your money.' "

It did not alarm the bankers that virtually none of the borrowing countries even pretended that they planned to pay off their debts. On the contrary, as Walter Wriston put it in a *New York Times* Op-Ed piece, governments could not—and should not be expected to—repay debts. It did not matter if loans were never repaid, as long as borrowers continued to make interest payments. The important thing was not a government's ability to repay its loans, but an everlasting supply of new loans. The new loans would pay the interest on older ones. The mantra was "Growth will take care of debt."

By 1978, one-quarter of all the money borrowed by non-OPEC Third World countries was used to pay interest on existing debt. The situation was particularly bad in Latin America, where borrowing doubled between 1976 and 1982, and 70 percent of new loans went to pay interest on old debt. The Bank's annual report acknowledged that "in recent years an ever larger proportion of new borrowing has been used to service outstanding debt" but emphasized that such loans "are important for increasing the level of investment in the developing countries."

By 1982, the situation had become truly absurd. Latin America was borrowing hundreds of billions of dollars a year, and spending all of it—and more—on keeping up payments on its past debts. In March 1982, Moody's, the credit rating agency, downgraded the bonds of nine top U.S. banks from triple A to double A. It was a timely move.

---

In December 1981, Manufacturers Hanover Trust assured its clients that Mexico was "probably one of the most dynamic economies in the world today, . . . [able because of its oil revenues] to insulate itself from many of the problems plaguing other developing nations. Government and industry alike encourage foreign investment and offer attractive incentives." Nowhere was it mentioned that Mexico's foreign debt was the second largest in the world, trailing Brazil's by only a few billion dollars. In April 1982, the World Bank published, jointly with the IMF, its own report on Mexico, which concluded that "there is considerable scope for sustained additional borrowing," though by then the country was already spending virtually all the money it borrowed to service old debts.

Four months later, on August 13, 1982, Mexico put an end to the whole charade. The country's finance minister, Jesus Silva Herzog, walked into the offices of the U.S. Treasury Department and explained that Mexico could not repay the $81 billion it owed its foreign creditors. It is hard to say who was in worse trouble, Mexico or its creditors. However much its people would suffer as a result of its default, there still would be a Mexico. The same could not be said with certainty of the banks that had lent it money. Mexico owed its largest American creditor, Citibank, $3.3 billion—more than two-thirds of Citibank's net corporate assets. The Bank of Tokyo was even worse off: 80 percent of its net assets were at risk in Mexico.

The banks seemed suddenly to become aware of how much they had lent, especially to Latin America—and how little control they had over being repaid. Citibank, Manufacturers Hanover Trust, and Chase Manhattan each had outstanding loans in Latin America amounting to more than twice their net worth. Shortly after Mexico's stunning announcement, Barton Biggs, a managing director of Morgan Stanley, told *Fortune*, "Somehow the conventional wisdom of 200 million sullen South Americans sweating away in the hot sun for the next decade to earn the interest on their debt so that Citicorp can raise its dividend twice a year does not square with my image of political reality." If the top five Latin American borrowers (Mexico, Brazil, Venezuela, Argentina, and Chile) defaulted on only half their loans, the six largest banks in the United States would be bankrupt. And when Mexico's threat to default was followed in a matter of weeks by similar moves by Argentina and Brazil, this was not a far-fetched idea.

———

In previous centuries, governments had used military force to protect their citizens' assets from default by foreign powers. Britain, Germany, and Italy, for example, had blockaded Venezuela, and the United States had sent the Marines into the Dominican Republic, Haiti, Honduras, and Nicaragua. There was no such rescue in the 1920s, however, and millions of small investors had suffered. Now, with large banks, not individual investors, at risk, the creditor nations once again intervened, deputizing the IMF instead of the military to deal with the problem.

The Fund offered Mexico a large emergency loan on condition that it keep up payments on its foreign debts and cut back drastically on government spending. "The IMF is acting as enforcer of the banks' loan contracts," wrote Karin Lissakers, who later became the Fund's American executive director. But the Fund also used its muscle on the private banks. Jacques de Larosiere, then the Fund's head, threatened to let Mexico default unless the private banks came up with new loans of $5 billion by December 15, 1982. The deadline was met. William Lamoureux of Seattle's Rainier National Bank said, "The bank advisory group rep who called us said 'It's like Butch Cassidy and the Sundance Kid, let's all hold hands and jump.' "

As an inducement to the banks to keep lending, they were allowed to charge hefty fees, which borrowers had to pay up front, for rescheduling their loans. These fees made rescheduling a lucrative business. Speaking of one nearly insolvent developing country, one banker said, "That country is a cash cow for us. We hope they never repay!"

The United States also did much to encourage banks to keep lending, at considerable risk to their shareholders—and to the U.S. taxpayers, who had guaranteed a sizable proportion of the deposits that were being loaned out. U.S. banking law required banks to deduct six months of interest from their earnings for any loan that was sixty days in arrears. After Mexico defaulted, the sixty-day limit was extended to ninety days; the following year it was extended to six months. In addition, U.S. banks were allowed to count as current income, peso payments that were being held in escrow for them in Latin American central banks that were unable to convert them to dollars. By relaxing accounting and reporting regulations, the government was protecting banks that were making risky loans from the wrath of worried shareholders.

The American government, wrote Martin Mayer in his book *The Money Bazaar,* essentially bribed American banks to extend more loans to defaulting countries: "The examiners would not question these loans, no reserves would have to be taken against them, alleged profits could continue to accrue, and, despite the extraordinarily negative implications of such conduct both politically and economically, the banks would be permitted to increase their interest charges on renegotiated loans and to pocket gigantic 'rescheduling fees.' "

---

The World Bank did not stand idly by and let the IMF dominate the greatest international financial crisis since World War II. It had much at stake. Its loans were at risk, as was its reputation as a key player on the global financial scene. In addition, it was receiving what one independent study called "insistent appeals from the U.S. government, amongst others, to relieve financial pressure on the IMF and American commercial banks by lending into the arrears of the most heavily debt-distressed developing countries."

The Bank moved decisively to stake out its role. In February 1983, only six months after Mexico's crash, it announced a "special action program" to speed up its loan disbursements and increase its funding for projects that couldn't find the necessary cofinancing elsewhere. But project loans—however big, however fast—were not enough. The real need was for large, quick-disbursing loans that could be used to reduce a country's balance-of-payments deficit. As one Bank official expressed it to me, "Project loans are million-dollar pipelines. That's not enough anymore. We need billion-dollar pipelines now." Luckily, the Bank had billion-dollar pipelines. It had had them since 1980. Their construction had been one of McNamara's last important acts as president.

By the end of his term McNamara had recognized that his twelve-year assault on poverty had not had the hoped-for impact. Developing countries had spent billions of dollars of borrowed money to very little effect as far as their poor were concerned. They were still losing ground in relation both to the rest of the world and to the wealthy in their own countries. And they were being crippled by inflation and ever-growing debts.

The Bank had played a key role in this. For years, even decades, it had resolutely ignored all evidence that debt in the developing world was getting out of control. It had lent at an ever-increasing pace and had urged others to do the same. It had encouraged its clients to borrow more and more and had gauged its own success by the growth of its lending. Now many of its clients were on the verge of default, threatening the Bank's stability as well as their own. The Bank accepted some responsibility in this regard. Ernest Stern, head of the Bank's Operations Division and the leading champion of structural adjustment lending, admitted that in making its billions of dollars of loans the Bank had "failed to insist on any reasonable standards of efficiency for investment capital and the management of economies."

There was, however, a bright side to the crisis for the Bank, as economist Richard Feinberg explained. "As a result of the twin crisis of development and debt, the Bank finds new opportunities for influence in Third World countries and on international capital markets. Desperate for help, debtors and creditors alike are willing to devolve a portion of previously guarded management perogatives to a capable international agency, and the Bank alone is fit for such a task."

What the Bank decided to do was to make large, quick-disbursing loans in order "to assist countries . . . to meet an existing or to avoid an impending balance-of-payments crisis." But these so-called structural adjustment loans would only be available to countries that agreed to reform their economies in line with the Bank's advice. The Bank's Articles of Agreement allow it to make nonproject loans but only "in special circumstances." In the 1960s, the Bank had adopted a rule of thumb limiting "nonproject loans" to 10 percent of its annual lending. Most nonproject lending had been for emergency reconstruction after natural disasters, but the Bank had also made quite a few naked balance-of-payments loans to help important borrowers in desperate circumstances.

Structural adjustment loans would also be large, quick-disbursing loans to needy clients, but they were perceived as quite different from those of earlier nonproject loans. For one thing, they were not to be a mere emergency measure, but a key weapon in the Bank's development armory. McNamara acknowledged that the board's approval was necessary if such loans were to become a major element of Bank lending. But the board was less than enthusiastic about structural adjustment. In the first place, McNamara presented the matter to them in a very offhand manner, giving them a terse and uninformative briefing document. "They felt that they were not being given the full systematic presentation of why it was necessary to have structural adjustment lending," said Stanley Please, who designed the Bank's program of structural adjustment lending. Even Please felt that it looked like "the Bank was being just a little two-faced because it had said it had been able to effect all these policy changes in the 1970s, now it turned out they couldn't."

Many of the executive directors argued that lending money to countries with severe balance-of-payments deficits is the job of the International Monetary Fund, and that the Bank should stick to what it knows best, which is lending for specific projects. To allay concerns that it was treading on the toes of its sister organization, the Bank's management assured the board that only countries that were already in an IMF stabilization program would be eligible for adjustment loans. And being in such a program, said management, would constitute the "special circumstances" required by the Articles of Agreement for nonproject loans.

The board of directors also argued that because policy reforms do not cost money, they should not require loans. It worried that adjustment loans were no more than bribes—and bribes of dubious efficacy—that would open the Bank to charges of meddling, however ineffectively, in the internal affairs of its borrowers. In the end, however, the board, which had never been much more than a rubber stamp for the forceful, brilliant McNamara, put aside its reservations and in early 1980 reluctantly agreed to allow the Bank to make up to 10 percent of its lending in the form of structural adjustment loans. When the debt crisis broke, the Bank was ready to step in.

# Nine

## BILLION-DOLLAR PIPELINES

When the debt crisis hit, the Bank made good use of its new billion-dollar pipeline, pumping out money faster than it ever had before so that developing countries could keep up payments to their private creditors. This had the effect of converting short- and medium-term developing country debt held by private banks into long-term debt held by the Bank. The Bank "earned its keep" during the global debt crisis, said a grateful Kidder Peabody executive.

Not everyone approved of the Bank's efforts to postpone the Third World's day of reckoning. A 1983 *Wall Street Journal* editorial about the Bank's response to the debt crisis fumed that "the [B]ank is busily plotting new ways to shovel the money of U.S. and other developed nations' taxpayers out the door. . . . Little wonder it wants to keep pumping the money out. How many of [the Bank's] borrowers could maintain their perfect repayment records if they had to earn their way instead of getting fresh infusions of capitalist money whenever they began to experience some difficulty?" Liberals, too, criticized this approach to dealing with the debt crisis. Democratic Representative Charles Schumer of New York spoke of "Faustian finance"—the "bargains in which banks make new loans so that debtor nations have enough cash to continue paying interest on their old loans."

———

Robert McNamara did not preside over adjustment lending for long. He retired from the Bank on the last day of June 1981, only four months short of breaking Eugene Black's record as the institution's longest-serving president. The man chosen by the newly installed Reagan administration to succeed him was Alden Winship "Tom" Clausen, the former head of the Bank of America, the world's largest commercial bank. At Bank of America, Clausen had enthusiastically heeded McNamara's call for more lending to developing countries and had worked closely with the Bank, arranging parallel loans to numerous Bank projects.

Still, Clausen wasted no time in making it clear that McNamara's priorities were not his own. In a meeting with the Bank's top executives during his first week in office, he declared that he did not intend to continue McNamara's focus on poverty. Mahbub ul Haq, who was at the meeting, was disappointed to discover that Clausen had a sympathetic audience. "It pains me to say this," he said later, "but [apart from myself] . . . each and every one of the people sitting around that table said that McNamara's rhetoric on poverty was never the policy of the Bank. It was only Mahbub and McNamara's concoction." According to ul Haq, Clausen was "very convinced that the only constituency that mattered was the United States. He made that statement about ten to twelve times in the first meeting."

In the early 1980s, the governing economic philosophy in Washington, London, Bonn—and at 1818 H Street—was supply-side economics. This is a version of trickle-down, the economic theory that McNamara had declared a failure ten years before. Both supply-siders and trickle-downers hold that the benefits of economic growth trickle down from the rich to the poor, but supply-side theorists also maintain that growth is stimulated by the "supply side"—the private sector—rather than by the "demand side"— the government. It was Clausen's job to refocus the Bank away from its efforts to target poverty directly and back toward the promotion of economic growth, especially through the private sector.

Clausen replaced McNamara's chief economic theorist, Hollis Chenery, with Anne Krueger, an eager advocate of supply-side economics. According to Benjamin King, Krueger discouraged debate. "She cut off anybody who ever had any relationship with Hollis Chenery, irrespective of the person's merit." *Aid and Power,* a study of the Bank's structural adjustment programs by three British academics, described Krueger's impact on the Bank's economic work: "Dissent was little tolerated [in Krueger's department]. The Bank's research was reorganized more tightly around large projects designed to substantiate what everyone knew in their hearts already: that economic liberalization was right."

The Bank was—and is—convinced that the mechanisms of the marketplace would solve most of the problems its borrowers faced—inflation, unemployment, underinvestment, poor public services, inefficient public bureaucracies, unsustainable debt burdens, and even lack of personal freedom. For the marketplace to operate efficiently, it believes, countries must reduce public spending, lift trade restrictions, remove price subsidies, and create the legal and financial mechanisms necessary to a free-market economy. In essence, the Bank has a formula for economic life that, in the interests of ideology, administrative efficiency, and a desire to appear even-handed, it applies—or tries to apply—to all countries, regardless of their differing characteristics.

As part of its formula, the Bank presses its borrowers to adopt legal as well as economic reforms. In recent years, borrowers have written, amended, or repealed hundreds of laws in order to qualify for World Bank adjustment loans. Argentina weakened the legal protection for labor unions. Ecuador effectively eliminated communal land holdings. India scrapped laws limiting the amount of land one person could own. In fact, India alone has changed more than twenty major pieces of legislation at the behest of the Bank, including the Trade Unions Act, the Maternity Benefits Act, and the Industrial Disputes Act. Only countries in the most desperate circumstances would accept such intrusions on their sovereignty—but the debt crisis left many countries in that position. Shahid Husain, a vice president of the Bank, acknowledged that the Bank was making extraordinary demands on its borrowers. "These loans do go to the heart of the political management of an economy," he said. "We will have to approach them with humility."

Burke Knapp also advised the Bank to practice humility. In 1981, three years after retiring as the Bank's executive vice president, he said, "Let me declare myself as being skeptical . . . about the extent to which the Bank can design and enforce conditions on such lending. I'm just not sure we're wise enough—I'm sure we're *not* always wise enough—to design these structural adjustment programs and to formulate conditions that are relevant and productive." But Clausen and his top managers were not feeling humble or skeptical. Under pressure to deal with the debt crisis, they eagerly embraced the view that a combination of dramatic reforms, bolstered by large balance-of-payments loans, would solve the debt problems of most developing countries within a few years. They favored a total-immersion approach to adjustment rather than a gradual introduction of reforms—

and they gave little thought to the impact such dramatic changes would have on the citizens of its borrowers.

The Bank declared that adjustment for any country would require no more than five loans and would be completed within three to five years—in another two years the country would also have a sustainable balance of payments. Then, with adjustment behind it, the country could resume the task of long-term development, this time with more chance of success.

———

Turkey was the first recipient of an adjustment loan from the Bank. During the 1950s and '60s, that country had emphasized self-sufficiency and public investment in industrialization, with considerable success. But during the 1970s Turkey overborrowed spectacularly: In just three years the country's external debt tripled, and in 1977 Turkey declared itself unable to keep up its debt payments. This economic crisis was attended by a political crisis, in which control of the government bounced from one unstable coalition to another. Western countries, worried that Turkey might go the way of its neighbor, Iran, where religious fundamentalists were gaining popular support, were eager to help. First, however, they wanted the blessing of the global authority on fiscal policy, the International Monetary Fund.

But the IMF would not provide emergency help to Turkey, because its rulers refused to accede to its demand that they devalue the Turkish lira and reduce public spending. In January 1980, however, with annual inflation exceeding 100 percent, a new government adopted a tough new plan for economic reform. The plan, drawn up by a former World Bank official named Turkut Ozal, aimed to lower Turkey's foreign debt by encouraging exports and curtailing public spending. Less than two months later, the World Bank gave the country a $200 million structural adjustment loan (SAL), despite the fact that Turkey still had not reached agreement with the Fund on a stabilization program.

The Bank's action violated a pledge that McNamara had made to the executive directors less than two months earlier. In return for their approval of structural adjustment lending, McNamara had promised that the Bank would give structural adjustment loans only to countries that were already participating in an IMF stabilization program. The Bank's haste to make the SAL to Turkey was partly a result of pressure from Western nations eager to see the country stabilized, and partly due to its own eagerness to see structural adjustment in action. Over the next four years, Turkey received four more SALs from the Bank, for a total of $1.5 billion.

Both the Bank and Turkey expected a great deal from adjustment, as this summary of the goals for the first SAL shows: "Reduce inflation; rationalize foreign exchange and interest rate policy; increase utilization of production capacity; curtail and reorient public investment; improve domestic resource mobilization."

Turkey's adjustment loans came with many conditions attached, but most were remarkably vague—requiring the government to make "satisfactory progress" or "adequate progress" toward various goals without specifying a timetable or defining "satisfactory." Few of the goals were ever met, but the vague wording meant that the Bank never had to withhold or rescind a loan on grounds of nonperformance. Thus the Bank was spared the need to cancel a series of showcase loans—an act that would have been an admission of failure, while also opening it to charges that it was trying to dictate policy to Turkey.

The major success of adjustment in Turkey was a growth in exports, which rose from 5 percent of the GDP in 1980 to 14 percent in 1984. This rise, which was due in part to the government's devaluation of the Turkish lira and its 25 and 30 percent export subsidies, helped cut Turkey's international trade deficit by almost two-thirds over those four years. During the same period, Turkey's gross domestic product grew steadily, even taking into account an inflation rate that hovered around 50 percent in 1984. On the negative side, real wages fell substantially and the billions of dollars Turkey was borrowing from the World Bank and other lenders swelled the country's external debt and its overall deficit.

By 1984, Turkey had received its allotted five adjustment loans, but it had not yet met its goals. The Bank was learning that adjustment would take longer and cost more than anticipated. In order to keep Turkey afloat, it came up with a new kind of loan, the "sectoral adjustment loan," or SECAL, aimed at promoting reform in specific sectors of the economy. Between 1985 and 1988, the Bank gave Turkey $1.4 billion worth of SECAL for the agriculture, energy, and finance sectors. In addition to these huge adjustment loans, Turkey also received $4.2 billion in project loans from the Bank between 1980 and 1988. Thus the Bank's loans to Turkey during that period amounted to more than $7 billion.

Despite the continued influx of World Bank funds, 1984 turned out to be the high point of Turkey's adjustment program. In the second half of the decade, many of the initial gains were frozen or reversed, while some problems worsened. Turkey's adjustment began to falter in late 1983, when the military government was replaced by an elected civilian government headed by Turkut Ozal, the former World Bank official who had designed the country's adjustment plan. The problem with this otherwise welcome turn of events was that democracies are at a disadvantage when it comes to enacting unpopular measures.

Turkey's military government had abolished the right to strike, curtailed trade union activity, and imposed an incomes policy that "resulted in a decisive shift in income distribution away from wage-earners [to the wealthy]." Ozal's government had to relax some of these restrictions. In a 1989 review of Turkey's adjustment experience the World Bank's Faezeh Foroutan said, "Whereas the military regime in 1980–83 was able to implement its adjustment program, including the massive redistribution of income, with relative ease, the newly restored democratic government has had more difficulty traveling along the same path."

In an effort to satisfy the demands of both the Turkish electorate and the Bank, the Ozal government increasingly turned to the use of "extrabudgetary funds" (EBFs). These are funds raised by levies on certain imports but not included in the national budget. By increasing its EBFs and using them to subsidize social welfare programs, the government could technically—though not really—keep its promise to the Bank to reduce public expenditure, without risking the fury of its citizens.

In his 1989 report, Foroutan stated that "despite Turkey's substantial adherence to World Bank policy advice in the 1980s . . . [the country] today is facing some of the same pressing problems that afflicted its economy over ten years ago during the height of its debt crisis. Turkey's public sector deficit is high and growing, inflation is high and accelerating, and the foreign and domestic debt service burden is mounting while investment in key sectors is stagnating." These problems were not reflected in the Bank's assessments of Turkey's structural adjustment loans. A 1988 survey said that "Turkey's adjustment program was undoubtedly successful" and other Bank studies described Turkey's adjustment programs as having "achieved most, if not all, of the original objectives of the programs" and having had "no major shortcomings."

By 1995, despite its nearly $3 billion worth of adjustment loans, Turkey was deeper in crisis than ever before. One of its greatest problems is its $70 billion foreign debt. Keeping up payments on that huge debt takes almost a third of its export earnings. The government responded "by depressing wages and draining productive resources from industry to finance fiscal deficits and current expenditures," says Sozer Ozel, an industrialist and chairman of Ankara's Chamber of Industry. In 1994, according to the Organization for Economic Cooperation and Development (OECD), the average inflation rate was 118 percent—the highest in the history of modern Turkey; per capita income dropped from nearly $3,000 to $2,200; and

GDP fell by 3.9 percent—the biggest contraction since 1943. There was a "fragile" stability in the country's financial market, but it was achieved at the expense of a 15 percent cut in real wages, a real devaluation of the lira, and the loss of half a million jobs.

———

Adjustment did not live up to its billing as an intense but short process. It turned out to take much longer—and require much more money—than its sponsors had anticipated. By 1982 structural adjustment lending had already broken through the 10 percent ceiling approved two years earlier by the board of directors. By 1986, adjustment loans constituted between 25 and 30 percent of the Bank's lending. At some point during the mid-1980s, the board agreed to raise the 10 percent ceiling to 25 percent, though according to Kenlee Ray, the board's librarian, this does not represent a "hard-and-fast" limit. In fact, the Bank's adjustment lending exceeded 25 percent in 1989, 1990, 1991, and 1992.

By 1995, eighty-eight countries had embarked on Bank-funded adjustment programs and not a single one had kept to the Bank's original timetable of completing adjustment in three to five years. Many have received adjustment loans for more than a decade without making any discernible progress. In 1991, the Bank admitted that "instead of disappearing, adjustment lending intensified."

Senegal is an example of a country in which adjustment has dragged on for more than a decade, with no end in sight. It was one of the first countries to receive an adjustment loan from the Bank, which lent it $60 million in 1980. However, it flouted its loan conditions so flagrantly—for example, by funding state enterprises instead of privatizing them—that the Bank, in a rare gesture, refused to release the last $16 million of the loan. Between 1981 and 1986, Senegal received no adjustment loans, though it did get more than $200 million worth of project loans from the Bank. In 1986, the Bank accepted Senegal back into the adjustment fold and by 1995 had given it another ten adjustment loans, worth a total of $480 million. In 1989 Senegal's per capita income was lower than it had been in 1960.

Other countries that began adjusting in the early 1980s and are still doing so include Bolivia, which by mid-1995 had received $235 million in Bank adjustment loans; Jamaica, $380 million; Kenya, $760 million; and the Ivory Coast, more than $1.4 billion. In fact, these figures are probably understatements because the Bank often gives adjustment loans other names. In 1992, for example, the Bank categorized a quick-disbursing $52 million loan to Kenya as an education loan, not an adjustment loan, although its purpose was "to supplement the [$100 million] education sector–adjustment loan" that had been approved the previous year.

The Bank attributes the rising cost of adjustment and its ever-receding attainment not to any flaw in its reform prescriptions but to the fact that the economies of developing countries are much more "profoundly distorted" than it had realized—and therefore need more time and more money to adjust than anticipated. Another reason for the overrun, according to Bank officials—and one that seemed to reflect well on the Bank—was simply that so many countries wanted adjustment loans. "We did not anticipate just how popular structural adjustment lending was going to become," remarked Senior Vice President Ernest Stern.

Even as strong an advocate of adjustment lending as Stern acknowledged that there is something odd at the heart of adjustment. "People often ask," he once said, " 'Why bribe governments to do what they ought to be doing anyway?' " Indeed, in the early 1980s, a number of countries undertook far-reaching structural reforms without the inducement of large loans. In Africa, the World Bank's Lost Continent, sixteen countries had eased or eliminated controls on farm prices by 1984, though only six of them had received SALs. The most dramatic changes occurred in Zimbabwe, which was not then on a World Bank adjustment program. Now, however, it is a rare country that will adopt reforms without first asking the Bank for a large adjustment loan.

Whether because of national pride, ideology, political survival, or corruption, many governments have been unwilling or unable to adopt the tough measures on which their adjustment loans were conditioned. Few, however, openly thumb their noses at the Bank. It is far better to circumvent its requirements quietly, and borrowers have been remarkably inventive in finding ways to do so. Jamaica, for example, set up an Export Development Fund, as the Bank insisted, but failed to fund it. The Philippines got a high compliance rating on its first SAL by observing scores of trivial conditions—those calling for the hiring of certain consultants or for the commissioning of a small study—while ignoring the major ones. State enterprises have been "privatized" by being given to government officials. Other countries have, like Turkey, learned to hide public spending in extrabudgetary funds.

These machinations make it hard to evaluate how strictly a borrower is following the agreed-on path of reform. The Bank claims a fairly high level of compliance, but Elliot Berg, though a champion of adjustment, says that the Bank's assessors do not distinguish between "cosmetic compliance" and the real thing. Overall, says Berg, "the World Bank's capacity to supervise all this is extremely limited."

An internal Bank study admitted that Bank staff are "overly optimistic" in judging adjustment loans, and said that they downplay important defects in their eagerness to make positive pronouncements. For example, despite finding that the Bank's $50 million structural adjustment loan to Bolivia "was unsuccessful; reforms were minimal and shortlived," Bank auditors concluded that Bolivia "had complied with the spirit of the Loan Agreement." In fact, according to Stanley Please, the senior bank official responsible for developing structural adjustment lending, "Bolivia was a disaster from the beginning." Even when the Bank does identify a lack of compliance on the part of a borrower, it rarely takes action. It has, on occasion, expressed its annoyance with defiant borrowers by delaying the release of the second installment of a loan, but it has only ever canceled one SAL, Senegal's first.

The Bank is well aware that it cannot control the behavior of sovereign nations. It can bring great pressure to bear on disobliging borrowers by withholding its funds and its imprimateur, thereby effectively blocking a country's access to all other sources of external finance. But such a blunt instrument cannot be used to micromanage national economies, police recalcitrant governments, or control the behavior of the man in the street. In acknowledgment of this, the Bank now emphasizes the need for borrowers to, in Bank jargon, "own" their adjustment programs—that is, to want to make the reforms they promise to make.

———

The Bank has often held up Mexico, the nation that triggered the 1982 debt crisis, as a model for other nations undergoing adjustment. "The Mexican state," the *Financial Times* declared in 1992, "has become the darling of the [World] Bank's economists." U.S. Treasury Secretary Robert Rubin called Mexico the star pupil of free-market economic development.

Between 1983 and 1991, the Bank made a series of thirteen adjustment loans totaling $6 billion to Mexico. The Mexican government was a very cooperative partner with the Bank in the adjustment process. "The Bank does not need to force Mexico to do anything; the two sides agree on almost everything. . . . World Bank economists and Mexican officials often spend weekends together brainstorming on policy issues. Many are the graduates of the same U.S. universities, and friends," the *Financial Times* reported. The Bank, said Angel Gurria, Mexico's undersecretary of finance, is staffed by "the best people in the world. If you are convinced you are doing the right thing, often they will tell you how to do it better."

When, in preparation for the North American Free Trade Agreement, Mexico had to amend its constitution to divide the communal lands of the country's peasant communities, or *ejidos,* into small individually owned parcels, officials in the agricultural ministry asked their friends at the Bank for help. According to the *Financial Times,* it was a genuine collaboration: "The World Bank wrote issue papers; the Mexicans responded in kind. Draft laws were written and re-written. Eventually [in late 1991] a constitutional amendment was drawn up, and passed."

In mid-1994, the British economist and former World Bank official Sir Alan Walters listed Mexico's accomplishments under adjustment: "It has substantially opened its economy to world trade, reduced regulation, privatized much of its state sector, reduced the fiscal deficit to less than 2 percent of GDP and finally made the Central Bank independent of government." In addition, it lowered its inflation rate from 157 percent in 1987 to 7 percent in 1994. Keeping inflation down was essential to Mexico's adjustment strategy, because foreign investors demanded assurance that their peso profits would not be wiped out by inflation when they were changed back into dollars. To accomplish this, the Mexican government pegged the peso to the U.S. dollar. This managed exchange rate was, according to World Bank economist John Nash, the "anchor in [the government's] antiinflationary program."

Impressed with Mexico's success in opening its economy and controlling inflation, overseas investors gave the country a dramatic vote of confidence by making it the world's second-largest recipient (after China) of foreign private investment. By the end of 1994, a quarter of the Mexican stock market and half its government bonds were in foreign hands. The strong peso and the lifting of trade restrictions on imports fueled an import boom. American and European cars, appliances, and other consumer goods were in great demand among the upper classes. Many businesses also found it cheaper to buy equipment, tools, and raw materials abroad than domestically.

On January 1, 1994, Mexico became a partner with the United States and Canada in the North American Free Trade Agreement (NAFTA). Five months later, it also joined the "rich countries' club," the Organization for Economic Cooperation and Development (OECD). As the country whose economic difficulties had precipitated the debt crisis in 1982, Mexico's success was an important achievement for the Bank, evidence that its prescriptions for reform could, if strictly adhered to, achieve results.

But, although it succeeded in lowering inflation and attracting investors, Mexico did not achieve the main aims of adjustment—economic growth and poverty reduction. Production was stagnant. The Mexican boom was based not on real economic growth but on relentless borrowing, the provision of a safe haven to foreign investors, and the sale of state-owned enterprises. Between 1988 and 1994, Mexico's economic growth averaged 2.2 percent annually, barely enough to keep pace with its population growth.

The reduction in poverty that is supposed to accompany successful adjustment also failed to materialize. In fact, Mexico's remarkable transformation came at great cost to the mass of its citizens. In 1992, average wages were—in real terms—half what they had been ten years earlier. Aid to the poor—such as subsidies for milk, tortillas, and primary school breakfasts—had been drastically reduced or eliminated. Investment in health, education, and basic physical infrastructure was cut roughly in half, with predictable results. Between 1980 and 1992, infant deaths due to malnutrition almost tripled. Faced with reduced real wages and increased fees for books and tuition, many families withdrew their children from school.

But Mexico's adjustment did more than fail to eliminate poverty; it intensified it, making the rich richer and the poor poorer. A Bank report found that the way state-owned enterprises were privatized "worsen[ed] the already skewed and concentrated pattern of ownership distribution in the economy. . . . Only a small group of local conglomerates have been involved in purchasing public enterprises." In 1984, the top one-fifth of the population received 48 percent of the national income and the poorest one-fifth got only 5 percent. By 1992 the wealthy's take of the national income had grown by 13 percent and the poor's had fallen by the same amount. The country's richest man, Carlos Slim, had more money than the country's 17 million poorest people combined.

When Mexico, with the Bank's guidance, amended its constitution to convert communally owned lands to individual ownership, many of those who had obtained title promptly sold their lands to wealthy buyers. This had been anticipated by the government, which argued that the new owners would farm the land more efficiently. In the process, however, large numbers of poor peasants were displaced from the land on which they had depended for a living, and were thrown into destitution.

The Mexican government downplayed the problem of poverty. In its eagerness to be seen as having "graduated" from the Third World, it preferred to dwell on the fact that the number of billionaires in Mexico rose from two to twenty-four between 1988 and 1994. "Mexican poverty," said Finance Minister Aspe in 1993, "is a genial myth."

On January 1, 1994, however, Mexican poverty reared its head in a manner that no one could ignore. As the new year dawned, a peasant army named after the country's revolutionary hero, Ernesto Zapata, seized six towns in the southern state of Chiapas. More than 150 people died in several days of heavy fighting between the Zapatistas and the Mexican army. The rebels were protesting political corruption and economic policies they said favored foreign investors over Mexico's workers. "The Zapatistas are only saying what many Mexicans want," said Sergio Aguayo, a political science professor at the Colegio de Mexico. "That is why they have had such a strong impact." One poll found that 61 percent of Mexicans sympathized with the Zapatistas.

The uprising focused international attention on the grievances of Mexico's peasants and the wider issue of the growing gap between the country's rich and poor. Even the editors of The Economist acknowledged that the rebels' demands could not be ignored. "Mexico's Zapatist rebellion is not the only recent sign, merely the fiercest, that ordinary Latin Americans want more of the cake," they noted.

The apparent stability of Mexico's long-standing government—the Institutional Revolutionary Party (PRI) had held power since 1929—had been a source of confidence for investors. By bringing to light the depth of the social discontent in the country and its potential for sparking turmoil, the Zapatist rebellion undermined much of that confidence. Later in the year, when several top PRI officials were assassinated, investors became even more uneasy. As nervous investors will do, Mexico's began scanning the horizon for other problems—and they found some. The most worrying among them was the problem of the peso.

By pegging the peso to the dollar, the Mexican government had managed to keep Mexico's inflation rate about even with that of the United States. But there was a growing gap between the peso's real value and its official value. It became more and more expensive for the Mexican government to buy pesos at the artificially high official exchange rate. Still the government refused to lower the exchange rate—that is, devalue the peso— for fear of driving away foreign investors. Instead, in what The Washington Post called "a type of Ponzi scheme," it borrowed heavily from the World Bank and commercial lenders in order to obtain the dollars it needed to buy pesos at the high official exchange rate. This borrowing helped drive Mexico's foreign debt from $86 billion in 1982 to more than $120 billion in 1992.

Many economists and financial writers argued that Mexico should de-value the peso, but the World Bank put no pressure on the government to do so. Speaking in September 1993, Patrick Low, of the Bank's International Trade Division, said that foreign investors were putting so much money into Mexico that the country could afford to ignore pressures to devalue. "The Mexicans want to avoid depreciating their currency, but if you have a deficit that you can't finance through long-term borrowings or through investment or whatever else, then you may have to look at devaluation. And Mexico in the last couple of years *has* been running a very substantial balance of payments deficit, importing a lot more than it's been exporting. But that hasn't been a particular source of concern because there have been significant inflows of foreign direct investment and that has been financing the deficit. That has enabled them not to worry too much about devaluation."

Wealthy Mexicans, however, were not as sanguine as the Bank's economists. In November 1994, alarmed by the mounting degree of social unrest and fearing that the government would be unable to maintain the value of the peso much longer, they began changing their pesos into dollars and moving them out of the country. In a matter of weeks, Mexico's foreign reserves fell from more than $17 billion to $8 billion. Still the government refused to devalue the peso. On December 1, a new president, Ernesto Zedillo, was inaugurated. Less than three weeks later, his government devalued the peso by 15 percent, triggering an even greater rush of investors out of the country and further draining Mexico's foreign reserves. Two days later, Mexico abandoned the expensive pretense of maintaining the peso at its false official value and announced that it would be allowed to float. Its value at once plummeted.

With virtually no foreign currency reserves left and with $28 billion worth of dollar-linked bonds coming due over the next year, Mexico faced bankruptcy for the second time in twelve years. In early January 1995, the Zedillo government announced a fierce austerity program that included a wage freeze, a sharp cut in government spending, higher taxes, and limits on bank lending. In return, the United States agreed to provide Mexico with $20 billion in loan guarantees—with the IMF and several European countries contributing another $30 billion to the package. The World Bank also rushed to the rescue, sending a twenty-five-member mission to Mexico to "speed up disbursements and to start preparing new operations." Chief among those new operations was a $1 billion loan to Mexico's banks. That one loan, the largest the Bank has ever made, represented 4 percent of all Bank lending in 1995.

The effects of the government's austerity program were dramatic. In the first five months of 1995, though wages were frozen, prices rose by 29 percent. More than 750,000 people lost their jobs. Businesses went bankrupt by the score. Many people lost their homes and cars when interest rates on their loans rose to 90 percent a year. Armed robberies went up by 35 percent. In an effort to placate the middle class, the government announced that it would subsidize interest on consumer loans, mortgages, and credit cards, a mini bail-out that *The Economist* warned "sets a dangerous precedent." In June, the Bank lent Mexico $500 million to pay for "essential social services in education and health" and "to cushion the poor from the effects of the economic crisis."

Meanwhile, in the United States, critics of its $20 billion rescue package charged that American taxpayers were financing, in the words of *The Wall Street Journal,* "a bailout of a foreign country, plus a handful of investment firms . . . [including] the firm that Treasury Secretary [and World Bank Governor] Robert Rubin used to run, Goldman, Sachs & Co., which ranked as the No. 1 underwriter of Mexican stocks and bonds in the U.S. and European markets for 1992 through 1994."

Speaking to Rubin and Federal Reserve Board Chairman Alan Greenspan at a House Banking Committee hearing, Congresswoman Maxine Waters, a Democrat who represents some of the poorest neighborhoods in Los Angeles, said, "We marvel at the ability of all you guys to get together in a room and solve a crisis of this magnitude. We just wish you could apply some of that creativity and thinking and find some loan guarantees for us. We'd like to have it."

Treasury Undersecretary and former World Bank Chief economist Lawrence Summers hastened to assure critics that the United States' $20 billion would give it far-reaching control over the running of the Mexican economy. "We're going to [put] . . . conditions on their budget, conditions on the expansion of credit, conditions on how much money they can print, conditions that they have to move ahead with privatization, conditions that will ensure we'll get repaid, that they'll have healthy economic growth," he said.

Two billion dollars of Mexico's debt to the United States was due on October 31, 1995, but in early September, Presidents Zedillo and Clinton held a joint press conference to announce that Mexico would prepay $700 million of that debt with money raised by selling bonds in Germany. This was offered as evidence of Mexico's creditworthiness, but Carlos Heredia, formerly an official in Mexico's Finance Ministry and now a prominent critic of the government, argued that it was just the reverse. "Every dollar that Mexico has paid has not come from Mexico, but from external sources," he said. "The country keeps going into debt to pay its debts." The two presidents did not mention that Mexico had requested that the deadline for repaying the remaining $1.3 billion be extended. Lance Taylor, professor of economics at the New School for Social Research, said that Mexico had entered "the cycle of hype and bust."

The panic in Mexico sent stocks plummeting and weakened currencies in several other Latin American nations, notably Brazil and Argentina— and in Mexico's NAFTA partner, Canada. Economists in the U.S. government, the World Bank, and the IMF worried that Mexico's collapse would make other countries, as Clay Chandler of *The Washington Post* put it, "repudiate the liberal approach U.S. policymakers and academic economists have promoted so zealously for the past two decades." The World Bank's faith in that approach, however, was not shaken. It attributed the peso crisis to bad timing—Mexico should have devalued the peso sooner— rather than to poor policies. The Bank predicted a quick recovery. "Toward the end of '96," said the Bank's chief Latin American economist, Sebastian Edwards, "we may be surprised at how brisk the recovery will be."

Many independent economists argue, however, that the Bank was wrong to encourage Mexico to rely so heavily on foreign capital. That reliance, they argue, exacerbated Mexico's economic woes by making it vulnerable to forces it could not control. According to a study by Goldman, Sachs & Co., 80 percent of the movement in Mexico's financial markets in 1994 was caused not by domestic economic or political events, but by events elsewhere, such as a rise in interest rates in New York or Tokyo. An analysis by Anne Swardson and Martha M. Hamilton in *The Washington Post* asked whether "the free-market economic model [is] all it was cracked up to be. Were the nations of Latin America prepared for the vagaries of the business cycle, in which even well-managed economies plummet into recession at times? . . . And was the new world of wealth in Latin America helping its people, or were the benefits accruing to the global foreign investors who had made it all possible?"

At a 1989 Bank seminar, adjustment advocate Elliot Berg admitted that "many of the intellectual or analytical underpinnings of 1980s-style adjustment lending are contested—such fundamentals as the feasibility of export-led growth, the efficacy and beneficence of deregulated markets, and the desirability of market-determined interest rates or exchange rates."

One of the most controversial aspects of the Bank's adjustment programs is their emphasis on the need to increase exports. The Bank's borrowers generally export raw materials and import manufactured goods, mostly from industrialized nations. Recent research by the World Bank and others, including Jeffrey Sachs of Harvard University, indicates, however, that countries that rely on the export of natural resources actually grow more slowly than those that do not. This is partly due to the fact that there are a limited number of commodities in demand internationally and when dozens of countries simultaneously try to increase exports, the market becomes flooded and prices fall. Oxfam cites increased commodity exports in the 1980s and 1990s as a major factor in "the most protracted and deepest depression in world markets since the 1930s." Another reason for the slower growth of resource-dependent economies is that resource exploitation diverts capital and labor from manufacturing and industry. A third is that natural resource exploitation—such as oil, mineral, or timber extraction—tends to follow a boom-and-bust pattern. In such a cycle, producers and governments enjoy windfall profits, but only for a short time. The sheer volume of the cash flowing in invites waste and corruption, and experience shows that such large sums of money are rarely wisely invested. While less spectacularly profitable, an export program based on manufactured goods, say these researchers, is a more dependable contributor to long-term growth.

The Bank's adjustment policies are also intended to open developing countries to imports by lowering tariffs and removing administrative barriers to trade. This fact led U.S. Undersecretary of the Treasury and former World Bank chief economist Lawrence Summers to tell Congress in 1995 that, in view of the growing U.S. trade deficit, "even an extra one or two percent [in pledges to the World Bank] is justifiable." Since prices of manufactured goods are generally higher than those of raw materials, many developing countries are finding their increased export earnings more than wiped out by the cost of imports. Between 1980 and 1989, the terms of trade for developing countries—that is, the prices of commodities versus those of manufactured goods—fell by 52 percent.

According to Patrick Low, a World Bank trade specialist, however, it is wrong to judge the Bank's programs by their effect on a borrower's balance of payments. The Bank encourages countries to export not so that they will earn foreign currency, says Low, but so that they will become more efficient through competition with other nations. "If they keep their economy pretty well aligned—this is the theory—with relative world prices, that means minimal import restrictions, minimal differences between world

prices and their prices, they get more efficient. They're more likely to allocate their resources to the things they're best at doing; they're more likely
to find where their comparative advantage is. So export orientation for
these countries means that they're going to have to produce competitively
for world markets."

But, as Low acknowledges, world markets are not open markets: "An
interesting question is whether the industrial countries aren't inconsistent
in not giving good market access to developing countries." The barriers to
trade erected by rich countries against poor countries make a mockery of
structural adjustment. "[We] need structural adjustment in northern industrial nations to remove economic obstacles," says Paul Spray, head of policy research for the development charity Christian Aid.

Critics of the Bank, such as Doug Hellinger, cofounder with his twin
brother, Steve, of the Washington, D.C.–based nonprofit Development
Group for Alternative Policies (D-GAP), charge the Bank with promoting
policies that help the industrial world, and especially the wealthiest members of that world, at the expense of the poor. Hellinger, who before forming D-GAP worked as a consultant to the Bank on urban development,
says, "The Bank is saying that to join the world economy you have to
become more efficient and you have to be able to compete against imports
from around the world. But the purpose is not to develop Brazil or develop
Ghana. They could give a damn. The U.S. is trying to stay competitive with
Europe and Japan and the Bank is helping to provide the government's
friends in business with cheap labor, a deregulated atmosphere, and export
incentives. It isn't a development strategy, it's a corporate strategy."

McNamara's former deputy, Mahbub ul Haq, was another who believes that the market inevitably favors rich countries—and individuals—
over poor ones. "Those who have the money can make the market bend to
their own will," he has written. "When we start from a position of gross
inequalities, the so-called market mechanism mocks poverty, or simply ignores it, since the poor hardly have any purchasing power to influence
market decisions." The language of the market is a limited one; it understands only the movement of money. It can signal that prices are too high
or too low relative to the demand of those with money to spend, but it is
silent as to whether there are people without money who are hungry. It is
equally unable to respond to the needs of the environment because it cannot know and does not signal that economic forces are causing ecological
damage—at least, not until the damage appears in economic form—the
need to buy bottled water, for example, or an increase in hospitalizations
due to lung disease.

Some of the Bank's members agree that it has overemphasized the importance of an unfettered market and underrated the role of the state in achieving economic growth. Many of the countries that the Bank holds up as economic models, countries such as South Korea, Singapore, and Japan, have taken a very different path than the one the Bank advocates. In these countries, the state has played a strong role in setting prices, controlling imports, overseeing industries, and redistributing land and income.

Hoping to convince Bank management that there are viable alternatives to its development model, in 1992 the Japanese executive director and several others asked the Bank to produce a report on the development experience of Japan and the "Four Asian Tigers"—South Korea, Singapore, Hong Kong, and Taiwan. Japan had to exert what one observer calls "considerable pressure"—and agree to pay the $2 million cost of the study—before the Bank agreed to undertake such a study. The report, *The East Asian Miracle,* acknowledged that in these economies, "The government intervened—systematically and through multiple channels—to foster development." It concluded, however, that the success of the Asian Tigers "was primarily due to the application of a set of common, market-friendly economic policies" and that nations wishing to achieve similar growth should, first and foremost, adopt similar market-friendly policies.

Japan and the other subjects of the study were angered by its conclusions. They believed it understated the contribution of government intervention to economic growth in favor of the market-friendly policies the Bank has long championed—and that the understatement was deliberate. As the financial writer Michael Lewis observed in *The New Republic,* they were convinced that "the Bank cooked the study so that it came out the way it wanted, that it was a willful misreading of the Asian experience."

In the beginning, the Bank gave little thought to how adjustment programs would affect ordinary people, other than to assume that everyone would benefit from an improved economy. But the sorts of economic changes called for in World Bank adjustment programs can make life harder for a good part of the population—at least in the short term. It is not only the poor who are affected by adjustment. Currency devaluations, for example, hurt the rich by making imported cars and other luxury goods more expensive and raising the price of educating their children abroad.

Middle-class city dwellers are particularly vulnerable to cuts in government-funded services, because they are the main beneficiaries of such amenities as subsidized housing, health, sanitation, public schools, and staple foods. Many in the urban middle class are public employees or workers for state-owned industries; these risk falling into the urban poor when they lose their jobs owing to government cutbacks. Those who are not laid off may find that labor and health protection laws are loosened in an effort to attract foreign investment. Moreover, the rise in unemployment drives wages down. Ten years after Mexico embarked on its adjustment program, real wages were half what they had been in 1982.

The riots and demonstrations that have accompanied adjustment programs all over the developing world have, to a large degree, been urban revolts. Thousands of housewives demonstrated in the streets of Caracas against the rise in food prices. Coal miners in Poland struck when the government froze their wages. Taxi drivers and car owners in Jordan rioted when the government raised the price of gasoline. In Buenos Aires tens of thousands of government workers, students, and pensioners took to the streets to protest the effects of structural adjustment. In Bolivia, teachers and telephone workers led a national strike. Industrial workers rallied in Bucharest to protest wage freezes. Cities throughout Zimbabwe were filled with demonstrators protesting cutbacks in social spending and increases in hospital fees.

Though the rural poor are generally worse off than their urban counterparts in absolute terms, the circumstances of their poverty are different. Agriculture is the main occupation in rural areas, and commercial farmers benefit when food prices rise, though that benefit may be canceled out by the higher prices charged for imported pesticides and fertilizers once the local currency is devalued. Subsistence farmers, however, are largely outside the marketplace and are therefore unlikely to be much affected by such economic reforms. The rural poor are also less likely to be hurt by reductions in government spending on hospitals, schools, and housing because they have limited access to such services in the first place. On the other hand, sharecroppers and farmers without legal title are likely to lose their access to land if government support for export crops causes large farmers to expand production.

In the face of widespread discontent in adjusting countries, it has become harder and harder for the Bank to argue, as it did in 1988, that adjustment has "a favorable effect on the poor." In 1987, the United Nations Children's Fund (UNICEF) published a scathing review of the social effects of adjustment. Called *Adjustment with a Human Face*, the survey found that "the number of people in poverty in many 'adjusting countries' increased." It reported that the availability of food per person declined in more than half the countries that received adjustment loans between 1980 and 1987 as adjusting governments promoted food exports, let food prices rise, and pressured wages downward. It documented a deterioration in child welfare throughout Latin America and Africa and in some Asian countries and found that adjustment policies "have been an important contributory element." Some form of economic reform is necessary for most developing countries, said UNICEF, but there are ways to achieve reform without damaging children's health or reducing their chances of an education.

Two years later, in its annual report, *The State of the World's Children*, UNICEF labeled the 1980s "the decade of despair." It cited harsh adjustment policies in many developing countries as a major contributor to the misery of the poor. "It can be estimated," said UNICEF, "that at least half a million young children have died in the last twelve months as a result of the slowing down or the reversal of progress in the developing world." Among the reverses cited by the report are a 10 to 25 percent drop in average incomes during the 1980s throughout Africa and in many Latin American countries; a 50 percent reduction in per capita spending on education and a 25 percent reduction in per capita spending on health in the 37 poorest countries in the world; and the falling enrollment of children in primary school throughout the developing world.

Of Bank-sponsored adjustment programs and their predecessor, the lending frenzy of the 1970s, UNICEF declared, "It is hardly too brutal an oversimplification to say that the rich got the loans and the poor got the debts. . . . The fact that so much of today's staggering debt was irresponsibly lent and irresponsibly borrowed would matter less if the consequences of such folly were falling on its perpetrators."

Gradually the Bank began to acknowledge that adjustment does indeed have serious drawbacks. Its 1990 *World Development Report* admitted that "in the short run, some of the poor may lose out." In 1993, Sebastian Edwards, the Bank's chief economist for Latin American and the Caribbean, acknowledged that "in some countries the structural adjustment programs have been excessively costly and have made income distribution worse, although the cost of making no adjustment is also great." A study by Edwards's office found that between 1980 and 1989 in Argentina, Bolivia, Brazil, Mexico, and Panama the proportion of people in poverty (defined by the Bank as having a monthly income of $60 or less) increased, as did the percentage in extreme poverty (defined as having an income of $30 or less). Other Bank studies acknowledged that in many adjusting countries unemployment rose, while primary school enrollment and nutritional levels of the poor both fell. The Bank agreed that "adjustment operations should give greater emphasis to the social costs of adjustment."

Ironically, these findings provided the Bank with a defense against the argument that adjustment loans were mere bribes to induce governments to reform. Precisely because adjustment is so hard on the poor and the middle class, goes the Bank's new rationale, adjustment loans are necessary to enable governments to "increase social sector expenditures targeted toward the poor." Without them, it argued, governments will not be able to "sustain reforms against the opposition of those who are adversely affected." Accordingly, by 1995 the Bank was claiming that "the share of adjustment lending that addresses social issues" was 50 percent, up from 5 percent a decade earlier. Ironically, this is in direct contravention of the intentions of the Bank's founders. They created an institution whose purpose was to lend foreign currency to countries that needed to purchase goods and services abroad. They had insisted that the Bank would not get into the trap of lending foreign currency for domestic expenditures. "It will not be possible for any member to finance his national work or relief programs with money obtained from the Bank," the promotional literature for the Bank had said.

In any case, despite the Bank's recent efforts at mitigation, the social costs of adjustment have stubbornly remained high and its critics have remained bitter. The Bank launched its 1993 World Development Report, which focused on health, in Zimbabwe, a country that has the kind of community-based health-care system the report advocates. When Dr. Timothy Stamp, the national health minister, was called on at the press conference to say a few words, he startled the Bank officials in attendance by declaring, "This book should be called Catch-22. Zimbabwe has carried out virtually all the recommendations and proposals in this report to improve health care and yet, during this period of economic structural adjustment, we are now seeing our health standards drop every year."

In 1996 Bank Vice President Shavid Burki agreed that the Bank's "targeted interventions" and other efforts to minimize the ill-effects of adjustment on the poor had not been successful. "We're saying we have failed," he said. "We need to move in a different way." But, added Burki, "we are not moving away from [the basic adjustment] model," merely seeking new ways to reduce its social cost. The British development charity Oxfam argues that a new model is needed because "simply 'bolting-on' social welfare provisions to Structural Adjustment Programs does not amount to a strategy for reducing poverty, especially when these programmes reinforce its underlying causes."

Even supporters of the Bank's adjustment policies are beginning to wonder whether they may be better suited to more advanced countries than to the poorest ones, which may need *more* state investment in infrastructure and in social programs before they can hope to thrive in the international marketplace without enacting unacceptable human costs. A report prepared for the 1994 meeting of the assemblage of finance ministers known as the World Bank–IMF Development Committee found "little evidence of strong results from adjustment programmes in lower income countries" and recommended "a reconsideration of the link between supporting finance and policy reform" in such countries.

Bank officials remain adamant that, whatever the hardships attached to adjustment, countries must make radical changes in order to forestall economic collapse. They must rid themselves of high inflation, overvalued currency, huge external debts, and massive national deficits. Countries will either subject themselves to an "orderly" adjustment, under its guidance, or be forced into a series of panic measures whose social costs will be far greater than those of adjustment. There is "no evidence that adjustment lending increases the overall misery of the poor," says the Bank. "On the contrary, orderly adjustment, supported by Bank lending, seems to be less costly for most of the poor and for the general populace than disorderly adjustment without Bank support."

––––––––

The aim of adjustment is to bring "about higher, sustainable growth and a consequent reduction in poverty." A country's success in meeting the first goal—higher, sustainable growth—is measured by the growth in its GDP, exports, and domestic investment, and by the fall in its rate of inflation and a reduction of what the Bank calls "excessive external borrowing." Once these conditions are achieved, the Bank believes, a reduction in poverty will naturally follow. Objectives do not, of course, come with road maps showing how to reach them. In the words of *The Economist* magazine, "The Bank and the Fund set out to influence policy, but this does not mean that they do influence it, or that the policies they favor are the right ones."

There is broad general agreement on several points in the many studies of adjustment that have been conducted by the Bank and by independent researchers. It is clear that in most cases adjustment does succeed in increasing exports. It does not, however, appear to reduce inflation or contribute to significant long-term growth of GDP or of investment. In 1992, in fact, the Bank concluded that adjustment is associated with a "statistically significant drop"—not increase—in investment. A few select countries, primarily in Latin America and East Asia, have experienced a dramatic surge in foreign investment. But very little of that was committed for the long term; most was so-called "hot money"—invested in easily divested stocks and short-term bonds. Between 1990 and 1993, for example, the amount of foreign capital in the stock markets of the seven largest Latin American nations increased by 23 times, but as Mexico discovered in 1994, that money can leave as quickly as it came in.

Adjustment has certainly not succeeded in reducing foreign borrowing. Almost all adjusting countries are deeper in debt now than they were before they began adjusting. Between 1980 and 1992, Third World debt more than doubled, from half a trillion dollars to $1.2 trillion. More significantly, in virtually every developing country, external debt was a much greater proportion of GDP in 1992 than it had been in 1980. In Chile it rose from 45 to 49 percent; in Indonesia from 29 to 67 percent; in Mexico from 30 to 35 percent; in Morocco from 53 to 77 percent; in Jamaica from 78 to 153 percent; and in Guyana from 147 to a staggering 768 percent. The only significant decreases occurred in Argentina, Bolivia, and South Korea.

"It is not even clear," according to the independent British study *Aid and Power,* "whether the net return, in terms of growth of gross national product, on the $25 billion which the Bank has so far invested in policy-based lending is positive or negative." *The Economist,* with its usual bluntness, put it more simply: "It isn't working. And the Bank knows it." It remains to be seen, however, whether the Bank will ever lose faith in its creation or whether it will follow the example of its former chief economist, Lawrence Summers, who, when confronted with evidence that adjustment wasn't achieving the desired results, said stoutly, "Well, the theory is right."

# Ten

## WHEN PEOPLE FIND OUT

In 1983, Bruce Rich, a senior attorney for the Environmental Defense Fund, and Patricia Aufderheide, a professor at American University, wrote an article about the World Bank for *Defenders,* a magazine published by the conservation group Defenders of Wildlife. The article drew attention to the environmental and social damage being caused by World Bank projects in the Amazon rainforest and asked readers to write to the Bank and demand that it stop funding such "debacles." A few weeks after the article appeared, Rich heard from an acquaintance at the Bank:

"That goddamn article of yours has caused an uproar over here."

"It has? What do you mean?" Rich couldn't help but be flattered; it was rare for the Bank to take notice of its critics.

"Well, we've been swamped with letters from animal lovers," his informant said.

"Really? How many?" Rich was trying not to sound too pleased.

"At least twelve!"

---

Letter-writing campaigns and other forms of grassroots protest were new to the Bank. For decades it had been able to count on the goodwill of the church-sponsored and humanitarian organizations that worked directly with the poor in the Third World. These nonprofit groups, whose workers spent more time in the field than Bank staffers did, knew as well as anyone that the poor were slipping further and further behind and that many development projects did more harm than good. But they were conscious of the Bank's superior resources and they deferred to it. In the mid-1970s, Patricia Adams, now executive director of the Canadian aid watchdog Probe International, was a volunteer worker in the West Indies for CUSO, Canada's version of the Peace Corps: "I remember . . . the reverence in which the World Bank was held. It had an army of economists, Ph.D.s by the thousands, and a cool-headed quasi-scientific approach to development that few thought—and even fewer dared—to challenge."

At about the same time, environmental groups in America and Europe were beginning to turn their attention to international issues. One of the most gripping was the fate of the world's remaining tropical rainforests. These fragile ecosystems were among the last undeveloped places on earth and the Bank was pouring huge amounts of money into their development—building roads and dams, sponsoring cattle ranches and colonization projects. These efforts had a devastating effect, not just on the forests, but also on the people who had for centuries made their homes there. All over the developing world, native people were being forced off their land and into homelessness and destitution. Environmentalists and campaigners for the rights of indigenous people soon discovered that they had a common cause.

In the 1970s, scientific journals devoted increasing amounts of space to the complex biological life of the tropical forest ecosystem, while, for the most part, ignoring the fact that it was being rapidly destroyed. It was left to local activists to document the destruction of the forest and the effects of that destruction on the poor. This information made its way from a variety of grassroots organizations in Brazil, Indonesia, the Philippines, and other rainforest countries to environmental and human rights groups in North America and Europe. Those groups got the word out as best they could—though newsletters, pamphlets, and slide shows in church basements. "These activists didn't have a history with the Bank," says Patricia Adams. "They weren't in awe of the World Bank, and they sure weren't impressed by what they saw. The Bank was treating Third World people and their environments in ways that would never be tolerated in the industrialized world."

The World Bank was hardly alone in pushing for the modernization of what one of its senior economists called this "undeveloped frontier region." Governments, multinational corporations, other development agencies, and various arms of the United Nations all played their part in the process. But by virtue of its global presence, of the funds at its command, and of the respect in which it was held, the Bank was a dominant force in the assault on the rainforest. It was also the most visible target for critics of that assault. Opposition to the Bank was at the heart of the worldwide network of grassroots activists that emerged in the early 1980s.

These activists introduced a new note into attacks on the Bank—firsthand evidence. They visited Bank project sites and took photographs and collected testimony. They raised money to send people who were affected by Bank projects to Washington to confront the Bank. This changed the nature of debate between the Bank and its critics. As one Bank staffer put it, "It's a lot easier to argue endlessly about policy approaches to energy conservation in the abstract than to find that someone's just returned from Indonesia and has photographs of what you just finished saying couldn't possibly be happening." Richard Webb, formerly an economist at Peru's central bank and the coauthor of an authorized history of the Bank commissioned to mark the institution's fiftieth birthday, predicted that this new brand of critic would "turn the Bank into a real swamp . . . because it involves a new kind of people—religious people, who have no particular respect for traditional forms of quantification and who insist on looking at the long run. They are people who are prepared to place much greater weight on uncertainties than has been the case. So there will be lots of noise, lots of delays."

The Bank did not dignify its critics by directly acknowledging their charges, but references to its high environmental and social standards began to appear more frequently in the speeches of its top executives. In a 1981 lecture, for example, Clausen assured his listeners that the Bank had dedicated itself to protecting the environment and the rights of the people affected by its projects: "As a matter of policy, we won't finance a project that . . . causes severe or irreversible environmental deterioration." To this end, he continued, all Bank projects are "reviewed by a special environmental unit . . . and I'm pleased to say that it has been possible to incorporate protective measures in all the projects we have financed over the past decade."

Indeed, the Bank had created an environmental office in 1970, well before any other development institution had done so. McNamara had proudly informed delegates to the landmark 1972 United Nations Conference on the Environment that the Bank's environmental office conducted "careful in-house studies" on all of its projects and "intensive on-site evaluation[s]" for those with serious problems. Each project was loaded with "safeguards" and designed with an awareness of "not merely physical and health-related factors, but cultural considerations as well."

With the Bank making nearly 150 loans every year, the environment office's task must have been a daunting one—the more so in view of the fact that until 1978, the office consisted in its entirety of Dr. James Lee, a veterinarian with experience in wildlife conservation. Lee's mandate was to "make sure that every project was looked at in terms of the impact it would have on the environment and on health" and to ensure that projects involving resettlement were well managed. He was, in short, the Bank's environmental and human rights watchdog, but one with a bark and no bite. Lee's job was all responsibility and no power. He had to rely on persuasion if he wanted colleagues to change a project—and few were eager to be persuaded. In an oral history recorded in 1993, Visvanathan Rajagopalan, who had been Lee's supervisor, said, "We used to think that Jim Lee was a bloody nuisance. He was someone who had to be tolerated because the President has put him there, but he was not taken too seriously."

In 1970, when Lee arrived at the Bank, he found that its library had no information on the environment or on health. "My file cabinet became the Bank's environmental library," he later recalled. Lee concerned himself primarily with the health effects of industrial pollution, rather than with the environmental aspects of the Bank's lending. It was, in fact, an outsider, Prince Bernhard of the Netherlands, who was behind the first revision of a Bank project for environmental reasons. At Bernhard's request, the Bank rerouted an electrical transmission line so that it would not cut through Tanzania's Mikuni National Game Park.

Not until 1978 did the Bank hire its first professionally trained ecologist, Robert Goodland, a specialist in tropical ecology and environment assessment. Goodland was supposed to review each of the nearly 250 loans the Bank was by then making each year and to conduct more detailed analyses of the one-third or so that were likely to have a significant social or environmental impact. By 1984 the environmental staff had grown to five, including one sociologist, but Goodland was still the only trained ecologist among the Bank's 5,700 employees. The Bank had an impressive set of environmental guidelines, running to several volumes, but they dealt only with problems of industrial pollution. They contained no advice on how to avoid environmental or social damage from the Bank's most common projects—agriculture, irrigation, dams, and roads. In any case, the guidelines were suggestions, not commands—and few staffers even knew they existed.

In 1983, after several years spent gathering information, a coalition of American environmental groups decided to take their case against the Bank to Congress. Representative Jerry Patterson of California, head of the House Subcommittee on International Development Institutions and Finance, agreed to hold hearings on the impact of Bank-funded projects on the environment. On two days in late June, a parade of environmentalists, anthropologists, and indigenous rights activists presented the subcommittee with evidence that many Bank projects were harming the environment *and* the poor.

Critics cited scores of Bank projects: some that had required the forcible relocation of tens of thousands of people; some that had seriously damaged local fisheries and local livelihoods; some that promoted the use of chemicals, such as DDT, banned elsewhere in the world; some whose disruption of the ecological balance was so severe that it resulted in the spread of dangerous diseases; some that caused severe deforestation and irreversible soil damage; some that displaced poor people on behalf of large mining, logging, ranching, or farming companies; and a few that accomplished all of the above.

Although taken aback by the testimony they had heard, most of the committee members did not believe that the Bank's overall impact was as harmful as its critics claimed. They asked the Bank to respond, which it did in a forty-eight-page document. At the heart of the Bank's defense was the argument that it was unfair to point to its past mistakes, because it is constantly learning from experience. "The statements [of critics]," it said, "may create the misleading impression that past trends continue." This was to become an enduring theme in the Bank's self-analysis; it should not be criticized for past failures, because it has learned from them and moved on.

The Bank conceded that some of the projects it funded had high environmental and social costs, but it argued that the damage would have been worse without its participation. "Attention should be paid to the human and ecological costs of *not* going ahead with projects," it warned darkly. This is another of the Bank's key beliefs: However bad a Bank-funded project might be, it would be worse without the Bank's influence. "What they're really saying," one Treasury official remarked to Bruce Rich, "is that there is no project so costly, and so disastrous, that the Bank won't throw hundreds of millions of dollars into it to try to make it better."

In its response to Congress, the Bank also asserted that "every project proposed for financing comes to the attention of OEA [the Office for Environmental Affairs] early in the project cycle . . . to ensure that the environmental effects of the project are avoided or kept to a minimum." But this assertion was false, as the Bank's top officials privately admitted during a meeting of the Bank's Operational Policy Subcommittee two months later. A memo of the closed meeting, which was chaired by senior Vice President Ernest Stern and attended by four other vice presidents, several top managers, and the head of the Environmental Office, states that "as a matter of routine, environmental issues are not considered, but . . . they are taken into account in specific instances when environmental consequences are pointed out by the Bank's environmental adviser, the press, or special interest groups in host countries."

The Bank did make a few changes in response to the concerns aroused by the public airing of its environmental and social record. In 1984, for example, it amended its operations manual to state that it would "not finance projects that cause severe or irreversible environmental deterioration, including species extinctions, without mitigatory measures acceptable to the Bank" and would "not finance projects that displace people." But it failed to live up to its new high standards and it demonstrated again and again in its daily actions the conviction that its critics were shortsighted and misinformed. "The Bank slammed the door in our faces," said Patricia Adams. "Then it opened it to tell us why we were wrong."

In the spring of 1984, Clausen gave an audience to a small group of environmentalists—a rare occurrence. He wanted to dissuade them from lobbying against the Bank's pending request to Congress for an increase in its contribution to the International Development Association, the soft-loan arm of the Bank. According to Rich, who attended the meeting, Clausen argued that making an issue of protecting the environment would have a devastating effect on the poor. "Don't hold IDA hostage to the environment," he said. "Think about poor people." "We *were* thinking about poor people," says Brent Blackwelder, president of Friends of the Earth, who was also at the meeting. "It was the poor, the people on the ground, who brought these problems to our attention." The Bank still tends to equate criticism of its policies with callous indifference to poverty. In response to charges that it invests too much in expensive new sources of thermal power and hydropower and not enough in renewable sources of energy, in energy efficiency, or in energy conservation, the Bank in 1994 issued a statement accusing its critics of "implying that the developing world will have to make do with dung for cooking and their feet and bicycle rickshaws for transport. Such insensitivity to the economic plight of millions of people in the developing world is appalling."

In refusing to hear its critics, the Bank drove others—in and out of Congress—to listen to them perhaps more closely than they otherwise would have. One of those who took up the critics' cause was Senator Robert Kasten, a right-wing Republican from Wisconsin. As head of the Senate subcommittee responsible for appropriations to the World Bank, Kasten was an important—if unlikely—ally for environmentalists. Other powerful members of Congress also took up the issue. Notable among them was Congressman David Obey, a Democrat from Wisconsin and chairman of the House subcommittee in charge of World Bank appropriations. During the mid-1980s, Congress held at least twenty hearings on the environmental and social impact of Bank projects. The record of abuses and errors created by these hearings—and the Bank's stubborn insistence that it had matters under control—convinced many that there was something terribly wrong with the World Bank.

James Conrow, head of the U.S. Treasury Department's Office of Multilateral Development Banks, defended the Bank's environmental record before Patterson's subcommittee in the summer of 1983. The following year, however, he returned to say, "In appearing before you in June 1983, I could honestly say that I was unaware of particular problems." But in following up on the testimony presented, he "found substantial corroboration of the information presented by most of the witnesses." The effect of revelations on conservative Senator Kasten was even stronger, driving 1986 to say to a British documentary filmmaker: "When people find at's been going on, you're going to see people out in the streets 'My God, did you read this information? Why are our dollars being used to fund this kind of destruction?' "

Even a few of the Bank's executive directors (EDs) had begun to ask that question. In June of 1986, the U.S. ED, Hugh Foster, cited environmental considerations in voting against a proposed $500 million loan to develop Brazil's power sector. Brazil planned to use part of the loan to finance the completion of several large and controversial dams, including one the Bank itself had termed "the notorious Balbina dam." The Bank had refused to fund Balbina directly because it was so badly planned. It was to flood more than 600 square miles of rainforest—including an Indian reservation that was home to 2,000 people—in order to produce a mere 125 megawatts of power. The Indians had not been consulted, nor had the government any plans to relocate them.

Critics claimed that by making a general loan to Brazil's power sector instead of separate loans for each project, the Bank was attempting to bypass responsibility for the individual projects on which the loan money would be spent because it knew that they would violate the Bank's environmental and social standards. The Bank insisted that Brazil had promised not to spend the loan on any controversial projects, but, as Foster pointed out, once the funds were disbursed, Brazil could spend them on whatever it wished.

Despite Foster's opposition, the loan was approved—and in due course Balbina was completed. Subsequently, however, engineers discovered that, due to an unfortunate error in mapping, the 600-square-mile reservoir did not hold enough water to turn the turbines. The dam was useless. According to Jason Kelman, the president of the Brazilian Association of Water Resources, "Everybody in the country agrees that it was a stupid mistake to build Balbina." To cover its embarrassment, the state power company hurriedly came up with a new plan: to raise water levels by damming another river and diverting it into the Balbina reservoir, putting another Indian reservation under water.

Still, Foster's lone vote against the Brazil Power Sector loan was the first time in the Bank's history that there had been a vote against a project on environmental grounds. This tiny revolt sent a shockwave through the Bank—and thrilled environmentalists, who began, prematurely, to dream of victory.

———

It was not Balbina, however, but another Brazilian project—the Northwest Region Integrated Development Program, or Polonoroeste—that dealt the most severe blow to the Bank's reputation for honesty and competence. Beginning in 1981, the Bank lent more than half a billion dollars for this massive highway-building and colonization project covering 150,000 square miles of the Amazon. From its inception, Polonoroeste had many critics—in Brazil and outside. They predicted that there would be violent clashes between colonists and the Indians whose land they would clear, and warned that much of the soil would be unsuitable for farming. The Bank took these concerns seriously enough to make its loans conditional on Brazil's implementing an impressive array of measures designed to protect the environment and the rights of the indigenous people. The measures included the establishment of fifteen Indian reserves with health facilities, two biological reserves, four research stations, and a national park. In addition, there would be no settlement on soils that were unsuitable or of unknown quality. Thanks to its influence, the Bank boasted, Polonoroeste was a model of ecological and social planning.

By 1984, reports from the project region indicated that matters were not proceeding in line with the Bank's plans. Hundreds of thousands of eager settlers had poured into the area, many attracted by a government-sponsored ad campaign, only to find that the schools, health clinics, water wells, and other promised services were not in place. After clearing thousands of square miles of forest with axes and fire, the colonists had discovered that the soils were unsuitable for farming. They moved on, clearing more forest and then abandoning it, and then clearing more, so that in just a few years 50,000 square miles, an area roughly the size of the state of Wisconsin, had been devastated.

NASA called the burned forest, which was visible from space, the largest man-made change to the earth's surface. Meanwhile, the indigenous population was being pushed off its land by colonization and killed by newly introduced diseases; the Catholic church estimated that by the end of the decade 85 percent of the region's native people had died through violence or disease. The ecological breakdown also resulted in an epidemic of malaria, which by 1984 was infecting 150,000 people in the project area every year—and spreading from there to the rest of the country. (By 1988, the infection rate had nearly doubled; the following year the Bank lent Brazil $99 million so that it could spray the project area with 3,000 tons of DDT.)

In September 1984, the House Subcommittee on Natural Resources, Agricultural Research, and the Environment held a special hearing on Polonoroeste. One of the witnesses was agronomist Jose Lutzenberger, later to be Brazil's minister of the environment, but at that time a mere thorn in the flesh of its military government. Lutzenberger told Congress that Polonoroeste was "designed as a safety valve for the political and social pressures" caused by the large numbers of farmers who had recently lost their land in the fertile south of Brazil to powerful agricultural interests. He blamed the Brazilian government and the World Bank for promoting a shift in that rich region from small-scale peasant agriculture to "only cash crops, monoculture for export. . . . There is in fact no shortage of land in the South except the shortages caused by the concentrations of land holdings. The Polonoroeste project is a method of decreasing the risks and increasing the security of the large landowners."

The Bank, however, was staunch in its defense of the project, assuring Congress that Polonoroeste is "an opportunity to develop sustainable agriculture" in areas with "relatively better soils." And once again, it presented the Bank as a force for restraint, arguing that its involvement was necessary in order to prevent "the unavoidable alternative [which] is to expose the region to continued shifting cultivation and land degradation."

In October 1984, shortly after the congressional hearings, Bruce Rich and Steve Schwartzman, a University of Chicago anthropologist, sent the Bank extensive evidence that Brazil had violated the conditions of its loan agreement. Their dossier was accompanied by a letter signed by thirty-two representatives of citizen groups in eleven countries asking the Bank to cease disbursements on Polonoroeste until Brazil complied with the conditions of the loans. The Bank responded with a brief and condescending note: "Polonoroeste is a carefully planned regional development program, which seeks to stabilize and maximize the economic development of the regions, while minimizing the risks to the regional ecology and Amerindian population. . . . You can be sure that the Bank is continuing to monitor the situation closely, and that your concerns will be considered as Polonoroeste continues."

The Bank's cool confidence about Polonoroeste was all for show. Things were more complicated inside the institution. Some years later, Rich obtained a series of unpublished memos, dating from the time when the Bank's technical staff was appraising the project before presenting it to the board, that summarize the Polonoroeste story.

January 8, 1980, Lee to Rajagopalan: "To use unproven technologies as a basis for agricultural settlement under extremely adverse soil conditions would be a highly risky undertaking and would prove disastrous for the settlers themselves."

February 25, 1980, J. C. Collins, Bank agricultural specialist, to Robert Goodland: The environmental protection measures "in no way will . . . offset the possible harmful effects of project—deforestation, particularly of lands unsuitable for sustained agriculture, use of unsustainable agricultural production systems and the invasion of tribal reservations."

May 20, 1980, Lee and D. C. Pickering, an agriculture specialist in the Bank's Brazil department, to Dennis Mahar, senior Bank economist in charge of Polonoroeste: "Certainly there would seem to be better opportunities to increase agricultural productivity elsewhere, but there is no consideration of such alternatives in the report."

July 9, 1980, J. C. Collins to Dennis Mahar: "The tone of overall optimism does not seem warranted."

November 19, 1980, Lee and Pickering to Mahar, Rajagopalan, and Brazil division head Robert Skillings: "The total milieu in which this development is being undertaken is hardly promising of success."

December 19, 1980, James Lee, memo to files re phone conversation with Skillings: "[He] went on to state that the World Bank was above all else an economic development institution and should not align itself with or 'take up' a cause such as the one under consideration [protection of indigenous peoples' rights]."

June 9, 1981, Lee to Vice President Warren Baum via Rajagopalan: Lee asks Baum to insist on stronger measures to protect Indians and the environment. The memo was returned to Lee later that day, with a scribbled note from Rajagopalan: "Mr. Baum does not want these details to be discussed at the Vice-President's level."

On December 1, 1981, the board of directors unanimously approved three loans to Polonoroeste, for a total of $320 million. The directors knew nothing of these staff memos or the problems they highlighted. Instead, as the board minutes note, "Several [directors] congratulated the Bank staff and Brazilian authorities for their conception and design. . . . Most of the speakers who supported the projects pointed to their truly integrated nature and the comprehensive approach to development they represented: they also cited the balance among infrastructure, agriculture, health and even ecology and Amerindian welfare."

In March 1982 the board approved $26 million for a new phase of the program, Polonoroeste II. Behind the scenes, however, the project was still falling far short of Bank standards. In March 1983, the Bank sent a telex to Brazil's minister of interior complaining that "little progress has been made in demarcating Amerindian reserves [in the project area]." Despite the continuing problems, the Bank approved yet another Polonoroeste loan in October 1983—$65 million to encourage more colonization in the region. The Bank's press release about this loan emphasized that it would be disbursed as quickly as possible—not withheld until the loan conditions were met—"as part of the World Bank's Special Action Program . . . to help developing countries maintain economic momentum in the face of the current international economic crisis." Two months later, the Bank put another $23 million into the project.

In January 1985, Senator Kasten wrote a letter to Clausen, chiding him for his failure to respond to the issues raised in the letter written to him about Polonoroeste some three months earlier. "As you know better than anyone else, securing support for U.S. contributions to multilateral development institutions is difficult at best," he wrote. "The questions and concerns raised in the [environmentalists'] . . . letter are legitimate and deserve a credible and responsive answer. I, therefore, put these questions and concerns to you and ask that you respond to me as Chairman of the Foreign Operations Appropriations Subcommittee."

Kasten's letter, the congressional hearings the previous autumn, mounting public criticism of the Bank's role in the project, and the growing scale of the disaster in the project area itself, forced the Bank, in March 1985, to halt disbursement of its Polonoroeste loans until emergency measures to protect the environment and Indian lands were carried out. This was the first time that the Bank had halted disbursements on a loan for environmental reasons. In August, however, the Bank declared that the situation had improved and that it would resume disbursements.

In the spring of 1987—after all the loans had been paid out—the Bank publicly acknowledged that Polonoroeste was plagued with problems and apologized for having that "misread the human, institutional and physical realities of the frontier." In 1990 the Bank's Operations Evaluation Department undertook a review of Polonoroeste. "It is evident," states the unpublished report, "that Polonoroeste contributed both directly and indirectly to the acceleration of environmental degradation in Northwest Brazil." Moreover, it said, the project "benefitted land speculators and ranchers, together with high value mining, prospecting and logging ventures, as much as, if not more than, its intended small-farmer target population."

The report attributed the program's failure partly to "the distorting influence of powerful economic and political interests behind the program or which subsequently benefited from it, together with the Bank's failure to adequately anticipate the potential impact of these influences." It faulted the Bank for not having "suspended disbursements at a considerably earlier date." The study also refuted the Bank's oft-repeated claim that its involvement made a bad project better. "In the absence of the Bank's support, which provided legitimacy—as well as financial resources—to the program. . . . the hordes of migrants which arrived in Rondonia during the early and mid-1980s would probably not have materialized as quickly or in such large numbers as they did."

Also in 1990, however, the Bank discovered a silver lining in the Polonoroeste disaster. In its first annual report on the environment, it boasted that "Polonoroeste . . . has fostered a growing political and public commitment to preserve the Amazon's remaining natural resources." A smaller and less spectacular debacle might not have achieved that.

# Eleven

In June 1986, Clausen returned to his old post at the Bank of America. During his five years at the World Bank, he had made $10 billion worth of adjustment loans to thirty-eight countries and turned the Bank into an impresario for what Ronald Reagan, addressing the board of governors in 1983, had called "the magic of the marketplace." But Clausen's lack of political finesse was a burden the Bank could not bear. His hard-line adherence to supply-side economics and his belief that environmental concern was a luxury only the rich could afford had aroused anger in the borrowing ........ and mobilized critics in the rich countries.

To succeed Clausen, President Reagan turned to Barber Conable, a long-serving and popular Republican congressman from western New York. Conable was chosen largely for his understanding of the workings of the U.S. Congress. His assignment was to convince his former colleagues that the Bank was reforming itself and that it deserved continued funding by the American taxpayer. He was also expected to improve the Bank's public image, which, in a remarkably short time, had become that of an enemy of the poor. To this end he publicly acknowledged the validity of many of the criticisms about the social impacts of adjustment lending. He dismissed the hard-liners in the Research Department, and declared that the Bank would learn from its mistakes.

Conable had no argument with the Bank's basic operating premise, that the Bank's mission was to foster growth and "that market forces and economic efficiency [are] the best way to achieve . . . growth." He believed, however, that the Bank needed a thorough shakeout, and one of his first tasks was to institute a massive reorganization. According to Eugene Rotberg, the Bank's treasurer, the reorganization was intended to "dampen the criticism from the U.S. Treasury that the Bank was inefficient" and to "move Ernie off to the side somewhere." "Ernie" was Ernest Stern, the economist who had been the de facto power in the Bank since McNamara's retirement. Stern was a Dutch Jew who had sought refuge from the Holocaust in the United States. He came to the Bank in 1971 after a spell at the U.S. Agency for International Development. He was tough, forceful, and very smart, and he rose swiftly in the Bank. His power derived from his mastery of the institution's internal workings, something Clausen had never acquired. Under Clausen, Stern's title had been vice president for operations, but by all accounts his real job was running the Bank.

Conable wanted to cut the staff of six thousand by 10 percent. He began by asking every employee to resign and apply to be rehired. Working from the top, he then appointed four vice presidents: Moeen Qureshi from Pakistan for operations; David Hopper from Canada for policy, planning, and research; Willi Wapenhans from the Netherlands for administration; and Ernest Stern for finance. Stern's inclusion was something of a climbdown for Conable, but as Rotberg put it, "Conable realized that Ernie had more friends at the Bank than he had, and that he wasn't about to move Ernie out. . . . I think he realized that he needed Ernie." Each of the four vice presidents then chose their subordinates, who did the same, and so on down the managerial line, creating what one observer termed "a Christmas tree of yes-men."

Indeed, Conable's reorganization fostered a rampant cronyism in the Bank. One sure way to survive the cutbacks was to attach oneself to a powerful patron, and the patronage system produced some strange appointments. Shahid Javid Burki, a countryman and protégé of Moeen Qureshi, was made director of the important China department, though he had no experience running a country department and spoke no Chinese. He in turn passed over more qualified applicants to select as his top aide someone who shared his tribal origins, but had no experience of China. Responsibility for Brazil, one of the Bank's largest borrowers, was given to Armeane Choksi, a Stern loyalist who spoke no Portuguese. Many of the subordinates Choksi appointed were notable more for their long-term connections with him than for their knowledge of Brazil.

It is no overstatement to say that the reorganization put the staff in an uproar for months. Consideration of loans took second place to interoffice intrigue, counterplots, resentment, and depression. "The day-to-day task of financing development [came] to a halt," reported the magazine *Institutional Investor*. "For five months the familiar shuffle of loan documents was replaced by muted whispers at the water cooler. Poisonous, hurtful memos poured from the pens of executive directors and staffers alike." The *Financial Times* declared, "The Bank has become riddled with faction and distrust."

Observers judged the gentlemanly Conable to be "hardly a match for the Bank's wily, politically attuned bureaucrats." His efforts to free the Bank from the grip of powerful long-time managers failed. He was forced to rely on the very insiders he wanted to control, conceding that "the average congressman doesn't understand the World Bank, and I was the average congressman." He was, commented the *Financial Times*, "a 'hands-off' leader who does not quite know where to lead." Many of the best and most experienced Bank officials took the generous severance package and left—more in anger than in sadness. One of those was Eugene Rotberg, who said, "What they call bureaucracy, I call care and prudence." Rotberg went to Wall Street, but many of those who left were later rehired by the Bank as consultants, at significantly higher wages. The reduction in staff was short-lived: Within four years of the reorganization, the workforce was back up to six thousand.

------

Parallel with the main reorganization, Conable expanded and restructured the Bank's tiny environment office. He created a central environment department to conduct research and draw up environmental policies and guidelines for the rest of the Bank, and he put satellite environmental divisions into each of the Bank's six regional lending departments. The regional divisions were supposed to review each loan proposal, conduct closer investigations of those likely to have important social or environmental impacts, oversee remedial work on problem projects from the past, and monitor scores of ongoing projects.

Conable's purpose in putting environmental divisions into the regional lending departments was to put environmental thinking into the heart of the Bank's operations, but one result was a loss of independence for the Bank's environmentalists. They are now subordinate to managers whose main concern is getting loans through, not getting them right. The environment divisions have neither the budget nor the authority to visit project sites. For that they need the permission of the project manager, and as one environment staffer said, "If you're a hard-liner, you don't get invited to go; if you're soft, you're asked back time after time."

The character of the environment department changed radically as it grew. For nearly ten years, Robert Goodland had been the Bank's sole ecologist and its environmental conscience. He was greatly admired outside the Bank and largely ignored within it. He stood up against the Bank's worst projects, to little avail, and he devoted much time to developing enlightened policies that few of his colleagues thought they would ever be expected to follow. As his worldwide reputation grew, and the policies he had pushed through came back to haunt the Bank, he progressed in the eyes of his superiors from a nonentity to a nuisance to a threat.

As the department expanded, Goodland's distinctive voice was gradually drowned out. Most of the new voices belonged not to ecologists or sociologists, but to economists who had been reassigned from other positions at the Bank. The environmental department was built up, said one staffer, "by a recycling program that turned superfluous economists into environmental economists." One of the new senior environmental officials, Thomas Blinkhorn, came from the Bank's public relations department, for example. Blinkhorn, who was put in charge of the environmental aspects of the Narmada project, was described by a long-serving staffer as "the World Bank's strongest anti-environmentalist." By 1991, the environmental staff numbered 140, of which only six were trained ecologists. Visvanathan Rajagopalan, the vice president responsible for the department, complained about "the absence of skills" among its staffers and tried in vain to bring "people who had specialized in the sciences" into the department. Rajagopalan was himself a water engineer, not an ecologist.

In 1992 Andrew Steer—a conventional economist with no environmental credentials—was made deputy director of the Bank's Environment Department. Two years later he was promoted to director. Under Steer, says one staffer, the department "has gone totally technocratic. It's full of self-important greenies who think the key to being loved is to translate everything into economic terms. Their interest in local communities is purely rhetorical." Steer is not popular among the more pro-environment members of his staff, who see him as a sort of warden whose job is to keep things quiet in the department. "Steer has a long track record of being anti-environment," complained one official. "They know we're rocking the boat, but instead of saying maybe we've got a point, they put someone on top of us to suppress us.

In 1989, the Bank committed itself, for the first time, to conduct environmental-impact assessments for all loans likely to have a significant impact on the environment. About 10 percent of loans, those the Bank considers likely to cause major environmental disruption, receive a full environmental impact assessment. Another 35 percent, those likely to have only a minor impact, receive a limited assessment. More than half of all Bank loans, however—including all adjustment loans—are considered unlikely to have any impact—and thus receive no assessment.

Unlike his predecessor, Conable had a genuine concern for the environment. He also understood its importance as a political issue. In contrast to Clausen's foot dragging on the matter, Conable declared that environmental protection went hand in hand with development and that environmental degradation canceled out the Bank's development efforts. "Sound ecology is good economics," he said. He pledged the Bank to demonstrating "greater sensitivity to the long-term environmental effects" of Bank-funded projects, to listen to the concerns of nongovernmental organizations (NGOs), and to begin funding projects whose main purpose was to protect or improve the environment. Conable's pledges and his reputation for integrity convinced many erstwhile critics that the Bank really was turning over a new leaf.

As one sign of the Bank's new committment to the environment, Conable pledged to quadruple the Bank's lending for forestry, which, as one of his staff later said, "he thought synonomous with environment." For most of the Bank's history, its forestry loans had been notably anti-environment—devoted almost exclusively to logging equipment, sawmills, and papermills. In 1978, however, the Bank had announced that in the future it would pay more attention to "afforestation and raising incomes and productivity of poor farmers" and to "the ecological considerations of projects." After 1978, the Bank continued to promote industrial forestry, logging, and the export of tropical hardwoods—indeed, by 1990 its average annual investment in such projects had risen from $10 million to $75 million. As its 1978 policy paper declared, "The developing countries contain the world's main reserves of tropical hardwood . . . [and] the extraction of this resource provides valuable foreign exchange." But after 1979, more than half the Bank's forestry lending was for afforestation and what it terms "social forestry." Social forestry projects are intended to establish community-managed plantations to meet local needs for fuel wood, fodder, small timber, and minor forest products.

Instead of bringing the Bank praise, however, these projects provoked heated protests from affected villagers. The plantations created were owned and managed not by the local communities they were supposed to serve but by the wealthy farmers on whose land they were established or by government forestry departments that created plantations on communal lands and then kept those lands under tight control. Peasants, used to gathering fuel wood and fodder free from local forests, could not afford the prices charged for this new supply, so timber merchants and pulp mills became the main customers. To satisfy their demands, fast-growing exotics, such as eucalyptus, were planted. Eucalyptus produces straight trunks with few branches and leaves that are unpalatable to cattle—good qualities in a timber tree, but not when fodder and fuel wood are wanted. Moreover, the plantations were monocultures, not forests, so they did not support wildlife or provide the variety of resources—nuts, thatch, different types of timber, basket-making materials—on which peasant communities depend. Critics charged that the major beneficiaries of the Bank's social forestry projects were the rich, not the poor. Even the Bank conceded that its own "audits and [project] completion reports have cast doubts . . . about how much these projects have benefited the poorest of the poor." Moreover, despite the Bank's emphasis on making the projects pay their way, an internal review found that "these projects are beset with financial problems."

In India, which was the main recipient of the Bank's social forestry funds, hostility to the projects was intense. The damage poor farmers suffered through having their communal lands taken over by plantations of trees they could not use moved many to public protests and demonstrations. In August 1983, in one of several such actions, villagers in the Indian state of Karnataka marched on a project site, ripped out all the eucalpytus seedlings, and replaced them with tamarind seedlings. When they were arrested, so many other villagers swarmed into the fray, demanding to be arrested also, that the police retreated.

Soon after taking office, Conable ordered the Bank to adopt a new approach to forestry, and in 1987, it endorsed the Tropical Forestry Action Plan (TFAP), a "global program to support tropical forest conservation." TFAP was sponsored jointly by the Bank, several UN agencies, the Rockefeller Foundation, and the World Resources Institute, a Washington-based think tank. Drawn up with the help of timber industry executives, it blamed deforestation largely on poor farmers. It envisioned spending more than $1.5 billion a year—to be contributed by rich countries and international aid agencies—logging tropical rainforests, creating plantations, and teaching peasants better ways of farming on forest soils.

In order to get some of the promised TFAP millions, countries had to draw up "national forest plans." Most were far from conservationist documents. Cameroon's plan, for example, prepared in 1989 with funding from the World Bank and the United Nations, recommended that the country commit itself to becoming Africa's biggest timber exporter by the year 2000. It called for the logging of 30 million acres of intact rainforest, the construction of a 360-mile highway through the forest, and the establishment of tax incentives and subsidies to encourage loggers.

In short order, conservation and indigenous rights groups all over the world were up in arms about TFAP. They were angry that it ignored the involvement of large-scale development and big ranching, mining, agribusiness, and timber companies in deforestation; angry that no one who lived in or near a rainforest was consulted in drawing up the plan; and angry that the plan would consume every penny available for tropical forestry projects worldwide. The final ignominy for TFAP came in 1990, when even the leaders of the world's top seven industrialized countries, hardly radical environmentalists, singled it out for criticism at their summit meeting in Houston, Texas. The Bank quietly backed away from TFAP, but it continued with the forestry projects to which the plan had given birth.

One of these was the $8 million Guinea Forestry Management Project, which the Bank described as a plan to protect the last remaining rainforest in the West African nation of Guinea. The project called for the construction of 45 miles of roads and logging of about two-thirds of the forest. Environmentalists called the project a *de*forestation scheme. In late 1989, however, the Bank's executive directors unanimously approved it.

The Bank later disavowed many of the original aspects of the Guinea Forestry project. In 1991, the official in charge of the project assured NGOs "that the Staff Appraisal Report [the key project document] was outdated and no longer served as the basis of the project, which had shifted its focus entirely to forest protection." But a report by representatives of the Environmental Defense Fund, the German Rainforest Campaign, and a Guinean group, the Association of Friends of Nature and the Environment, who visited the project site in late 1991, found no such change of heart reflected in the way the project was being managed. A key project official told them "that he was following the SAR to the letter" and "the [project] coordinator . . . described it as 'his bible.' " In 1996, the Bank prepared a $13 million follow-up loan.

In 1990, the Bank made an even bigger forestry loan—$80 million to the Ivory Coast. This loan also had its genesis in TFAP. Environmental

groups gave members of the board copies of secret Bank documents re-
vealing that the project would force at least 40,000 and as many as
200,000 people to move, making it one of the largest dislocations ever
financed by the Bank in Africa. Alarmed, U.S. Executive Director Patrick
Coady asked Bank staff for more information about the loan. The staff
refused to provide him with any of the project documents, but management
finally agreed to conduct a briefing for interested EDs. With Coady casting
the lone "no" vote, the project was approved, even though—in violation of
Bank policy—there was no resettlement plan.

Although his was a lone voice against the Ivory Coast loan, Coady did
persuade his fellow directors to demand that the Bank develop yet another
new forestry policy. That policy, formally adopted in 1991, promised a
"special emphasis on expanded public participation" and greater consideration of "the needs and welfare of forest-dwelling people," and stated that
"the Bank does not—under any circumstances—finance commercial logging in primary tropical moist forests." The Bank held up this self-imposed
ban as proof of its concern for the environment, but the institution really
had no choice. Its Articles of Agreement allow it to lend only "when private capital is not available on reasonable terms" and, in the Bank's words,
"logging is one aspect of the [forestry] sector which is sufficiently profitable
to attract capital on a strictly commercial basis."

Under Conable, the Bank became more aggressive in "advertising" its environmental activities. In 1989, it began categorizing as "primarily environmental" those projects in which the costs of environmental protection
measures or the benefits to the environment make up at least half the total
costs or benefits. Projects for which that figure is greater than 10 percent
are said to have a "significant environmental component." In 1991, Conable's last year, the Bank made fourteen "primarily environmental" loans.

In its literature, the Bank often refers to these "primarily environmental" projects simply as "environmental projects," a term that is in many
cases misleading. Most of the projects that merit that description are aimed
at pollution control. In that category, the Bank has financed the establishment of a government agency to oversee water quality in the Brazilian city
of São Paulo; disposal facilities at several Chinese ports for ships' wastes
that would otherwise be dumped at sea; a sewage treatment system in
Ankara, Turkey; and industrial pollution control programs in several Indian states. In addition, the Bank is a participant in several multiagency

programs to reduce pollution and reverse biological decline in regional seas and river basins, among them the Mediterranean, Black, Baltic, Aral, and Caspian seas, the Danube River basin, and Lake Victoria.

The Bank's attempts at protecting the natural environment have been far more controversial. The notorious Guinea Forestry Management Project is classed as an environmental project, as is the $80 million forestry sector loan to the Ivory Coast. Other "environmental projects" that do not deserve the title include a $20 million loan to Pakistan to increase agricultural production in the Punjab by replacing 1,300 government-owned tubewells with 13,000 smaller privately owned ones; a $59 million project to replace productive mangrove forests in Ecuador's Gulf of Guayaquil with shrimp farms; a $72 million loan to Malaysia that will finance expansion of a government-sponsored colonization program in a forested region of Borneo; and a $42 million loan to Belarus designed to increase logging and boost timber exports.

Many of the Bank's environmental projects are intended to mitigate the negative consequences of earlier Bank loans. Critics say that often the follow-up projects are no improvement on the original ones. The $167 million Rondonia Natural Resources Management Project, known in Brazil as Planoflora, for example, was supposed to undo the damage done by the disastrous Polonoroeste Project—into which the Bank put half a billion dollars. Among other things, Planoflora was to finance four biological preserves and eight Indian reserves that were supposed to have been, but never were, demarcated and protected under the first Polonoroeste loan in 1981.

The most innovative aspect of Planoflora was to be its establishment of so-called "extractive reserves," legally protected, communally managed land dedicated to sustainable harvesting of about thirty products of the forest, from rubber to nuts to fruit. Chico Mendes, the charismatic leader of the Union of Amazonian Rubber Tappers, promoted extractive reserves as a way to support local communities and protect the rainforest, but Mendes was no fan of Planoflora. In October 1988, shortly before his assassination by cattle ranchers, he wrote a letter to Conable warning that "the extractive reserves included in [Planoflora] only serve to lend the governmental proposal to the World Bank an ecological tone, so much in fashion lately, in order to secure this huge loan. . . . What will be created are not extractive reserves, but colonization settlements with the same errors that led Polonoroeste I to the current disaster."

Soon after Mendes's death, Brazil abolished the Urueuwauwau Indian reserve, the largest in the state of Rondonia. Over the next few years, a coalition of Brazilian NGOs bombarded the management and board of the

World Bank with information about the Brazilian government's having sponsored cattle ranching, road building, and colonization in many of the areas it had agreed to set aside as extractive reserves, Indian reservations, or biological sanctuaries. The NGOs also alerted the Bank to many instances in which the project violated its own policies on forestry, wildlife, public participation, and indigenous communities. Eventually, at the Bank's insistence, Brazil re-established the Urueuwauwau reserve, but the Bank ignored the request of Brazil's environment minister, Jose Lutzenberger, that it postpone consideration of the loan because there had been no consultations with local people. On March 17, 1992, Planoflora was formally approved and became one of the nineteen "environmental projects" the Bank funded that year.

---

In 1989 France and Germany told Bank officials that they were willing to make large contributions to a "green fund" that would make grants to help poor countries tackle environmental p̶ lems whose causes transcend national borders, such as loss of b̶⋯ and global warming. They asked the Bank to suggest ho⋯ ⋯ight operate. The finance department, under Ernes⋯ ⋯e idea with enthusiasm. Working quickly and in secrecy—co⋯ ⋯ther the public nor the Bank's own environment department—a task ⋯ took less than four months to come up with a plan for the new fund: It would be administered by the World Bank with technical assistance from two UN agencies, the Development Program and the Environment Program. The Bank would prepare and execute most of the projects. Grants of less than $10 million could be approved by a group of senior Bank managers without reference to the board. Grants of more than $10 million would be linked to an ordinary World Bank loan and would need the approval of the Bank's board of directors. Private companies, as well as governments, could initiate projects.

In November 1990, twenty-eight governments (including twelve Bank borrowers) committed $1.2 billion to a three-year pilot program called the Global Environmental Facility (GEF). The fund was to focus on four areas: limiting emissions of greenhouse gases, protecting the ozone layer, preserving biodiversity, and protecting international waters. During its three-year pilot phase, the GEF authorized $730 million worth of grants to 115 projects. These included $7.8 million to 29 countries for national biological surveys; $11 million to build a privately managed power station to be fueled by methane gas from a garbage dump near Lahore in Pakistan; $3 million for the construction of a wind power plant in Costa Rica; and a small grants program that distributed $13 million among hundreds of NGOs in developing countries for such things as a local tree nursery in Burkina Faso, an electric fence in Botswana to protect farmers' fields from elephants, a survey of rare wildflowers in Jordan, environmental education workshops for teachers in Pakistan, a network of bicycle paths in Poland, and production of one hundred copies of a recipe book for solar cookers in Belize. The GEF also began working with the International Finance Corporation, the Bank's private-sector affiliate, to establish a venture capital fund that would make deals with traditional communities to pay them for sharing their knowledge of plants, animals, and the local area—knowledge that could be useful for private companies wanting to develop ecotourism or patent new drugs or crop varieties.

————

By early 1990, the commotion caused by Conable's reorganization had died down. In the words of one veteran staffer, "Everything had gone back to the way it was before"—with Stern in charge and staff numbers up. Then, on March 30, 1990, *The Wall Street Journal* published an open letter to the Bank from Dr. Michael Irwin, the Bank's director of health services and formerly its vice president for personnel. The letter, which was also Irwin's resignation, was in the form of an Op-Ed piece titled "Why I've Had It with the world Bank." The piece opened with a reference to the Bank's "bloated and overpaid bureaucracy, wasteful practices, poor management, and unjustified arrogance" and went on from there. It threatened to undo all that Conable had achieved in Congress, reviving the image of the Bank as a haven for "foreign loafers with tax-free salaries."

Irwin's name was already well known throughout the Bank. Several months earlier a letter he sent to the staff magazine had provoked one of the biggest internal rows in the Bank's history. In that letter Irwin criticized the Bank's policy of allowing staffers to travel first class on any flight of more than nine hours, a category that covers nearly all overseas flights from the Bank's Washington headquarters. He argued that business class travel is good enough for employees of an institution dedicated to the reduction of poverty. He also pointed out that the United Nations allowed only its top two officials to fly first class.

Irwin's remarks elicited scores of letters from outraged Bank staff. Many argued that first-class travel and first-class accommodations were necessary both for the dignity of the World Bank and to protect Bank officials from the worst effects of jet lag. One letter to the Bank magazine called Irwin's proposal for ending first-class travel "a chilling statement" and warned that such a move would result in an increase in "post-mission travel-induced strokes." When the row became public, the Bank's chief press officer explained to *The Washington Post* why flying first class was so important: "Because in many places in the Third World if you don't fly first class you can be subject to overbooking. They also tend to lose your luggage."

*The Wall Street Journal* piece was not the first public attack on the Bank's extravagance, but it was unprecedented in its forceful and detailed censuring of the inner workings of the Bank and in that it came from an insider. Irwin's former Bank colleagues were less concerned with the charges he made than with the question of why he betrayed what *The Washington Post* called "the one unbroken commandment to which they [World Bank employees] all adhere without question . . . one never, never goes public." Not going public is "like a blood oath here," a senior Bank official told the *Post*, adding that he could not understand why someone of Irwin's "respectable background" would have broken that oath. Another mystified Banker said, "No one can imagine why in the world he's doing this."

Irwin was not a lifetime Bank employee, but neither was he inexperienced in the ways of bloated international bureaucracies. He had come to the Bank in 1989 after thirty-two years with the United Nations, but that had not prepared him for the degree of luxury he encountered at the Bank. Salaries in both institutions are tax-free (U.S. citizens must pay taxes, but they receive a special allowance for that purpose). On average, Bank staffers are paid 30 percent more than UN employees of equivalent rank and Bank pensions are 25 percent higher than UN pensions. Leaving aside the top-paid executives, the *average* salary for Bank professionals in 1995 was $86,000 tax-free (equal to $114,000 before U.S. taxes)—an amount that rises to $144,000 when benefits are taken into account. The president's salary is $305,000 net of taxes. Though many private banks pay their presidents much more, the Bank's president fares very well in comparison with the chairman of the U.S. Federal Reserve Board, whose $133,000 salary is subject to taxes.

"If you want to compete and get the best people, you have to be able to attract them," Armeane Choksi, one of the Bank's seventeen vice presidents, told *The Washington Post*. "Many of these people could go to their home countries and live extremely comfortably and make a hell of a lot more money." A 1995 survey by the U.S. government's General Accounting Office found, however, that Bank pay rates "exceed [those] in the public sector in all surveyed markets, as well as in the United Nations." In addition, it noted, "Benefits for all employees are more generous than those available in the United States."

In his work for UNICEF, Irwin had spent much time abroad and had noticed, he said, that "the World Bank representative always seemed to have the best house in town." When he came to the Bank, he was astonished to discover that, unlike the UN, it provides free housing for all its employees stationed overseas. Overseas jobs are rare in the Bank—90 percent of the employees of this international development agency work in its Washington headquarters. In an effort to take the sting out of living in the Third World for the other 10 percent, the Bank provides lavish benefits. These include free furnished air-conditioned housing with all utilities paid; an annual $5,000 "assignment allowance;" a "cost of living adjustment allowance" for those posted to cities where the cost of living is higher than Washington; and, in many countries, an additional "hardship allowance" amounting to a bonus of from 15 to 25 percent of one's base salary.

Upon joining the Bank, all employees—whether assigned to Washington or abroad—receive a "settling-in" grant amounting to four weeks' salary, eight weeks' if they are married or have children. If the new employee has to move house, he or she also receives a "relocation grant" of $3,450, plus $1,725 for each dependent. The Bank also pays for all moving and travel costs. On leaving the Bank, employees receive a "resettlement grant" of $2,760, plus $1,380 for each dependent, plus all travel and moving costs to their new home.

Staffers who are stationed outside their own country, whether in Washington or not, also receive education grants for all children below college age. The amount of the grant varies according to the country in which the child is schooled. In 1995 the annual education grant for a child in primary or secondary school in the United States, for example, was $8,570. Bank employees only receive grants to send their children to college if they are stationed outside Washington. The grants vary in value by the location of the college. Students attending American colleges receive $13,040 a year.

All Bank employees are entitled to home leave every two years. They receive the cash equivalent of the cost of a full economy fare air ticket to their home country, plus a "home leave allowance" of $1,070 for each staffer and $535 for each dependent. If the trip involves a layover, they receive an additional "subsistence allowance." Traveling to India, for example, is considered a three-day trip, for which staffers are entitled to an extra $560 in each direction. Because Bank employees do not pay taxes, they miss out on the dependency tax allowances available under most tax systems; to make up for this, the Bank gives them annually an extra $600 for each dependent child and up to $3,500 for spouses who earn less than $30,000.

The Bank is an enlightened, as well as generous, employer. It gives new employees twenty-six working days of vacation and fifteen days of sick leave a year. It provides generous medical and pension plans, and sets the retirement age at sixty-two. It offers staffers low-interest mortgage and education loans. It assists in selecting schools for World Bank children and in finding jobs for World Bank spouses. It offers family counseling, advice on office ergonomics, and help in renting and buying homes. Its Legal Assistance Service provides help with personal legal problems; its insurance representatives offer domestic coverage. It has an active Staff Association, with several full-time salaried administrators, an elaborate grievance resolution system, and a credit union that makes loans, gives investment advice, and deals with personal bankruptcies. It also has its own ethics office, which addresses, not the Bank's work problems with Bank projects, but offenses by Bank staffers. Among the most common of these are tax evasion and the keeping of domestic help from developing countries in conditions of slavery by the Bank employees who brought them to Washington.

The headquarters complex is much more than a workplace. It is nearly a self-contained world, offering almost every service and facility a person could need. It provides day-care facilities, a meditation room, a dizzying array of subsidized eating places from cafeterias and snack bars to cafés and fancy restaurants, and a fitness center indistinguishable from expensive private clubs in terms of decor, equipment, exercise classes, and quantity of showers and saunas. It also boasts a newsstand stocked with every publication from *Time* to *World Development Review* to *Soldier of Fortune* magazine. These many services help explain the Bank's high running costs, more than $200,000 per employee, 25 percent higher than the IMF and 72 percent higher than the United Nations.

The Bank and its employees engage in many charitable works. Its community relations office stages free weekly concerts at the Bank, and urges staffers to donate their used clothes and extra airline toiletry kits for distribution to homeless shelters. Its dining rooms donate their leftovers to soup kitchens. Its environment club promotes recycling. The Bank also provides meeting space for more than forty staff clubs, catering to all interests from artistic (stamp collecting, ballroom dancing, and photography) to sporting (bicycling, windsurfing, and softball) to spiritual (several Bible study groups, a Transcendental Meditation circle, and the four hundred–member

Spiritual Unfoldment Society). In addition, employees are entitled to join an exclusive club in nearby rural Maryland where they can enjoy golf, swimming, tennis, and send their children to summer camp. The Bretton Woods Recreation Center, as it is officially known, is something of a touchy subject at the Bank. Outsiders often make the mistake of referring to it as a country club, a description the Bank considers an inflammatory distortion. According to the Bank's press office, the club is not an indulgence, but an expression of principle, having been "established in the 1960s when similar facilities in the Washington area were racially exclusive." And anyway, adds the press office, the club is managed by the Fund, not the Bank.

# Twelve

## THE NEW MAHARAJAHS

The Bank gives its press officers a briefing book with answers to frequently asked questions. Reading it, one learns that "the Bank does not interfere in a country's internal political affairs." It is certainly true that the Bank's Articles of Agreement state that "only economic considerations shall be relevant to [the Bank's] decisions." Nonetheless, the Bank's claim to be apolitical is both inaccurate and implausible. Bank literature is replete with statements of its need and right to take an active role in the domestic affairs of its borrowers. In fact, John McCloy, its second president, felt that the Bank was "too much politics, too little finance."

But the Bank's emphasis on politics is unavoidable, according to economist Raymond Mikesell, who took part in the Bretton Woods meeting and has been a consultant to the Bank: "One of the most important functions of a development assistance institution is to influence the politics and strategies of aid recipient countries." In 1965 the Bank told its borrowers not to be "hypersensitive about suggestions originating outside their national boundaries. . . . So long as developing countries depend on foreign aid, they should accept the [fact] that the promotion of development is a joint enterprise involving the extenders and the recipients of such assistance."

Power is political and the Bank has a great deal of power. It has the power of the money it can lend and the power of its sway over other lenders. And it exercises that power to an extraordinary degree. It seeks to influence its borrowers on such politically charged domestic issues as land reform, industrial policy, and foreign trade. This puts it smack in the middle of important national debates. "In the typical case," say the authors of the Bank's authorized history, "the Bank finds itself supporting certain elements in the government or in the community against others."

The Bank has often been the deciding factor in supposedly internal contests. By threatening, in the 1960s, to cut off its telecommunications loans to India unless modern accounting and management practices were introduced to that sector, the Bank gave the Ministry of Posts and Telegraphs the clout it needed to prevail over the powerful Ministry of Finance, which opposed the suggested reforms. In 1968, Brazil's central bank succeeded in deregulating the cattle industry—over the objections of rival government departments—only after the Bank made deregulation a condition of a $40 million livestock loan. And when Philippines President Marcos was unable to push a tax increase through the Congress, the Bank strengthened his hand by making all new lending conditional on such an increase. The Bank is often on the side of right in these battles—pushing incompetent ministries to become more efficient, forcing an end to patronage and waste—but such interventions are not apolitical.

In a conversation with the historian Robert Oliver in the mid-1980s, Julian Grenfell, formerly George Woods's speechwriter, vividly recalled an instance of the Bank's willingness to influence domestic politics. In 1965, Grenfell was in Uganda with Woods and Abdullah El Emory, then the director of the Bank's Africa Department. The Bank had ceased lending to Uganda some years before on the grounds that the leftish government of Milton Obote was pursuing unsound economic policies.

At breakfast on the terrace of the Lake Victoria Hotel, just before Woods was to meet privately with Obote, remembered Grenfell, "He asked El Emory, 'How important politically is it that we resume lending?' El Emory said, 'It probably means the difference between Obote staying in power and Obote going. If the World Bank does not announce that it's going to resume lending after your visit, this is a real blow to a man.' Woods said, 'Do we need to keep him in power? Is there somebody else who could do the job better?' El Emory said, 'No, there is only the army. If you lose Obote, you lose most of the good people who are with him at the moment, and the army takes over.' Woods said, 'I guess we'd better make the loan.' "

Grenfell found this conversation astonishing: "I was sitting there as a very junior staff member, eating my cornflakes and wondering, 'My God, is this the way the Bank operates?' But that was very much Woods. He would always get down essentially to what was the critical political issue."

---

The Bank has gradually expanded the range of domestic issues in which it expects to have a say. In its earliest days, it asked little of borrowers except that they be creditworthy and their projects be financially and technically sound. Under Eugene Black, it began to draw up national development plans for its borrowers. In George Woods's time, the Bank got involved in the formulation of fundamental economic policies, pressing India to devalue the rupee, for example. Structural adjustment lending intensified the Bank's engagement in the domestic affairs of its borrowers; its involvement now extends to almost any issue with economic ramifications—from labor law to health policy to military spending. Even the Bank admits that with adjustment lending its "role in a country tends to become more politicized."

With the Bank's entrance into balance-of-payments lending, traditionally the exclusive territory of the IMF, the two institutions have begun— grudgingly because each is convinced of its own superiority—to learn to work together, coordinating their demands on borrowers. "The cross-conditionality between the Bank and the Fund is very strong," says Deepak Nayyar, who as the Indian government's chief economic advisor negotiated that country's first loan from the Fund in 1991. "They are like Tweedledee and Tweedledum. For IMF, read IMF-hypen-World Bank . . . but the Bank gets much more involved; the Fund is more distant, like the gnomes of Zurich. The Bank is very active in the structural adjustment program in India, and exercises a very considerable influence on the process of reform in terms of speed, direction, and activity. . . . The Fund and the Bank have begun to see themselves as the new maharajahs." And to a great degree they are treated that way. In 1992, the government of India submitted its draft budget to the Bank for comment—and incorporated most of the Bank's recommendations—before sending it to Parliament.

In the last few years the Bank has taken another step into the internal affairs of its borrowers. It has asserted that many Third World countries suffer from "a crisis of governance" that is undermining efforts at development. Among the problems the Bank has identified—and declared its readiness to help correct—are corruption; inequitable distribution of income; failure to respect human rights such as freedom of expression and association; government secrecy, unaccountability, and inefficiency; and outdated legal systems.

In 1990 the Bank's general counsel addressed the question of whether the Bank has the power, under its Articles of Agreement, to insist that its borrowers adhere to its definition of good governance. He found that, although the Bank is prohibited from making political judgments, it may take into consideration the "direct economic effects" of "internal or external political events." Human rights advocates and champions of democracy have been heartened by the prospect of the Bank's using its leverage to further their causes. But this new inroad by the Bank into national sovereignty raises questions that are not easily answered. In Deepak Nayyar's eyes, "They're seeing themselves more and more as a world government."

"The Bank is eager to internalize its thinking in the governments it lends to," says Nayyar. "And it does so through an amazing revolving door activity, not just in India, but in Africa and Latin America as well." In the long and close relationship between India and the Bank, for example, many officials have moved back and forth between the two. In 1993, during a period of heavy negotiations with the Bank, Shankar Acharya, India's chief economic advisor and the government's principle negotiator with the Bank, was on a leave of absence from the Bank. Acharya's boss, Finance Secretary Montek Singh Ahluwalia, was also a former Bank official, as were high-ranking economic advisors in several other government departments. And India is not unique. Officials from many countries have passed through the revolving door—some several times. Attila Karaosmanoglu, for example, came to the Bank in 1966 from Turkey's state planning organization. He returned to Turkey in 1971 to serve as deputy prime minister, and in 1973 went back to the Bank as one of its three managing directors until his retirement in 1994. Among the Bank officials who have held high government positions in recent years are Henri Konan Bedie, president of the Ivory Coast; Nicephore Soglo, president of Benin; Jose Cordoba Montoya, considered the second most powerful official in the administration of Mexican President Carlos Salinas de Gotari; and Pedro Malan, Brazil's finance minster.

Graduates of the Bank's Economic Development Institute occupy positions of influence in nearly every government in the world. "In Korea the old school tie meant the old members of EDI. They more or less ran the country," said the institute's first director, Sir Alexander Cairncross, after a visit to Asia in the late 1970s. "Pakistan [also] has a great many ex-EDI men who quite consciously were pulling together and having an influence on development." As the Bank's historians note, the concentration of EDI graduates in top jobs invites speculation: "So infiltrated with strategically placed EDI alumni are the governments of certain less developed member countries that some representatives of the new left profess to see in the situation evidence . . . of a system whereby the Bank can influence or dominate policymaking in the interest of something more sinister than sensible use of available resources."

———

Just as the Bank exercises its influence over would-be borrowers, so its major shareholders exercise theirs on the Bank. The United States is the Bank's most powerful member. Originally, it was not only the Bank's major shareholder, but also the only market for its bonds. By 1995, however, the Bank's bonds were denominated in more than twenty-five currencies, and only about a quarter of its borrowings were in dollars. The United States' shareholding has dropped from 40 percent to 17 percent. Nonetheless, it is still the largest single shareholder in the Bank; it still chooses the head of the Bank; and it is still the only country with a veto over amendments to the Articles of Agreement.

Part of the United States' power derives from its vigilant oversight of the institution. No other country maintains such a close watch on the Bank—and none other has been so demanding of it. Alone among the Bank's members, the U.S. reviews each loan proposal in detail, and officials of the Treasury Department are in daily contact not only with the U.S. executive director but directly with Bank officials.

The Bank has jumped many hurdles in its efforts to placate America's presidents and its Congresses. One of the first was in 1948, when the Bank negotiated a $45 million loan for the rehabilitation of the Polish coal industry. The United States did not want the Bank to lend money to a Communist country and instructed its executive director to vote against the loan. With only the United States opposing it, the loan would have received majority approval, but Bank President McCloy did not wish to defy his major subscriber. He decided, therefore, not to send the loan to the board for approval. Poland, understanding that the Bank was unlikely ever to grant it a loan, resigned shortly thereafter.

In its annual report for 1948, the Bank strained to make its conduct in this incident consistent with its claim to political impartiality. Its unimpeachable explanation was that politics and economics are inseparable. "The Bank is fully cognizant of the injunction in its Articles of Agreement that its decisions shall be based only on economic considerations. Political tensions and uncertainties in or among its member countries, however, have a direct effect on economic and financial conditions in those countries and upon their credit position."

During the 1950s and 1960s, only a few congressional isolationists took an active interest in the Bank. They accused it of supporting socialist regimes, financing competitors to American business, and having an overpaid and bloated bureaucracy. The "fat cat" issue heated up at least once every decade. In the early 1960s, recalled Pieter Lieftinck, an executive director at the time, "There was that childish criticism in the [U.S.] Administration and the Congress that . . . the salaries were higher than U.S. civil servant salaries." In 1975 a Senate subcommittee charged Bank officials with claiming "to be dedicated servants of the poor" while "receiv[ing] unseemly compensation for their service." There were many more angry reports over the years, and many opportunities for Congress to make its anger felt, particularly with respect to IDA, which is dependent on the cash contributions of the Bank's rich members.

By 1996, there had been eleven replenishments of IDA—and almost every one had run into trouble in the U.S. Congress. The first was flatly rejected by the House, which reversed itself only after a lobbying campaign by the Eisenhower administration. For the second, George Woods sought a commitment of $3 billion to be paid over three years. The negotiations dragged out for four years as the U.S. government tried unsuccessfully to get its fellow members to allow it to limit its contribution to the amount American businesses received in business from IDA. In the end, the Bank received pledges totaling only $1.2 billion, of which the U.S. share was about one-third.

Congress also dragged its feet on the third replenishment, giving its approval only at the last moment. In negotiating the fourth replenishment in 1975, Congress insisted on stretching out its IDA payments to four years instead of three, forcing its fellow members to come up with emergency funds to keep the organization afloat. It was also late in authorizing the fifth replenishment. But it was the sixth replenishment, Robert McNamara's last, that was the most controversial.

Under McNamara's leadership, the Bank had became the object of much more congressional scrutiny and suspicion. His celebrity and his ambitious plans for the Bank attracted attention. As secretary of defense he had made enemies on both the right and the left. Supporters of the war in Vietnam regarded him as untrustworthy and suspiciously dovish; opponents considered him untrustworthy and a warmonger. During his long tenure at the Bank, both sides kept a close eye on him.

William Simon, President Ford's secretary of the treasury and, ex officio, governor of the World Bank from 1974 to 1977, became the standard-bearer for opposition to the Bank. Simon charged McNamara with creating a monstrous bureaucracy more interested in propping up socialist regimes than in stimulating private investment. Simon also wanted the Bank to slow its lending to heavily indebted countries. McNamara's right-hand man at the Bank, William Clark, dismissed Simon's criticisms as the fruit of institutional envy: "He felt the World Bank had become more powerful than the U.S. Treasury, and he wished to show who was master."

When Jimmy Carter was elected president, Simon and a cadre of fellow conservatives kept up the anti-Bank rhetoric. If anything, Simon out of office was even more aggressive than Simon in office. He succeeded in stirring up congressional opposition to the Bank's requests for funds by depicting it as a power-hungry, secretive institution full of overpaid time-servers. This view was also promoted by conservative think tanks, such as the Heritage Foundation, and expressed in *The Wall Street Journal*, whose editorials excoriated the Bank, calling its projects "harebrained schemes."

Though generally well disposed toward the Bank, the Carter administration pressed it to drop its support for regimes with bad human rights records. This the Bank was unwilling to do, on the grounds that it could not make distinctions of a political nature. The Bank did bow to Carter's demand that it impose an across-the-board salary cut after a congressional investigation said its officials were overpaid. That "bought us years of peace" one of McNamara's aides said. But the staff was unhappy with what Deborah Shapley, McNamara's biographer, calls "the symbolism of McNamara's paying his own people less to get more money for the poor." Shapley tells of one loan officer "who complained that he [McNamara] was trading part of their livelihood to help the poor."

In 1978, over the strenuous objections of the United States, the Bank made a $60 million loan to Vietnam, its first to that country. McNamara's decision to bring the loan to the board for approval was partly intended to demonstrate his resolve to withstand political pressure. The loan outraged American conservatives, who maintained that this loan and five others that were proposed to follow would fund not a simple irrigation project, as the Bank claimed, but the forced relocation of farmers into government-controlled communes. The House of Representatives then attached an amendment to the foreign appropriations bill that banned U.S. funds from being used for loans to Vietnam and five other countries, all of which were deemed "unfriendly to the United States." The amendment would have crippled IDA—which, like the IBRD, cannot accept earmarked funds—by forcing it to refuse the entire U.S. contribution.

The matter was resolved only by McNamara's sending a letter, drafted by the U.S. treasury department, to Clarence Long, chairman of the House

Subcommittee on Foreign Operations, stating that the Bank would make no more loans to Vietnam on account of its lack of a "rational development policy." (The Bank maintained its embargo on loans to Vietnam until 1993.) McNamara's letter resolved the crisis, but did lasting damage to the Bank's efforts to be seen as above political influence.

In 1981, the newly installed Reagan administration announced its intention of cutting back on foreign aid. The Bank and other "organs of international aid and so-called Third World development," wrote Reagan's budget chief, David Stockman, "were infested with socialist error . . . turning Third World countries into quagmires of self-imposed inefficiency and burying them beneath mountainous external debts they would never be able to repay." One year later, when the debt crisis hit, liberals and some conservatives accused the Bank of using taxpayers' money to bail out the private banking industry. Suddenly, the Bank was a target of what John Makin, author of *The Global Debt Crisis,* called "a unique coalition of liberals who hated the [big private] banks and conservatives who hated the thought of more foreign aid for . . . corrupt, communist-inspired borrowers."

In 1982 the Reagan administration asked the Treasury Department to investigate the World Bank. The department's report was generally favorable to the Bank. It found that "the United States is without question the major influence in the bank" and concluded that the Bank usually acts in support of long-term American political and strategic interests. Among the instances the report cited were McNamara's 1979 pledge not to lend to Vietnam, the Bank's refusal to lend to Chile while Allende was in power, and its willingness to lend generously to friends of the United States, such as Zaire, Indonesia, Thailand, and the Philippines, even when they failed to meet the Bank's normal standards of creditworthiness.

The Bank's behavior during the debt crisis earned it the gratitude of America's big banks, a fact that caused the Reagan administration to take a new look at the Bank. It concluded that structural adjustment lending could be a useful tool because adjustment loans were conditional on borrowers' agreeing to move toward a market economy. From then on, the administration regarded the Bank as an important instrument of its foreign and economic policy. Paul Volcker, then chairman of the Federal Reserve Board, later told Catherine Gwin of the Overseas Development Council that the U.S. Treasury and the Fed "directed" the Bank's lending in the years after the debt crisis.

Despite its newfound respect for the Bank's usefulness, Reagan administration officials apparently did not trust its managers to keep them fully informed. In the summer of 1983, according to former U.S. Attorney General Elliot Richardson, the administration had a "spy" software program secretly installed on Bank computers. The program contained a secret "trapdoor" that allowed the National Security Administration to clandestinely monitor the Bank's activities. Richardson, who is the lawyer for the developers of the original, noneavesdropping version of the software, called PROMIS, says that the installation was motivated by the CIA's desire to have "early warning" of the failure of Latin American banks. A Justice Department source told *Thomson's International Banking Regulator,* an industry newsletter, that senior officials from that department had met with top Bank officials in June 1983 to discuss installation of the modified PROMIS software, which, he said, was needed "for security tracking purposes." World Bank computer specialists have confirmed that a program called PROMIS "suddenly showed up" on a key Bank computer in mid-1983.

In early 1994, at Richardson's request, the Bank's general counsel, Ibrahim Shihata, ordered a search for the software. When Bank technicians found nothing, he ordered them "to look again more carefully." Asked in late 1995 if he had learned anything more about the alleged installation, Shihata declined to comment.

Congressional attitudes toward the Bank do not follow standard party lines. Pro-business types like the contracts the Bank funnels to American companies. Isolationists argue that the Bank takes American money and uses it to build up America's competitors. Free-marketeers appreciate the Bank's efforts to make the developing world a business-friendly place. Left-wingers see the Bank as a tool that Western political and commercial powers use to further their control of developing countries. Liberals want the United States to contribute to the Bank's antipoverty efforts. Progressives deplore the Bank's environmental and human rights record.

Supporters and opponents alike, however, believe the institution can be improved. Both groups have in common the desire to exert more control over the Bank. And they view the annual appropriation for IDA as an opportunity to do just that. Congress routinely attaches amendments to its IDA appropriations with instructions to the U.S. executive director on how to vote under particular circumstances. Congress has, for example, directed the U.S. ED to oppose all loans for projects that would create competition for American businesses, and all loans to countries that have expropriated the property of American citizens without compensation, countries that have a consistent pattern of gross human rights violations, and countries that have nuclear weapons, but have not ratified the Treaty on Nuclear Non-Proliferation.

Congressional directives to the U.S. ED are largely symbolic, however, because the United States does not on its own have the number of votes needed to veto a loan. Nor have the frequent U.S. nay votes or abstentions sparked debate on the board. "When the U.S. ED says 'I have to abstain' on this issue," says one board member, "no one even bothers to ask why anymore." The United States first voted against a loan in 1971, on the grounds that the borrower, Guyana, had expropriated the property of American citizens. Since then, the U.S. has voted against or abstained on more than 120 World Bank loans, but all were approved by the board nonetheless.

Congress's most effective weapon against the Bank has been not its directives, but its threats to reduce or cut off funding for IDA. Nowadays, nearly all its contributions are conditional on the adoption of specific reforms in the Bank's approach to such issues as the environment, human rights, and freedom of information. This tactic has been quite effective, particularly when the U.S. administration is also concerned about the issue in question and adds its pressure to that of the Congress. It has been a major factor in the Bank's adoption of several important reforms, including a wider use of environmental impact assessments of Bank loans, improvements to the Bank's information policy, and the establishment of an inspection panel with limited powers to review disputed projects.

The IBRD, which raises its own cash by selling bonds, is thus much less dependent for its funding on the good graces of the United States and the other rich countries. Nonetheless, from time to time it must ask its members to subscribe more capital so that it can increase its borrowing on the bond market. The first such occasion was in 1959, when the Bank's members agreed to double its capital—after Eugene Black said that they did not have to contribute any additional cash. Black regarded this capital increase as a one-time-only event. "I don't think we'll ever have to do it again," he said later, "because now, in the meantime, we're getting repayments. It's going to be revolving to a large extent."

In fact, Black's capital increase was only the first of six over the years. These have brought the Bank's capital from $10 billion in 1946 to $175 billion today. Most of that amount, of course, is in the form of pledges; only a small proportion has been paid in cash. The United States, for example, has subscribed $30 billion to the IBRD, but has actually paid in less than $2 billion. In the most recent capital increase, in 1988, the Bank's members pledged an additional $75 billion. The U.S. share of that was $14 billion—of which 3 percent, or $420 million, was to be paid in cash, spread over six years. Congress appropriated the $420 million, but showed its hostility by spreading the payments over seven years, instead of six, to do so. The IBRD says it is now adequately capitalized and will not ask for another capital increase before 2005, though its former treasurer, Eugene Rotberg, estimates that it will need a new infusion of capital at least five years earlier.

--------

The Bank has often cut off loans to a country with which its major share-holders, in particular the United States, have some quarrel. In 1970, for example, Salvador Allende was elected president of Chile on a platform of land reform and nationalization of foreign industries. President Nixon's secretary of state, Henry Kissinger, said, "I don't see why we need to stand by and watch a country go communist because of the irresponsibility of its own people." Nixon, who was, in Kissinger's words, "beside himself," gave orders to "make the economy scream." According to the Bank's reasoning in the earlier Polish case, this degree of hostility by a major economic power was reason enough to conclude that Chile was, or soon would be, uncreditworthy. The Bank made no loans to Chile during Allende's time in office. In 1974, a few months after Allende was killed in a military coup, the Bank resumed its lending.

The Bank's key members are also sensitive to loans for projects that might compete with their own industries. Under Conable, the Bank was especially sensitive to the United States' concern about its worsening trade deficit. It stopped or cut back on loans for such things as the production of steel, oil, and copper. A $20 million steel loan under negotiation with Pakistan was one casualty, as was a $12 million copper loan to Zambia, and a $20 million IFC loan intended to increase Brazil's exports of iron ore.

Perhaps the most dramatic result of the Bank's bowing to political pressure, however, occurred in the case of the Aswan High Dam. In the early 1950s Egypt spent three years negotiating with the Bank for a $200 million loan to finance this massive dam on the Nile. In 1955, the British and American governments announced their support of the project and said they were considering providing an additional $70 million along with the Bank loan. For a number of reasons, however, feeling in both Parliament and Congress turned against the dam: Britain became convinced that Nassar was trying to undermine its influence in the Middle East; some

American Senators objected to financing foreign dams when there were still undammed rivers in the United States; and both countries were impatient with Nassar's failure to take sides in the Cold War.

Nassar's recognition, in May 1956, of the Communist government in China was the last straw. On July 19, the U.S. government announced its withdrawal from the Aswan scheme. The next day the British did the same. With its most important members now opposed to the project, the Bank stopped negotiations on *its* loan. A week after the loan collapsed, Egypt annexed the Suez Canal—an act that launched the Suez War.

---

The Bank comes under political pressure to make loans, as well as cancel them. One example is the $1.25 billion loan it made to Argentina in October 1988. Officially, the Bank made four separate project loans—for housing, trade policy reform, and electric power—all on the same day. In reality, it was a balance-of-payments loan to a deeply indebted country that had been unable to reach a standby agreement with the IMF, due to what the Fund considered its irresponsible fiscal policies. The Bank made the loan, over the heated objections of the Fund, at the request of U.S. Treasury Secretary James Baker, an old political ally of Barber Conable. Baker, who resigned his post shortly thereafter to join George Bush's presidential election campaign, wanted to forestall social unrest in Latin America during the run-up to the U.S. presidential election. The experience was deeply embarrassing for the Bank, partly because the political maneuvering was far from secret and partly because Argentina failed so signally to live up to its promises that the Bank was forced to cancel the loan within a few months.

In the fall of 1993, less than two months before the U.S. Congress was due to vote on the North American Free Trade Agreement (NAFTA), the Bank put together a $918 million package of loans to finance environmental improvements in Mexico. In an unusual move, it held a press conference and signing ceremony to announce its intention to make these loans—though board approval of them was nine months away. Among those present were Mexican Finance Minister Pedro Aspe and U.S. Treasury Secretary Lloyd Bentsen, who praised the loans as "an important complement to the programs we have developed in the North American Free Trade Agreement." As Bentsen implied, the Bank's loan package was part of the U.S. government's effort to convince Congress that in approving NAFTA it would not be linking the United States to a polluted country with second-

rate environmental standards and no budget for environmental improvement. The Bank's project summary for one of the three loans, the Northern
Border Environmental Project, elaborated on that theme: "Arresting and
reversing environmental degradation [on the border] has become an urgent
government priority, with international considerations linked to the debate
on the North American Free Trade Agreement." In due course, all three
projects were approved.

It may be inevitable that the Bank takes pains to mollify its major
shareholders, but it is to its advantage to be seen to do so. A reputation for
evenhandedness enables the Bank to prescribe harsh medicine that would
otherwise likely be rejected. As *The Washington Post* explained in a 1981
editorial, "successive American presidents have found the World Bank and
the International Monetary Fund extremely useful. Both, with their international staffs, can set enforceable conditions for aid without threatening
the infringement of national sovereignty or national pride." The *Baltimore
Sun* concurred: "Better, sometimes, to have multilateral agencies like the
World Bank prepare the path for direct Western corporate investments than
for the U.S. to dictate to foreign governments."

Indeed, the Bank does not always bend to the United States. In 1980, at
the height of the civil war in El Salvador, the Bank cut off funding to that
country, citing concern for the safety of its personnel. In doing so, it defied
the Reagan administration, which supported the Salvadoran government
and wanted the Bank to do the same. And in 1993, just a few hours after
U.S. Secretary of State Warren Christopher called Iran "an international
outlaw" for its support of terrorism, the Bank made a $165 million energy
loan to it.

———

The Bank has its own ideology, independent of its members' politics. Its
creed is to lend. Acts that appear to be political may merely be an expression of this deep-seated drive. The Bank's stance toward South Africa is an
example. Between 1948, when the country officially adopted apartheid,
and 1966, South Africa borrowed a quarter of a billion dollars from the
Bank, making it one of the Bank's biggest clients. The Bank had doubts
about lending to an avowedly racist government, but they were of a financial, not moral nature. It worried that the South African people would
overthrow the government and repudiate its debts. Instead of protecting
itself against this eventuality by refusing to lend to South Africa, the Bank,
in 1953, simply shortened South Africa's repayment schedule from the
usual thirty years to ten. In 1965 the General Assembly of the United

Nations—whose membership is more or less identical to the Bank's own—passed a resolution asking the Bank to refrain from lending money to South Africa as long as that nation maintained its policy of apartheid. The Bank refused, arguing that its charter prohibited such politically motivated actions. Although this incident did the Bank's reputation as a defender of human rights no good at all, its actions were dictated more by a desire to demonstrate its independence and an eagerness to keep up its lending than by any particular sympathy for apartheid.

Much the same thing happened in 1992, when Western donors decided to cut off all nonhumanitarian aid to Malawi until the country improved its human rights record. This loss of an estimated $74 million was more than made up for by the World Bank, which within weeks stepped in and lent Malawi $199 million. In 1992, a survey of the Malawi by the Economist Intelligence Unit, an offshoot of *The Economist* magazine, cited a report that claimed that "internal World Bank documents indicate that at least some of the new money was specifically provided to cover the shortfall in government finances caused by suspension of bilateral aid." The Bank also funds projects in East Timor, the former Portuguese colony whose annexation by Indonesia in 1976 was opposed by the local population and is not recognized by the United Nations. The Bank says, however, that since the mid-1980s, all its projects in East Timor have been "designed to help the poor."

The Bank does not have a history of taking a strong stand on human rights. It prefers not to address the issue directly. As former Vice President Burke Knapp has said, "You don't want to be accused of tolerating, or even providing positive support, to obnoxious regimes who are engaged in the suppression of human rights and oppression of their peoples. On the other hand, we felt we were the agent for fostering the development of peoples and not of regimes and that in the long run, if we hewed to the task of development in the interest of the people, the undesirable regimes would come and go."

The World Bank lent more than a billion dollars to Ethiopia during the repressive Marxist regime of Colonel Mengistu Haile-Mariam. Mengistu began his fourteen-year reign in 1977 with a campaign of violence against his political enemies that became known as the "red terror." In 1986 alone—the year that *The Economist's* *World Human Rights Guide* declared Ethiopia's human rights record the worst in the world, the Bank lent Mengistu's government more than $100 million. During the great famine of the 1980s, Mengistu's government prevented famine relief from reaching disloyal sections of the country.

The Ethiopian famine was exacerbated by an agriculture policy the Bank helped fund. In an effort to nationalize agriculture and eliminate rebel activity in the countryside, Mengistu's government forced millions of its citizens off their land and into government-run "villages." This "villagization" program was run by the Ministry of Agriculture, to which the Bank made numerous loans. It tried to keep its hands clean by specifying that its loans should not be used for forced resettlement, but Yonas Deressa, president of the Ethiopian Refugees Education and Relief Foundation, warned at the time that the regime would not comply with the Bank's stipulation. "They just take the money and laugh. Over the past two decades the World Bank has contributed as much to agricultural disaster in Ethiopia as the governments themselves."

Possibly the worst human rights outrage ever associated with one of the Bank's projects occurred in Guatemala. In 1978 the Bank lent that country $72 million to build a dam on the Chixoy River. Facing displacement, the local people, mostly indigenous Achi Indians, began to organize, refusing to move without receiving fair compensation. On March 4, 1980, a group of people gathered in the church in the village of Rio Negro to rally against the coming evictions. Three soldiers assigned to guard the project site fired into the crowd, killing seven people.

Though frightened by this event, the people of Rio Negro continued to condemn the government's resettlement plan as inadequate. On February 13, 1982, the villagers were ordered by the army to attend a civil defense meeting in a neighboring town. Seventy-four villagers went, and seventy-three of them were assassinated. The surviving men of the village took to sleeping in the hills, while the women and children, presuming they were safe from military attack, stayed in their homes. Early in the morning of March 13, however, a group of armed men came to the village, rounded up all the women and children and marched them to an isolated area. They raped many of the women and young girls before killing them and the children, then pushed the dead bodies into a ravine. A few escaped, however, and later led others to the site of the massacre. In 1993, an international team of forensic scientists exhumed 177 bodies of women and children who had been garrotted, slashed by machetes, or smashed against the rocks. Another 117 villagers were killed in two separate incidents shortly before the reservoir began filling.

There was a civil war going on in Guatemala at the time of the massacres, but the Rio Negro murders took place not to punish local people for harboring guerillas, but to punish them for opposing the dam. According to the Guatemalan anthropologist Rolando Alecio, "INDE [The government electricity authority], the Army, and the financial backers of the dam did not want the example of resistance by Rio Negro to spread to the other communities which were being forcibly resettled." A church worker from the region said, "The Chixoy dam was built with the blood of the inhabitants of Rio Negro."

The Bank's report on the dam does not mention the atrocities that preceded the filling of the reservoir. It must have been aware of them, however, because, as the Bank's chief resettlement expert has delicately expressed it, "The turmoil surrounding resettlement in Guatemala's Chixoy dam project eventually became so severe that the entire area was declared a national emergency zone." The report admits that the resettlement plans "were seriously flawed," but says that "the World Bank did not consider it to be appropriate to suspend disbursements in order to obtain compliance with covenants."*

It is often argued that in lending money to an undemocratic regime, the Bank enables it to ignore the will of its people. "Providing a tyrant with fifty-year interest free loans inevitably increases his power," says James Bovard, a right-wing critic of the Bank. In 1989, the Chinese astrophysicist and political dissident Fang Lizhi pleaded with the World Bank to suspend loans to China, saying, "We must make our government realize that it is economically dependent on its citizens." Isabelle Letelier, the widow of Orlando Letelier, the assassinated former Chilean ambassador to the United States, referred to the same phenomenon when she wrote, "Repression in Chile can continue precisely because the military junta can rely on outside sources of financing."

The deciding factor in whether or not the Bank withholds funds from a country with a record of human rights abuses is not how abusive the regime is, but how rebellious its people are. In an oral history of his time at the Bank, former vice president Burke Knapp said: "If a regime became so unpopular in a country and the Bank continued lending money to it, we felt it quite possible—certainly something we should take into consideration—that successive regimes might denounce the obligations incurred by that government." It was fear of such a development that dictated the Bank's

---

* In July 1982, four months after the massacre, the empty village of Rio Negro disappeared under the rising waters of the Chixoy reservoir. But when the dam was completed, it was discovered that, in the words of one Bank staffer, "the damned thing wouldn't work." Not only had it been built on heavily fissured rocks in an area known for its active seismic faults, there were so many engineering errors that it stopped producing electricity after only five months of operation. The Bank lent another $47 million to help pay for the repairs. Poor planning, corruption, and mismanagement ultimately raised the cost of the dam from the original estimate of $340 million to $1 billion.

decision to insist that its loans to South Africa be repaid in ten instead of thirty years.

The Bank's reluctance to use human rights as a yardstick for lending explains its checkered history with respect to abiding by international sanctions. Like all other donors, it cut off aid to Haiti after the military coup that deposed President Aristide. It also suspended aid to China after the 1989 massacre in Tiananman Square, but a few months later it began lending again, saying that "economic development should come first, before so-called political liberalization."

In the rare cases when the Bank has refused on human rights grounds to make loans—to the Dominican Republic under Trujillo and to Equatorial Guinea under Macias—it has been loathe to admit the fact. Knapp recalled that when the Bank stopped lending to Uganda during the regime of Idi Amin, "I personally had the unhappy duty of explaining to successive Ugandan Ministers of Finance why we had quit. I didn't want to say we had quit because of human rights issues but what I did say was that we thought that the government was no longer exercising effective control, or perhaps I used the words, would no longer be able to employ funds effectively and put them to productive use."

——————

The Bank is often accused of favoring right-wing governments, whereas what it actually favors are strong governments. As James Morris pointed out in *The Road to Huddersfield,* the Bank has always lent to dictators: Franco, Tito, and Haile Selassie were among its first customers. The Bank's weakness for strongmen is still evident, but it can take comfort from the theory that angering people on both sides of an argument is evidence of fairness. While critics on the left are angered by its sponsorship of favoring such right-wing dictatorships in Nicaragua, Chile, and the Philippines, the right has been outraged by its support of left-wing tyrants in Tanzania, Ethiopia, and Romania.

The reason for the Bank's enthusiasm for dictators is simple: Autocratic governments are more capable of instituting and seeing through the unpopular reforms the Bank often prescribes for its clients than are democratically elected governments, which rely on the support of the public. A former Bank economist describes a belief in the Bank that "a courageous, ruthless, and perhaps undemocratic government is required to ride roughshod over . . . special interest groups." Several years ago, the Bank's chief economist, Lawrence Summers, tried to convince his colleagues that totalitarianism is not essential to development. Writing in *Finance and Develop-*

*ment,* a magazine published jointly by the Bank and the Fund, he said, "We have learned an important lesson over the last decade: authoritarian regimes are not necessary to bring about growth."

Nonetheless, some observers argue that the Bank is more indulgent with dictators than with democratic governments, and that it actually undermines the latter by demanding more of them. Throughout the 1980s, for example, Bangladesh was under the corrupt rule of General Ershad, among whose abuses was diverting World Bank funds to his supporters. In 1990, a popular uprising forced Ershad to resign, and a democratically elected government took his place. "The Bank knew about the corruption under Ershad, but said nothing about it all those years," says Tasneem Siddiqui, a Bangladeshi sociologist who has acted as a consultant on Bank-funded projects, "but now that there's a democratic government in power, the Bank says it must repay all that was stolen." The Bank, charges Siddiqui, expects more of democracies than of dictatorships but does not allow for the fact that they cannot move faster than the public will tolerate. "The Bank forced this government to impose a 15 percent sales tax only two months after taking office. It raised a lot of money, but it put the government in a precarious position when it should have had time to consolidate support, not alienate people. Land reform is another example: this government is under pressure from the Bank to do something about it, but Ershad wasn't."

The Bank *does* have a long history of demonstrating markedly more enthusiasm for dictatorships than for democracies. Brazil is one example among many. From the mid-1950s to the early 1960s, Brazil was plagued with high inflation rates, which exacerbated its already serious balance-of-payment problems. A succession of elected governments were unable, in the face of massive popular opposition, to institute the stringent economic reforms that might have reduced inflation. During this period, the Bank cut off lending to Brazil because of the government's refusal to bring inflation under control. In April 1964, the elected government was overthrown in a violent military coup. Once in power, the army used violence and intimidation to impose harsh reform measures on the public. A twenty-man World Bank mission rushed to Brazil "to study the Government's economic development program," and Brazil once again became one of the Bank's major borrowers.

Tanzania became one of the Bank's favorites in the late 1960s and the 1970s, thanks in part to the political stability it enjoyed under its socialist president Julius Nyerere. A 1989 Bank report concluded that in Tanzania, "with one-party rule, stability was the feature of governance that the Bank found attractive." The Bank also found its own new concern with poverty alleviation echoed in Nyerere's political philosophy. Finding itself in sympathy with Nyerere, the Bank backed him devotedly, even blindly. It helped fund the "villagization" scheme, part of his plan for *Ujamaa*, or African socialism. Under this scheme the army forced millions of peasants out of their scattered homes and herded them into densely packed settlements where they were put to work on government-run farms. According to Bernard Nossiter, author of *The Global Struggle for More*, "The villagers knew what Nyerere did not, that their soil was not suitable for intensive farming. Crop output fell swiftly. Despite Nyerere's use of an armed militia and the burning of recalcitrant peasants' huts, the farmers drifted away from the settlements and back to their plots."

Bank staff and consultants had identified many of the problems besetting villagization, other Bank-funded projects in Tanzania, and the Tanzanian economy in general. But their reports, the Bank later acknowledged, were "downplayed or ignored, because the results might slow down lending and interfere with the achievement of overall regional lending targets. . . . By turning a blind eye to such matters, the Bank could sustain or increase lending to . . . stable countries—often with unhappy consequences." In 1991, the Bank cited Tanzania as an example of "when aid can be ineffective." With no apparent shame or irony, it condemned unnamed "external agencies [that] continued to provide aid to Tanzania while the country experimented with disastrous rural policies and institutions."

Perhaps the most extraordinary example of the Bank's susceptibility to despots was its protracted enthusiasm for Communist Romania. Romania joined the Bank in 1972. Though its leader, Nicolae Ceauçescu, was harsh and maniacal, his calculated rebuffs to Moscow had earned him the patronage of the West. The Bank handled Romania with kid gloves. It was not required to settle its outstanding debts before receiving loans; it was exempted from reporting important economic information to the Bank; and—most striking of all—it was considered creditworthy despite the complete domination of its economy by the state. Romania received its first World Bank loan, $60 million to build a government fertilizer plant, in 1974. Over the following eight years the Bank lent Romania more than $2 billion for large-scale power, agricultural, and industrial projects. During this period Romania was pursuing brutal assaults on the country's ancient villages and farmlands, forcing people into urban tenements in the name of modernization. Ceauçescu's—and the Bank's—economic program failed to put Romania on a solid economic footing. Instead, by 1982 the country was so heavily in debt that Ceauçescu stopped all borrowing and forced a cripplingly harsh austerity program on its people.

Though Ceauçescu was ruining the country, the Bank consistently gave his government good marks for effort and achievement. Its most thorough report, a 1979 study titled *Romania: The Industrialization of an Agrarian Economy under Socialist Planning,* predicted that "Romania will have taken off and become an industrialized economy by 1990, on a level with many other countries considered to be developed." Using statistics supplied by Ceauçescu's government, it reported that the national economy had grown at the remarkable rate of 10 percent a year for twenty-five years— clearly a ludicrous claim. This success, the Bank noted, "was made possible by the state's control of the major productive resources and its monopoly over foreign trade." *The Wall Street Journal* editorialized that the Bank's decision to publish the report—against the advice of its own publication committee—was due in part to its hope that "a sympathetic review of a Communist economy would entice others—perhaps even China—into the fold of the bank."

Indeed, the Bank did want desparately to lend to China, with its huge borrowing potential. There was a problem, however: China owed millions of dollars to buyers of its pre-revolutionary bonds—more than $40 million in the United States alone—and the Bank had a long-standing policy requiring borrowers to negotiate a settlement with creditors to whom it was in default. But the Bank had violated this policy for Romania, and it did so for China, which was welcomed into membership in 1980. Twelve years later it was the Bank's largest borrower. The Bank's embrace of China reflected its ideology—its enthusiasm not for communism, but for lending.

# Thirteen

## SUPREMELY SELF-CONFIDENT

The professional self-esteem of World Bank staffers is legendary—and, by most accounts, amply warranted. They are widely regarded as hard-working, highly qualified specialists who are attracted to the Bank not only by the generous salaries it offers, but also by the opportunity to work with some of the brightest minds in the field. Four to five thousand people apply each year for the Bank's Young Professionals program, a one-year internship that leads almost automatically to a permanent job. Applicants must have at least a master's degree in finance, economics or (since 1992) a technical field, such as irrigation engineering, urban planning, or health management. Of these thousands of applicants the Bank hires only about thirty-five, most of whom have a Ph.D. and several years of work experience.

"You don't last at the World Bank unless you are very, very good," says the business guru Peter Drucker. "They are the best and the brightest," agrees CalTech socioeconomist Thayer Scudder, a frequent consultant to the Bank and to many other development agencies. "None of the others," he says, "are anywhere near as good as the Bank." But even admirers often feel that, as James Morris observed more than thirty years ago, the Bank has "tendencies toward the stuffy and the patronizing." "They're arrogant sons of bitches, many of them," says one observer, "but when you belong to the best organization and you get the highest salaries and you have all the perks, it goes to your head." Most Bank staff would argue that they are—as one put it—"not so much arrogant as supremely self-confident."

In recent years, however, the Bank has been worrying about the quality of its staff. In June 1989, Vice President Willi Wapenhans told a gathering of top executives that "there had been a deterioration in the skills of Bank staff." Shortly thereafter, Vice President for Personnel William Cosgrove warned in an internal memo that "borrowers may now be more skilled than Bank staff." One reason for the deterioration is the Bank's over-reliance in recent decades on academic qualifications. A Bank study found "a reduced proportion of staff with hands-on implementation experience in their pre-Bank careers." Thus, many Bank officials have spent their professional lives telling people in countries where they have never lived how to do things they themselves have never done. It was not always so: As Wapenhans said in another report, "Until the 1970s many of the Bank's technical staff had long experience in managing business functions in developing countries."

Now, however, most staffers are recruited to the Bank early in their careers, and few leave. Turnover at the Bank is low: The average age of Bank staff increases by nine months each year. In a internal survey conducted in 1992, three-quarters of the staff cited "deficient skills" as a major problem in the institution. According to the Bank's 1993 annual report, the institution lacks skilled staff "in the areas of procurement, private-sector development, environment, the financial sector, the social sciences, population and human resources, and public-sector management."

Whether it has the right skills or not, the Bank's staff is ever-expanding. In 1990 there were approximately 6,000 Washington-based employees. In 1995 the Washington-based staff numbered 8,500. In addition the Bank issued 8,000 contracts for short-term consulting work that year. During that five-year period, the Bank's administrative budget increased by 55 percent, though the number of loans and the amount of money it lent stayed roughly level.

The increase in staff numbers has not brought quality, according to Hans-Eberhard Kopp, director of the Bank's Operations Evaluation Department, who told the magazine *Euromoney* that "we can't find a connection between staffing and the level of success" enjoyed by Bank loans. The Bank, Cosgrove said in 1989, "could do twice as much with its present staff or only needs half the staff for the present workload." The question, however, is which staff? For as the Bank has expanded, fewer people than ever are doing the real work of the institution: overseeing projects. In 1981 there were twenty-one staff members for every loan approved; by 1992, the ratio was twenty-seven staffers per loan. In the same period, the workload for task managers, the people who oversee individual projects, doubled. Instead of being assigned three or four projects at once, each one was overseeing five or six at a time. Task managers have considerable control over how a project is designed, appraised, and implemented. They can insist on true consultation with local people or ignore them; they can push for in-depth appraisals or rush things through. They can also follow projects closely or neglect them, learn from successes and failures or fail to do so. With less time to devote to each project, and a promotion system that rewards quantity rather than quality, it has become harder and harder for even conscientious task managers to do their jobs well.

———

The reason the Bank has found it so "difficult to remove deadwood," as Cosgrove put it, is that it is hard to find a better job. Besides the generous salaries and perks, a Bank job comes with an American visa—something that is highly prized by many of the three-quarters of the staff who are not American citizens. Moreover, adds Moises Naim, who has been minister of industry in Venezuela, a Bank official, and an executive director, "For many, the Bank is one of the few places in the world where there is a demand for their highly specialized skills. . . . Losing a job at the Bank becomes an event of catastrophic proportions. This extreme dependency . . . is a pervasive and crucial element of the Bank's culture."

But even velvet chains can be oppressive. The sense among many Bank employees that they cannot leave their jobs, whatever their dissatisfactions, has contributed to a serious problem with morale. One person who works in the Bank compares the atmosphere to "what it must have been like to be in an Eastern European dictatorship just before the collapse. People just don't believe in their work the way they have to pretend to," he said. "A lot of the problem is the failure of adjustment [lending]. It's all a game, really. You give money to a government and you don't know where it goes."

Indeed, an internal survey, conducted in 1988 for the Staff Association, found deep cynicism among the staff about the value of the work they do. Less than half believed "that borrowers' most important needs are being met by the Bank's lending policies. And 30 percent indicated that the Bank's move toward structural adjustment or policy-based lending has *decreased* their feeling of commitment to the Bank." On a scale of 1 to 6, the overall level of job satisfaction at the Bank was 2.8.

Four years later, another internal survey found that things were no better. Only 17 percent of the staff "felt that analytical work done during project preparation was sufficient to ensure the achievement of project quality." Three-quarters reported that task managers are "overwhelmed by responsibilities for which they have little or no pre-Bank experience or in-Bank training." More than half said their bosses lacked either the time or the expertise to help them prepare good and realistic projects.

One problem is that the Bank is mired in red tape—a certain sign of an insecure bureaucracy. Its official operations manual fills several volumes. Division chiefs spend 52 percent of their time interacting with colleagues, 29 percent of their time documenting their work, and only 2 percent dealing with borrowers. Task managers, who are closer to the action, spend a greater proportion of their time dealing with borrowers—7 percent.

In 1992, Bank employees also testified to a "declining level of job satisfaction," and to being "preoccup[ied] with salaries and promotions." One consequence, says Moises Naim, is an increasingly inward-looking staff that has formed into "clanlike groups whose members support and promote each other in a muted but intense rivalry with other clans." At the apex of this clan system, according to management consultant Michael Macoby—whom the Bank hired in 1988 to review the institution's internal operations—are the Bank's senior managers, many of whom he characterized as "dukes, running their departments or offices like fiefdoms."

———

The proof of the Bank's competence lies not in the professional qualifications or high IQs of its employees, but in the success of its projects and programs. The Bank's system for ensuring that its projects meet its standards—that they are technically sound, economically feasible, socially desirable, and well-executed—is called the project cycle.

The first stage of the project cycle is identification. This is when the Bank, in consultation with the borrower, decides that a particular project merits further consideration. The project must fit in with the borrower's overall development plan and make technical and economic sense. Once a project is formally identified, it is incorporated into the Bank's five-year lending plan for that country. If a project crosses this hurdle, it will most likely end up receiving formal approval from the Bank's board of directors.

The projects considered for identification may be proposed by the Bank itself, by the borrowing country, foreign aid agencies, consultants, or even a private firm. The whim of an influential individual, in fact, may be all that is necessary to set a project in motion: The billion-dollar Bangladesh

Flood Action Plan (FAP) has its origin in a 1987 visit to Dacca by Danielle Mitterand, wife of the then president of France.

During her visit, the monsoon stuck with more than its usual force and Mrs. Mitterand was deeply touched by the plight of the many people left homeless. She begged her husband to do something to alleviate their misery. As it happened, the government of France was looking for a good deed to celebrate the two hundredth anniversary of its revolution. What better than to help poor Bangladesh erect concrete embankments along the length of its three mighty rivers—the Bramaputra, the Ganges, and the Meghna—in order to protect its citizens from their raging waters?

Many scientists and engineers in Bangladesh and elsewhere pointed out serious flaws in the project's conception and design, beginning with the fact that the flooding that causes most of the damage in Bangladesh comes not from rivers overtopping their banks but from cyclonic storms along the coast. But Mrs. Mitterand's idea won the immediate support of the French construction industry, which was facing a dearth of large-scale projects at home. When the construction lobbies in other donor nations found out about the French plan, they pushed their governments to secure a share of the action for them. Soon an unseemly battle broke out over who would get to concretize Bangladesh's rivers. The World Bank stepped in to settle the squabble and now acts as coordinator for the twenty-six FAP projects. It has made a $120 million loan for one of the embankment projects. Responding to public concern about cyclone damage, it has also funded a $35 million cyclone-protection project that is not part of FAP. Public opposition to FAP in Bangladesh is still strong, but in late 1995 the Reuters news service reported that "government officials said they were trying, with the help of the World Bank, to reverse public discontent by renaming the project the 'Bangladesh Water and Flood Management Strategy.'"

The next stage in the project cycle is preparation. In this stage, the borrower draws up a detailed project plan. Preparation is supposed to be solely the responsibility of the borrowing country, but the Bank has always played an active role in it, believing that passively waiting for borrowers to submit well-documented preparation reports will not produce enough projects to meet its five-year lending targets. In recent years, however, the Bank has stepped up its role in project preparation, a fact that former Vice President Willi Wapenhans has deplored because it "threatens the institution's ability to assess with disinterest the merits of a financing proposal." Increasingly, the Bank lends its borrowers money so that they can prepare projects that the Bank will be asked to fund. In 1995 alone, it lent Russia

$40 million for this purpose. The Bank also administers nearly fifty "consultant trust funds" that donor countries have established. These trust funds provide borrowers with grants so that they can hire consultants to prepare projects for them. Virtually all the funds require the recipient to hire consultants from the donor country, thus increasing the likelihood that the project design will call for materials and expertise available from that country. In 1992 such funds provided $25 million to borrowers; by 1995, the figure was up to $64 million.

Many developing countries feel that through such devices they have been reduced to the role of passive collaborator in the planning of their own futures. In 1992 the Bank held a seminar on project management with officials from borrowing governments. One of the conclusions of the meeting was that "project design and preparation too often . . . reflect policies the Bank currently favors instead of the country's felt needs." Despite the Bank's active involvement in preparation, an internal review of a decade's worth of projects concluded that only 20 percent were well prepared.

———————

Once a project has been identified and prepared, the Bank conducts its own appraisal to ensure that it is technically and financially possible and economically desirable. The Bank's appraisal techniques have come a long way in fifty years. The technical report for its first loan to Mexico—$34.1 million for several hydroelectric and thermal power plants—read in its entirety:

> I visited Mexico several times during the last year, and made inspections of the properties of the Mexican Light and Power Company and the Federal Electricity Commission. I checked over the proposed programs of expansion and am satisfied that they are reasonable and in line with good engineering practice. The staffs of both the Mexican Light and Power Company and the Commission are competent and I feel sure can carry out the program proposed.

The Bank's early economic analyses also left something to be desired; for many years they did not take into account the fact that governments often set the interest on its loans to public agencies at below-market rates. Such artificially low rates are basically government subsidies on capital that make high-cost projects seem cheaper that they actually were. Because the Bank failed to recognize such subsidies, it overinvested in capital-intensive projects such as hydroelectric dams.

It was not until the early 1960s, after what Benjamin King called a "palace revolution" by the Bank's economists, that its analysts regularly considered not only a project's financial rate of return, but also its economic rate of return—what it would generate for the country in increased taxes, employment, exports, and so forth. Several Bank economists had advocated such an approach in the early 1950s, but they got nowhere. As Jonas Haralz, an Icelandic economist who worked for the Bank in its early days and was later an executive director, explained, "The top people were not economists. They were either financial people or engineering people, and things like economic rates of return were new to them."

The adoption of economic rate of return (ERR) as an analytical tool was a great advance for the Bank, because it enabled it to compare the value of several different projects in a given country. Soon the economic rate of return became the chief yardstick by which loans were evaluated. No project whose projected ERR is below a certain level—at present 10 percent—is sent to the board for approval. "At one time," says a Bank official, "the figure 14 percent was popular as a cut-off point; now it's often 10 percent. Whatever is used, it's quite arbitrary." Moreover, once a project is completed, the primary gauge of its success is whether it produces the ERR it was predicted to produce.

But an economic rate of return is merely an opinion rendered in numerical form. "Though they are cited as measurements by the Bank," says economist Richard Feinberg, they are simply "indicators (sometimes convenient myths) that often serve to formalize what staff members subjectively know or believe in response to institutional requirements for 'the numbers.' " ERRs are easily manipulated; they are the product of the assumptions—arbitrarily chosen—that go into their calculation. The ERR of India's Narmada Dam, for instance, was originally calculated at just over 11 percent. At the time, however, the Bank's board was unhappy with ERRs lower than 12 percent. By redoing the analysis, using different assumptions, the staff was eventually able to obtain a 13 percent ERR. This done, the project was presented to, and approved by, the board.

Slavish devotion to ERRs gives rise to absurd decisions. Agronomist David Hopper joined the Bank in the late 1970s as vice president of the South Asia department. He had spent a decade working on agricultural projects in India and was determined "that no irrigation investment would be unaccompanied by appropriate drainage and . . . farmer demonstration and education." But when Hopper tried to add these elements to a new irrigation project, his staff objected. They explained, he later said "that the project in question barely met the test of a 10 percent economic rate of return, and that if drainage or demonstration or education were added, the extra cost would make the project uneconomic and, thereby, eliminate it from the lending program." And judging by the ERR, Hopper had to agree: "It was obvious that they were right. Proper drainage would have tripled the cost of the investment." Installing drainage would be economic, however, if the land to be drained was water-logged and saline as a result of earlier irrigation projects. Only then, said Hopper, did drainage projects "meet the economic rate of return, because unproductive acres were to be returned to productive use. But the costs were high, much higher than if the investment had been made concomitantly with the initial irrigation project."

In the early 1990s, the Bank, in an effort to satisfy Venezuela's urban residents who were in an uproar over that country's adjustment program, decided to finance some projects for the urban poor. It was a frustrating experience for the team that went looking for suitable projects because, as one member later explained, in terms of ERR "it turned out that putting water into slums wasn't half as good an investment as putting new sidewalks and parks into middle-class neighborhoods."

The Bank's efforts to invest only in projects with attractive ERRs were always plagued by what Mervyn Weiner, a former director of the Operations Evaluation Department, called "the old dog of a question that never goes away: whether the Bank isn't really financing, not the projects it thinks it is, but a miserable marginal project that nobody ever knows about and that isn't worth financing. This argument has merit. But I think this happens less than is often asserted." Weiner was describing the "fungibility problem," so called because the money from any given loan is fungible—that is, interchangeable with money from any other source. Thus it is impossible to say with certainty whether a Bank loan was spent on a new highway, or whether the government, having already set aside funds for the highway, used the Bank money to give a pay raise to discontented civil servants or build a palace for the president-for-life. In fact, one of the Bank's very first loans, the $195 million reconstruction loan it gave the Netherlands in 1947, is widely believed to have financed that country's war against Indonesian separatists.

For Warren Baum, however, who served as vice president of projects under McNamara and Clausen, "The fungibility argument is a red herring." This is because the Bank contributes more than money; it contributes expertise and experience. Thus, says Baum, "Our projects, when we have completed . . . them, are very different types of projects than they would have been had the Bank not been involved."

Underlying the Bank's obsession with judging projects by their economic rates of return is its desire to gauge the contribution of its loans to the gross national product (GNP). GNP was devised in the 1930s in response to economists' and government planners' demand for a uniform measurement of national production. It blossomed during World War II when Britain and the United States used it to gauge their war-related production. GNP counts all manufactured goods and paid services, but does not count anything that is not bought or sold, such as unpaid labor, clean air, or home-grown food.

Neither does GNP distinguish between productive and destructive contributions to the national income. Any monetary transaction adds to GNP. An oil spill produces clean-up jobs, a war produces jobs in weapons factories, a crime wave produces jobs for prison guards, a virulent disease produces hospital jobs. All add to the GNP. Moreover, GNP regards the consumption of natural resources as income. So a developing nation that clearcuts its forests and sells the timber sees its GNP go up year after year—until the year when the last tree is cut and the GNP suddenly crashes.

GNP is a measure of national income, albeit a deficient one. But the Bank, and almost all economists, use it as an index of social welfare, a task for which it is completely unsuitable. Its inadequacy on this score has long been realized. Robert Kennedy spoke about it on the first day of his 1968 campaign for the presidency:

> Gross national product counts air pollution and cigarette advertising and ambulances to clear our highways of carnage. It counts special locks for our doors and the jails for the people who break them. It counts the destruction of the redwoods and the loss of our natural wonders. It counts napalm and it counts nuclear warheads and armored cars for the police to fight the riots in our cities. . . . Yet the gross national product does not allow for the health of our children, the quality of their education, or the joy of their play. It does not include the beauty of our poetry, or the strength of our marriages, the intelligence of our public debates, or the integrity of our public officials. It measures neither our wit nor our courage, neither our wisdom nor our learning, neither our compassion nor our devotion to our country. It measures everything, in short, except that which makes life worthwhile.

There is a growing demand for an index or measurement that would reflect a wider range of values, including education, health, civil liberties, and so forth. This would not only give a more useful snapshot of a country's position, it would also permit planners to gauge more accurately the costs and benefits of proposed projects. In recent years, several such measures have been devised. One of the first was the Index of Sustainable Economic Welfare, devised by the economists Herman Daly and John Cobb, who are known internationally for their efforts to convince economists to incorporate notions of sustainability into their work. In 1990, the United Nations Development Program began producing an annual Human Development Index, which ranks countries by their citizens' level of education, life expectancy, and purchasing power. And in 1995, a San Francisco–based group calling itself Redefining Progress presented its plan for a Genuine Progress Indicator. The World Bank did not adopt any of these proposals, even though Herman Daly, now professor at the University of Maryland's School of Public Affairs, was for some time a senior economist at the Bank.

Daly was hired in 1988 at the urging of Robert Goodland, who hoped to broaden the view of the Bank's economists. "A lot of what's wrong with the World Bank, in my opinion," says Daly, "can be traced right back to where the Bank's officers got their training. They're mostly economists, and whether they came from Zaire or California, they all went to the same few schools—Harvard, MIT, Stanford, Oxford, Cambridge, Chicago—and they all learned the same thing. . . . They're coming here, trying to apply what they learned, and it's not working."

It was Daly's quixotic task to try and convince the Bank's economists that there are ecological constraints on economic growth and that taking those constraints into account in the choice and design of projects will produce better, more sustainable projects. "The Bank said it was in favor of sustainable development," he said, "so we tried to show how it could be done. The trouble is that the Bank wanted to keep sustainable development very vague. It was kind of like pornography: We'll know it when we see it, but it's too hard to define. The only part of the Bank that took up the idea that depletion of natural capital is a cost was the natural gas section. In the other areas, there was no attempt to apply it. We just never were able to get the idea of sustainable development taken seriously. And the reason is that the Bank is basically a money pump. It wants to get money out the door and anything that gets in the way of that—like careful accounting and environmental review—is frowned upon." Daly stayed at the Bank six years before resigning out of frustration at its resistance to change.

In 1995 the World Bank unveiled its own new system for measuring national wealth. This method defines a country's wealth as the sum of the value of its natural resources, its manmade assets, and the health, literacy, and productive capacity of its people. Like the other alternative indices, the Bank's system produces unexpected rankings: On a per capita basis, Surinam is wealthier than Belgium, for example, and Botswana is wealthier than Saudi Arabia.

Though the Bank's system was devised by its environment department, it largely ignores the value of a healthy environment. For instance, it assigns a higher value to forest land that has been logged than to a standing forest. Even its creator, John O'Connor, says, "If anything, the method is too businesslike." Daly questions the wisdom of putting human, natural, and manmade capital into separate categories. "It looks like the Bank is saying that it's okay to run down natural capital, as long as you build up your human or manmade capital to compensate. This system assumes that these are separate items that can be substituted for one another, but they aren't; they're interdependent. It doesn't do you any good to have thousands of highly educated petroleum engineers if you've run out of oil." Whatever its faults or virtues, the "wealth index" will have a minimal impact on the Bank's operations because GNP is still its key measurement and its touchstone of progress.

———

Appraisal is supposed to be the Bank's chance to make an independent assessment of a project, but, as its authorized history notes, the Bank often finds itself "working both sides of the street," appraising projects it has already proposed, identified, and prepared. Having decided that a project is worth so much work in the first place, the Bank is unlikely to cancel or reject it when it makes its own appraisal. A 1992 internal task force found that "many Bank staff perceive appraisals as marketing devices for securing loan approval and achieving personal recognition."

According to longtime Bank economist Benjamin King, an institutional bent toward overoptimism is inevitable: "If I'm expected to put a loan through, I'm going to assume that all the factors that could be favorable or unfavorable are favorable. You don't actually have to lie; you just have to be rather biased." Another Bank report confirmed this view, finding "substantial evidence that appraisal estimates are usually overoptimistic, sometimes strikingly so." One reason is that Bank analysts rely too much on best-case scenarios. In forecasting the productivity of agricultural projects, for example, they often use production figures obtained on government-managed model farms or on the demonstration plots run by fertilizer companies. As the Bank's own reports have pointed out, however, these pampered plots are often two or three times as productive as real farms.

In their eagerness to have projects approved, many top managers discourage questions that might produce unwelcome answers. For example, Martin Karcher, the official in charge of population and human resources in the Bank's South Asia Department, was unable, he said, to obtain the economic analysis for a huge hydroelectric scheme for Nepal, the Arun dam, "until quite late in the project processing cycle. Somehow that information wasn't being shared very readily." When he finally did read the staff appraisal report, in January 1994, he "found many problems with the analysis," including the assumptions on which it was based. "How is it possible that you can assume that the average Nepali consumer would be willing to pay something like 53 cents per kilowatt hour, when we in Washington pay something like 7 or 8 cents? Obviously, if you use these kinds of values, then any project becomes feasible and justified."

"My feeling," said Karcher, "was that the project was not being handled in an objective and evenhanded manner. Since senior management seemed to be committed to the project, a serious and open debate was no longer possible, and even common sense questions were being dismissed." So determined was the Bank to push the Arun dam through that it pressured Nepal to reject an $800,000 grant from Japan for "a project that would be directly targeted at the poorest people in Nepal, [because] the feeling was that it would distract too much of the government's attention." Arun was the last straw for Karcher, who quit the Bank in July 1994 after serving twenty-nine years: "I had serious reservations and misgivings, [and] I felt that one way of making that statement more effectively than through my previous memos would be to say I no longer want to be part of the decision-making process."

Another Bank staffer described how lending programs get out of control. "When I worked on Bangladesh," he said, "we decided at a country program division meeting that the lending program for the next year should be slowed, because Bangladesh could not absorb any more money. Everyone agreed. Then the division chief spoke. He said he also completely agreed, but if he went to his director and told him the lending should be slowed down, 'Tomorrow you will have a new division chief.' "

"The Bank has set up a system where they measure themselves by the quantity of money they lend," says Patrick Coady, who was U.S. executive director during the Bush administration. "So you have—both on the senior level and the individual task manager level—a lot of incentives not to be tough. And a lot of pressure not to be tough, a lot of games going on to reduce or bypass conditions." Coady's observation has been confirmed by numerous internal reviews that have described "pressure to lend as a pervasive aspect of the Bank's culture."

"One of the things that drove me crazy at the Bank," says Coady, "was the sense that you couldn't talk to a country unless you lent them a lot of money. The staff is not comfortable doing it. It's like 'What, you expect me to get off a plane in Quito, Ecuador, and deliver a hard message and tell them we're not going to lend? They won't receive me.' I say, 'Fine. Don't go to Ecuador. Go to someplace else.' There are lots of reasons for this. On a personal basis it's obviously a lot easier to talk to someone if at the end of a nice dinner you can pledge $500 million and they promise to do a little bit. I mean, that's a pleasant way to go through life."

———

Appraisals are conducted by small teams of Bank staffers, often supplemented by outside consultants. These teams or missions (Bank jargon for what one participant has called the "parachutings in by Washington-based officials of various backgrounds and training") generally spend three to four weeks in the borrowing country. The Bank chooses people for its missions on the basis of their technical or academic expertise, not their knowledge of the country.

The ignorance of many Bank-funded consultants regarding the countries about which they make multi-million-dollar judgments is a source of great annoyance to locals—and of chagrin to at least some within the Bank. The Dutch executive director, Eveline Herfkens, complained to journalist Paul Sweeney that "any transnational corporation—like Royal Dutch Shell—would make you go through a training program before sending you to a foreign country. But that's not how the Bank works."

In 1985, economist Robert Klitgaard made his maiden voyage to Equatorial Guinea as part of a small World Bank team charged with designing a project to rehabilitate the country's economy. The Bank wanted to make a fast-disbursing $10 million loan to the debt-ridden country and it was up to Klitgaard and his colleagues to find a suitable project. (Klitgaard explains that in Equatorial Guinea $10 million is "more than $30 per capita or, in a calculation possibly more relevant in government circles, more than $500,000 per cabinet minister.") The team was also supposed to coordinate the project with the country's medium-term development strategy, though, as Klitgaard soon discovered, Equatorial Guinea had no such strategy. The three-week mission ended in May 1985, and "the reports of the

team members were assimilated at the World Bank into an economic rehabilitation project," which the Bank duly funded with the promised $10
million.

The Bank prides itself on the fact that 38 percent of its professional
staff are citizens of developing countries, but those staff are drawn from the
ranks of the privileged, not the poor. By education and life-style, Bank
officials from developing countries have more in common with the political
and social elite in industrial nations than they do with the poor farmers and
laborers who form the majority of their compatriots. This was all too
evident to Jose Figueres Ferrer, president of Costa Rica in the 1950s and
one of the leaders of the movement that gave the country a democratic
constitution. In an oral interview recorded in 1970, Ferrer recalled his
experiences with Bank missions: "They were horrible. The people in the
World Bank were extreme reactionaries who came to Costa Rica and listened to what the oligarchy here, which we had just overthrown, was saying, and repeated all the arguments [to] us. . . . They were against
anything that meant social progress."

Since then the Bank has made little progress in becoming acquainted
with the hoi polloi. Recently, at an in-house seminar, a group of Bank
officials, most of whom were from developing countries themselves, were
asked how much time they had spent with rural people. Less than a quarter
had spent even one night in a village. "In other words," said someone
present at the meeting, "these were urbanites who took Ph.D.s at Oxford
or Harvard or Cambridge, but didn't really know too much about the
needs of the low-income majority in their own countries."

---

People affected by World Bank projects desperately want the outside world
to know of their circumstances. In April 1993, a visitor to a small settlement in the Indian state of Orissa was surrounded by a group of women,
all trying to tell their stories. The place where they were living was not their
real home. They had been ousted from their old village by a controversial
Bank-funded hydroelectric dam being built on the Muran River. Theirs was
a sadly familiar tale—of being forced suddenly to leave their land, of broken promises, of not receiving enough compensation to buy new land, of
receiving no compensation at all if abandoned by their husbands, of having
no temple, no well, no food, of having to walk 10 kilometers just to buy
salt, of struggling to keep their community together and their spirits up.

"We have nothing in our houses, nothing to give you," they apologized. Despite all they had suffered, however, they had not given up: They

had built new mud and thatch houses and planted crops in the floodplain of the seasonal river nearby, and now they were waiting for the water to come. They didn't know that the engineers upstream had dammed the river and that it would never water that land again. "You are a woman and we are women," one said. "You can see our situation and our children and you must understand. We can tell you things, many things. You are a literate person from a big country. You understand these things that are happening to us. So please, as a woman, help us." A man standing nearby added, "The human society living in America must know what is going on in another human society living in India. And they are responsible, because we're all humans, living on earth. They can't escape, you know. If I starve, you also bear a responsibility."

"We must look at our world through the eyes of the underprivileged," Barber Conable declared in 1986. But the Bank rarely encounters the underprivileged. Certainly not in Washington, D.C., where most of its work is done—and not even when traveling abroad on Bank missions. Few things annoy Bank staffers more than the oft-repeated charge that they live in unwonted luxury when they are abroad. But it is true that Bank missions rarely venture far from the major cities, where they stay in the best hotels and spend their time with politicians, bureaucrats, and business leaders.

"The team has to stay together and you won't get financial analysts and economists to go to a village," explained a frequent Bank consultant. "Anthropologists do that kind of thing; Bank officials don't. I've never been on a Bank mission, ever, where anybody on the mission stayed in a village. Sometimes we stay in government guesthouses, which are very nice. Usually they're on the edge of a small lake or in some other scenic setting."

Another consultant described a three-week Bank mission to an Asian country to appraise a massive mining investment.

We met every morning at the hotel dining room for breakfast and then each went our own way during the day—to meetings with various officials. At the end of the day we regrouped and swapped notes. In terms of cultural experience, you might as well have stayed in Washington, aside from working with the [local] officials. I was really lucky; I got out for almost nine days into the country-side.

This consultant did visit some of the sites selected for "his" project. Still, he saw only those places to which government officials escorted him and he had no chance to meet privately with local people. Even apparently casual encounters between Bank personnel and "real people" are generally carefully stage-managed. "We used to refer to the 'World Bank farmers,' said a consultant on a huge Bank-funded resettlement scheme in Sri Lanka. "Those are the ones to whom the Bank is led—and they're carefully selected by the government. A good consultant will go off and find someone else to talk to. But most just want to get it over with. They don't ask extra questions, or look beyond what they're shown."

This attitude is slowly changing, says a Bank staffer. "There's a perceptible shift since the late 1980s. We still get a fair number of the ones who stay in the capital and look at blueprints, but I'd say there's generally an expectation that you visit the field and talk to people, even if visits are too short and conversations less than spontaneous."

The Bank has published several papers touting the benefits of a technique called "beneficiary assessment." This involves commissioning local consultants, NGOs, and academics to spend several weeks living among those who will be affected (presumably beneficially) by Bank projects. It is a time-consuming but relatively inexpensive way of gathering information about what local people actually think about a planned project.

In one case, a team of Malians from the Ministry of Education, a local research institute, and a local consulting firm spent a month in 1988 living in rural villages in an attempt to learn more about people's attitudes toward education. They discovered that parents felt the costs of their children attending school outweighed the benefits. Among the problems: the walk to school was on average five miles in each direction; it was expensive to provide food for children during school days; families needed their children's help in the fields; the school buildings were deteriorating; the curriculum was of poor quality; and, most important, schooling did not improve the chances of obtaining a job. Using the information obtained from this exercise, which took six months and cost $20,000, the Bank altered a planned project so that it addressed some of the concerns expressed by the parents. The redesigned project included a subsidy for school lunches and a campaign aimed at persuading parents "of the importance of literacy and numeracy skills to the selection of seeds and fertilizer appropriate for better crops."

A Bank study of 121 rural water supply and sanitation projects, funded by the Bank and other agencies, found that beneficiary assessment was the single most important element in determining success. Nonetheless, beneficiary assessment has been slow to catch on at the Bank—in twelve years it was used in no more than fifty projects. Lawrence Salmen of the Bank's environment department attributes the institution's reluctance to use this apparently helpful technique to the fact that "many Bank staff and borrower-government personnel felt they knew what needed to be known regarding a development activity, including the people's perspective."

Although most Bank employees regard beneficiary assessment as unnecessary, a few regard it as an inadequate substitute for true local control of development. "It's a case of 'We know what the project's going to be and let's spend a little time finding out what refinements the beneficiaries would like,' " said one Bank official. In the case of the Mali education loan, for example, the beneficiary assessment resulted in some improvements to the project but left unaddressed the parents' main concern—the lack of employment opportunities for young people, whether educated or not. "What is really needed," the official continued, "is to find out what the people want and what they think, before projects are planned, when the overall development strategy is being worked out."

Governments tend to discourage rather than encourage consultations with local people. Members of a Bank mission to a Latin American country kept "trying to convince first the national and then the local officials that we were interested in the *poor* poor families—the ones without water. They kept taking us to middle-class neighborhoods where the sidewalks needed repaving, or where they wanted to put in a park, or the mayors would suggest building markets or slaughterhouses to increase municipal income."

Many Bank staffers and consultants complain that those who show the greatest indifference to the suffering of the poor are the bureaucrats of the borrowing countries.

"When I go with a task manager and our government escort to talk to people, it may or may not be the first time the task manager has seen the impacts of their project," one Bank anthropologist said, "but it definitely will be the first time that anyone from the first seven tiers of the government's project management team will have visited the area. Most probably they still won't see the impacts, or if they do, all it takes is a wave of the hand to solve them—through dismissal. How many times have I been told on a first-time visit that 'they're complaining only because outside agitators rile them'? Or, more bluntly, 'it's none of the Bank's business.' I remember one village meeting with very upset farmers, watching the government officials fall asleep one after the other as the farmers made their desperate petitions to stop the evictions from their forest homelands."

It is such incidents that fuel the Bank's conviction that virtually any project is better for its participation. "Nowhere does the Bank tell governments to lower their social and environmental standards," one official argued, "and in several places committed task managers and others have raised them." But the Bank can only raise standards so far before governments take their business elsewhere. In recent years, several countries have canceled—or refused to seek—Bank loans for projects to which they fear the Bank would attach burdensome environmental and social conditions. In 1993, for example, Bangladesh informed the Bank that it did not wish to proceed with a planned loan for a controversial urban renewal project on the outskirts of the capital, Dhaka. The reason for the cancellation, according to Christopher Willoughby, then the Bank's resident representative in Bangladesh, was "so they don't have to bother with World Bank–style resettlement."

Borrowers sometimes employ elaborate ruses to get World Bank loans without having to bother with World Bank–style resettlement. This is particularly true with urban loans because the Bank's urban department, long a refuge for what one staffer calls "Peace Corps guys from the seventies," has the most stringent resettlement policies in the Bank. These include a rule of thumb that it will not fund projects that will displace more than 5 percent of the affected population. As a result, says one Bank official, borrowers often "clear people out before they ask the Bank for funds." Kenya used a different tactic with a Bank-funded slum upgrade project in Nairobi. "The Bank was very good about this project," said one observer. "They put in a condition that the government could not bulldoze the shantytowns. They upgraded all around the shantytowns and in them, putting in sewers, water lines, and so forth. On the day the project ended, the government went in and burned down all the old buildings."

The Bank worked for several years on a loan to China for the Three Gorges Dam on the Yangtze River, a controversial project that will displace at least 1.2 million people. But the Bank would have imposed many burdensome conditions before agreeing to fund such a project. Instead China is trying to go ahead without the Bank's help. As one staffer explained: "They figure—rightly, because the Bank still does have approximate lending targets—'We'll get $3 billion from the Bank, whether it's for the Three Gorges or for education. So why expose ourselves to their resettlement demands?'"

Jochen Kraske, the Bank's historian and previously the head of its New Delhi office and of the Nepal, Bangladesh, and Sri Lanka Department, says the Bank must learn to be more accommodating to its borrowers. If it insists on imposing unrealistically high standards, however admirable, warns Kraske, the Bank will become irrelevant. It will be left out of "projects that are environmentally and socially controversial. It will not [be asked to] fund dams, irrigation projects, power projects, and all those things. That will be left to somebody else. We will fund only health, population, nutrition projects." The British development aid group Oxfam argues that the Bank should not lower its standards, but apply them more widely. It wants the Bank to "introduce effective cross-conditionality, in which all project lending is made conditional on compliance with social and environmental guidelines in every project."

––––––––––

Appraisals that ignore local knowledge, wishes, and concerns give rise to poorly designed and often fatally flawed projects. A case in point is the Bank's 1973 $50 million loan to rejuvenate Indonesia's once-vibrant sugar cane industry by rebuilding old sugar mills. Once the mills were ready, however, it turned out that Indonesian farmers did not want to grow sugar cane. The reason was simple: They could make twice as much growing rice. In some areas the disappointed mill owners resorted to keeping their mills busy with the help of local officials who forced unwilling farmers to grow cane at gunpoint.

It is not only local people who get short shrift in many appraisal reports; the land itself is often ignored. A survey of the Bank's appraisals of hydro projects between 1978 and 1989 explained that "in most SARs [Staff Appraisal Reports], references to the type of land [to be flooded] are understandably vague, as appraisal missions tend to visit mainly the dam sites. The reservoir area of the Karakaya Project in Turkey was described in terms of the gorge and surrounding steppe land immediately upstream of the dam site. The fact that large areas of alluvial plain lay further upstream, and a highly productive apricot industry that was situated on the lower slopes above the plain would be inundated, was overlooked." In fact, 40 percent of the appraisal reports studied did not state how much land the dam would flood.

The effect of such self-imposed ignorance is illustrated by the Bank-financed El Cajon dam in Honduras. Completed in 1985, El Cajon was designed to generate 300 megawatts of electricity—64 percent of the country's normal consumption. But deforestation in the surrounding watershed sent so much silt into the reservoir that in less than a decade the dam's electricity production was cut in half. By agreeing to lend money for a dam while ignoring the obvious degradation of the dam's watershed, the Bank encouraged Honduras to take on an $850 million debt it could ill afford. Moreover, because this poorly planned dam was allowed to dominate the national electricity supply, Hondurans must, in addition to paying for an overpriced project, endure crippling energy rationing and bear the cost of providing expensive emergency power from diesel generators.

Over the past half-century, the Bank has destroyed traditional cooperative irrigation systems and water-user organizations all over the world—insisting that they be replaced by modern state-run irrigation schemes, very few of which have lived up to expectations. Now the Bank has decided that the key to irrigation success is "farmer participation," a supposedly new idea it is enthusiastically promoting—and energetically lending for. The Bank has finally discovered what peasant farmers have known all along: "If the irrigators are involved in the design, you get a much better designed system."

Not that the Bank is alone in its disdain for local knowledge and esteem for engineers. Governments throughout the world share its confidence in modern technologies and top-down bureaucracies and its impatience with the unschooled masses. Near the Yanhee dam stands an enormous plaque on which Thailand's Electricity Generating Authority has inscribed a heartfelt statement that might serve as a motto for the World Bank. "Those who would carry on great public schemes must be proof against the worst fatiguing delays, the most mortifying disappointments, the most shocking insults, and, worst of all, the presumptuous disparagement of the ignorant upon their designs."

———

The imbalance between theoretical knowledge and local experience produces what the Germans, who have a word for everything, call a *Fachidiot*, a specialist-idiot. Michael Lejeune, who was director of the Bank's East Africa Department in the 1970s, later explained that the reason so many of the projects in that region were failures was that "none of us, I must confess, really understood how African society worked. We did not speak the local languages. . . . These people communicated in their tribal languages, or possibly in Swahili or some other lingua franca which none of us knew."

Sometimes the Bank bends over backward to maintain its ignorance. In 1980, it hired American anthropologist David Price to report on the likely impact of its Polonoroeste project, the massive colonization scheme in the Brazilian Amazon, on the Indians of the region. Price, who had lived and studied in the area for many years, was sent on a two-week trip, an amount of time which he later described as "highly inadequate in a very inaccessible region." In subsequent testimony before the U.S. House of Representatives, he explained:

> I came home. I wrote my report . . . and my report was very, very negative—it could not be other than negative. . . . The [government's] plan to assist the Indians in the area was puerile and trivial and I could not believe that it has ever been intended to be taken seriously. . . . I made this very, very clear in my report to the World Bank. However, I found out after I had submitted it that the report was seen by no one except the two World Bank staff members who accompanied me to Brazil and the head of the [Bank's] Latin America and Caribbean regional office. . . . When the World Bank produced a general evaluation of the Polonoroeste project, my findings were watered down, distorted and changed.

In 1995, human rights activist Harry Wu accused the Bank of funding forced labor camps in China through its $125 million Tarim Basin irrigation project. The Bank says the project is intended to improve food production on the edge of the Taklimakan Desert in Xinjiang Province. The project area is known as China's Siberia, because it is dotted with *laogai*, forced labor camps. "The World Bank would have us believe the project primarily benefits Xinjiang's minority population," said Wu, who insists that the true beneficiaries are the military farms attached to the region's seven large *laogai* and its many smaller prison camps. In responding to Wu's charges, the Bank at first pleaded ignorance. A spokesman, Graham Barrett, said the Bank was unaware of the scores of prison camps in the project area. "China does not tell us about its military installations and camps. Inevitably, Bank projects are going to be located in areas where they may have these things. . . . But we have no knowledge of any link in this project to the military or to forced labor." A subsequent Bank inquiry found that the government agency that implements the Tarim project is also "responsible for administering some prisons and adjacent farms for the central Ministry of Justice," but concluded that there is "no evidence to substantiate [Wu's] claims."

---

The strain of going "on mission" (in Bank jargon the article is omitted) has less to do with jet lag than with the need to ignore the gulf between the messy, complex real world and the neat tidy "official" world. In "The

Development Game," a short story about a mission to northwest Pakistan written by a longtime development consultant, a young Dutch sociologist makes the rest of the team uncomfortable.

This Dutch girl is a nuisance. . . . For her it is an important discovery that the official world does not match the real one. She visits villages and reports back to us at dinner that the irrigation schemes are not working the way the government says they are, or that the veterinary employees are selling drugs they should give away. She tells us that money for building primary schools has gone into the pockets of contractors and local politicians. The official figures on truck transport are wrong because they neglect the Afghanis who own most of the trucks. And so on. She's like a detective excited at uncovering a vast conspiracy. We make non-committal replies and try to change the subject. The older Japanese says nothing and finds an excuse to leave the table.

Most successful consultants have gotten beyond the stage in which the Dutch girl finds herself. Like the narrator of "The Development Game," they have learned that to do their jobs they must treat the official account as the truth: "The real world is infinitely complex, and even the people who are part of it don't understand it. And we are here for only four weeks, most of that in office meetings. When you discover that the official world does not correspond to the real world, you can either accept the official version or make your own judgement. It's always best to take the government figures."

Thayer Scudder, a frequent participant in Bank missions, knows well the frustrations—and the hopes—to which they give rise.

You embark on a mission in the hope that you'll play a role in enabling people to raise their living standards—in a sustainable fashion. Very rarely have missions I've been on achieved that goal. I end up either saying "The project's no bloody good" or "Well, you should implement it, but only in this certain way"—but that's not done. . . . The most frustrating thing is your increasing realization that the problem lies at the center: not just in Washington, but the capital of Botswana, the capital of Zambia, the capital of Cameroon, where the local elite want to maintain their power. They don't want to decentralize fiscal control, they don't want to decentralize decision making; they don't want to do the things which a consultant feels are absolutely necessary. In other words you're dealing with bastards, guys who don't give a damn.

For many years, Majibul Huq Dulu, a community organizer in Bangladesh, has been working with the people who are to be displaced by the country's massive Flood Action Plan. He offers to take consultants out to see the people whom their work will affect. A few have gone with him. "They listen to the people," he said. "They are sympathetic; they want to be nice. Then as soon as they get back to Dhaka, they forget. Some of them do write a good report, but if it doesn't serve the purpose, their team leader or someone in the World Bank throws it out." As David Lilienthal explained a quarter-century ago, "Consultants are generally supposed to agree with the Bank staff."

Consultants who wish to make a life of it have to learn to close their eyes to certain aspects of the real world. Those who refuse to do so are not popular teammates. They slow things down with their disturbing questions and incessant worrying. Most international consultants—certainly the most successful ones—have learned to narrow their vision, to focus only on their small piece of the puzzle, to ignore the larger questions and those that fall between the cracks, so that they can do their work quickly and efficiently, collect their substantial paychecks, and move on to the next mission without pausing to have a nervous breakdown.

———

Once a project has been appraised, the Bank enters into negotiations with the borrower. This is when the formal loan documents are drawn up and the parties agree on the conditions to be attached to the loan. When the negotiations are complete, the loan is submitted to the board for its approval.

In theory the board is the ultimate authority in the Bank: It alone can approve or deny loans. By tradition, however, the board may not propose loans, so its power is a negative one, the power of rejection—a power it has never exercised. The board consists of twenty-four executive directors (EDs). The five countries with the largest capital subscription—at the present time, they are the United States, Japan, Germany, the United Kingdom, and France—each appoint one director. The remaining nineteen directors are elected for two-year terms by the governors of the other countries, each director representing those countries whose votes he or she receives. The vote is divided among the directors in proportion to the shareholdings of the countries each represents. The U.S. ED casts 17 percent of the vote; the

Japanese ED 6.3 percent; and so on down the line. At present the smallest vote, 1.58 percent, is cast by the ED who represents Benin, Burkina Faso, Cameroon, Cape Verde, and nine other African countries.*

The shared-director arrangement makes for some strange bedfellows. One director, for example, casts his 2.92 percent of the vote on behalf of Antigua and Barbuda, the Bahamas, Barbados, Belize, Canada, Dominica, Grenada, Guyana, Ireland, Jamaica, St. Kitts and Nevis, St. Lucia, and St. Vincent and the Grenadines—some borrowers, some donors, some North American, some Latin American, and one European country. At least this group has English as an official language in common. The entry into the Bank of the countries of Eastern Europe and the former Soviet Union has created even stranger mixes. One constituency now comprises Austria, Belarus, Belgium, the Czech Republic, Hungary, Kazakhstan, Luxembourg, the Slovak Republic, Slovenia, and Turkey.

It is taken for granted that management would not propose a project that is technically, financially, or otherwise unsound. Therefore the chief concern of the EDs is how a project will affect the political and business interests of their countries. Former U.S. ED Patrick Coady mourned the fact that most screening of World Bank loans by the U.S. government concerns "U.S. congressional sensitivities or the philosophical tendencies of the administration. I didn't get the support I wish I had in considering whether the actual concept of the loan is good, whether it's going to be implemented properly, whether the disbursement schedules were right, whether the country's underlying policies were appropriate. . . . There was none of that input and I think that was a real shortcoming on the board because I had more of that interest than most directors."

The board has never failed to approve a project that came before it. EDs from industrial countries vote for loans because they want the lucrative consulting and engineering contracts that big projects bring. Borrowing countries do so because, as a developing-world ED explained, "If I vote against today's project, then my colleague will vote against my project tomorrow."

Eveline Herfkens, an ED who represents a mixture of borrowers and donors, explained why she would not vote against a project even if she disapproved of it. "I represent borrowers. I know how difficult it is to get a penny out of this institution. And this project will have gone through one and a half years of negotiations by the time it gets to the board. If I only

---

* These figures apply only to votes on IBRD loans. IDA's shares are distributed somewhat differently. In IDA the United States, though still the largest shareholder, has only 15.4 percent of the vote, for example, whereas Japan has 10.5 percent.

then spot it, it's my mistake. [It means] I haven't been doing my homework, you see, in the early stages."

Many EDs from donor nations regard bringing business home as their main job at the Bank. Several, including the American, the Canadian (who represents thirteen countries), and the Italian (who represents five), have full-time staffers whose job it is to help their nationals get contracts for Bank-funded projects. Other board members disapprove of this. "I think there's a serious conflict of interest if someone who is on the board of an institution in the meantime tries to do procurement for his country," says Herfkens.

There is also a potential for conflict of interest of a more personal nature. In the late 1970s, Jacques de Groote, a Belgian banker, became the ED for Belgium, Austria, Hungary, Luxembourg, and Turkey. De Groote, described by *The Wall Street Journal* as "something of a bon vivant, with a taste for the finest in clothes, restaurants and residences. . . . [and] at times hard-pressed for cash," also advised Zaire's dictator, Mobutu Sese Seko, on his dealings with the Bank. By his own account, de Groote provided Zairean officials with information about views of "the higher echelons of the IMF and the World Bank" and about the Bank's instructions, which, he admitted, were supposed to be "given to no one, apart from the team of negotiators." Despite increasing disquiet about extraordinary government corruption and mismanagement, Zaire continued to receive World Bank loans throughout de Groote's tenure.

In 1990, two leading opposition figures in Zaire called for an investigation into de Groote's activities. Because the Bank has no written code of ethics for its EDs, officials said it was up to the Belgian authorities to investigate any alleged improprieties. In 1991, de Groote stepped down from his post at the Bank. Zaire has not received a loan from the Bank since then.

EDs do not find out about a project in any detail in its early stages unless it becomes an object of controversy or they search out information on it. In general, EDs are given briefing papers on projects fourteen days before they come to the board. For many years, management fed information to the board very sparingly; all "internal" documents, including even the Bank's operational memos, which clarify its policies and procedures, were denied to them. Today the EDs have access to any document in the Bank. The trick is that in order to ask for a document, it is necessary to know of its existence.

Sometimes, before being allowed to see a Bank document, directors are required to sign a "confidentiality agreement," or to agree not to copy it or discuss it with anyone else. In 1989, the Bank's then director of external affairs, Francisco Aguirre Sacasa, warned senior managers that if documents were more readily available to board members, there was a danger that their governments would have time to make "too many comments." In a farewell speech to his colleagues, economist Herman Daly questioned this attitude, saying, "Why one part of the Bank has to hide things from other parts of the Bank, and especially from the executive directors, has always puzzled me."

Former U.S. director Patrick Coady says he relied on "the environmental community and the other NGOs" to supply him with information he did not get from the Bank. "That was generally the case. Initially I was embarrassed by that, but after a while you learn to live with the fact that there are just a hell of a lot of documents that you're not on the distribution list for, and there are people that care about them and get them—and send them to you." He added, "The overriding principle is that the management is in charge of managing the Bank and they should only provide the directors with the information they feel the directors need. 'Treat them like mushrooms: Keep them in the dark and feed them shit.' I think that's the guiding principle."

---

The EDs are full-time employees of the Bank. The Bank pays their annual salaries and provides them with secretaries, offices, and all the other perquisites of Bank employment. The board meets formally twice each week and in committee on most days. At one time governments sent top officials to serve on the board. Lately the job is increasingly treated as a reward for faithful service, a pleasant posting at the end of a career. "Nowadays, executive directors have come from the second and third tiers of their respective administrations," says former Vice President Visvanathan Rajagopalan. "They are not the topmost people." Taking care to be more tactful, Moises Naim, himself a former ED, agrees: "The generalized, and admittedly subjective, anecdotal and perhaps even uninformed, perception among observers is that the caliber of the board has tended to decline."

With only twenty-four positions to share among 178 countries, most directors serve for just one or two two-year terms before leaving to make room for someone else. In that short time, says Moises Naim, "It is impossible, even for the few of them that have a good prior understanding of the institution, to master the overwhelming array of complex issues on which they are supposed to develop an independent opinion." As a result, says Naim, the board, which should be overseeing the Bank's management, instead relies on it for information and guidance. Naim sums up his former colleagues as "divided," "overwhelmed," and "no match for a usually brilliant group of professionals with decades of experience at the Bank." Bimal Jalan, ED for India, Bangladesh, Sri Lanka, and Bhutan, finds the situation satisfactory, however. "It's a pretty good system," he told me. "If you have any questions, they tell you which staff member to talk to."

For a brief, glorious moment in 1946, the board of executive directors was the dominant power in the Bank. Led by the U.S. director, whose power derived from his government's role as the Bank's main funder, it set policies, initiated loans, and oversaw the running of the infant institution. It was, in fact, his inability to control the board that drove the Bank's first president, Eugene Meyer, to resign after only six months. Meyer's successor, John McCloy, took the job only on condition that he could replace the U.S. director with his own man. McCloy was followed by three strong presidents, Eugene Black, George Woods, and Robert McNamara—all of whom kept a tight reign on the board.

McNamara kept the board under particularly strict control, recalled Warren Baum, the longtime vice president of the Bank's central projects department. "Directors never spoke to each other and they never spoke to the staff; they spoke only to the chairman, and he was the filter between them and the staff." Board subservience continued even under the weaker, one-term presidents who followed—A. W. Clausen, Barber Conable, and Lewis Preston. Over the years, there have been intermittent flashes of independence on the board's part, efforts to maintain a minimum level of self-respect in the face of a general feeling that the board was, as the U.S. Government Accounting Office once put it, little more than a rubber stamp for the Bank's president. The debt crisis made the borrowing countries even more reluctant to quarrel with the Bank's management. According to former Vice President Willi Wapenhans, "They were more than ever dependent on the Bank, and not only on its money, but also on its good offices" in dealing with other creditors.

The problem has continued. "Rich-country directors, mostly upper-middle-ranking civil servants, know they have little to gain from confronting a Bank president who can get through on the telephone to their bosses, the finance ministers, at any time of the day or night," says *The Economist*. "And poor-country directors hesitate to confront top managers if they think they might jeopardize capital flows to their countries."

In recent years, however, the board has shown some signs of taking a more active role. The board—and its expanding staff—is now the fastest-growing item in the Bank's administrative budget. In 1989, Timothy

Tahane, a Bank vice president and the secretary to the board, warned his fellow vice presidents that "increasingly, the skills of the executive directors' advisors were superior to some of the Bank staff they have to deal with." The Bank's senior management does not want the board taking a more active interest in its lending operations. As Wapenhans put it: "The Board is ill-equipped to deal with operational detail, nor should it! . . . It should become focused on policy, strategic direction, and institutional oversight."

The board appears to agree that a close oversight of individual loans is not its role. In late 1992 it decided that its time would be better spent considering the Bank's general policies and its overall development strategies for individual countries, than its projects. "The projects were just too complex for the board as such to make a meaningful contribution," said Jonas Haralz, the ED for the Nordic countries, who chaired the committee that recommended the changes. "Unless something was terribly wrong, project discussions were best carried out, not in the boardroom, but directly with the staff. As ED, I had few opportunities to evaluate individual projects thoroughly." The problem is especially acute toward the end of the fiscal year, when loan officers are scrambling to push up their lending levels. Roughly a quarter of the year's loans come to the board in June, the last month of the fiscal year. Patrick Coady, the former U.S. ED, deplored this pattern. "I can't possibly perform my oversight duties in such a brief period of time. Projects get approved that shouldn't be." In 1993, Coady's last year in office, the board approved 245 World Bank loans, 30 percent of them in May and June, and another 185 for the IFC.

In response to this situation, the board in 1992 adopted a procedure for "streamlining" loan approval. This means that nowadays most loans are approved by default without a formal board meeting, unless a board member, all of whom receive project summaries in advance, raises an objection. The only loans that cannot be "streamlined" are adjustment loans, debt-reduction loans, and loans for projects that are unusually large or "involve complex issues or innovative features."

---

After a project is approved, the loan agreements are signed. These are the legal documents in which both the Bank's and the borrower's obligations are spelled out. Once upon a time, before the Bank was making hundreds of loans a year, there was a formal signing ceremony for each loan, with much taking of photographs and giving away of pens. James Morris attended one such, in which the borrower was a small nation. "Lofty indeed was the condescension with which the Bank, whose purpose is the making of loans, agreed to make this one, and fawning to a degree was the deference with which the money was accepted, the borrowers' representative assuring the management that he was positively grateful for the difficulties the Bank had placed in their way, which had made them feel not only richer, but happier and more civilized too, and had convinced them, he seemed to suggest, that such obstructive and delaying tactics ought properly to be applied to the governing of all human affairs." On the other hand, there is also the story about an Indian delegate who, when "reminded fulsomely that the Bank had lent his country a total of $600 million, turned with a sweet but abrasive smile upon the management and offered them his hearty congratulations."

# Fourteen

Once a loan is signed, the implementation stage of the project cycle begins. A great deal is at stake during this stage: Bank projects are cornucopias of business for private companies. Each year they result in the awarding of several thousand multi-million-dollar contracts and tens of thousands of smaller ones to construction companies, engineers, equipment makers, and other businesses. Since its founding, the Bank has paid out more than a quarter of a trillion dollars to the providers of the goods and services used in its projects. In 1995 alone it disbursed $17 billion.

Contracts for Bank projects are awarded under a system devised by the Bank called international competitive bidding. This system is supposed to ensure that contracts are awarded fairly and to the lowest bidder. Local bids are discounted by 10 to 15 percent, to improve the chances of domestic firms competing with large foreign companies. Partly due to this, about 44 percent of the Bank's funds are disbursed to companies within the borrowing country, mostly for construction work. The rest, 56 percent of all the money the Bank lends, is paid to foreign companies, mainly those from rich countries. As one Bank official said, "Most of our money doesn't go to the South, it goes straight from Washington to Pennsylvania, where they manufacture the turbines, or Frankfurt, where they produce the dredging equipment."

Business from the Bank is one of the chief inducements to membership for the rich countries. As Mason and Asher explained in their authorized history of the Bank, *The World Bank Since Bretton Woods*, "Major subscribers of Bank capital tend to regard the procedure as somehow unfair or insufficiently responsive to 'political realities' if their own share in total procurement falls significantly below the share of their subscriptions in the total capital resources of the Bank." In other words, the Bank's rich members expect to get at least as much out of the institution—in the form of contracts—as they contribute to it.

And they do. Year after year the Bank's most powerful members are awarded contracts roughly in proportion to their shareholdings in the Bank. The Bank's five top shareholders, the United States, Japan, Germany, France, and the United Kingdom, are also the top five beneficiaries of World Bank expenditures on foreign goods and services. Together, they receive half the money the Bank spends on foreign procurement.

Over the years, American firms alone have received $24 billion in business from the World Bank—exactly what the U.S. government has contributed in cash to IBRD and IDA. If the two institutions are considered separately, however, a different picture emerges. The $1.94 billion the United States has paid to IBRD has brought in more than ten times that much to American businesses, whereas the $22 billion it has paid to IDA produced only $4 billion of business for American firms. Britain has done even better then the United States: It has given the Bank $7 billion and received $12 billion in Bank-funded contracts. Its contributions to IBRD, like those of the United States, have been much more lucrative that its contributions to IDA.

---

In 1991, *The Economist* painted an idealized view of the Bank's behavior after a loan is approved. "As the loan is disbursed, typically over five–ten years, the Bank stays involved—checking on progress, monitoring the procurement of materials and labour, ready with advice when difficulties crop up." In reality, the Bank tends to lose interest in its projects once they are approved by the board. Though it is supposed to supervise the projects' implementation by the borrower, numerous internal surveys have found, as did one in 1992, that "the promotion and reward system in the Bank [is] biased towards new lending; supervision [comes] nowhere." Even the Bank's official publication on the project cycle describes supervision as "the least glamorous part of project work." The way time is allocated in the

Bank reflects supervision's lowly status: The staff devotes less than 14 percent of its time to supervising projects, 21 percent to making loans, and 26 percent to "overhead tasks."

Borrowers are legally required to provide the Bank with a steady stream of financial statements and other information so that the Bank can, in the words of its charter, "ensure that the proceeds of any loan are used only for the purposes for which the loan was granted, with due attention to considerations of economy and efficiency." But a study carried out in 1993 by the Bank's accounting division found that more than 60 percent of the financial information due to the Bank is received so late it is "inconsequential for project management purposes." The format of the statements, when they do arrive, is often so confused that "it is even impossible to make reconciliations between the records of the projects and those of the Bank." Moreover, most of the financial reports the Bank receives are carried out by government auditors, "many of whom lack independent and skilled staff, particularly for the audit of commercial type entities."

These problems are compounded, said the task force, by the fact that the Bank has "a severe shortage of financial specialists" and "a lack of sufficient interest and understanding by the staff" in such matters. As a result, "Financial statements frequently are not reviewed, or are reviewed by staff without the necessary skills to identify significant problems and to take appropriate action." The study concluded that "project management itself is not under control."

————

With billions of dollars at stake, many foreign firms hire local agents to act as their liaisons with governments. Agents are freelancers who get a percentage of the value of the contracts they win. "The agent's job is to develop a relationship with the client [the borrowing country] and feed back information on the best ways of winning the project," explained one international consultant. "The danger, of course, is that—especially with the larger projects—there's a great temptation to start offering money to the key individual. Or not money but cars. In countries that are quite poor, a car means a lot."

Corruption is notoriously difficult to quantify or pin down. Most incidents of which the Bank becomes aware are discovered only by chance. In one recent case, a Canadian company was awarded a consultancy contract for a project in Burundi after an open-bidding process that was judged by an international panel of respected experts. The winning company contracted to use some employees of a second firm. The heads of the two firms went to meet with the Burundian head of the panel, "who very openly took out a list of panel members, including himself, to whom bribes should be paid." The head of the second firm refused, left at once, and severed his company's connection with the project. He later told the story to a friend who works at the Bank. That friend reported it to someone connected with the project, and the contract was rebid. No record was made of the embarrassing incident. "In the normal course of events," one of the people involved said, "no inspector would ever have discovered this."

Many businesses would like the Bank to keep a closer eye on the awarding of contracts. "Saying 'Well, it's really up to the government' is just asking for trouble," says one official of an engineering firm. "Government salaries tend to be quite low and if someone has a low income and power over huge amounts of money and people who want contracts offering them 'rewards,' what do you expect will happen? In Africa, literally, prices are enhanced by 10 percent or more to pay for corruption. . . . It's no good saying that's the way things are. It's the Bank's money and the Bank should have a more transparent [i.e., open] bidding system."

――――

The Bank has not received much support from its members in its efforts to control corruption. The United States has had a law against bribing foreign officials to get business since 1977, but no other country has such a law. Germany recently decided against adopting one, and in many countries, including Australia, Canada, Spain, Austria, Denmark, Switzerland, and Germany, bribes to foreign companies are tax-deductible. In 1993, several former Bank officials and international businessmen founded Transparency International, a nonprofit group dedicated to combating corruption in international development and trade. Corruption on a grand scale has "become almost universal in major international contracts between the North and the great majority of South countries," says the organization.

The bigger the project, the higher the official whose interest it will attract. Assuming, for example, that 5 percent of a project's cost is spent on bribes, Transparency International offers the following rough guide to the hierarchy of graft: "Five percent of $200,000 will be interesting to a senior official below the top rank; five percent of $2 million is in the top official's area; five percent of $20 million is real money for a minister and his key staff; five percent of $200 million justifies the serious attention of the head of state." The group cautions that "the amounts will vary from country to country" and states that 5 percent is a conservative figure: "Recently figures like 10 and 15 percent are often heard."

In 1977 *The Wall Street Journal* reported "authoritative estimates" that corruption inflates the cost of Bank-funded projects by 10 to 15 percent in Indonesia. Sixteen years later the leading Indonesian economist and former finance minister Sumitro Joyohadikusumo set the figure at 30 percent. "If waste and corruption is soon tackled," he said, "we [will] basically no longer need foreign aid." In 1993 the Hong Kong–based Political and Economic Risk Consultancy rated Indonesia, China, and the Philippines as the most corrupt countries in Asia. That same year, Indonesia, China, and the Philippines also ranked as the first-, second-, and third-largest recipients of World Bank loans to East Asia.

International competitive bidding is, in the Bank's own words, supposed to "ensure that the requisite goods are procured in the most efficient and economical manner." Nevertheless, an internal survey revealed in 1992 that "staff considered borrowers were getting away with much misprocurement." There are many ways of abusing the procurement process. Some Bank-approved procurement contracts evoke the Pentagon's infamous $640 toilet seat. In their book *Food First,* Frances Moore Lappé and Joseph Collins cite the high prices paid for electronic gear in a 1977 agricultural project in Thailand: 420 hand calculators at $50 apiece; 30 desk calculators at $160 apiece; 30 16-millimeter film projectors at $1,200 each; and 12 21-inch color TVs at $1,050 each. The authors comment: "Sounds more like a Harvard graduate course in mass media than a rural development project in Asia!"

For a Bank-funded tubewell project in 1970, the Bangladeshi government contracted with one of its wealthiest citizens to provide tube wells. The local Bank representative considered the price agreed on unnecessarily high—$12,000 per tubewell—and recommended to his superiors in Washington that the contract be canceled. Washington insisted that the contract go ahead. In the *Far Eastern Economic Review*'s account of the incident:

> World Bank officials were apparently told that the highest Government authorities in Dacca were involved in placing the contract, and to cancel the whole scheme now would create embarrassing political problems in an area where the Bank hopes to have increasing influence in years to come.

Corruption, of course, raises the cost of development projects. More worryingly, it also lowers their quality. In 1989 a major Bank review of irrigation projects found that 60 percent suffered from "premature deterioration of civil works." This is largely the result of corruption: substandard materials substituted for the more expensive ones called for in the contract, and work paid for in full but performed inadequately or not at all.

Evidence of corruption—even on a massive scale—is not enough to cause the Bank to cancel or suspend a loan. The Yacyreta Dam on the river that divides Argentina and Paraguay was to have provided 2,700 megawatts of electric power at a cost of $1.5 billion. The project is the result of a 1973 agreement between Paraguayan dictator General Alfredo Stroessner and Argentina's then vice president, "Isabelita" Peron. The World Bank got involved in 1979, when it lent Argentina's military government $210 million for the dam.

By 1983, when Raul Alfonsin was elected president of Argentina, replacing the military junta, the dam had already consumed $1 billion, though construction had scarcely begun. There was much support in the new civilian government for abandoning the costly venture before it was too far advanced. According to an article by reporter Judith Evans in the *Joint Annual Meeting News,* "The only thing keeping the project alive was the promise of [more] World Bank and IDB [Inter-American Development Bank] financing." The cabinet split over the issue, and "the tie was broken by Roque Carranza, an engineer who was then minister of public works and a long-time consultant to the World Bank." In 1988, the Bank made a second loan, for $252 million, to Yacyreta.

In 1990 Argentine President Carlos Saul Menem called Yacyreta "a monument to corruption." The dam was still less than 60 percent finished, and had already consumed $3 billion. The 50,000 people in the reservoir area had still to be relocated, a process that reportedly worried Menem due to the rich possibilities for corrupt land deals. In 1991, *The New York Times* reported that the "World Bank raised questions at various times about accounting and record-keeping procedures but did not try to conduct extensive oversight."

Also in 1991, Judith Evans reported that "suspicions have been raised about every one of the bidding awards involving international firms." Much of the Yacyreta money is believed to be resting comfortably in overseas bank accounts in the names of Argentinean and Paraguayan officials responsible for awarding contracts on the project. A portion may have made its way into Argentina's military budget: Some Bank staff call Yacyreta "the dam that financed the Falklands war."

In 1992, over vigorous protests from many quarters, including the likely oustees, the Bank approved a third loan for the dam, this one for $300 million. Since then, things have only gotten worse. In mid-1995 an inspection team visiting the dam found that many of the 15,000 people who have been forced from their homes have received neither land nor financial compensation. A fish elevator that was installed at a cost of $25 million only allows fish to move upstream, although the river's migrating fish need to travel in both directions. The most conservative estimate of what Yacyreta will finally cost is the World Bank's figure of $6 billion. President Menem put the figure at $12 billion.

---

Virtually every Bank project mandates the use of consultants during the implementation phrase—to conduct studies, to provide training, or to manage entire projects. The Bank is the single largest source of work for the international consulting industry. Development Bank Associates, a firm that provides information on the business opportunities offered by the World Bank, calls it a "goldmine of consultancy business." The Bank pays out more than a billion dollars a year for the hiring of consultants.

Many developing countries resent what they see as the Bank's imposition on them of both the consultants and the studies. "Generally, governments know what they want to do: They want to build something. The rest is a bit of a nuisance," says an experienced international consultant. "The first reaction is 'Why the hell do we need someone else to tell us what to do?'"

Borrowers have various ways of skimping on studies and consultants. In one recent case, a government official simply painted out the number of man-months to be devoted to a particular study in the Bank-approved terms-of-reference document given to bidders, and wrote in a smaller one. Bidders understood that the department was more interested in a low price than a thorough job. The Bank may discover such efforts and press the borrower to go back to the original terms, but by then bidders will have gotten the message. "You can improve your chances of winning the contract by lowering your price, because even though so many man-months are there in the bid, you don't really plan to do that much work," one consultant explained. "The government understands that that's the reason for your lower bid and that's fine with them."

In its publications, the Bank declares its preference for local consultants, because they have a better understanding of local "conditions, procedures, and customs" and because they are cheaper. In practice, however, the Bank presses borrowers to hire consultants from the United States and Western Europe. A recent Bank report put it this way: "The borrowing country insists that they want local consultants A, B, and C, and the World Bank says, 'No, unless you have D and E' (expensive consultants from

London and New York)." More than 80 percent of the foreign consultants hired for Bank projects are from industrialized countries, primarily the United States, Britain, and France.

In 1962 David Lilienthal was trying to help Colombia's Cauca Valley Corporation, a public agency modeled on the Tennessee Valley Authority, develop its own engineering expertise. The Bank was a major funder of CVC ventures. On August 1, an angry Lilienthal wrote in his journal:

> Yesterday I leaned that Bernardo Garces of CVC had a World Bank money-pistol put to his head, forcing him to give up his plan—and ours—for establishing a Colombian staff of design engineers in place of a foreign U.S. firm. . . . In other words, the idea of a CVC engineering staff is out the window. It is a foreign firm or no money. The day when Colombian engineers will be "experienced" enough will, of course, *never* come, if the holders of the money-bags, the Bank, never lets them get the experience.

---

Foreign consultants are expensive. Not only do they command salaries that are extraordinarily high by local standards, they also expect to be provided with first-class housing, transport, and office facilities. The Bank claims to have no figures on the overall cost to its borrowers of hiring consultants, but in 1990 Bangladesh's Ministry of Finance commissioned a study on that subject.

The study found that between 1971, when Bangladesh became independent, and 1986, 93 percent of all the consultants it hired were foreign, mostly from Western Europe and the United States. The average monthly salary the government paid these consultants was $7,250, though some received more than $13,000 a month. They were also provided with housing, transportation, and offices, at an additional average monthly cost of $9,500 per consultant. These wages and benefits are now more than a decade out of date; consultants' salaries in Bangladesh have roughly doubled since the time of the study, as has the cost of providing housing and transport.

Attended by chauffeurs, maids, cooks, and gardeners, foreign consultants enjoy a level of luxury in their overseas postings that is beyond their reach at home. And, because so many of their expenses are paid for by the borrowing government, they can put most of their large salaries into savings accounts in New York or London. All this is regarded as reasonable compensation for the hardship of living in a developing country. For someone accustomed to the ease and relative efficiency of middle-class life in a highly industrialized country, working in many parts of the Third World can be extremely frustrating. Bad telephones, constant power outages, and roads clogged with smoke-spewing vehicles are aggravating facts of life. But some consultants—strange to say, because they have chosen a line of work that requires them to spend much time abroad—also regard foreign languages, unfamiliar food, and curious customs as annoyances from which they deserve to be protected. Many consultants take care to live in an expatriate bubble, rarely, if ever, encountering local people on their own ground.

This lavish and isolated life has earned the resentment of many in the developing world, who believe that their countries do not get their money's worth from these expensive advisors. "The foreign experts come, they get discouraged, and they take it as easy as they can. . . . [They] make sure they have their air-conditioning and cars and trips . . . and then many of them do not even come to work," commented one African official.

In a 1992 letter to the World Bank, a Guinean citizens group, the Association of Friends of Nature and the Environment (ASSOANE), complained that "a tiny portion of the salary of an expert is spent in the recipient country, the rest is transferred to banks in rich countries . . . while innocent people incur debt and interest obligations. . . . One can truly ask who is aiding whom?" ASSOANE's letter was prompted by a Bank-funded forestry project in Guinea whose ten foreign consultants, the group claimed, exercise undue power over the project. "It is foreign personnel that controls, directs and makes all the decisions," they wrote. Korinna Horta, of the Environmental Defense Fund, who visited the project site in the fall of 1992 with a group from ASSOANE, reported that

> the most visible of project results in the forest regions has been the construction of villas built to the specifications of the individual foreign experts in the small town of Seredou. The expert enclave, consisting of four distinctly European suburb-style houses, represents a striking contrast to the dilapidated building of the regional forestry administration, which has neither running water or electricity, and is just a short walk away.

The impoverished Guinean forestry department has only six guards to patrol the 260,000-acre forest. By coincidence, six is also the number of guards assigned to protect the consultants' houses.

Foreign consultants are not automatically more knowledgeable or better educated than local ones, though that often seems to be the assumption. Forty-two percent of the experts brought in to advise Bangladesh had a graduate degree; another 28 percent had a bachelor's degree only. However, 15 percent had only a high school diploma, and 2 percent had no formal schooling at all. Half had worked only in their own countries and had no prior international experience. Inexperienced consultants don't necessarily come cheap; it is not uncommon for consulting firms to charge for the services of a senior staffer, but send a junior to do the work.

The question of whether the developing world is getting the cream of the international consulting profession's crop is answered in the negative by economist Robert Klitgaard, who in the late 1980s returned to Equatorial Guinea to spend two years overseeing the Bank-funded project he had helped design in 1985. In his 1990 book, *Tropical Gangsters,* Klitgaard describes some of his fellow consultants. He tells of the macroeconomist from South America who worked for the Planning Ministry and who once "drew a graph that made it clear he literally did not grasp supply and demand. The Ph.D. in economics his German consulting firm claimed for him had to be as bogus as the orange tint in his hair."

Klitgaard's colleagues also included a Canadian hydrocarbon expert whose job was to interest Canadian companies in the local gold mines, but who, thanks in part to his habit of keeping to a four-hour workday, managed over the course of eighteen months to elicit only one interested response. There was, in addition, a Frenchman in his late twenties who was hired on a short-term contract to negotiate with Equatorial Guinea's creditors and train local officials to do the same, but whose contract was renewed again and again—for a total of nearly half a million dollars—because he failed to train his coworkers, whom, he insisted, "cannot even add and divide." Consultants' contracts often call for them to train their local counterparts to take over their job. It is easy to see that success in this endeavor might not be in the interest of the consulting company. Some consultants have made a career out of a single project, which may have begun as a short-term contract. "Seventy percent of the problems [with consultants] could be solved by professional integrity," says Upendra Gautam, a leading Nepalese development consultant.

Nepal is a very poor country, but it has a good number of highly qualified technical experts. Few, however, are hired to work on internationally funded development projects in their own country. This galling fact comes up over and over again in conversations with Nepalese engineers and scientists, who are angry at being treated as less capable of making important decisions about Nepal than people who have spent only a few months or years there. Asked about this, Joseph Manickavasagam, the Bank's resident representative in Kathmandu, speculated that Nepalis are particularly sensitive about the predominance of foreign consultants in their country because Nepal has never been colonized.

This ingenious theory is undermined by the robust resentment of foreign consultants that is apparent even in countries that have had the benefit of centuries of foreign domination. Indeed, in Bangladesh a local wit insisted that "consultantization is the next step after colonization." A Bangaldeshi engineer remarked that the Flood Action Plan "could be in Iceland, because it's about the employment of northern consultants." In 1994, the Indian state of West Bengal refused a World Bank loan for a $64 million shrimp culture project rather than agree to the Bank's demands that the project employ foreign rather than local consultants.

Edward Jaycox, the World Bank's vice president for Africa, said in 1993 that the use of foreign consultants "is a systematical destructive force which is undermining the development of capacity in Africa. And most of this technical assistance is imposed. It is not welcome. There is no demand for it really except on the donor side. And when I talk about donors I am including the Bank." Jaycox also criticized "that business where you make the project and then you discover a gap on the implementation side and try to fill the gap with expatriates." Projects should, he said, "fit within the domestic capacity."

---

Shortly after a loan's final disbursement, the task manager, the Bank official in charge of the project, prepares a Project Completion Report (PCR), which is submitted to the board. Managers are under pressure to give their projects a good rating because, according to an internal survey, "Management tend[s], often unfairly, to blame staff for poor project performance." Perhaps for this reason, completion reports have little credence within the Bank. Speaking to the board in 1992, Vice President Willi Wapenhans called the PCR "an unloved chore—of little use to anyone . . . [and] hardly read."

One reason PCRs are ignored is that they seldom provide a full and accurate portrait of the project. In 1987 the Bank made an $80 million emergency loan to Ecuador for the reconstruction of several oil pipelines damaged earlier that year by two powerful earthquakes. The project included plans for helping people that would be displaced by the work, for clearing up oil spills caused by the earthquake, and for monitoring water quality. The project completion report was a ten-page document that made no mention of any of these components. Nor did it explain why the pipeline itself, whose cost was estimated at $4.4 million, ended up costing $21.1 million—an increase many Ecuadorians attributed to corruption.

One of the Bank's most ambitious efforts to improve primary education was the Brazil Northeast Basic Education project. This $92 million project (for which the Bank provided one-third of the funds) was launched in 1980 in 218 rural countries in Brazil's poor northeast region. Its aim was to improve primary school resources, increase achievement levels, and reduce failure and dropout rates. It was to provide local schools with textbooks, writing materials, furniture, and other equipment, as well as teacher training, the development of appropriate curricula, and an improved local education administration structure. It also included funding for "an unusually comprehensive program of data collection and analysis to assess whether [the program] was meeting its objectives."

In 1992 the Bank published the results of the decade-long self-evaluation that the project had funded. This document drew on the work of a large team of Brazilian and Bank researchers. The examiners found that the promised resources were indeed delivered to the schools. To their considerable surprise, however, they found that academic performance did not improve as a result. Rather, it deteriorated relative to schools in the same region that had not participated in the project. "These estimates of the impact of [the program's] resources do not provide very strong support for its efficacy," the report said. "This finding offers little comfort to the education planner whose common sense and professional credo both indicate that increasing the supply of learning resources will translate reliably into higher achievement." As for reducing the number of failures and dropouts: "Nowhere . . . did [the project] achieve its objective of increasing promotion rates." Despite these failings, the Bank's completion report rated the project satisfactory (as opposed to the alternative rating of unsatisfactory).

Project completion reports do, however, make it clear that most appraisal reports are overoptimistic. The average Bank project costs 22 percent more, takes 50 percent longer to finish, and has an economic rate of return 25 percent lower than was predicted at appraisal. Though the Bank says it will not fund projects whose rate of return is less than 10 percent, a quarter of completed projects have an ERR below that minimum—and 8 percent have a negative rate of return. The gap between forecast and reality "has increased considerably over time," according to a 1989 internal Bank review.

It is absolutely critical that the Bank investigate the results of its lending, because unlike private banks, it is not automatically made aware of its failures. As Willi Wapenhans has pointed out, "In commercial banking you know something's wrong when you don't get paid back." The Bank is always paid back, but that says nothing about the quality of its loans. Nonetheless, the Bank made an effort to evaluate its projects until 1970, when it established its Operations Evaluations Department (OED) in response to threats by the U.S. Congress to have its own research arm conduct audits of World Bank projects. At first, however, Bank evaluators did not have the freedom to make truly independent judgments, at least in the estimation of Congress, which continued to press for a truly independent auditor. Finally, in 1975, the Bank removed the OED from the institution's normal chain of command and made it directly answerable to the board of directors. The board appoints the head of the OED, who is generally a Bank official on the verge of retirement. He has a relatively small staff—about forty-five professionals and twenty-five support staff. The professionals are rotated from jobs in other parts of the Bank, and, according to one, "It can be hard to get back in—if you are hard on them while you're here, you may not get asked back."

The OED only audits about 40 percent of Bank projects—among them all the Bank's adjustment loans. The audit is conducted a year or two after the project is completed, and the OED investigator bases his evaluation on the completion report, the project files, interviews with the staff, and sometimes on a four- or five-day visit to the project site and to the appropriate officials in the borrowing country.

Each project is rated either "satisfactory" or "unsatisfactory." A project is judged satisfactory if it achieves at least a 10 percent ERR. If the ERR is less than 10 percent or if it was impossible to calculate an ERR at all, the project may still receive a satisfactory rating if it has produced "other significant benefits" based on "an evaluator's qualitative judgment about performance." According to one evaluator, "The two main questions to be answered are, Was this a good thing on the whole? And did the project meet the objectives it had when it was presented to the board? . . . In all but 7 or 8 percent of cases, everyone agrees on whether a project is 'satisfactory' or not. Of course," he added, "it's that 7 or 8 percent that is the most interesting."

Between 1974 and 1993, the OED audited nearly four thousand Bank operations. Fewer than two-thirds were rated satisfactory. The percentage of satisfactory operations has been in a more or less steady decline for twenty years: 85 percent of operations approved before 1974 were rated satisfactory; for operations approved between 1974 and 1979 the figure is 71 percent; and for projects approved since 1980 the figure is 68 percent. Since 1989 the OED has also evaluated the sustainability of the Bank's projects. Out of 1,300 operations, 44 percent have been judged likely to be sustainable. Fewer than a third have been rated as both satisfactory and sustainable.

Given the subjective nature of the task, there are many oddities in OED audits. A dam in Southeast Asia that was built on time and on budget and is producing electric power received a "satisfactory" rating, even though the appraisal report had overestimated the amount of rainfall in the area and it is now clear that two-thirds of the anticipated irrigation benefits from the dam will never materialize. It is cases such as this one that led one OED official to remark, "I don't attach much credence to these ratings myself."

The OED studies a few, a very few, projects in detail five to eight years after completion, when their long-term performance can be judged. These Impact Evaluations are more thorough than project completion reports or audits, but only a handful of projects—an average of two per year—receive this in-depth scrutiny. As of 1995, only ninety loans had been the subject of Impact Evaluation Studies.

———

The heart of the OED's work is not the rating of satisfactory or unsatisfactory it gives each project, but the detailed evaluations of the projects contained in the accompanying reports. Though their tone is bureaucratic, OED audits and impact evaluations can be brutally frank about the shortcomings of Bank operations and often contain information from which future operations would benefit. Nonetheless, they are largely ignored by the staff and the board. It seems, indeed, that few board members or staffers even read the reports. Due to a production error, one-third of the paragraphs in a 1990 OED report on a $40 million agricultural project in Indonesia ended in midsentence. Two years later no one outside the OED had asked for the full text. In fact, it may be critics of the Bank who have learned the most from these reports—though outsiders are not supposed to see most of them.

The OED has concluded that the Bank "focusses on what is intended, not on what is actually being delivered." This means that the Bank is unlikely to learn from its past mistakes—unless those mistakes are discovered and brought to its attention by outsiders. In recent years, the Bank has made several efforts to force lending staff to pay attention to the OED's findings. When a project is in the preparation stage, the task manager is supposed to cite lessons learned in evaluations of similar projects and explain how they will be taken into account in the new project. A senior OED official says that compliance with this requirement "is not as good as we would like, but we see an improvement; people are taking it more seriously than when it was first introduced." But many staffers say they are unaware of this several-year-old rule. "It's not making a difference that I can see," said one.

LDCs—intrinsic rights to certain goods, moral reasons, social concerns" and points out that all of these arguments "could be turned around and used more or less effectively against every Bank proposal for [trade] liberalization." Thus, Summers is saying that if the arguments for more pollution are wrong, then so is the economic philosophy at the heart of the Bank's adjustment lending.

In June 1992, just as the furor over the Summers memo had died down, the Morse Commission published its report on India's Sardar Sarovar dam. The report, prepared at the Bank's request, detailed a long history of the Bank's ignoring the warnings of its own experts and violating its own policies. The Commission members had been asked to suggest ways of improving the project, but their findings so concerned them that instead they recommended that the Bank "step back" from it. Management provided the board—few members of which seem to read entire documents—with a summary of the Morse report that caused Bradford Morse to write Louis Preston a letter accusing the Bank of having "seriously misrepresented the main thrust of our report." Ten days later, the board voted to continue its funding of the dam.

---

The day before the board's vote on Narmada, Willi Wapenhans presented the results of his review of project quality to Preston and his top managers. It was sobering news. Wapenhans opened by saying, "There is reason to be concerned!" He explained that the proportion of projects experiencing major problems during execution "almost doubled" from 11 percent in 1981 to 20 percent in 1991. In the same period, the proportion of completed projects that were judged unsuccessful more than doubled, to 37.5 percent.

The report also found that clients were flagrantly ignoring the conditions of their loan contracts: "The evidence of gross non-compliance is overwhelming." Borrowers obeyed only 22 percent of the financial covenants they had agreed to; in Africa, the figure was 15 percent. The report attributed this "gradual, but steady deterioration in portfolio performance" to "deep-rooted problems," including a "systematic and growing bias towards excessively optimistic rate of return expectations at appraisal," an "approval culture" in which "staff perceive appraisals as marketing devices for securing loan approval (and achieving personal recognition)," and the Bank's "nearly exclusive focus on new commitments" at the expense of older projects. It was clear, Wapenhans told the board, that "something is not quite right."

One of the problems Wapenhans identified was that the Bank does not hold officials responsible for project quality. For at least twenty years, numerous internal surveys have pointed out that career advancement in the Bank depends almost entirely on the amount of money an employee has helped lend and not at all on the quality of project design or implementation. In 1993, Luis Fernando Jaramilo, Colombia's ambassador to the United Nations, used the occasion of his last speech as chairman of the Group of 77, the developing nations club, to chastise the Bank on this point: "We all know the way in which structural changes are imposed and how projects are formulated. And how subsequently, when many of these policies and projects fail, their authors disappear . . . [and] nobody is then held accountable for anything." Bank historian Jochen Kraske, who headed the India Department during the Sardar Sarovar years, says there are two reasons why "Bank staff can't be individually accountable for projects they are involved with: the time lag for judgment of the projects is too long to take account of in their personnel evaluations and there are too many variables to assign blame to any one [person]."

Even in the face of the Wapenhans Report's shocking revelations, the Bank's senior managers were remarkably complacent about the institution's problems. As David Hopper told a Canadian parliamentary hearing, "After all, in the horse racing game only 33 percent of the favorites win, and I think the Bank's record is substantially better than that." Management's official response to the Wapenhans Report was a platitude-ridden document called *Next Steps*. In it, the Bank pledged to "foster genuine partnership with borrower[s], . . . ensure the participation of the poor in operations directly affecting them, . . . improve . . . project design," and "redirect the Bank's internal incentives, toward a better balance between approving new operations and ensuring the success of those in progress." In a rare moment of resolve, the board initially rejected *Next Steps* as too weak and too vague. It had "Ernie's fingerprints all over it," one director said, referring to Ernest Stern, who was by then more or less running the Bank. Stern made some minor changes to the document and in July resubmitted it to the board, which this time approved it.

The final version of *Next Steps* outlined eighty-six "actions" the Bank would take to achieve a better success rate. More than two-thirds of the actions amounted to preparing reports or conducting studies, and many of the rest involved holding workshops or forming new committees. The few action-oriented actions were so vague as to be nearly meaningless: number 27 was "Give more attention to risk/sensitivity analysis and ability to implement it;" number 45 was "Increase attention to supervision planning." The Bank's mania for padding drove it to include number 15, which pledged the Bank to "Produce [a] report on Bank's environmental policies and activities"—the Bank had been producing such a report annually since 1990. The last two actions pledged the Bank to enact the previous eighty-four actions and then to check that it had done so: Number 85 was "Provide leadership in implementing the reform plan"; Number 86 was "Assess implementation status of the reform plan."

The parade of scandals continued. The one for May 1993 concerned the Bank's new headquarters building, then under construction. The Bank had long since expanded its occupation of 1818 H Street from two floors to the whole building and then to nineteen other buildings. It is now, apart from the federal government, the largest tenant in Washington, D.C. In 1989 the board authorized a $186 million plan for a new headquarters building that would bring almost all the Bank's Washington offices under one roof. In 1990 the cost rose to $206.5 million. In May 1993, the Bank discovered that the actual figure would be $250 million.

Preston ordered one of his top officials, Managing Director Sven Sandstrom, to conduct an internal inquiry into the burgeoning headquarters budget. In July 1993, Sandstrom reported that the project's true cost was actually $290 million—56 percent over the original budget. His report attributed the cost overrun to "mismanagement and misconduct." Eventually one senior administrator in charge of the project was fired and three others were demoted. Preston called Clausen's decision to build in central Washington "insane," but said it was dictated by the desire to be near the U.S. Treasury Department. Bank spokesman Tim Cullen declared that the Bank had learned from its mistakes and would, if necessary, change its procedures to ensure that they were never repeated. Only a few months later, however, the cost of the project had risen to $314 million.

The uncomfortable fact that the world's leading development institution was unable to complete a straightforward construction project within its budget was made even more embarrassing by an ancilliary revelation. Leaked documents showed that several EDs, arguing that the Bank's ban on smoking was an infringement on their personal liberty, had pressed for the installation of a special air-conditioning system in their private offices and in the boardroom so that they could continue to smoke. Such a system would cost an extra $5 million, a sum that, as The Economist did not hesitate to point out, was equivalent to the cost of "200,000 child immunizations in the third world."

In January 1993, Preston was finally able to enjoy a public relations victory. Striking a small blow for sanity, the Bank announced a new policy restricting Bank staff to business class on air journeys of less than twelve hours. A year later, the Bank further restricted first-class flights and required staffers traveling within the United States and Canada to fly in economy class. At the same time, it declared fifty-seven five-star hotels, among them the Excelsior in Rome, the Mandarin in Hong Kong, the Savoy in London, and the Ritz and George V in Paris, off limits to traveling staffers. The Bank calculates that these changes reduce its annual costs by $12.5 million.

Later in 1994, Preston pledged that the Bank would cut its administrative budget by at least 10 percent, or roughly $150 million, by June 1997. Alarmed by rumors that as many as eight hundred jobs would be cut, the Staff Association wasted no time in declaring that savings of $16 million could be had by cutting unnecessary expenses in the offices of the Bank's senior managers—its twenty vice presidents and eighty division directors.

———

In April 1994 the Bank produced another embarrassing report—this one on involuntary resettlement. It revealed that between 1986 and 1993 the Bank approved nearly two hundred projects that required people to leave their homes and property. When they are completed, these projects—dams, roads, pipelines, canals, plantations, and urban renewal—will have dislocated 2.5 million people.

"Forced resettlement," the CalTech anthropologist Thayer Scudder has said, "is about the worst thing you can do to a people, next to killing them." Recognizing this, the Bank in 1986 adopted the policy that involuntary resettlement "should be avoided or minimized whenever feasible." When it is unavoidable, displaced persons should be "compensated for their losses at replacement cost, given opportunities to share in project benefits, and assisted with the transfer and during the transition period at the relocation site." These obligations apply also to indigenous people and others with only "informal customary rights to the land or other resources taken for the project." The "fundamental goal of the Bank's policy is to restore the living standards and earning capacities of displaced persons— and when possible to improve them." For more than a decade, Bank executives had pointed to this and to the Bank's numerous other high-minded policies as evidence of its commitment to high social and environmental standards. But it was a commitment honored chiefly in the breach. Though Conable had pledged to change that, the evidence from the ground was that the Bank was still flagrantly violating its own standards.

The resettlement review confirmed this. More than half the projects reviewed had no resettlement plan when the board approved them—a clear violation of Bank policy. If there were a resettlement plan, its estimates of the number of people to be moved were most likely based on mere guesses, not on a reliable survey. And if a survey had been conducted, it most likely produced a gross underestimate of the number of people affected. The appraisal report for Turkey's Izmir Water Supply Project, for example, indicated that 3,700 people would have to be moved; the actual number was 13,000. Surveys showed that an urban renewal project in Cameroon would displace 12,500 people; the real figure was twice that. The Bank stated that 63,000 people would be displaced by the Andhra Pradesh Irrigation II Project in India; the correct number was 150,000. The review did not find a single project in which the Bank met its "fundamental goal" of raising household income for all oustees.

The Kedung Ombo dam on Indonesia's Serang River was one of the projects reviewed. The dam, for which the Bank lent Indonesia $156 million in 1985, displaced 30,000 people. Officials tried to place them in the Transmigration program—the controversial mass colonization program in whose expansion the Bank had said in 1987 it would no longer participate. When 80 percent of the people refused to join Transmigration, officials promised to help them resettle near their old homes instead. But because the compensation offered was less than half what was needed to buy replacement land, more than half the population refused to leave their homes in the reservoir area. The Bank was unaware of all this, because instead of visiting the site, it relied on reports from the government of Indonesia, which claimed that everything was proceeding on course.

But in early 1989, when the reservoir began filling and more than five thousand people took refuge on rooftops and in trees, the problem could no longer be ignored. Through the combined efforts of the Bank and the Indonesian government, about three thousand people were persuaded to accept resettlement. The rest, however, refused to move, and are now farming in the reservoir greenbelt, an activity certain to damage water quality and to shorten the life of the dam. According to an internal Bank report, however, these farmers are doing better than those who agreed to move. The report found the Bank's supervision of the Kedung Ombo project "incomplete, concentrating on the project's physical works to the neglect of the unfolding resettlement disaster."

Unlike the people of Kedung Ombo, whose plight became known to an international audience when newspaper editors ran dramatic pictures of them clinging to the roofs of their homes, most oustees suffer in obscurity.

The six thousand farmers who were moved to make way for Kenya's Kiambere Hydropower Dam on the Tana River are one such group. The project was approved despite the absence of a resettlement plan. Bank documents show that in the process of being forced from their homes the oustees lost much of their livestock and wound up with only half as much land after the move as they had had before it. Their incomes fell by an average of 82 percent, not only because they had fewer livestock and less land, but also because their new land was not as good as that which had been taken over for the dam.

When the findings of the Bank's resettlement review were made public (in a press release headlined "World Bank Guidelines Aim to Protect People Displaced by Development Projects"), Preston downplayed the extent of the problem: "My understanding is that the Bank is involved in only 3 percent of world resettlement problems and I believe its record is better than the projects in which it is not involved," he told a news conference at the Bank's fiftieth annual meeting.

Preston was supported by Ismail Serageldin, newly named to the newly created position of vice president for environmentally sustainable development, who declared that "involuntary resettlement is an inevitable result of development." Rather than abandoning projects that displace people, he added, the Bank wanted "to see our standards adopted more widely, by projects affecting the other 97 percent of people who are involuntarily resettled." Neither man dwelt on the fact that projects involving forced resettlement account for a substantial portion of the Bank's lending—14 percent the year the report was released, for instance. In 1994 and 1995, the Bank approved another twenty-eight projects that will displace more than half a million people.

A year later, in April 1995, the Bank faced another dam problem—not resettlement this time, but safety. Pratap Chatterjee, a journalist with the Inter-Press Service, obtained a memo about a study of dam safety conducted by the Bank's Asia Technical Department. The study looked at twenty-five dams in India and found that none were designed to withstand a major flood. It warned that this was "only the tip of the iceberg" because India has thousands of dams. One of the most worrisome discoveries was that the Bank-financed Ghandi Sagar Dam on the Chambal River was designed to contain less than 15 percent of the water that could enter it during a heavy storm. In "Ghandi Sagar the consequences of a dam failure during a major flood would have to be described with some adjective beyond disastrous," said the memo. "The failure of the dam Machu II in India in the 1980s killed over two thousand people. We must remember that there is no comparison between the downstream development in the relatively remote area of [Machu] and the highly populated . . . Chambil [*sic*] valley." At first the Bank refused to confirm that the memo was genuine. A day later, however, a Bank official acknowledged its authenticity but insisted that "mere data cannot be used to pass a judgement on the condition of dams."

———

The Bank has always vigilantly guarded the information in its possession. In 1947, when it became a "specialized agency" of the United Nations, it reserved the right to withhold from that body both "confidential" information and any whose release might "interfere with the orderly conduct of its operations." With its classifications of "restricted," "confidential," "internal," and so on, and its burn bags and shredders, the Bank is still a difficult institution to get information from. In 1994, *BankCheck,* a watchdog newsletter published by the Berkeley-based International Rivers Network, published an appeal to World Bank and IMF staff from which one can obtain an idea of the wide range of documents the Bank keeps secret:

> Until such time as the World Bank and IMF implement effective information policies, we will continue to rely on you to provide us with the appropriate documents to ensure accurate reporting. So, before you leave work each day, look around your office and pop into the mail any of the following: yellow- and green-cover Staff Appraisal Reports; Letters of Intent; Back-to-Office Reports; Draft Country Economic Memorandums; Loan Agreements; Executive Project Summaries; Policy Framework Papers; Article IV Consultations; Memoranda of the President; Country and Economic Sector Work Reports; Aide Memoires; and any other tidbits you think might be of interest.

The fact that a small proportion of internal documents is leaked to journalists and critics of the Bank is not evidence of openness, though Bank officials often act as if it were. The Bank "wants, in a sense, to make its concerns known to the outside world, or many people do, [so] . . . it leaks like a sieve," longtime Bank official Stanley Please said in an interview shortly after his retirement. Testifying before a Canadian parliamentary committee in 1992, David Hopper argued that a previous witness's reference to "internal Bank documents" proved that "the World Bank is one of the most transparent institutions. . . . He has all of these reports. They go out of the Bank by just about every means possible."

In 1992, the U.S. Congress threatened to cut off all Bank funding unless it made more information public. In response, the Bank set up a working group which, in 1993, split into two factions—each recommending a different policy. One urged release of a wide range of Bank documents; the other suggested only minor adjustments to the status quo. The debate reached the board in the summer of 1993, when Lewis Preston was at home recuperating from quadruple coronary bypass surgery. In Preston's absence, Ernest Stern was officially in charge of the Bank. Unofficially, he had been in charge of the Bank since McNamara's retirement in 1981. He had triumphed over Conable's attempt to push him to the sidelines, and many observers concurred with Percy Mistry, a former high-ranking Bank economist, who said, "Ernie gives the impression of having accumulated even more power under Mr. Preston."

The board was not particularly eager to relax the Bank's disclosure rules, but Stern was convinced that some changes were inevitable, if only to staunch the leaks. To convince the board of this, he read it a list of all the documents the staff had leaked in the past year, many of which the board itself had never seen. Having persuaded the board that its information policy needed overhauling, he presented it with only one policy option—the more conservative of the two drawn up by the information working group. In August 1993 the board approved the new information policy, which Stern described as "a genuine attempt" at greater openness.

Under the new policy, the Bank created a Public Information Center from which members of the public can obtain at no charge simplified project summaries prepared especially for publication. The PIC also has environmental impact assessments for those projects that receive such assessments and staff appraisal reports, though the latter are not available until after a loan is approved. The release of other important technical and factual data, such as is contained in engineering studies, cost-benefit analyses, and site plans, is entirely at the discretion of individual task managers, from whose decision there is no appeal. Moreover, governments have a right to bowdlerize any documents they helped the Bank prepare, as a condition of agreeing to their release.

"Under the new policy, there is supposed to be a presumption in favor of openness, but we've had very bad luck convincing people that they should give us those kinds of documents. As far as task managers are concerned, it's not in their interest to give them out," says Chad Dobson, director of the Bank Information Center, a nonprofit group that helps citizens of developing countries obtain information on Bank projects. The project summaries are free, but the PIC charges $15 for all other reports. Citizens of developing countries may obtain, at no cost, documents relating to their own country from the Bank office in that country, but overseas activists say that local Bank offices rarely have the desired documents—or manage to obtain them in a timely fashion.

The new openness policy applies only to projects proposed after January 1994: Information on older projects is still unavailable through official channels. Moreover, the Bank still does not release its project completion reports, OED audits, studies of the economic and policy issues confronting its borrowers, its own strategic advice to borrowers, and minutes or summaries of board meetings. In addition, all Bank papers and reports are in English, the Bank's official language. A few are also published in French and Spanish, but virtually none are translated into other languages. Even project documents are not published in the language of the borrowing country.

The volume of paper generated by the Bank has grown to the point where it is now sending many older documents to a storage site in Pennsylvania. Moreover, the Bank no longer maintains a centralized list of all its internal documents. With the increasing likelihood of documents being permanently misplaced or forgotten, it will be more and more difficult to obtain a clear record of the Bank's past actions.

In late 1993, also under intense pressure from Congress, the board created a three-member "independent inspection panel" to review complaints that the Bank has violated its own policies in a project. Only members of the board or people who live in the borrowing country and who can demonstrate that the Bank's violations "may materially harm their rights or interests" can ask the panel to undertake an investigation. If it decides to do so, it must first ask the board for permission and get the consent of the country in which the project is located.

If both these permissions are granted, the panel receives "full access to all pertinent Bank records and staff." However, the complainants have no right to address the board before it decides whether to allow an investigation to proceed, no right to appeal a rejection or to be told the reasons for that rejection, and no right to examine or cross-examine the evidence supplied by the Bank. At the end of its investigation, the panel submits its report and non-binding recommendations to the board and to Bank management. The complainants do not get to see the report for another eight weeks. During this time a board considers the Bank's response to the panel's report and decides what action, if any, to take.

In its first eighteen months of operation, the panel received four formal requests for investigations. The projects were the IFC-financed Pangue dam on Chile's Bio Bio River, another large dam in Tanzania, the Planaflora project in Brazil, and Nepal's Arun dam. The first was rejected because the panel has no jurisdiction over the IFC. The second was deemed unworthy of investigation. The panel asked the board for permission to investigate Planaflora and the Arun dam. The board denied the former and gave limited agreement to the latter. "The panel has been very, very constrained about what they can and can't do," says one long-serving staffer, "but it has improved things just by being here. Its existence fosters compliance with the Bank's own policies. The message has gone out: There are sanctions if you don't comply."

―――――――

The Global Environment Facility, which the Bank had hoped would improve its environmental profile, ran into controversy almost from the start. Many of its projects involved moving local people from their homes so that nature reserves could be established. A $6.2 million project to establish a protected zone for two species of endangered monkeys along Kenya's Tana River, for example, called for moving the five thousand Pokomo people who have lived in the area for more than six hundred years. According to the Bank, the human and primate populations could not coexist in the region.

But at a public meeting in May 1993, representatives of the East African Wildlife Society argued against moving the Pokomo, stating that the conservation effort would fail without their active involvement. It was, they said, the Pokomo who had alerted scientists to the existence in the area of one of the primate species. The conservationists maintained that the real threats to the primate population were the Kiambere dam and the Bura irrigation scheme, two Bank-funded projects on the Tana River that had done severe damage to the environment and the people of the Tana River region. The Bank's assertion that the resettlement would be voluntary was also questioned. "The so-called voluntary resettlement is in reality an eviction program," said the society's Nehemiah Rotich.

Critics, such as Friends of the Earth, describe the GEF as "a blatant attempt to buy environmental respectability for the Bank while the Bank continues to [fund] . . . environmentally and socially destructive projects." Many of its projects are intended to undo, on a small scale, damage the Bank is doing on a much larger scale. An example is a $5 million GEF project that aims to protect Lake Malawi's biological diversity, primarily by encouraging local people not to overfish. The project does not tackle other major threats to the lake, such as commercial overfishing or the choking of feeder streams due to erosion from the deforestation of its watershed. In fact, the GEF's Lake Malawi project is linked to a larger Bank project, the $9 million Malawi Fisheries Development Project, which is aimed at greatly increasing commercial fishing in the lake by supplying fishing vessels and building access roads, shore facilities, and fish-processing factories. If experience elsewhere in Malawi is anything to go by, the roads will bring loggers into the lake's watershed. Despite this and despite a warning in the staff appraisal report that "the Lake ecosystem is delicate and could be destroyed by over fishing and pollution," the large-scale fisheries development project was not subjected to an environmental impact assessment before receiving board approval in early 1991.

Another example of a GEF project whose purpose is undermined by larger Bank projects is a $7.2 million grant to help Ecuador improve the management of its biological reserves, many of which are being damaged by oil drilling. This grant is supposed to mitigate the effects of a 1994 $20 million technical assistance loan that helped Ecuador adopt legal reforms aimed at making the country more attractive to foreign oil companies. The government wants the companies to exploit the oil reserves that lie under five million acres of its rainforest. "The World Bank has paid for the rewriting of Ecuador's laws and the privatization of its oil industry, which threatens the entire Amazon," says Glenn Switkes of International Rivers Network. "If the Bank wants to save Ecuador's biodiversity, it should stop making loans that are at cross-purposes with that goal."

In 1994, the GEF approved six projects worth $60 million that are intended to slow the buildup of carbon dioxide in the atmosphere, the chief cause of global warming. Among them are a $3.3 million grant to help Costa Rica develop windpower, one for $10 million to Mexico for high-efficiency lighting, and a $30 million geothermal energy project in the Philippines (which faces opposition from the indigenous people of the area). But the good these projects may do is cast into insignificance by the $6 billion the Bank lent the same year for energy and transportation projects, the great bulk of which support increased use of carbon dioxide–emitting fossil fuels.

The GEF gets its fair share of criticism from Bank employees as well as from outsiders. One common complaint is that it is inefficient. "It has some very good people and has pioneered some good ideas, but at least half their time is spent on interbureaucratic wrangling," said one Bank staffer. "Too many people with too many agendas have too much access. It is a form of torture to sit through meeting after meeting to get some agreement on what should be done. I'd be surprised if you could find any operating staff who wanted to keep the GEF."

Privately, some Bank officials also complain that the GEF has undermined the Bank's hard-won progress on environmental issues. "After a long battle, we finally agreed to allocate from 1 to 5 percent of each loan for environmental work," said one veteran staffer, "but now countries are saying, why should we borrow money for the environment when we can get GEF grants? The trouble is, GEF money can only be spent for four international issues, so everything else, everything local—and that includes spending on resettlement—is suffering."

One of the most compelling criticisms of the GEF is that it encourages the Bank to externalize the cost of the environmental damage done by its projects. The cost of avoiding or mitigating the damage done by large Bank projects is shuffled off to the GEF instead of being considered as a cost of the project itself. This violates the widely accepted principle that the polluter should pay for the damage he or she causes. It also makes the project seem to have a higher rate of return. And when a GEF project is attached to a privately funded project, the environmental cost is not only externalized, it is transferred from the private sector to the state.

In late 1993, an independent panel, formed at the request of the GEF donors, produced an evaluation of the fund's first two years. This confidential study disputed the Bank's claim that the GEF is "committed to working with non-governmental organizations." Rather, it found "a consistent, biased exaggeration, if not falsification, of the amount of consultation and participation with governments, NGOs, and affected communities in the project documents." The panel also characterized the relationship between the Bank and the UN's environment and development programs as one of "unproductive competition and antagonisms" and noted a "lack of agreement among industrial and developing countries on the raison d'etre, objectives and strategies of the GEF." It called for "changes in the GEF's strategies, structure, and operational arrangements" and warned that "the many instances of unsatisfactory practices by the GEF's implementing agencies point to the need to pause and rethink policies and practices."

In March 1994, one month before the pilot program was due to expire, eighty governments agreed to make the GEF a permanent institution and to contribute $2 billion to it over the next three years. The agency is headquartered at the World Bank; its chairman is Mohamed El-Ashry, the former director of the Bank's environment department. A thirty-two-member

executive council meets twice a year. Like IDA, the GEF will have to ask its
members to replenish its funds every three years.

———

By the early 1990s, environmentalists had begun to examine the Bank's
record as an energy lender. The Bank is the most important source of
external financing for energy development in developing countries. And
energy is important to the Bank, which has lent more money for it than for
any other sector of the economy apart from agriculture. The Bank regards
increased energy consumption as a key indicator of development. In 1992
it announced that "developing countries have made some progress in energy use. Their consumption increased from 20 percent of the world's total
in 1970 to 33 percent in 1988."

The bulk of the Bank's energy financing has been for fossil fuel–based
technologies as opposed to less polluting or renewable sources of energy.
Not until 1992, in fact, did the Bank make its first renewable energy loan—
$190 million to India for a series of renewable-energy subprojects. Less
than 2 percent of the Bank's planned energy loans are for renewable energy.

Producing energy is expensive as well as pollutive, and energy investments account for a large proportion of external debt in many developing
countries. As worldwide energy demands increase, the expense and the
ecological consequences of using energy inefficiently are becoming increasingly intolerable. Several Bank studies have shown that investing in energy
efficiency is a more cost-effective way of meeting increased demand than
building new power plants. In 1990, a Bank report said that if developing
countries could increase energy efficiency enough to reduce their commercial energy consumption by 20 percent, they would save $30 billion per
year. This amount, the report pointed out, is "about 60 percent of the net
flow of resources out of developing countries for debt service in 1988."

The Bank argues that energy waste is best reduced by taking action at
the macroeconomic level—that is, by creating the conditions for a competitive market. In that way, it says, prices will be set at a realistic level that
discourages waste, and energy monopolies will be replaced by efficient producers motivated to reduce the vast losses of electricity to technical defi-
ciencies and theft—"commonly greater than 20 percent," according to the
Bank—that many developing countries suffer.

But several studies have found that so-called end-use conservation measures—such as the use of variable-speed drives for industrial motors and

more efficient lightbulbs—also result in more efficient use of energy. A 1991 study carried out for the Bank by the U.S. Agency for International Development, for example, said that India could reduce peak power demand by at least 22,000 megawatts by the year 2005 if it used half the available cost-effective end-use energy conservation measures. Such a move would produce savings of at least $8 billion, because the cost of producing energy by building new power plants is two and a half times as expensive as "producing" it through conservation measures.

The Bank, however, has resisted making loans for end-use conservation. According to the International Institute for Energy Conservation, during the 1980s the Bank devoted less than 1 percent of its energy lending to such measures. In 1992, the Bank explained that investment in efficiency must await an increase in consumption since if only "small amounts of energy are used, there is little room for efficiencies to create savings."

In early 1993, the Bank finally announced a new policy on energy efficiency that pledged to find and fund ways of increasing end-use energy efficiency. But eighteen months later, according to a survey by Greenpeace, less than 1 percent of the projects the Bank was preparing promoted end-use energy efficiency. Moreover, a 1994 study prepared jointly by the Environmental Defense Fund and the Natural Resources Defense Council concluded that only two of forty-six energy loans the Bank was preparing complied with the Bank's own policy on energy efficiency.

One of the biggest recipients of Bank energy loans has been India. Despite the massive potential in that country for saving money and energy by investing in end-use conservation, the Bank has dramatically stepped up its investment in new coal-fired plants. In December 1993, it made a $400 million loan to India's National Thermal Power Corporation. This was the first installment a $12 billion series of loans for the construction of more than 16,000 megawatts of new coal-fired generating capacity. The loans are controversial: The first one was approved over the objections of the German, Belgian and U.S. governments because the plants—which will not be equipped with desulphurization equipment—will add more than 100 million metric tons of carbon dioxide and nearly 2 million metric tons of sulphur and nitrogen gases to the atmosphere each year. This will, according to the Environmental Defense Fund, "in all probability be the single biggest new source of greenhouse gas emissions on earth."

———

No bureaucracy likes criticism, but the World Bank seems to be particularly sensitive to it. There is a general feeling in the Bank that the nobility of its mission ought to shield it from censure, that because it means to help the poor it should not be attacked for failing to do so, and that to criticize the Bank is to be indifferent to the poor. In a 1994 Op-Ed piece in the *Financial Times,* Tim Cullen, the Bank's chief spokesman, asked why "the World Bank come[s] in for so much criticism—especially over its lending for dams that create electricity and for other large projects?" The reason, he concluded, is that critics "would like the Bank to steer clear of any activities that challenge the right of people to live in pristine poverty if there are any negative side effects." But "the Bank does not have the luxury of turning its back on that which may be controversial or difficult." To do so, Cullen declared, would be to condemn the Third World's poor "to the state described by Hobbes—'poor, nasty, brutish, and short.' "

Bank officials dismiss some of their most effective critics, such as the Environmental Defense Fund, Probe International, and International Rivers Network, as knee-jerk "Bank bashers," rich Westerners who care more about wildlife than people. But these groups, as many Bank staffers acknowledge, have built up a formidable body of knowledge and experience—and forged close links with grassroots groups around the world. "Steve Schwartzman [of the Environmental Defense Fund] knows Polonoroeste better than anyone in the Bank," one Bank official said. "The same with Lori Udall [of International Rivers Network] and Narmada."

The real trouble with these groups, according to another staffer, is that "they broke through the Bank's self-image. Nobody likes that. They revealed a lot of institutional hypocrisy, and a lot of well-entrenched liars. For a long time, Bank people lived in a miasma of good intentions. People genuinely believed that for all the ugliness brought about by their projects, poor people—poor countries—were better off because the Bank was involved than they would have been without the Bank. They still do. In fact, for many projects, I believe that too: I truly, honestly, believe that the two dams I worked on are better off because the Bank was involved than if the power utility had done them itself."

In early 1993, Preston warned his vice presidents that the Bank was losing the public relations battle and had to become more aggressive in putting its case forward. Speaking of the threat posed to the Bank by "well-organized environmental and human rights groups," Preston cast the Bank as David fighting an unequal battle against the fearsome Goliath of environmentalism. Another high-ranking officer complained that the Bank's weakness had allowed its critics to "become a virtual parallel institution."

The Bank hired media guru Herb Schmertz to help it devise a new PR strategy. Schmertz, formerly director of public affairs for Mobil Oil and the author of *Goodbye to the Low Profile: The Art of Creative Confrontation*, is known for his belief in responding aggressively to criticism. He conducted interviews with Bank staff and produced a report recommending that the Bank tell each of its "key constituencies"—identified as borrowers, donors, private financial institutions, NGOs, academics, businesses, and staff—that "we want to be your partner."

One of the first fruits of the Bank's PR rethink was its aggressive response to the publication, in early 1994, of a book by Bruce Rich, a long-time critic of the Bank's environmental policies. A few days before publication, Alexander Shakow, then chief of external affairs for the Bank, sent an urgent memo to twenty-two of the Bank's senior managers, asking them to drop everything in order to prepare a critique of Rich's book, *Mortgaging the Earth*. "The President's Office places a high priority on the speedy and effective preparation of the Bank's views in a readable and easily used form. Andrew Steer [head of the Bank's Environment Department] and I will guide the preparation of the material; Lesley Simmons [a senior press officer] will devote nearly all her time to the task in the next week or so."

A key part of the new strategy was to "tell success stories from the field." The Bank followed up on this by including in its fiftieth anniversary press kit a list of one hundred Bank projects, describing each in a paragraph or so. The projects, however, were not referred to by their official names in the text, making it impossible to identify the precise education project in Botswana or irrigation scheme in Pakistan for which the Bank was claiming success. Despite repeated requests, the Bank refused to supply the loan numbers or exact titles of the projects. Eventually, however, the Bank's press office provided names and a list of sources for its descriptions of thirty-six of the one hundred projects—there was no documentation for the other sixty-four. Most of the sources were internal documents that the Bank would not release. It was, however, possible to track down Bank documents or independent reports on a few of the projects. One was the Atlantic Railway in Colombia, which was depicted glowingly in the booklet as "the first reliable form of transportation in Colombia" and "one of the most pioneering feats the World Bank has financed." Years earlier, however, the Bank had described the railroad as having "had dubious results" and having contributed to "a widespread misuse of the region's natural resources."

Another part of the Bank's revised PR strategy was to respond force-fully to critics. Its new toughness was much in evidence at the Bank's fiftieth annual meeting, held in Madrid in 1994. While King Juan Carlos welcomed the delegates, several protesters climbed into the rafters of the conference hall, unfurled a banner reading: "World Bank: No Dollars for Ozone Destruction," and showered dollar bills carrying such slogans as "50 Years of Destruction" down on the bemused dignitaries. British Chan-cellor of the Exchequer Kenneth Clarke took it in his stride. "A very im-pressive piece of climbing," he told the Reuters reporter. "It added a certain amount of light relief." The Bank, however, went on the attack. The new head of external affairs, political consultant Mark Malloch Brown, called the action a "piece of cheap theatrics" and charged the dem-onstrators with caring "less about the ozone layer and a lot more about fund-raising."

At a press conference a few days later, Lewis Preston used very similar language in condemning the protesters: "Part of the problem is that there are, on the fringe, a number of NGOs whose business involves theatrics, involves getting attention and thereby presumably funding. I don't think they played a particularly constructive role." Addressing them directly, he said, "My message is simply this: We will not be distracted. We are more committed than ever before to help the poor and we have the renewed support of our global membership to do it."

In addressing the general public, however, the Bank is neither pugna-cious nor self-pitying. It is disarmingly ready to admit past faults and to reiterate its commitment to change. In a 1994 radio interview, Andrew Steer bent over backward to accept responsibility for the Bank's past mis-takes, while emphasizing that they were made "in the past":

I would certainly agree that in the past we have failed to take adequate note of the environment. Yes, I would definitely accept that. In a well-meaning desire to promote economic development, economic growth that enables people, including poor people, to get jobs, we have, in the past, neglected the impact on the environ-ment. So, for example, we, in the past, have supported roads which were designed to help poor farmers get their crops to market, which would give them higher incomes and enable them to live better lives. Those roads, at the same time, have unintendedly, encouraged people to move along them into the forests, for exam-ple, and to destroy some of the natural ecosystems. Yes I would accept that very much indeed. I think we've documented very clearly how projects that we've supported have, in fact, in the past led to adverse impacts.

In case his audience had missed the point, Steer reminded then that the past is past. "The important thing is that we learn from that, and we make sure that this kind of thing is changed for all future projects."

# Sixteen

I n 1990, for the first time in decades, the Bank's lending contracted instead of expanding. Since then, it has hovered at about the $22 billion level. This was some $3 billion less than the Bank's conservative lending projection and nearly $10 billion less than its optimistic one. Mark Malloch Brown, the Bank's chief of external affairs, called this leveling off "a striking feature of the Preston Bank," adding, "and you don't find many people around the Bank who expect that to reverse."

By contrast, the International Finance Corporation, the member of the World Bank Group that lends to the private sector, expanded dramatically in the same period. In 1994 it financed 231 projects, nearly twice as many as it had in 1990, and invested $2.5 billion, a billion dollars more than in 1990. It was still smaller than the Bank, but it was closing the gap. In 1984 the Bank lent forty times as much as the IFC; in 1994, only eight times as much. To accommodate its growing staff, the IFC broke ground for a new office building, expected to cost a quarter of a billion dollars, or just over $200,000 for each of the corporation's 1,200 employees.

In 1995 the IFC lent or invested $2.8 billion on its own account, and mobilized another $2.6 billion from private investors through its syndications and underwriting. In addition, it claimed that investors who followed its lead put another $14 billion into developing country enterprises. "IFC's presence in a project provides comfort," the corporation says of itself.

"Large companies value IFC's presence not because of funding the Corporation can provide, but because of its detailed knowledge of local business practices." Overall, says the corporation, every dollar it lends or invests attracts nearly six dollars from other sources.

The IFC was riding the crest of a wave created in part by the Bank's enthusiastic promotion of private enterprise, a wave the Bank itself could not ride. The IFC has the power to do what the World Bank can only preach—give support directly to the private sector. Although the Bank is willing—indeed, eager—to help the private sector, it is bound by its charter to work through governments. Eveline Herfkens, one of the Bank's directors, expressed the Bank's role succinctly: "The best thing that the Bank can do to help the private sector is to straighten out the public sector." As the private sector has become more and more central to the Bank's concept of development, a certain rivalry has developed between it and the IFC.

The IFC is part of the World Bank Group, but distinct from the World Bank itself. It shares a board and president with the Bank, but has its own leader, whose title is executive vice president of IFC. It also has its own offices, its own staff, its own corporate culture, and, most important, its own mission and philosophy.

Most of the IFC's funds are invested in large mining, manufacturing, and construction concerns: garment factories in Pakistan and Fiji; banana plantations in Ecuador and Indonesia; open-pit gold mines in Peru and Uzbekistan; pulp and paper mills in Brazil and Jordan; oil fields in Russia and Nigeria; and cement plants in India and Venezuela. Though it cannot accept government guarantees, it can lend to state-run companies. In China, for example, most of its projects are large-scale joint ventures with the country's debt-ridden state-owned enterprises—the very sort of agencies that have long looked to the Bank for funding. It also invests in a variety of smaller enterprises, including rose farms, luxury hotels, and a dried fruit processing company. In 1995, the IFC made its first investment aimed at helping so-called microenterprises. It invested $3 million in a Latin American investment fund that specializes in banks that make loans of as little as $50 to small and very small businesses in Latin America and the Caribbean.

The IFC has also entered the territory most identified with the Bank—large infrastructure projects. One-third of its financing now supports such projects. At present, governments and multilateral agencies provide 93 percent of the money spent on infrastructure in developing countries, but the IFC is urging private investors to take on a much greater share of the job. It is helping to finance privately owned dams in Chile, Belize, and Nepal;

power plants in the Philippines and Oman; telephone systems in Hungary and Uganda; sewage plants in Mexico and Argentina; ports in Pakistan and Mexico; a hospital in Jakarta; a railroad in Argentina; and a mass transit system in Bangkok.

One of the IFC's major activities is helping to establish capital markets and financial services. In 1994 alone it provided lines of credit to investment banks in Lebanon and Thailand; invested in private banks in Kazakhstan and the Philippines; underwrote stock offerings in India and Poland; and participated in venture capital funds in Mauritius, China, Morocco, Chile, the Slovak Republic, Ukraine, and Indonesia. It advises governments about such matters as how to conduct privatizations, how to reform laws governing financial dealings, and how to create stock exchanges and futures markets. And it offers financial advice to individual companies on a variety of topics, from finding new investors to setting up pension funds.

The corporation is not inclined to be deferential toward its elder sibling. On the contrary, its leaders have shown a tendency to gloat over what they see as the Bank's growing irrelevance in the changing economic climate. In 1994, shortly after stepping down from his post as head of the IFC, Sir William Ryrie called on the Bank to turn over more of its money to the corporation, arguing that there should be "a shift away from lending to governments and toward the private-sector-supporting activity in which the IFC engages." Said Ryrie, "It is a reflection of the changed economic environment in which we are living, that the IFC is experiencing demand for its financing well in excess of its ability to supply, whereas the Bank for some years has been having difficulty meeting its lending targets."

Later that year another titled former Bank official, Margaret Thatcher's economic guru, Sir Alan Walters, chimed in with his recommendation that the World Bank be abolished. Until then, he said, new lending by the Bank should be restricted and any increase in lending should be handled by the IFC. Ryrie's successor, Jannik Lindbaek, was equally blunt, calling the IFC "almost the only game in town."

Walters, Ryrie, Lindbaek, and others argued that the Bank was institutionally incapable of, as Ryrie put it, "using its influence to bring about a reduction in state activity." Though the market economy offers the best prospect for economic growth, they said, the Bank was stuck lending to governments. The requirement in the Bank's Articles of Agreement that its loans be guaranteed by governments made it, at bottom, an unsound institution. The IFC, by contrast, refused to accept government guarantees, arguing that "funds—including IFC funds—that are subject to full commercial risk are more likely to be efficiently used."

In short, said the critics, the Bank was a propper up of governments and, by the same token, an underminer of the private sector. Ryrie listed the ways in which the Bank did both these things: It made "large loans to governments to enable them to recapitalize state-owned banks; loans to government-owned financial institutions for on-lending to private companies on non-market terms, and loans for the rehabilitation of state-owned enterprises which could be privatized."

The Bank did not sit idly by and let itself be portrayed as yesterday's development agency. It welcomed the increased role of the private sector in development, which, it said, would allow it to concentrate its funds on the social sector, the environment, and other aspects of development that the private sector was unlikely to finance. Preston also took care to point out the Bank's role in the rise of the private sector. "Bank-supported adjustment programs," he said, "have helped to liberalize trade, free prices, dismantle state monopolies, and establish a climate conducive to private enterprise." Again, the IFC disagreed. Ryrie argued that "the changes in these countries were in the main generated in the countries concerned. The extent to which they were the result of pressure from the World Bank or the IMF is often exaggerated."

---

The IFC has invested in nearly one hundred countries, but most of its financing has gone to the same small group of Asian and Latin American countries that private investors favor. Sixty percent of its investments are in ten countries. Argentina alone has received nearly 10 percent of all the money the IFC has ever invested—more than went to all of sub-Saharan Africa. In 1995 only 11 percent of the IFC's funding went to Africa, and more than half of that financed three oil projects and a gold mine.

Much of the IFC's money is invested in companies that would seem able to obtain sufficient private capital on their own. These include Chevron Nigeria, Tata Iron and Steel (India's largest private steel company), Elf Congo, the Nairobi Hilton, Ashanti Goldfields, Barclays Bank of Zimbabwe, Hoechst Pakistan, and British Gas Tunisia. IFC officials say, however, that its participation gives confidence to investors who may be nervous about the pitfalls of doing business in developing countries.

In its impatience to grow, the IFC has taken on some characteristics of its big brother, the World Bank. Its officials, like the Bank's, are under pressure to make loans. "They're salesmen," says an American oil executive who deals often with the IFC. "They may call themselves vice president for northern Africa, but they're salesmen, eager to sell you loans." This eagerness has, predictably, resulted in overly optimistic appraisals of projects. Returns on the corporation's projects have almost always been lower than estimated, leading its chief economist to ask "whether there is a systematic bias to optimism in project evaluation." Nonetheless, the corporation is profitable overall, with a net income of $188 million in 1995.

Private investors also charge the corporation with invading their territory. Article III of the IFC's charter states that "the Corporation shall not undertake any financing for which in its opinion sufficient private capital could be obtained on reasonable terms." The corporation's opinion, however, is not always widely shared in the financial community.

In 1986, for example, the IFC launched the Emerging Markets Growth Fund, a mutual fund that invests in businesses in developing countries. The fund drew hostility from financiers even before it began operating. Portfolio managers complained that the new fund would compete with the Third World mutual funds recently set up by private firms, such as Merrill Lynch's India Fund and Bangkok Fund. One Hong Kong investment banker asked, "Why on earth should the IFC be doing deals when private investment banks desperately want to do them? The IFC has become a pain in the backside over the past few years."

"The problem is this," said *Forbes* magazine: "Some developing countries have developed to the point where they can attract private investors without the IFC's help. The IFC argues that it has worked hard—and made many high-risk loans—in an effort to get developing countries in better fiscal shape. Why, then, shouldn't the IFC get a chance to participate in profitable deals now that they're available?"

The IFC's plans to put $180 million into a 132-mile-long gas pipeline through fragile wetlands in the Ogoni region of Nigeria demonstrates just how strong is the corporation's craving for sure success. The lead investor in the pipeline project is Royal Dutch Shell, whose thirty years of oil extraction in the same region has devastated the land—through roads, pipelines, and numberless oil spills—without providing any benefits to local people. So intense has the hostility to the oil industry become in Ogoniland that the government imposed martial law on the area in an effort to allow the oil drilling to continue.

Activists in Nigeria and elsewhere argued, on environmental and human rights grounds, that the IFC should not support more oil extraction in the region. The corporation ignored their pleas and bitter criticism, however, even after the Nigerian government had condemned to death Ken Saro-Wiwa, the leader of the opposition to Shell's destructive activities, and eight of his colleagues. Saro-Wiwa was a bitter critic of the World Bank

Group, not just for the IFC's proposed investment in the pipeline but also for the Bank's harsh structural adjustment policies. In his posthumously published jail writings, he said, "The World Bank has to accept that its real instrument of torture is its insistence on growth, its economic theorizing at the expense of human welfare."

After the nine men were hanged, the IFC withdrew from the project. And within four days of its doing so, the other members of the consortium took up its share of the investment. This seriously undermined the IFC's claim that its involvement was necessary to attract private funders to the project.

In December 1995, IFC chief Jannik Lindbaek acknowledged that "our partners in the financial community have complained that IFC was competing unfairly with . . . the private banking community." In future, he pledged, it would not do so. Instead, the IFC would be, as one of its officials put it, "the stormtroopers of privatization," investing in countries and businesses that banks had avoided. But the Institute of International Finance, which represents 198 banks and financial firms, criticized the corporation's promised reforms as inadequate. It called on the IFC to cut back on its advisory business and its securities underwriting and to spell out a "graduation policy" for developing countries that no longer need the IFC's special help. "IFC has graduated a few countries, such as Spain, Greece, and Israel," said IIF director Charles Dallara, "but it is still operating in Chile, Colombia, Turkey, Thailand, and other countries that have substantial access to international capital."

_____

As the IFC has grown, it has been scrutinized more closely—not always to the advantage of its reputation. In 1992, it lent $5.5 million to and invested $2 million in Bosques y Maderas S.A. (BOMASA), a newly established Chilean timber company that logs hardwood forests and produces pulp and paper. The company lost money rapidly. In 1993 it applied for more IFC financing to help it stave off bankruptcy by logging its 144,000-acre hardwood forest in order to produce particle board. Chilean environmentalists opposed the scheme. A spokeswoman for one Chilean environmental group, Defensores del Bosque Chileno, described the forest in question as "one of the largest and finest remaining forests in the country." Environmentalists believed that if BOMASA did not get the IFC funding, it would be willing to negotiate the sale of its property for the creation of a national park in the region. In 1994, however, IFC agreed to invest another $2.8 million in the company.

In 1981, the IFC put $8 million into a Brazilian company, Companhia Brasileira de Agropecuaria (COBRAPE) for an irrigated rice project in the Amazon. The land the company acquired had been farmed for several decades by more than a hundred small farmers, who had thus acquired the legal right to stay on the land or, if dislocated, to be compensated. But COBRAPE, according to the Pastoral Land Commission of the Catholic Church in Brazil, "waged a systematic campaign of terror and intimidation against the residents" in an effort to force them out with no compensation.

In early 1987, in response to many protests from local church groups, the IFC sent a mission to meet with the company and Brazilian officials. It concluded that "the Government was acting responsibly in investigating this situation and that the current proceedings were likely to result in a fair and equitable solution which would take into account the concerns of all the parties involved." Six months later, the local public prosecutor filed charges against COBRAPE's managing director for participating directly in acts of violence against the occupants of the land and for having hired gunmen to displace them by force.

In 1989, the Brazilian government expropriated (with compensation) about two-thirds of the company's land and turned it over to the residents, but forty families were left out of the settlement. COBRAPE continued its efforts to make the remaining families leave and continued—according to local farmers and to the Brazilian government's Environmental Institute—to dump pesticides, gasoline, and oil into local streams. In January of 1990, the local town council wrote to COBRAPE protesting the company's illegal erection on a public highway of a roadblock manned by armed employees who subjected local people to arbitrary searches. It had, the council wrote, created a "climate of tension and insecurity" in the region.

In answer to demands from the Pastoral Lands Commission and others that the IFC make an effort to mitigate damages the company caused to residents of the area and to the local ecosystem, the corporation said that "it would be inappropriate for IFC to interfere or otherwise become involved in legal or political proceedings in Brazil. . . . We recommend that the church groups and other parties who feel aggrieved, refer their specific concerns or issues to the appropriate authorities in Brazil which are charged with resolving such matters."

COBRAPE was a financial failure as well as a social and environmental one. According to an internal IFC review, "The project suffered large losses due to inexperienced management, low crop yields, cost overruns, excessive debts, and lower-than-expected rice prices." After several years of negotiations, COBRAPE was restructured and IFC pulled out as an investor, though it still has several million dollars in outstanding loans to the company.

———

As the IFC has become more and more involved in financing infrastructure projects, the number of people displaced by its projects has grown. Between 1991 and 1994, it approved seven projects, mostly power plants, that will ultimately force about three thousand people from their homes. The IFC says that its "projects must comply with applicable World Bank environmental policies and guidelines," including those regarding resettlement. Until 1991, IFC projects were reviewed by the Bank's environmental staff. The corporation now has its own environmental division with a ten-person staff that is charged with reviewing all proposed IFC projects and with monitoring current ones. In 1995 the environmental unit reviewed 290 projects. But it is even harder to get information from the IFC than it is from the Bank—for two reasons.

The first is that IFC moves much more quickly than the Bank. In general only three to six months elapse from the time it begins to consider a project to the time the project is approved by its board. Bank projects, by comparison, take one to two years to go through the same process. This means that the IFC has less time in which to analyze the potential social and environmental effects of its projects or to engage in consultation with the public. Moreover, like the Bank, the IFC has a "streamlining" procedure that allows loans to be approved without a formal board meeting.

Second, citing the need for commercial confidentiality, the IFC keeps even more project information secret than the Bank does. Unless a project is subject to a full environmental impact assessment—and very few are—no information is available until thirty days before the project is presented to the board, when the IFC files a brief summary with the Public Information Center. In 1995 only 14 out of 213 projects received a full environmental impact assessment. These are carried out by the borrower, reviewed by the IFC, and made publicly available at least sixty days before a board vote. The project appraisal report is never made public, nor is the postproject evaluation report, or even the loan agreement itself. Without access to these documents, the public has no way to know if borrowers are keeping to the conditions of their loans. A Chilean environmental group has been trying since 1992 to get a copy of the eighty environmental and social covenants that are apparently part of the IFC's loan agreement with the company that is building the Pangue Dam on the Bio Bio River.

The IFC's environmental division also advises MIGA, the Multilateral Investment Guarantee Agency, on the environmental and social aspects of projects it insures. MIGA is another private sector arm of the World Bank Group. It was established in 1988 to offer foreign investors insurance against noncommercial risk such as expropriation, war, and civil disturbance. It can guarantee up to 90 percent of an investment, with a limit of $50 million per project and $175 million per country. It is one of the biggest investment risk insurers in the world. Relative to the Bank and IFC, however, MIGA is a small agency; its members have put up $1 billion in capital—$100 million in cash and the rest callable. It is supposed to be self-sustaining, funding itself out of its insurance premiums and the income from its investments.

MIGA has no hard-and-fast social or environmental standards for its investments, and the IFC's reviews of its projects are only cursory, involving no travel to the project site, for example. One consequence is that in its few short years of existence MIGA has developed an appalling record on the environment and human rights. Its first client was PT Freeport Indonesia, a subsidiary of the U.S. mining giant Freeport McMoran Copper and Gold, whose board of directors includes Henry Kissinger and William Cunningham, the chancellor of the University of Texas. Freeport wanted to expand its copper, gold, and silver mining operation in Irian Jaya, the west half of the island of New Guinea, but was having difficulty raising money to do so, partly because of bankers' concerns about political instability in the province, many of whose residents have never accepted Indonesian rule. MIGA claims to have "played a catalytic role in assembling the final financing package by providing the initial $50 million in coverage."

The local indigenous people claim that Freeport has expropriated, with government approval, roughly 24,000 acres of lands they have traditionally farmed and hunted. Since receiving MIGA's backing in 1990, the company has tripled its production. It is now the biggest gold mine in the world. As a consequence, it dumps more than 100,000 tons of tailings every day into the Agawaghon River system, upon which the local people depend for drinking water. The company has an environmental plan, but Indonesian NGOs say that it does not meet government standards. "The dumping of tailings into the river has caused flooding, re-routing of the rivers, and destruction of the forests and indigenous hunting grounds," said Emmy Hafield of WALHI, an Indonesian environmental group that filed suit against the company in 1995.

In 1994, local people held several rallies on and near company property to protest the company's activities. At least sixteen people who took part in these demonstrations were later murdered, and the homes and property of several others were destroyed. The Irian Catholic Church and the Australian Council for Overseas Aid conducted investigations and concluded that the killers were Indonesian soldiers who had been assigned to guard company property. Indonesia's official human rights commission then conducted its own investigation, which reached the same conclusion. According to Marzuki Darusman, deputy chief of the commission, eleven people, including women and children, were slaughtered in a village near the company's headquarters. The other five were tortured to death at a Freeport workshop. In addition, Darusman said, the military was implicated in several "disappearances," plus "excessive surveillance" and property destruction. The soldiers may have assumed, he said, that the protests were inspired by separatist rebels.

Freeport denies all responsibility for the killings, as does MIGA. As for the environmental problems caused by the company, said Gerald West, a senior MIGA manager, "it is not really our problem. It would be a little like appealing to your car insurance company after you were accused of murder." Freeport also had $100 million in "political risk insurance," issued in 1990 by the Overseas Private Investment Corporation (OPIC), a U.S. government agency. In contrast to MIGA, OPIC canceled Freeport's insurance in November 1995. In a letter notifying the company of its decision, OPIC's associate counsel general wrote, "Freeport's implementation of the Project, especially its tailings management and disposal practices, have severely degraded the rainforests surrounding the Ajkwa and Minajeri Rivers. Additionally the Project has created and continues to pose unreasonable or major environmental, health and safety hazards with respect to the rivers that are being impacted by the tailings, the surrounding terrestrial ecosystem and the local inhabitants." The decision, rare in OPIC's twenty-five-year history, was taken despite energetic lobbying of the U.S. State Department by Henry Kissinger and a personal appeal to President Clinton by Indonesia's President Suharto.

———

The fall of the Berlin Wall in 1989 led to the greatest increase in the Bank's membership since the mass enrollment of the newly independent countries of Africa and Asia thirty years earlier. For years the Bank had had only one Communist member, Yugoslavia, a country that took pains to distance itself from the Kremlin. The Soviet Union, though a participant in the Bretton Woods conference, did not join the Bank. Poland and Czechoslovakia did, but both resigned within a few years when it became clear that the

United States was implacably opposed to their receiving any World Bank loans. Then, between 1990 and 1994, the Bank acquired twenty-five new members, almost all of which were from the former Soviet Union or its eastern satellites—ex-Communist governments eager to adopt some version of capitalism. This influx of crumbling economies with dissatisfied populations and nuclear weapons put the Bank under intense pressure. It was expected to act as a guide through terrain that was unmapped, indeed untraversed. The new members were unlike the countries the Bank had been used to dealing with. Many were already industrialized, with a skilled and educated citizenry and an extensive, if decaying, infrastructure.

*The Economist* described the dilemma facing the Bank and the Fund:

In the third world, the Bank and the Fund have usually had a clear idea of the policies they thought were needed: until recently their main task was to bully and/or bribe unwilling governments to adopt them. In Eastern Europe, and at least in parts of the Soviet Union, the reverse is true. Except in general terms, the Bank and the Fund do not have a clear idea of the policies that are needed— nobody does, because this is uncharted territory—but governments need no persuading of the case for reform.

The Bank responded enthusiastically to the flood of new customers. It set up field offices in almost every ex-Communist capital, added 140 staff to its Europe and Central Asia office, and developed theories and policies on how to transform centrally planned economies into free-market ones. Between 1993 and 1995, 16 percent of the Bank's lending went to the countries of the former Soviet Union and to its Eastern Bloc neighbors. When the transforming economies that have not abandoned communism— such as China, Laos, and Vietnam—are taken into account, the proportion increases to 32 percent.

Russia is the biggest of the Bank's formerly Communist members, and it has received the lion's share of the Bank's lending to that group. The Bank's loans to Russia have overwhelmingly been for emergency support and institutional and macroeconomic reforms, rather than for specific projects. In its first three years of borrowing from the Bank (1993–1995), Russia received $4.6 billion, roughly divided four ways: $1.2 billion for essential imports; $1.2 billion for the rehabilitation of its oil and gas fields; $1.4 billion to fund government reforms, privatization, and the creation of such innovations as a private housing market and a commercial banking sector; and $630 million to rehabilitate the nation's highways and its urban transport systems.

Since joining the Free World, Russia has fallen into the same pattern that many of the Bank's other borrowers have. Its foreign debt has soared, and it has lost billions to capital flight. Between 1990 and 1995, Russia's foreign debt grew by 80 percent—or $47 billion. It is unable to keep up repayments on this burgeoning debt, and has already been forced several times to ask its creditors for more time to repay. In the same period, Russia's wealthiest citizens spirited an estimated $50 billion out of the country.

———

Whatever its enthusiasm for the task, the Bank seems singularly ill placed to advise anyone on free markets, private enterprise, and the beauty of competition. Despite its ideological commitment to these principles, the Bank has more in common with governments than with private enterprises. Its history and circumstances make it an unfit guide to the rough-and-tumble of the market place. It is protected from lawsuits. It is not subject to taxes or tariffs. Its breathtaking profitability stems not from its funding of successful projects but from the fact that its loans are guaranteed by the world's wealthiest governments and its borrowers buoyed up by an endless succession of new loans. In short, it knows nothing of self-support, accountability, risk taking, or many of the other facts of commercial life. In many ways, in fact, it resembles the elitist technocratic bureaucracies that used to flourish in the Soviet Union and its satellites, staffed with workers who were highly educated, intelligent, arrogant, privileged, and quite isolated from the people over whose lives they exercised so much power.

If a Bank project fails, the Bank suffers no penalty. Its borrowers, on the other hand, suffer twice—from the direct consequences of the failure and from having to repay the loans that financed it—and very often, another loan for a new project to put things right.

During the 1970s and early 1980s, for example, the Bank made more than $90 million worth of project loans to several state-owned agriculture agencies in Madagascar, agencies the Bank had helped to establish. Shortly after approving the last project, however, it concluded that the agencies, through their domination and mismanagement of the agricultural market, were largely responsible for Madagascar's having turned from a net exporter of rice to a large importer of it. While continuing to disburse the older loans, the Bank "proposed a market-based reform" of the country's entire agricultural sector, and provided Madagascar with $60 million in agricultural adjustment loans for that purpose. All the agencies were closed or marginalized and "all four projects failed because of their incompatibility with the new policy environment." The agencies collapsed and the projects were failures, but for many years to come Madagascar's people will have the debt to remember them by.

Critics charge that many Bank loans still tend to strengthen, even bloat, the state. In 1988, the Bank made a $300 million loan to the ten largest cities in the Indian state of Tamil Nadu. Part of the money was to be used for "improving the efficiency of the urban transport system." In 1991, a local businessman described the loan's effect on his city, Madurai:

> This town, Madurai, had an excellent network of private busses giving efficient, good and punctual service. It was taken over by the government with [a] World Bank loan. Now we have nationalized transport which is continuously running in loss and giving extremely poor service. . . .
>
> The whole state of Tamil Nadu had several private busses running profitably and efficiently and they were all nationalized with World Bank loans and all the state-run corporations are running in loss. . . . Interestingly, the World Bank loans [were] used only to take over busses from private sector and not to add new services where private sector was not operating. In the same way, the World Bank is giving loans to [the government's] inefficient Railways, Telecom system, etc. which can be run more efficiently by the private sector.

Inefficient enterprises can obtain huge loans from the Bank—if they are large enough and government-owned. In early 1995, the Bank lent India $700 million to bail out and restructure six state-owned banks "in an effort to make them more competitive." According to India's *Economic Times,* the six banks were among the country's biggest financial failures, losing $828 million in the 1993–94 financial year alone.

When the Bank *has* tried to support the private sector, its efforts have not been particularly fruitful. Some would say they have been counterproductive. This is particularly true in the case of its loans to financial intermediaries. The Bank's ability to lend to private firms is limited by the fact that very few—mostly vast industrial conglomerates—can absorb World Bank–size loans. In an effort to reach beyond these behemoths, the Bank has channeled two-thirds of its industrial lending through intermediaries—in effect, investment banks—that use the funds to finance smaller firms. By 1990, it had lent $26 billion to financial intermediaries.

Before the Bank could fund such institutions, however, it had to create them. There were not enough private investment banks to lend on the scale the Bank had in mind, so, beginning in the 1950s, it helped to establish scores of so-called development finance institutions (DFIs) in developing countries. These include Turkey's Industrial Development Bank, the Development Bank of Ethiopia, India's Industrial Credit and Investment Corporation, the Industrial and Mining Development Bank of Iran, and the Philippines' Private Development Corporation. Through Black's and Woods's reigns, most DFIs were, in theory at least, privately controlled, but they were sponsored and financed largely by their governments (using World Bank loans). As the Bank's authorized history says, "Under these circumstances it is an open question whether such DFIs can be said to be privately controlled."

In any case, McNamara removed the restriction against lending to government-controlled DFIs and allowed them to invest in state-owned as well as private enterprises. By the end of his term in office, most DFIs were state-run and they passed on much of the Bank's money to wealthy individuals and state-run enterprises. The result, the Bank later acknowledged, was that "borrowers willingly defaulted because they believed creditors would not take court action against th[em]." Indeed, a 1985 Bank survey of 150 or so Bank-funded DFIs found that almost half had 25 percent of their loans in arrears, and a quarter had more than 50 percent of their loans in arrears. Four years later, the Bank reported that, on average, Bank-funded DFIs had half their loans in arrears.

In 1993, the public got a rare glimpse inside this system when Pakistan's caretaker prime minister, Moeen Qureshi, a former vice president of the World Bank, published a 1,300-page list of people who were at least one year overdue on repayments of one million rupees ($33,000) or more to state-owned banks. According to Mohammad Rafiq, executive vice president of Pakistan's Banking Council, "Almost all big politicians, industrialists and businessmen are included." The total owed to the state was estimated at $3.2 billion, almost exactly the amount of the national deficit.

Another reason for the high level of defaults among DFIs is that many lend money at artificially low interest rates, thus encouraging borrowers to take on more debt than they can support. In the 1980s, for example, the Bank provided about $700 million to seven state-run banks in Yugoslavia for on-lending to small and medium-sized enterprises—even though the banks were charging interest rates that were negative in real terms, as low as minus 10 or 20 percent. By 1989, all seven banks were insolvent, with liabilities of from $300 million to $1.2 billion.

The 1985 survey found that "few [Bank-funded DFIs] have become financially viable, autonomous institutions capable of mobilizing resources from commercial markets at home and abroad." Instead, many have been bailed out again and again by the Bank. And to little purpose, because the average cost of creating a single job by channeling money through DFIs is roughly $20,000 to $30,000—and has run as high as $540,000.

In the mid-1980s, in an effort to address these problems, the Bank began shifting much of its DFI lending back to the private sector. In 1988, for example, almost 40 percent of the Bank's DFI loans were to privately owned banks or financial institutions. Yet internal Bank studies continue to describe DFIs as grossly inefficient and as prolonging the economic distortions they are supposed to curtail. "The subsidies received by DFIs have often far exceeded the profit presented in [their] audited financial statements," said one 1992 report. In 1993, another Bank study found that although DFIs were the Bank's "key instrument for transmitting support to the private sector," they "proved to be deficient in most cases." In 1992, an OED study of DFI loans declared that "the Bank now limits its DFI operations." Three years later, however, the Bank channeled $1.8 billion, 8 percent of its total lending, through DFIs, many of them publicly controlled.

Despite its poor record, the Bank wants more than ever to be useful to the private sector. It has pledged to continue working to reform the public sector "in order to provide the assurance to private investors that they will have no nasty surprises in carrying out their plans." It has devised a host of ingenious new instruments, facilities, and services aimed at businesses. It has conducted studies of every aspect of the new world economy and held innumerable conferences, seminars, and training sessions through which to share its insights with Third World officials and businessmen. It has established, in conjunction with the IFC and MIGA, a "foreign investment advisory service" to help governments attract foreign private investment. By 1994 more than a third of all its lending was aimed at the private sector. That year the Bank paid tribute to private enterprise in the way it knows best: It established a new vice presidency for finance and private sector development.

In 1995 the Bank also announced a new guarantee program to encourage private banks to lend money to infrastructure projects in developing countries. The program does not cover commercial risk, but it will cover losses resulting from a government's failure to adopt open market reforms. In essence, the Bank is offering structural adjustment insurance, which it says will only be necessary until the reforms it has been promoting since 1980 "take root." The aim of the program, said Preston, is "to get commercial banks back into the project lending they were involved in during the 1960s and 1970s. That's the business they should be in. The problem is the expertise they had then is now lacking." The fact is that "the expertise they had then" helped bring about the worst global debt crisis in history, but that has not discouraged the banks from having another go. "Many big banks are falling over themselves to lend [for large projects in developing countries]," said *The Economist* in 1995, "tempted by the fat fees for arranging loans. Moreover, margins on the loans can be anything up to 30 times those that banks can charge top corporate borrowers at home."

———

Though a great deal of private capital is now flowing into the developing world—far more than the amount of development aid—it is concentrated in only a few countries. Of the $167 billion of private capital that entered developing countries in 1993 (up from $44 billion only five years before), more than 75 percent went to just twelve countries, mostly in East Asia and Latin America. China alone received 27 percent; sub-Saharan Africa got less than 3 percent. And much private capital has gone into stocks, bonds, and other financial instruments, rather than bricks and mortar. In October 1994, Preston said, "I think we should be concerned about the volatility of some of these funds . . . which tend to move on interest movements." A month later, Mexico proved him right, as worried investors pulled $9 billion out of the country in a few weeks.

Nonetheless, at least some of the Bank's borrowers are now capable of obtaining private capital for many of their foreign exchange needs—and according to the Bank's Articles of Agreement it may not lend if "private capital is available on reasonable terms." The Bank, however, has continued to lend large sums of money to countries such as Argentina, Venezuela, Chile, and South Korea long after, in the opinion of some observers, they have developed the ability to obtain private financing for many of the projects the Bank is funding. In 1992, for example, the Bank lent $100 million to South Korea for a liquefied natural gas project, and in 1995, $155 million to Thailand for natural gas production.

James Burnham, the U.S. ED from 1982 to 1985, pursued this issue during his term in office, only to discover, in his words, that "no one [at the Bank] had taken this article very seriously for many years." The staff's response to his questions was "a marvelous document of high bureaucratese that, in effect, stated that since the Bank was interested in 'policy change, institution building, and technology transfer' it could ignore the terms and conditions of alternative private-sector finance whenever it wished." In its many decades of operation, only two developing countries have "graduated" from the Bank—Barbados in 1993 and South Korea in 1995. Twenty-five countries have graduated from IDA to IBRD and nineteen have made the reverse trip, starting out as IBRD borrowers and later becoming so poor that they could only borrow from IDA. Recently, a group of senior financiers and economists recommended that the Bank adopt a "more aggressive policy of graduation from both IDA and the Bank as a whole."

The Bank insists that it has no desire to compete with private investors. "We are prepared to lend in countries that can use the money," said Preston in 1994, "but there is no point in shoveling it at countries who could get private-sector funds." Instead, he said, the Bank would continue to invest in all kinds of projects in countries that do not have access to private capital, and in those that do, it would concentrate on investments in education, health (a category that includes nutrition and family planning), environmental protection, and less profitable infrastructure projects, such as construction of rural roads.

The Bank's growing emphasis on health and education is partly in response to the drastic cuts in those sectors that its adjustment programs have forced borrowers to make. Having lent massive sums to encourage governments to cut public spending on social services, the Bank is now making new loans for the restoration of those services. This is fueling a vicious circle in which the increasing debt load of developing countries reduces the funds available for social services, and leads to more borrowing in an effort to maintain those services. Uganda, for example, spends $3 per capita on health services, and $17 per capita on foreign debt repayments. Between 1992 and 1995, it borrowed $205 million from the Bank for a structural adjustment program and another $190 million for social projects.

The benefits to a nation of better health and education are so great that there is a tendency to assume that any loan for these purposes is desirable. But getting education and health care right is at least as difficult—as fraught with technical problems and opposing theories—in developing countries as it is in rich ones, where dissatisfaction with the existing services and disagreements over how to improve them is a major social and political problem. Investments in social services, much more than those in industry or infrastructure, require intimate understanding of local mores and conditions.

Between 1990 and 1993, the Bank gave a rating of unsatisfactory to 27 percent of the education projects it evaluated, 40 percent of the health projects, and 44 percent of the water supply and sanitation projects. The cost of failure for these projects is high in financial and in human terms. The billions lent for them must be repaid whether they succeed or not, and each failed experiment, each wasted year, means that millions of people will never receive the education and health care they deserve.

Since 1990, education's share of the Bank's overall lending has been steady at about 9 percent, almost twice what it was during the previous two decades. It now lends $2 billion each year, but that is less than 1 percent of developing countries' total expenditure on education. Therefore, the Bank says that its "main contribution must be advice." The Bank's advice at present is that developing countries should shift their financing away from higher education and toward primary schooling. Though most developing countries already devote the largest part of their educational budgets to primary education, secondary schools and colleges are much more heavily subsidized on a per-pupil basis, even though the students tend to come from richer families. The Bank advocates raising fees for secondary schools and colleges, and using that money to subsidize primary schools.

This approach has not been universally welcomed. Some critics maintain that the Bank has abandoned higher education out of a conviction that developing countries are destined to be little more than sources of cheap labor for the West. "The Bank's basic economic premise is that an unfettered global market best decides which jobs are located in which countries. The main goal of their education efforts is to prepare people for the jobs that the global market offers . . . low-skill, poorly paid jobs that produce goods for North Americans, Europeans, and Japanese," says Argentinean development economist Jose Luis Coraggio. He argues that developing countries also need "literate people, entrepreneurs to hire them, engineers to build the society, social workers to heal the wounds of poverty, plus researchers, administrators, and intellectuals." Armeane Choksi, who, as vice president for human capital development, oversees the Bank's education loans, argues that such objections are a form of sour grapes. The Bank's emphasis on primary education has run into criticism because, he says, it "means taking away the subsidies from the rich and giving it to the poor [and] . . . it is the rich that provide the funds for political campaigns."

Another idea the Bank promotes enthusiastically is the need to educate girls. About 40 percent of its education loans are now aimed at ensuring that girls go to school. This, says the Bank, is the most cost-effective investment a country can make. Educated mothers tend to have healthier, better educated, and smaller families. They also tend to be more productive farmers, or, if they work outside the home, to earn higher wages. A Bank report estimates that for every 1,000 girls in India that receive an additional year of primary schooling, there will be 300 fewer births, 43 fewer infant deaths, and 2 fewer maternal deaths.

The Bank's education loans are chiefly spent purchasing equipment, materials, and books. But 25 percent goes to pay consultants and other experts to devise training programs, design curricula, and give advice on improving local administration and national management. In fact, education loans employ a higher proportion of advisors than any other category of Bank lending. Virtually all education projects include a component aimed at improving institutional capacity. But since 1989, when the Bank began evaluating projects on this score, only a quarter of education projects have been judged to have met their goals in this regard. This is largely, says Choksi, because "the best and the brightest in government end up in the finance ministries and not in the education ministry."

---

The Bank is also increasing its spending on health. In the 1980s it devoted only about 1.5 percent of its overall lending to this category. In the 1990s, the proportion has been 5.5 percent—about $1.2 billion a year. In 1995, more than 10 percent of that—about $150 million—was devoted to AIDS prevention and treatment programs.

To a great extent, the Bank regards these loans, like its education loans, as vehicles by which to introduce its ideas and advice on health to its borrowers. The Bank wants countries to shift their health investments from expensive Western-style hospitals to local clinics that offer prenatal care, family planning, and treatment for common diseases like measles. It also prescribes a variety of low-cost but efficient public health measures. The most cost-effective way to improve public health, says the Bank, is to vaccinate young children and to give them iodine and vitamin A supplements to protect against malnutrition. It also recommends education and control measures for contagious diseases such as tuberculosis and AIDS. But according to Oxfam, the Bank's rhetoric and its lending are not in line. "In many countries, too much of that [social sector] support is directed towards spending on teaching hospitals and universities, rather than towards basic health care, primary education and rural water and sanitation supply, where benefits to the poor are maximized."

"It is regularly pointed out in Bank reports," points out a Bank report, "that the poor are the hardest group to reach . . . and, by implication, to understand because they are distant—physically, culturally, and socioeconomically" from planners. Judging by the Bank's experience, it is certainly harder to design a successful project that reaches the poor than one that improves life for the middle or upper classes. Many Bank-funded medical clinics, for example, have failed because neither the Bank nor the national health ministry understood the people they were supposed to serve.

Rural health clinics are often underutilized because they are run by what the Bank's representative in Bangladesh calls "uncaring government bureaucrats." But even when the Bank has attempted to replace uncaring bureaucrats with a corps of local people trained in preventive health, mis-understandings may remain. A village health worker program in Lesotho that was created in the 1980s with Bank funds, failed because villagers preferred the traditional healers who possessed remedies, whereas the health workers were trained only to give advice and were not provided with drugs. Lacking the power to cure they also lacked status in the eyes of the villagers. And in one region of Ethiopia, where pregnant women rarely attended nearby health centers, it was eventually discovered that they stayed away because "it was considered weak and improper for women to admit to any pain or discomfort." This information, noted a Bank report, "was new to the public health officials in Addis Ababa [and] was considered useful."

---

The question of whether it makes sense for a country to borrow money abroad to invest in health, education, and other areas that do not require foreign currency is an awkward one for the Bank. The need for social investments is unquestioned, but the wisdom of making them with the aid of loans that must be paid off in foreign currencies is not. The Bank was long reluctant to take on social lending, and when it did, it tried to choose those projects that would produce the highest yields. At first, for example, it limited its education loans to vocational and technical training and sec-ondary schools, which were judged more likely to be financially productive than primary schools. Robert McNamara, however, put an end to this small attempt at prudence. He told staff not to worry about maximizing financial yields for education loans, an order that enabled the Bank to triple its education lending between 1974 and 1979.

Nowadays the Bank says that education loans do produce a good eco-nomic rate of return. "If a few years back, Bank staff had said what they say now, that investment in education shows a Bank return, people would have snorted disbelievingly," Mark Malloch Brown told a press confer-ence. "Now it is part of the new orthodoxy." One way social projects can show a "Bank return" is if the users of schools, hospitals, piped water, and latrines pay for those amenities.

Until recently, the Bank regarded the provision of water pipes, sewage lines, and sewage treatment plants as the work of government. But it no longer believes that these "large public investment schemes" make sense. According to John Briscoe, chief of the Bank's Water and Sanitation Policy Unit, most have "become vehicles for the interests of powerful groups—the upper- and middle-class consumers, the contractors, the workers in the water utility, and the politicians." The result, says Briscoe, is corruption, inefficiency, and a system that subsidizes services to the wealthy while, more often than not, bypassing the poor. Recognizing these problems, the Bank in the 1980s recommended abandoning the effort to bring full-fledged services to the poor. Instead it suggested that they be provided with cheap, simple technologies—outdoor standpipes instead of piped-in water, for example, and improved pit latrines instead of sewers.

In the 1990s, however, the Bank changed its mind about this bare-bones approach to providing services to the poor. It now believes that the poor should have better services—but not for free. In Briscoe's words, "Poor people want and are willing to pay for services of a relatively high quality, and they will pay substantially more if the service is reliable." Charging users, the Bank argues, allows the authorities to provide a level of service the poor actually want, without overburdening the public treasury. In general, says the Bank, people are willing to pay for water supply and for removal of waste from the vicinity of the household, but not for waste treatment and disposal.

City planners in New Delhi, where 70 percent of the population has no access to toilets or latrines, are considering a "pay-and-use" system of street latrines for the poor. It is estimated that using these latrines would cost a three-member family almost $16 a month in a country where the average annual income per capita is $300. The Bank recognizes that not all individuals or communities are willing to pay for water supply and sanitation, either because they cannot afford to or because they don't think they should have to, but as Briscoe points out, "Once government paternalism ceases, those who [feel this way] might express a willingness to pay."

———

The Bank is constrained by the scale of the operations it undertakes from helping the largest part of the private sector, poor entrepreneurs. It would dearly love to have the spectacular success that the so-called microbanks have enjoyed over the past twenty years. The pioneer in this field is the

Grameen Bank, founded by Muhammad Yunus, formerly an economics professor at the University of Chittagong in Bangladesh. In 1976, Yunus tried to convince several commercial banks that poor people would be good credit risks. "The poor have skills," he argued, "or they wouldn't have been able to survive. All you have to give them is access to capital. Most of them can take it from there." The banks disagreed, so Yunus took out a personal loan and began lending small amounts of money himself.

He found that as little as $5 or $10 could make all the difference in the world to a basketweaver, say, who wanted bus fare to take her baskets to market directly instead of selling them to a middleman, or to a farmer's wife with plans to buy, fatten, and sell a pig and use the profits to open a noodle stall. Nearly all his borrowers were women intent on improving life for their families. Instead of asking for collateral, Yunus required his borrowers to organize into groups of four or five. Each member of the group is liable for the repayment of the other members. The combination of mutual support and peer pressure has meant that borrowers nearly always succeed in meeting their obligations.

The Grameen Bank, as Yunus's experiment became, is now owned by its two million borrowers, 94 percent of whom are women. It is active in more than half the nation's 68,000 villages. In 1995 it made half a billion dollars' worth of loans, averaging $140 each. Its interest rates are slightly higher than those charged by commercial banks, to cover the extra administrative costs of handling millions of small loans. Nevertheless, Grameen's repayment rate is 98 percent; by comparison the repayment rate for Bangladesh's private banks averages 27 percent. One survey found that in two and a half years, per capita income among Grameen borrowers increased 35 percent. Another found that after ten years of borrowing from Grameen, 46 percent of female borrowers had raised their household incomes above the poverty line, compared to only 4 percent of women who did not borrow. There are now microbanks serving the poor in some forty countries, including the United States.

The Bank has long been eager to participate in Grameen's success. In the late 1980s it offered funding to Grameen several times, but was refused. Finally, in December 1993, the newly established Grameen Trust, which will work to set up similar banks in other countries, accepted a $2 million grant from the Bank. In 1995 the Bank joined with a number of other international agencies and countries to establish a new body, the Consultative Group to Aid the Poorest. CGAP, which is headquartered at the Bank and headed by a Bank vice president, has $200 million, $30 million of which is from the Bank. It will make loans and grants to NGOs, unions, banks, and other organizations for on-lending "to poor people of working age." These institutions will in turn make loans as small as $100 to individuals. Some will also make loans of $1,500 or less to "micro-firms that employ less than 10 people and help to create employment for the poorest." CGAP's funding is "really peanuts compared to the need," said Minh Chau Nguyen, who is in charge of gender analysis in the Bank's Poverty and Social Policy Department. "But . . . [the idea is] to demonstrate to governments that it works."

---

The Bank no longer sees itself as a mere "purveyor of capital." It describes itself now as "a knowledge-based institution" whose clients value its advice as highly as the cash it can offer. At least, it would like its clients to feel this way. "We need to find a way to become an advisor without always having to be a lender at the same time," says Malloch Brown. The Bank has long fantasized about its borrowers finding its advice as enticing as its loans, but as Mason and Asher pointed out in 1973, borrowers are more appreciative of the Bank's advice when it is "lubricated by lending operations."

The Bank spends nearly $100 million a year on research. It employs five hundred full-time professionals (and the equivalent of two hundred full-time consultants) to collect, analyze, and disseminate information. According to former Vice President Willi Wapenhans, the Bank "maintains perhaps the largest 'development research university' in the world."

This "university" generates hundreds of reports annually—a steady stream of commodity forecasts, debt tables, surveys, working papers, discussion papers, policy papers, research papers, study papers, technical papers, and occasional papers. Many are published—though the public version often differs from the internal one. Recently, a staffer who was asked when a particular document would be available replied, "The department is busy gutting it now for public release." The Bank also produces seventeen free newsletters, a monthly magazine, and several academic journals, as well as an array of teaching materials, from posters to textbooks to videocassettes, to introduce schoolchildren from first grade on up to its work.

In 1995, Mark Malloch Brown warned the Bank's vice presidents that "publishing Bank-wide has exploded in volume and deteriorated in relevance and readability." Nevertheless, some of the Bank's publications are enormously influential, particularly its annual *World Development Report*, which has the largest circulation of any international economic report in the world. Every June, when it appears, newspapers all over the world, taking a sudden interest in international development issues, run articles reflecting the report's conclusions, warnings, and recommendations. The Bank also produces a number of massive, well-presented annual statistical compilations, such as *World Debt Tables, Social Indicators of Development, Trends in Developing Economies,* and *The World Bank Atlas.* Journalists, teachers, academics, and government officials around the world rely on these statistics.

As the global clearinghouse for national economic statistics, the Bank is better placed to detect trends in the global economy than any other international or national institution. Nonetheless, its record as a forecaster leaves much to be desired. It failed, for example, to anticipate the oil price rises of 1973, 1979, or 1985. The Bank's researchers tend toward overoptimism. Its predictions have frequently exceeded not only reality, but even the estimates of other agencies. In 1986, for example, it said that Equatorial Guinea's export earnings two years in the future would be 42 million Central African francs; this was 23 percent higher than the United Nations' estimate, 44 percent higher than the IMF's, and 64 percent higher than the actual 1988 figure of 15 million CFAs.

In 1989 the board's Joint Audit Committee urged the Bank to "try to improve the quality of its agricultural price forecasting." But throughout the 1990s the Bank has been wrong, consistently overoptimistic, in its estimate of a key statistic, world grain supplies. In 1992 the discrepancy between the Bank's projection and reality was 56 million tons; in 1995 it was 225 million tons. These inflated forecasts have led the Bank to predict that grain prices will continue to fall until at least the year 2010. The Japanese government, however, foresees scarce grain supplies and says that by 2010 the world price of wheat and rice will be double what they were in 1992. Lester Brown, of the Washington-based think tank the Worldwatch Institute, says that the Bank overestimates the size of world harvests because it neglects to take into account the increasing impact on farmers worldwide of such problems as water shortages, soil erosion, and heat waves associated with rising global temperatures.

The Bank has also consistently produced overly rosy projections of economic growth, its holy grail. In 1981, for example, it predicted that between 1980 and 1985, Third World economies would grow annually by from 4.1 percent to 5.3 percent. The actual growth rate was 3 percent, meaning that the Bank's forecasts were off by between 33 percent and 75 percent. In 1991, the Bank acknowledged that its predictions of growth throughout the 1980s had been "too hopeful." It had, it explained, overestimated how fast world trade would grow, underestimated interest rates, overestimated the flow of capital to developing countries, underestimated how far oil prices would decline, and overestimated global savings.

The Bank's forecasts sometimes contradict one another. In April 1995, its economic department predicted that Latin America and the Caribbean would grow at 3.5 percent annually over the next decade. But in October of the same year, Shahid Javed Burki, the Bank's vice president for Latin America and the Caribbean, declared that "it is quite possible" that within five years the region would be growing at an annual rate of 6.5 percent.

In late 1993, two Bank economists, William Easterly and Lant Pritchett, came up with an explanation for the Bank's poor record of prognostication. "There is a surprisingly large volatile element" in economic matters, they wrote. "This volatile element . . . can be described simply as 'luck.'" They cited the Bank's erroneous prediction in the late 1950s that Burma and the Philippines would become economic powers to rival Japan; its belief in the early 1960s that South Korea's government was "ludicrously optimistic" in its economic projections; and its high expectations for Latin America in the 1970s. "Such mistakes could be repeated today, given the euphoric expectations for East Asia and gloomy predictions for the states of the former USSR," they warned.

————

From the earliest days, the Bank had been envisioned as a gathering place for information. It required its borrowers to collect and give it vital statistics about their economies. As a central pool for such data, the Bank had considerable power: It could make pronouncements about the world economy that no one was in a position to refute. Research, however, was not an important aspect of the Bank's work in its early days. When the Economic Development Institute, the Bank's "development university," was formed in 1956, there was some idea that it would be a center for research as well as for education. The emphasis stayed on training, though, because Bank managers felt that by and large the Bank should concentrate on its practical work and leave academic research to the universities.

McNamara was more ambitious for the Bank. He wanted it to become the world's intellectual center for development studies. His view was not universally accepted within the Bank. Mahbub ul Haq, for example, thought that the Bank would do better to finance research institutes in developing countries instead of creating a centralized research staff in Washington, D.C. "This whole desire to build a research empire here, to duplicate a Harvard or a Yale, to try to do better than they do, and publish, has been very counterproductive," he said. "There is a lot more of an argument to have indigenous research because it would be more suited to the cultural and to the peculiar patterns of each nation."

Though the Bank considers its research the equal of that carried out in the world's top academic institutions, there are two important differences. First, the Bank's research is not subject to peer review before publication, because the Bank is its own publisher. The Bank has isolated itself from the wider intellectual community, and this, says Wapenhans, "creates the perception that the Bank's operational research is exclusive, self-serving, and of insufficient objectivity."

Second, the Bank's researchers are not free to pursue whatever subject interests them; their work must serve their employer. "The [Bank's] research agenda," Wapenhans has written, is largely directed by "the need to substantiate politically inspired shifts in policy direction." Unlike most research institutions, the Bank has invested hundreds of billions of dollars in a certain approach to development. It is less than eager to be acquainted with facts that would seem to dispute that approach. Or, as Gustav Ranis, professor of international economics at Yale University, put it, "The Bank is inhabited by a large number of highly talented professionals, especially economists, who have shown little willingness to dissent or deviate from what the in-house conventional wisdom is seen to be at any point in time."

A close examination in 1994 by James Ferguson, of the University of California at Irvine, of a key Bank paper on Lesotho, a country entirely surrounded by South Africa, supports this view. In 1975, nine years after Lesotho achieved independence from Britain, the Bank produced a "country report," the baseline analysis that guides the Bank's lending decisions. The report describes Lesotho at the time of its independence as being "virtually untouched by modern economic development. It was, and still is, basically, a traditional subsistence peasant society. But [due to] rapid population growth . . . the country was no longer able to produce enough food for its people. Many able-bodied men were forced from the land in search of means to support their families. . . . At present an estimated 60 percent of the male labor force is away as migrant workers in South Africa."

The report contains figures for income and wealth distribution that its authors say are based on the country's 1970 agricultural census. But the census contains no information on income and states that more than half the population has no cattle at all, whereas the report gives a detailed breakdown of income distribution and claims that the poorest 40 percent of the population own 31 percent of the cattle. These figures, though unsupported themselves, support the Bank's contention that Lesotho is an egalitarian peasant society, which, due to population pressures, is in need of help in making the transformation to a more modern way of life.

Ferguson, however, cites numerous historical sources to demonstrate that Lesotho has produced cash crops for export to South Africa for nearly a hundred years and that the percentage of the male labor force that migrates to South Africa for jobs is about the same now as it was in 1906. "It is almost inconceivable," Ferguson writes, "that a serious scholar of Lesotho's history could . . . maintain that labor migration and the cash economy is something new in Lesotho's history." On the contrary, when the report was written Lesotho had for decades been fully incorporated into a regional industrial economy, in which it functioned as a reservoir of labor and commodities for South Africa.

Ferguson contends that the Bank's report "is not some sort of staggeringly bad scholarship," but a deliberate effort to cast Lesotho as a country in need of the standard development intervention the Bank offers to all its clients. The Bank's report ignores all evidence that the poverty of Lesotho's people owes anything to the country's domination by South Africa. As a result, says Ferguson, the Bank's "planners regarded the paralyzing bureaucracy of the government apparatus in Lesotho, with all its 'inefficiency,' as some sort of mistake—the result of poor planning, perhaps, or a bad organizational chart, or perhaps lack of education." They see government "as a machine for delivering services; but never as a way of 'governing' people, a device through which certain classes and interests control the behavior and choices of others."

The Bank has to look at things this way, says Ferguson, because it has only one solution to offer—the "development" solution—and "it must make Lesotho out to be an enormously promising candidate" for this solution. But many of the technologies the Bank suggests introducing to Lesotho, such as land terracing, erosion control, irrigation, and reforestation, were carried out on a large scale by the country's British colonial rules during the 1930s and 1940s. "If Lesotho is poor," says Ferguson, "it is not because no one has ever tried such 'development' before."

# Seventeen

## A RELATIONSHIP BANK

In early 1995, less than four years into his term, Lewis Preston was diagnosed with pancreatic cancer. For the next four months the Bank was led by a series of acting presidents, of which Ernest Stern was the first. Preston died in May 1995. Before his death, however, he had arranged for Stern to leave the Bank for a prestigious and lucrative position at J. P. Morgan, the investment bank Preston had headed for ten years. This was Preston's gift to his successor—an institution free of its éminence grise, the man who, in the words of a colleagues, "had virtually run the Bank since McNamara retired."

The man chosen to succeed Preston was a sixty-one-year-old investment banker, an Australian-born naturalized American citizen named James Wolfensohn. One of the factors that led President Clinton to name Wolfensohn to head the Bank was his willingness and apparent ability to serve at least two terms of office. Since McNamara the Bank had gone through three single-term leaders, none of whom had really been able to get a grip on the massive institution. The Bank had been at its most glorious, if not its most benign, under its two longest-serving leaders, Eugene Black and Robert McNamara.

Wolfensohn has something in him of both these men. Like Eugene Black, he is an investment banker with a deep interest in the arts. Like McNamara, he is confident, energetic, and concerned about the plight of the poor. Unlike the reclusive, puritanical McNamara, however, Wolfensohn is also gregarious, eager to be liked, and enjoys the company of the rich and famous. Leonard Bernstein once greeted him with "Look, it's my favourite groupie!" *The Washington Post* described him as a man who "relish[s] meeting heads of state on an equal footing," and *Business Week* called him "the Man with the Golden Rolodex."

Wolfensohn claims McNamara—and McNamara's key advisors, the late British economist Barbara Ward and Canadian businessman Maurice Strong, along with the pioneer development economist Albert Hirschmann—as his guiding lights in the field of development. Returning the compliment, McNamara, according to Wolfensohn, "identified me as a possible candidate" for the Bank presidency in 1981. Wolfensohn, then a partner at Salomon Brothers, wanted the job and—having taken out American citizenship the previous year—was eligible for it, but it went to Tom Clausen instead. Not yet fifty, Wolfensohn then formed his own investment firm and bided his time building up his fortune and his international circle of friends.

Fourteen years later, Wolfensohn finally achieved his goal, but the Bank he took over was at a low ebb. It was still reeling from the effects of its fiftieth birthday, which scores of critics and supporters had celebrated by offering their judgments on the past and their advice for the future. A global coalition of environmental, religious, and social action groups calling itself Fifty Years Is Enough coalesced around the general view that the Bank has done more damage than good. The coalition not only wanted the Bank to change the way it does business, it also wanted it to do less business. It argued that the Bank was too large and that its financial resources should be spread out among many public and private organizations espousing a variety of approaches to development.

It was not only the Bank's old familiar opponents who took the opportunity of the fiftieth anniversary to criticize the institution, though. George Shultz, who, by virtue of being U.S. secretary of the treasury was a governor of the World Bank and the IMF from 1972 to 1974, charged the Bank with "sponsor[ing] activities favored by government officials who know that their own taxpayers would not foot the bill." He called for the Bank to be merged with the IMF to create a "new organization that encourages emphasis on private contributions to development." Allan Meltzer, professor of economics at Carnegie Mellon University, said that the Bank had "reached a decent old age" and that it was "time perhaps to go to a retirement house." Management expert Peter Drucker agreed that the Bank's time was over. "The World Bank was one of the brilliant ideas of the

1940s," he said. "[But today] it does not work and it cannot work. The question is not whether it is too big, but whether it makes any sense." Toru Kusukawa, chairman of the Tokyo-based Fuji Research Institute, declared that "the structure and scale of international public financial institutions have grown beyond reasonable proportions. The World Bank is a case in point."

The high-level business and industry group known as the Bretton Woods Committee, which was formed to support the Bank and keep business interests at the top of its agenda, established an international commission to consider the future of the World Bank Group and the International Monetary Fund. The commission was headed by Paul Volcker, the former chairman of the Federal Reserve Bank and a man who once declared that "no one can reform international organizations." Volcker is also chairman and co-owner of James D. Wolfensohn, Inc., the investment firm Wolfensohn founded in 1980. (In 1996, Wolfensohn, Inc. was taken over by Bankers Trust.) The Volcker commission's major finding was that because "economic resource and growth potential have come to reside largely in the private sector," the Bank Group "must change the way it does business, emphasizing its role as a mobilizer of resources—private and public, intellectual and financial—and not as a lender of money to governments."

"The Bank has perhaps lagged slightly in making its case for relevance in the future," conceded Mark Malloch Brown, its head of external affairs, several months after Wolfensohn was named to his new post. If so, it is not from lack of trying. In recent years, the Bank has adopted—if only superficially—virtually every suggestion its supporters and critics have offered, with one exception. The exception is Ryrie's advice that the Bank practice "self-restraint." It is now committed—at least on paper—to helping the private sector, women, and the poor; to working with nongovernmental organizations and the people directly affected by its projects; to increasing its lending for education, health, nutrition, and micro-enterprises; to protecting or improving the environment; to reducing military expenditures and corruption; to promoting openness in government, the rule of law, and equitable income distribution—and to doing it all "sustainably."

Indeed, to listen to Bank officials, one would think that the Bank was now devoted entirely to working with the poor and protecting the environment. In 1995, according to Bank figures, one-third of its loans were targeted to the poor, one-third "included influential forms of participation by directly affected stakeholders," and one-third were "primarily environmental" or had "major environmental components." In addition, one-third of its lending was "devoted to improving women's status in education, population, health, nutrition and agriculture."

In 1995, as in five of the previous seven years, one quarter of the Bank's lending was for adjustment. But adjustment, too, is now largely a social program, according to the Bank. "Adjustment, as it now operates, is far removed from the structural adjustment of street demonstrations and popular myth," says Mark Malloch Brown. "It is now part of an integrated economic reform program, based on a complex combination of sectors and of sectoral lending, which combines health lending with a series of economic reform measures."

The Bank's rhetoric on the topic seems to have persuaded even some insiders that it has left its infrastructure days behind and become a social agency. "If you look at our portfolio in India," said Executive Director Eveline Herfkens in 1995, "most of it is going for primary education for girls. Just look at it." In fact, in 1995 India received thirteen loans, worth more than $2 billion, but only one, for $260 million, was for education. The previous year, the Bank lent India nearly a billion dollars, but nothing for education. And the year before that, India got $2.3 billion in Bank loans but only $165 million was for education.

When, shortly after leaving the Bank in 1993, Lawrence Summers advised the Bank to pay more attention to "educating girls and less to construction of power plants—more energy conservation and health clinics, and fewer airports and superhighways," his former colleagues were miffed. Said one, "Larry is being a bit naughty there. He knows it's been a number of years since we financed airports and superhighways."

True, the Bank hasn't built an airport lately, but in the 1990s, as in previous decades, the bulk of its funds go to agriculture, energy, and transportation. From 1990 to 1995, loans in these three categories totaled $56 billion, 42 percent of the Bank's overall lending. The fastest-growing categories of Bank lending are loans to the financial sector, which constituted 4 percent of Bank lending in 1993, 7.2 percent in 1994, and 13 percent in 1995, and loans to improve public sector management, which nearly tripled from 2.8 percent in 1991 to 7.5 percent in 1995.

Lately, the Bank has even taken up spiritual issues. At its 1995 annual meeting it cosponsored a Conference on Ethics and Spiritual Values, the aim of which was to "identify those values and beliefs that contribute to sound and sustainable improvements in the quality of life and the environment [and] generate a consensus around the critical ethical issues related to development that are confronting our global society."

One way in which the Bank has been trying to demonstrate its relevance is by "relaunching" important issues on which it has been working for years or even decades with no dramatic success. In April 1993, for example, American Congressman Tony Hall conducted a twenty-three-day hunger strike aimed at pressuring U.S. congressional leaders to take an interest in the issue of world hunger. Hall's action attracted support from dozens of celebrities. When many of them, including Susan Sarandon and Jeff Bridges, joined Hall for a single day, the Bank announced that it, too, had been inspired by Hall and would do its part to end "the growing scourge of hunger" by holding a conference on the topic. At a meeting of the Bank's top officers shortly after the conference, its organizer, Ismail Serageldin, vice president for environmentally sustainable development, stressed that "contrary to the views of some staff, the conference was not simply a public relations exercise. It was a reaffirmation of the Bank's focus on poverty and extreme poverty."

The Bank has always engaged in empire building, as demonstrated by its early transformation from the World Bank to the World Bank Group. Its impulse for expansion has not diminished over the years. It is, says one staffer, "an organization that wants to be everything." Thus, it not only makes its own loans, and acts as a coordinator for all aid flows to many of its borrowers through the consultative groups it chairs, it also offers refuge to a growing collection of semi-independent and ponderously named funds, facilities, groups, initiatives, and programs, among them the Consultative Group on Agricultural Research, the Special Program of Assistance, the Fund for Innovative Approaches in Human and Social Development, the Consultative Group to Aid the Poorest, and the Policy and Human Resource Development Fund.

In addition, the Bank has carved out a role for itself in many major international crises. It has funded, among other things, demobilization of troops in Uganda, land-mine clearing in Bosnia, and efforts to find alternative employment for nuclear scientists in Russia and the Ukraine. On the day the Bosnian peace accord was signed, Wolfensohn expressed his willingness to oversee the reconstruction effort. "This is subject to the wishes of the parties involved," he allowed, "but we will probably emerge in that role." The Bank has also been involved in the negotiations over Rwanda, the Middle East, Cambodia, and Eritrea. On these occasions the Bank acts not as a mere lender but as a deal maker whose advice and decisions can influence the shape of political agreements.

The Bank has even come to see itself as a peacemaker in such "post-conflict" countries. Steve Holtzman of its Social Policy and Resettlement

Division, says it can help rebuild "connections between people" by making loans that "break down the rhythms of war and build up the rhythms of peace."

The Bank would very much like to help rebuild South Africa—in 1992, shortly after Nelson Mandela was released from prison, it sent a team of twenty people to South Africa to scout out likely projects—but to its intense anguish the South African government has steadfastly refused its preferred loans.

Some observers worry that the Bank "has been used as a dumping ground for intractable world problems," but it has not been an unwilling conscript in this regard. On the contrary, it has consistently sought out new obligations—and powers. In 1994, for example, it made an unsuccessful bid to take control of the world's major seed banks, which are repositories for the earth's plant genetic resources and the hubs of research into new crop varieties. A few visionaries have suggested an even bigger role for the Bank. According to Jessica Matthews of the World Resources Institute, it may one day "be pushed into a new role as a conservator for failed nation states . . . or small new states unable to shoulder the full burdens of statehood. Obvious possibilities include Somalia, the former Yugoslavia, Sudan, the former Soviet Republics, Cambodia, and Afghanistan. Broadly, this role could be the economic and social, post-nationhood counterpart of the political trusteeships of the postwar era."

The Bank's expansionist tendencies and its readiness to adopt what Yale economist Gustav Ranis calls "ever-changing fads-du-jour" is criticized by many Bank staffers who believe that it has overextended itself. Speaking shortly after his retirement in 1993, Visvanathan Rajagopalan, vice president and special advisor to Lewis Preston, complained that the Bank lacks focus. "We tried to do everything under the sun," he said. "Human resource development, attention to natural resources management, poverty alleviation, women in development, environmentally sustainable development, and private sector development—these are all critical things, but then you can't do everything in every country." Jonas Haralz, an executive director from 1988 to 1991, recalled that "everybody agreed that there were too many goals and that we should cut some out, but nobody would suggest which goals should be cut."

Hans Tietmeyer, who as head of Germany's central bank, the Bundesbank, is a governor of the Bank and the IMF, has advised both institutions to "resist the temptation to take on tasks which they cannot solve and the pursuit of which would detract from their actual goals." But such criticism has had little impact on the Bank, which is eager to maintain its relevance by extending and expanding its activities. Recently it has adopted a slogan that stresses this fact: "Above all, the World Bank is a relationship bank, continually adapting its products and services to meet the changing needs of its clients."

It is not clear what, if any, impact the Bank's growing list of concerns and goals has had on its lending practices. Its increasing dedication to public participation, for example, is rendered nearly meaningless by its all-encompassing notion of participation. The Bank does not, for example, distinguish between information sharing, social surveys, or workshops with NGOs, and what most people would regard as true "stakeholder participation," that is, joint decision making or collaborative project preparation with those directly affected by Bank projects. According to Nancy Alexander of Bread for the World, "For many World Bank staff, the term 'participation' means—first and foremost—participation by, or partnership with, the client government. In Bank meetings, one continually hears staff saying that they have been 'doing participation' for years and years. It is defined so loosely that lots of staff can make this claim." "The claim that the Bank cooperates with NGOs is a pure hoax," says Sunil Roy, a critic of the Narmada dam who served as India's consul general in New York during the 1960s and later as its ambassador to several Latin American and Africa countries. "They only cooperate with the respectable NGOs, the ones who will tell them what they want to hear."

In 1994, the Bank's longtime treasurer, Eugene Rotberg, said, "I am not one of those who believe that the World Bank has changed over the last twenty years. I think the rhetoric has changed, the talk has changed, and maybe, at the margin, the lending has changed. However, most of the staff are not doing things differently than they did twenty or thirty years ago."

———

Like all World Bank presidents, Wolfensohn came into office determined to bring about change. He realized that the poor perception of the Bank in many quarters was "a question of substance as well as image," and he wanted to improve both. He made a dramatic start soon after taking office, when he unilaterally decided not to fund the controversial Arun Dam in Nepal.

The dam, which was to be built in a remote Himalayan valley, would generate 200 megawatts of electricity—eight times Nepal's current needs. With a cost estimated at nearly $800 million, the Arun Dam would be the largest single investment Nepal had ever made, equal to the country's total annual budget. In October 1994, a coalition of Nepali NGOs had filed a complaint, the first, with the Bank's new inspection panel. They alleged that the Bank's planned $175 million loan for the dam violated Bank policies on disclosure of information, economic analysis, environmental assessment, involuntary resettlement, and indigenous peoples.

After a preliminary review of the charges and the Bank's response to them, the panel was sharply critical of the Bank's failure to adequately explore alternatives to the megaproject, which it said "will have an extensive impact on living conditions throughout the country." The board, however, refused to give the panel the permission it sought to fully investigate the scheme. Instead, it allowed the panel to look only at the social and environmental aspects of the project. Shortly after Wolfensohn took office, the panel submitted its report, which found problems in both areas. It was the board's responsibility, based on the advice of Bank management, to decide what action to take.

Neither the board nor the Bank's senior managers wanted to cancel the project, because, as Bank Vice President Joseph Wood explained, "The signal we'd send out is that the Bank can no longer support infrastructure projects like this." In early August, however, Wolfensohn simply informed the board that the Bank would not fund the dam. One of his concerns, he said, was that the dam was so expensive it would crowd out needed investments in other sectors, such as health and education, an argument the dam's critics had been making for years.

Wolfensohn's cancellation of the project meant that the dam was dead, because both the Bank's funding and its blessing were essential to pull in other lenders. It was also the strongest possible signal that Wolfensohn intended to do more than pay lip service to reforming the Bank and being a strong leader. Although his action distressed some executive directors and top managers, it cheered many lower-ranking staffers, who saw in it both the promise of a change in lending practices and the possibility of a shake-up among senior management.

Even before his formal assumption of power, Wolfensohn had injected a long-absent sense of energy into the Bank. In a series of informal meetings with Bank staffers and with outside critics, he said that he wanted to be a strong leader of a proud institution. He enumerated the familiar criticisms of the Bank and expressed displeasure that the problems identified in the 1992 Wapenhans report—particularly the Bank's overemphasis on lending—had not been corrected. He impressed his listeners with his energy, his directness, his mastery of detail—and his prickliness. One staffer described him as "quick to go on the offensive when he thinks his motives are challenged or he is misinterpreted."

Wolfensohn made his attitude toward criticism quite clear in a "Dear Colleague" letter he sent to every member of staff on his first day in office. "I expect from you loyalty to the institution and to each other," he wrote. "Criticisms must be internal and constructive. . . . I will regard externally-voiced criticism of the Bank as an indication of a desire to find alternative employment." The letter was leaked on the day it was delivered and published in *The Washington Post* the following day.

To critics, Wolfensohn was by turns conciliatory and threatening. He acknowledged that "the World Bank has got things wrong," adding, "I don't need to be defensive about that." He spoke of his desire "to do my very best to make sure this is an institution that we can be proud of." He asked for critics' support and said he wanted to work with them as partners. And he acknowledged that he had no certain answers to the Bank's perennial problems. "I haven't come with any magic insight. Every one of the things I've uncovered, I think, has already been examined by my predecessors and the vice presidents."

Within days of taking office, Wolfensohn embarked on a trip to Africa, the first of a series that took him in his first six months to Asia, Latin America, Eastern Europe, and the former Soviet Union. The journeys were rushed—five African countries in ten days; Haiti, Jamaica, Colombia in one day each; and Brazil and Argentina in three days—and filled with formal meetings with officials. But Wolfensohn insisted that some time be set aside so that he could travel into the field to see the Bank's projects and to meet some of the people affected by them. These forays were brief, but in many ways they were the most important aspect of his travels.

Their purpose was to put out the message was that, for Wolfensohn, the field, not the boardroom, is where the important work of the Bank is done. "He wades into the slums, grabs people by the hand, and looks them in the eye," Edward Jaycox, the Bank's vice president for Africa, told *The Washington Post*. "I can tell you my [officials] were touched by this kind of thing, and it has really started to affect their behavior." Said another Bank staffer, "All of a sudden, we have a leader who has a voice, who's not hesitant to fight, and who shows he cares, in a way that no president since McNamara has."

Many Bank employees were delighted to finally have a leader who spoke in idealistic terms about the Bank: "We all work here because we care about the world: we care about poverty, the environment, social justice," he told his colleagues. Like many of his predecessors, he declared that alleviating poverty was the Bank's most important job, but unlike most of them, he seemed to see the task in human terms. He has, for example, repeatedly referred to the importance of "putting a smile on a child's face." Like McNamara, Wolfensohn has what one observer calls a "savior mentality." But Wolfensohn also brought to his new job a reputation for being, in the words of the *Financial Times,* "defensive, thin-skinned and insecure." These characteristics are joined to "a sharp temper and [a] tendency to humiliate his subordinates." "Jim's a screamer," observed one Bank economist soon after his arrival at the Bank.

———

The most immediate problem facing the Bank when Wolfensohn took over was the possible collapse of the International Development Association. The problem, as usual, involved the United States Congress. Despite its history of foot-dragging on appropriations to IDA, Congress had always ended up paying whatever the U.S. administration had promised to contribute. In 1992, IDA's donors agreed to the tenth replenishment of the association. They pledged to contribute $18 billion, to be paid over three fiscal years, 1994, 1995, and 1996. The U.S. administration promised to pay $3.75 billion of that—subject, as always, to congressional approval.

Also in 1992, the bank's board voted to continue funding to the Narmada project despite the negative findings of the Morse report. Soon after, NGOs followed up on their threat, made earlier in an open letter to Preston in the *Financial Times,* to launch an international campaign to urge taxpayers, donor governments, and environmental and social organizations to oppose the $18 billion IDA replenishment. American groups, in particular, threw themselves into the effort, but for the first time ever there was also a substantial effort to cut IDA funds in other donor countries, including Britain, France, Germany, Japan, Italy, Canada, Finland, and Sweden.

At the time, critics of the Bank had several important allies in Congress, notably the chairmen of the subcommittees that control foreign aid spending in the Senate and the House, Senator Patrick Leahy, and Congressmen David Obey. Barney Frank, the liberal Democratic chairman of the House Subcommittee on International Development Institutions, also took up the issue, demanding that the Bank change its ways as a condition of more funding. "We'll just have to start cutting off the money," said Frank. "It seems like there is no other way to get them to pay attention."

In fiscal years 1994 and 1995, Congress appropriated a total of $2.2 billion to IDA, leaving $1.55 billion to pay in 1996. But then control of Congress had moved from the Democrats to the right wing of the Republican party. Most of the key committees were chaired by isolationists and longtime foes of foreign aid, such as Senator Jesse Helms of North Carolina, the new head of the Senate Committee on Foreign Relations, and his counterpart in the House, Sonny Callahan of Alabama. As a result, the Senate's version of the fiscal 1996 appropriations bill included only $755 million for IDA, less than half the amount due, while the House's version lowered it to $575 million. IDA's other donors were threatening to reduce their contributions proportionally. Such a move could force IDA to cut its 1996 lending program by half.

In addition, the negotiations for the eleventh replenishment of IDA, due to be completed by the end of 1995, were in suspension as participants reassessed their positions in the view of the United States' waning support. The Bank surveyed other governments and discovered that for Congress "to persuade other donors [that] the United States would remain a major continuing player in IDA," it would have to appropriate at least $800 million for fiscal year 1996 and pledge to pay the rest in 1997 (when the first installment of the IDA eleventh replenishment would also be due). "We cannot assume in the current negotiations on financing IDA that the United States will make a contribution that allows a fair sharing of the burden among all IDA donors," said Germany's finance minister, Theo Waigel. "We and most of the other donors do not want to fill this gap," added Carl-Dieter Spranger, the German development minister. "It must be clear to everyone, including the developing countries, who is responsible for the financing gap." "We may be seeing the end of IDA," said one congressional veteran.

As soon as he was named to office, Wolfensohn threw himself into the effort to convince Congress to increase the IDA appropriation in the final version of the appropriations bill. With top Bank officials, he worked out a three-pronged strategy: to "reposition the Bank" as an effective agency and a cost-effective investment; to demonstrate that he was serious about reforming the Bank; and to reduce the chorus of criticism reaching the Congress.

In support of the first goal, the Bank in mid-May "unveiled a major campaign to put the case for continued strong U.S. support." The campaign debuted with full-page ads in major national newspapers focusing on how the Bank had helped American businesses. One featured a giant dollar bill under the headline "How do you get more bang for the buck? Ask the World Bank." The copy explained that the World Bank doesn't just lend money, it helps developing countries become tomorrow's markets. Just ask McDermott International, Inc. of New Orleans, Louisiana. Thanks to a smart World Bank investment in Africa five years ago, McDermott brought home a $255 million contract for offshore oil and gas construction that produced work for over 1,000 Americans.

The ads also explained how Bank programs help U.S. businesses indirectly. "Using a mix of policy advice and finance, the Bank assists [Third World] countries to . . . create a friendly environment for the public sector and a less encompassing role for government . . . [and] adopt outward-looking economic policies and open trade regimes." In addition, the Bank placed an ad in the congressional newspaper, *Roll Call,* asking lawmakers: "What has the World Bank Done for You Today?" The ad named corporations that have received Bank contracts and enumerated the jobs generated by them—all sorted by congressional district.

It was a short-lived campaign. U.S. lawmakers found open discussion of the Bank's contribution to American prosperity unseemly, especially when they learned that the ad campaign was costing $3 million. The U.S. ED, Jan Piercy, rushed to Capitol Hill to assure Congress that the ads had only been an experiment and that "there are no plans at present for further use of these ads." Bank officials now describe the failed campaign as a "pilot" project, though they continue to cast the Bank as "a self-interest Bank, which is serving both halves of the world."

Subsequently, the Bank concentrated on a more behind-the-scenes approach. It decided, according to an internal memo from the head of external affairs to the Bank's senior managers, to cultivate important allies in business, the press, academics, and NGOs. It would set up "Friends of the Bank" committees in key countries, with senior Bank managers "play[ing] an active oversight role (as 'godfathers') . . . specifically in the area of cultivating new allies." The Bank's press office would focus on "developing the long term relationships with key media outlets (at institutional and personal levels)." Like an American political campaign, it would also stay "on message," strive for "better news management," and try "to pump out information with great targeting and in higher volume than ever before." It even adopted a motto, which is now affixed to many of its publications:

The World Bank: A partner in strengthening economies and expanding markets to improve the quality of life for people everywhere, especially the poorest.

The task of getting congressional support for IDA was made much harder by NGOs' continuing criticism of the Bank. At meetings with NGOs in several countries during the spring, before he took office, Wolfensohn asked for a moratorium on criticism for the rest of the year, saying that he planned to spend his first six months visiting the Bank's borrowers and forming his views about the path the Bank should take. He emphasized that criticism of the Bank would "play into the hands of the right-wing antidevelopment lobby." He told NGOs, "I want to know right now who will work with me and who's going to be my enemy," adding, "If you want confrontation you can have it."

NGOs did relax their lobbying effort. Some did so because they felt the eagerness of the Republican majority to cut IDA funding needed no extra encouragement. Others wanted to give Wolfensohn a chance: Abdou El Mazide N'Diaye, president of Forum of African Voluntary Development Organisations, said "We see that change is coming and . . . my feeling is, we should support [the Bank] until we see something we disagree with . . . [then] we fight." Many NGOs also discovered that, when push came to shove, they did not think it right to destroy an agency, whatever its faults, that exists to make low-cost loans to the poorest countries. As Oxfam's Stewart Wallis put it, "Everybody with a commitment to poverty reduction has a shared interest and a shared responsibility to defend aid budgets."

In appearances before congressional committees, personal meetings with key congressional figures, and public speeches, Wolfensohn stressed that by cutting funds for IDA, Congress was not reforming the institution, but killing it. He reiterated again and again that IDA's "basic constituency is the world's 3 billion poorest people." Wolfensohn drew many into his campaign, among them Barney Frank, once one of the most vehement and powerful advocates of cutting IDA funds. Frank urged his colleagues to increase the U.S. contribution, saying, "The poorest people in the world, who I believe we should be helping, will be hurt by this." IDA borrowers also joined the campaign. Bolivia's President Gonzalo Sanchez de Lozada said, "We are really alarmed because we know that credit to the least developed countries is being reduced. . . . This is terrible, because countries like sub-Saharan Africa, Bolivia, Nicaragua, Haiti and Honduras do not have access to loans on the normal World Bank terms." President Clinton, too, took a stand for IDA and warned that "reckless cuts" in foreign aid would harm America's business and political interests overseas. As a percentage of GNP, the U.S. contribution to foreign aid is, at 0.15 percent, less than half what it was in 1970, and the lowest by far of its fellow members of the OECD.

Big corporations also lobbied for IDA, through the National Foreign

Trade Council, which represents many major beneficiaries of Bank lending, including Allied Signal, Caterpillar, Dow Chemical, and Motorola, and through the Bretton Woods Committee. This group of prominent individuals is dedicated to gaining government and public support for the World Bank, the International Monetary Fund, and the regional development banks and to seeing that they in turn consider the interests of American business. Its members include several dozen former cabinet officials, along with top investment bankers and representatives of companies that do business on Bank-funded projects: Caterpillar, John Deere, Westinghouse, Chrysler, DuPont, Browning-Ferris, Phillips Petroleum, Weyerhauser, Borg-Warner, Litton Industries, and others. Its prospectus puts forward several arguments for the Bank, including the fact that the Bank "works to lower trade barriers and open developing countries' economies to U.S. and other foreign investment" and that it has "agreed to take steps to protect U.S. and other producers from competitors in the developing world." In the end, however, it took a last-minute, late-night phone call from President Clinton to Sonny Callahan, the Republican chairman of the House Appropriations Subcommittee on Foreign Operations, just to boost Congress's appropriation from $600 to $700 million. This was $100 million less than what the other IDA donors had said was a minimum contribution—and $900 million short of what the U.S. government had promised to pay.

In March 1996, the donor nations reached an agreement on the eleventh replenishment of IDA. They agreed to contribute $11 billion over a three-year period—down from the $18 billion they pledged for the previous replenishment, IDA-10. The Bank had contributed $2 billion of its own money to IDA-10; to keep IDA functioning at its current level, it had said it will put $11 billion into IDA-11. The Bank's total reserves, including funds set aside to cover possible loans, are less than $19 billion.

For the first year, fiscal year 1997, the United States will not contribute to IDA-11. It will instead pay off the $900 million it still owes on its pledge to IDA-10. In each of the last two years of IDA-11, the United States will contribute $800 million. Or so the government hopes. Whether or not Congress will authorize and appropriate what the administration has pledged is, as always, a moot point. One stumbling block has already appeared: Because the United States is effectively taking a year off from IDA, the other donors declared that it would not be eligible for any contracts awarded with the $3 billion in contributions they would make that year. That decision outraged some U.S. lawmakers, including Alabama's powerful Sonny Callahan. "We're going to have great difficulty funding this whole IDA request under the best of circumstances," he said, adding, "I don't know if I can take it to the floor" if the ban on U.S. companies getting project contracts remains.

If the United States drops out of IDA, would it continue in a reduced form without American participation or would the other donors decide to give their soft-loan funds to other international organizations? Already some IDA donors are increasing their attention to other multilateral agencies, such as the European Economic Community's Development Fund, the European Bank for Reconstruction and Development, and the Asian Development Bank. All are smaller than the World Bank and none is dominated by the United States. This is a distinct advantage to many Bank members who feel that, for reasons of history and geography, the United States exercises more control of that institution than is warranted by either its financial contribution or its expertise. Despite its poor record of late, the United States made contributions during the 1950s and 1960s that have given it a shareholding far greater than that of countries that are currently more generous. Japan, for example, is frustrated by the fact that although it has provided 20 percent of the IDA replenishments in recent years, it is entitled to only 10 percent of the IDA vote.

———

If IDA is drastically cut back or comes to an end, the immediate question would be how a reduction—or even cessation—of funds to the Bank's poorest customers would affect their ability to maintain payment on their foreign debt—and by extension how it would affect the Bank's own financial stability. One hundred and forty countries are eligible to borrow from the Bank, and more than one-third of them are severely indebted. That is the Bank's term for any country whose outstanding debt is greater than 220 percent of the value of its exports. Many severely indebted countries have a ratio of debt to exports much higher than 220 percent: Guyana's is 407 percent, Madagascar's 659 percent, Nicaragua's 2,610 percent, and Somalia's 3,000 percent.

Almost all the severely indebted countries are also very poor and are eligible to borrow only from IDA, but many of the so-called middle-income countries that borrow from the IBRD are also in trouble. In 1992, the Bank's management told the board that thirty-five of its sixty-two IBRD borrowers were "high-risk" and warned that they "could pose a risk of protracted arrears to the Bank." Arrears have become a serious problem for the Bank. Throughout the 1980s, an increasing number of borrowers did not or could not make their repayments—at least not on time. More and more frequently, the Bank's borrowers were going into arrears—that is, falling more than thirty days behind on debt service. By 1991, more than $188 million worth of IBRD loans was in arrears. That year the Bank offered to reduce interest rates by a quarter of one percent for every country that had serviced all its IBRD loans on time during the preceding six months. That offer has succeeded in reducing arrears substantially, but at a cost to the Bank of several hundred million dollars a year.

The Bank claims never to have suffered a default, but that is partly because it refuses to regard prolonged failure to repay as default. As of 1995, eight countries had made no payments for at least eighteen months on Bank loans totaling $6 billion, or 3 percent of the Bank's outstanding loans. Two of the eight, Syria and Liberia, had made no payments since 1988. The Bank does not consider these countries to be in default. Rather they are "in nonaccrual status" and "they can stay there as long as they want, as long as they intend to repay," says Jessica Einhorn, the Bank's treasurer. "Our view has been that as long as we are in mutual respectful contact with them, they haven't defaulted. We hope that they'll be able to come back."

The pressure against openly defaulting on World Bank bonds is intense. Any government that dared to repudiate its Bank debt would likely find itself cut off from aid by all other multilateral lenders and virtually every donor country. For the sake of the Bank's reputation in the financial community, its members have a tacit agreement that it is to be repaid before all other creditors. The forty IDA countries that the Bank classifies as severely indebted owe less than 8 percent of their total foreign debt to the Bank, but they give more than 40 percent of their annual debt service payments to the Bank. By contrast, they underpay their bilateral creditors by some $7 billion a year.

The Bank's excellent repayment record owes a great deal to the sacrifices of its rich members. In 1992 alone they reduced or forgave $10 billion worth of debt owed to them by forty developing countries. In addition, much bilateral aid is simply handed over to the Bank as debt service payments instead of being invested in productive enterprises. The Debt Crisis Network estimates that between 1990 and 1995, $4 billion worth of aid was used to pay off debts to multilateral agencies, of which the Bank and the Fund are the largest, instead of being invested productively. In 1990, a group of creditor countries paid Guyana's World Bank and IMF arrears. In 1992, donors arranged grants and loans so that Nicaragua could pay off its arrears. The following year, France paid off Cameroon's arrears to the Bank, and the United States and Japan gave Peru a "bridging" loan so that it could do the same. In 1994, ten nations, led by the United States, paid $65 million to clear Haiti's arrears with the Bank and the IMF. In 1989, the Bank itself began paying off the commercial debt of its IDA borrowers. By 1995, it had made $300 million in such grants to eight countries, including Zambia, Bolivia, and Uganda.

The Bank also has a program, known as the Fifth Dimension, to help countries (nineteen in number as of 1995) that once borrowed from the IBRD, but have become so poor that they now borrow only from IDA. These countries receive loans from IDA specifically "to help them service their IBRD debt." By 1995, the Bank had converted $1.3 billion of interest-bearing IBRD debt to interest-free IDA debt.

At the instigation of U.S. Secretary of the Treasury Nicholas Brady, the Bank began making loans to reduce the debt owed by its IBRD borrowers to commercial lenders. The debtors use the Bank loans to buy U.S. Treasury bills, which they offer as security to their commercial creditors in return for some debt forgiveness or reduction. The renegotiated and newly securitized debts are then sold on the bond market. According to Jeremy Grantham, a founder of the Boston-based investment firm Grantham, Mayo, Van Otterloo & Co., Brady bonds are an excellent investment. "The yields on Brady bonds are just enormous, well over 20 percent. . . . You will do well even if half the bonds you buy default and you don't get your money paid back."

By 1996, twelve countries had reduced by one-third the $190 billion they owed to commercial banks with the help of Brady bonds financed by $4 billion from the World Bank and about $8 billion from other donors. There had at first been some question in the Bank about whether it should be making such loans, because, as an internal memo acknowledged, "Making specific loans that are explicitly for the purpose of debt and debt-service reduction . . . is not an activity that normally falls under the specific investments projects clause of the Articles [of Agreement]. . . . We have to justify such lending . . . in terms of growth and increased investment." This the Bank did by declaring that only countries with an adjustment program were eligible for these loans.

————————

Ideally, the Bank's borrowers will one day be able to obtain whatever foreign exchange they need from private investors. They will stop borrowing from the Bank and will eventually pay off all their debts to it. So far, however, only two developing countries have "graduated" from the Bank—Barbados in 1993 and South Korea in 1995. The others—even those such as Brazil, that are able to obtain all or nearly all their foreign exchange needs from private investors—want the Bank to continue making new loans to them. For the Bank to refuse would be to invite threats of default, if not default itself.

New loans are a sort of repayment insurance for the Bank. As Uwe Bott of Moody's Investor Services put it, "A perpetual increase in Bank lending isn't necessary to keep debts alive, but if the Bank didn't keep increasing its lending, it would undermine confidence in its commitment to development, and erode the borrowing countries' commitment to giving it preferred creditor status." Brazil's finance minister expressed the same thoughts rather more ominously in 1989 when announcing his intention of missing a $1.6 billion interest payment to private banks: "This is a two-way street, in which debt payments should open the way for new resources."

The problem is that, as interest has accumulated on earlier borrowings, many of the Bank's borrowers have become net providers of money to the Bank. In 1987, for example, three-quarters of the seventy IBRD countries were paying more to the IBRD in interest and principal than they were receiving from it in new loans. Overall that year, developing countries gave IBRD $1.5 billion more than they got from it. In 1991, the developing world paid the Bank $1.4 billion a year more than the Bank paid it, and in 1995 the figure was $2.1 billion.

The Bank tries to be a net provider of funds, at least to its most precarious borrowers, but this means that it must keep lending them more and more. "What we do with IDA countries," says board member Eveline Herfkens, "is sort of take care that there is a positive net transfer. I mean you sort of recycle. I don't perceive that as being a problem. . . . We have to make sure that those countries get more from us than they have to repay to us."

Of course, each new loan adds to a borrower's burden of debt. Continual lending will certainly end in bankruptcy unless the money borrowed is not just used to repay old debts, but is invested productively, invested in something that produces enough money to enable the loan to be repaid. Continual lending "obviously doesn't work if you have a static situation," concedes former Vice President Willi Wapenhans. "It only works if there is continual growth." Wapenhans, who believes that continuous growth is possible, calls this process "productive indebtedness."

Critics, however, call it defensive lending. Charles Schumer, a Democratic congressman from New York, has said that the Bank's lending "just amounts to new lending to pay old interest." Any loan can be used for this purpose, but adjustment loans are particularly suited since they are not tied to any project in particular and are so quickly disbursed. From time to time, Bank officials have worried out loud about this aspect of adjustment lending. Burke Knapp, for example, described adjustment loans as an easy "way of [borrowers] obtaining funds to service their external debts." And Andrew Kamarck, a former director of the Bank's Economic Department, said that many adjustment loans "are just fakes. Basically, what they are is an excuse, a way of giving a lot of resources to a country in a hurry."

The Bank acknowledges its desire to maintain positive net transfers, but it insists that it does so only with loans that are economically sound investments—not emergency bailouts or mere balance-of-payments support. This is a delicate matter, for if the Bank were perceived to be making new loans in order to cover old loans, its reputation for financial soundness—and possibly its ability to borrow—would suffer. When told that some Bank employees had characterized adjustment lending as mere balance-of-payments support, Uwe Bott responded, "If I were president of the Bank, I'd fire anyone who said that. That kind of remark can cause a very dangerous loss of confidence." Still, Bott acknowledged that there is no telling how a particular loan is spent. "Of course, money is fungible [economists' jargon for interchangeable] so you *could* say that it is used to pay debts," he said. World Bank treasurer Jessica Einhorn agrees. "Money is fungible and the government can spend what they borrow on whatever they want."

———

The IBRD is by far the largest borrower in international capital markets, as well as the largest nonresident borrower in every country in which it borrows. To keep up its present level of lending, it must borrow more than $10 billion a year. The big institutional investors—retirement funds, insurance companies, pension funds, bank trust departments, and mutual funds—that purchase World Bank bonds are not motivated by charitable impulses. They buy Bank bonds because they receive the top rating, triple A, from all the rating agencies.

The rating is not based on the quality of Bank-funded projects or the success of its development efforts. In 1992, when the Bank admitted that more than a third of its completed projects were unsuccessful, none of the agencies lowered its rating of Bank bonds. "It's not for us to judge whether the Bank has been successful as a development institution; that's not our business," says Uwe Bott of Moody's Investor Services.

There are two main reasons for the IBRD's excellent rating. The first is that the richest countries in the world have pledged to repay bondholders if the Bank's borrowers default. According to David Beers, director of Standard and Poor's international public sector ratings group, the "ability and willingness" of the wealthy countries to provide the capital they have pledged is of prime importance.

The second reason for the Bank's AAA rating is what Moody's Credit Report calls "its preferred creditor status." In law, a preferred creditor is first in line to have its debts repaid. The Bank, however, is not legally a preferred creditor. As its associate general counsel has conceded, "There is no specific commitment to preferred creditor treatment in our Articles of Agreement or loan agreements." Canada's auditor-general reached the same conclusion when he examined the Bank in 1992. "The preferred creditor status of the . . . development banks is not based on a formal or legal subordination of the debts owed other creditors to the debts owed to the banks. It is based on informal factors, like the willingness of the development banks to maintain a positive cash flow to their borrowing countries. One must ask whether these flows can be sustained indefinitely."

Until 1993, the Bank insisted on having a form of protection known as a "negative pledge" clause in all its loan agreements. In making a negative pledge, a government guarantees that, in case it should default, no other creditor will have a higher claim on its assets than the Bank. In 1993, however, after what one ED called "a rather dirty lobby of all the oil companies," the board agreed to waive the negative pledge clause for five years if any country in transition from communism to a market economy requests such a waiver. The change was the result of pressure from American oil companies who wanted to invest in the modernization of Russia's oil fields but did not want the Bank to have first call on Russia's assets in case of a default.

"The negative pledge clause has been in our loan agreements for forty years," said board member Eveline Herfkens. "Most of our borrowers, from Zambia and Chile on copper, to Venezuela and Mexico on oil, all of them for forty years have been asking, can we drop it, and the Bank has always said no, no, no. Now, suddenly, it's yes." Russia, Uzbekistan, and Kazakhstan were the first countries to be exempted from the clause. The decision to waive the negative pledge clause did not affect the IBRD's AAA rating. "It shouldn't make a lot of difference if it's not a widespread phenomenon, which I don't think the Bank intends it to be," says David Beers of Standard and Poor's. What counts, says Beers, is that "the Bank has always been repaid. The important thing is that the borrower countries understand . . . that it's in their interest to bend over backward to pay their money back."

Interest payments made by just five countries—Mexico, Brazil, Indonesia, India, and Turkey—accounted for 37 percent of the IBRD's income in 1993. If any one of these five were to default—and at least one, India, has recently threatened to do so—the IBRD would be hard-pressed not to call on its unpaid capital. However, even if there were a major default, bondholders would probably be repaid. With paid-in, usable capital and reserves of about $23 billion in 1995, the Bank believes that it can withstand a default on the part of one or two major borrowers without having to ask its members to pay out their callable capital. Not everyone is so sanguine. At a hearing on the 1995 foreign aid bill, Senator Pete Domenici of New Mexico expressed concern that there might be an "S&L crisis sitting out there" that would require taxpayers to pay up the capital they have pledged.

One thing that everyone agrees on, however, is that calling in its unpaid capital would spell the end of the Bank. "The scenario is you'd call your callable capital, you'd pay off your bondholders, and you'd wrap up," says Jessica Einhorn, who hastens to add that she does not believe that such a scenario is remotely likely. If that day ever does come, though, the Bank may find it difficult to pry out of its shareholders the money they owe it. Most countries have not set aside the billions of dollars they have pledged to pay the IBRD.

The United States is an exception. Up until 1981, Congress appropriated not only the paid-in portions of its subscription to IBRD, but also the callable portion. These funds, amounting to $8 billion, were set aside in what is called a "no-year appropriation." Figuratively speaking, says Jonathan Sanford of the Library of Congress's Congressional Research Service, "It is sitting in a shoebox under the Secretary of the Treasury's desk," ready to be paid out to the IBRD when it is called. Since 1981, however, Congress has not been asked to appropriate the callable portion of the United States' subscription to IBRD. Thus, in an emergency, Congress could be asked to appropriate another $21 billion. "Can you imagine going to Congress and asking for 20 or 30 billion dollars to bail out the Bank?" asks one longtime Bank staffer.

Lawmakers in other countries, too, may be reluctant to pay in billions of dollars to the IBRD in case of an emergency. Doubtless many do not even realize that their governments have pledged the money. In a 1992 study of the Bank, Canada's auditor-general found that the 1988 law authorizing a $1.5 billion increase in Canada's subscription to the Bank refers only to the 3 percent that must be paid in cash and has no mention of the $1.455 billion that the government has agreed to pay when asked to do so. "Therefore we are concerned that Parliament is not made fully aware that it is approving a potential financial commitment." Parliament's lack of awareness does not diminish Canada's legal responsibility to pay, but it may affect Parliament's willingness to meet that legal obligation.

Most financial analysts, however, argue that the Bank's members—at least the wealthy ones—will pay up if asked. Mark Pinto, of Fitch Investor Services in New York, is certain that "none of the OECD countries would renege on their pledges, because there would be a strong, swift reaction from the markets if they did. Governments make pledges to the market all the time, and reneging on any one pledge would affect all of its debt—Treasury bills, bonds, all kinds of government debt. There would be a huge domino effect."

_____

Forgiving unwisely incurred debts will, it is often argued, encourage more overborrowing. Partly for this reason, the Bank has always refused to forgive the debts owed to it. But in recent years, the debt burden—a burden carried not so much by the borrowing governments as by their long-suffering populations—has grown so heavy that the Bank has come under increasing pressure to write-off some of the debts owed it by its poorest borrowers, most of whom are in Africa. In 1993 the Organization of African Unity called on the Bank and the Fund to reschedule or forgive the debts owed them by impoverished African countries. "The debt has to be addressed," said Solomon Gomes, the OAU's special political affairs officer, adding that "there is nothing Africa can do" in terms of economic development until then. In 1994, religious leaders around the world marked the Bank's fiftieth birthday by calling on it to "cancel or substantially reduce" the debt of its poorest countries. The following year, the Pope, during his visit to Cameroon, added his voice to the clamor for debt forgiveness. "I also make a pressing appeal to the International Monetary Fund and the World Bank and all foreign creditors to alleviate the crushing debts of the African nations," he said.

The Bank insists, somewhat defensively, that it "is not part of the [debt] problem, but it is part of the solution." Many outside the Bank have suggested that it would be more so if it would use some of its $19 billion in reserves to write off the debt of its poorest borrowers. Though this would not violate the Bank's Articles of Agreement, the Bank argues that it would send the wrong message, both to its borrowers and to the financial community. It asserts that "writing off World Bank loans would hurt rather than help borrowing countries."

In 1995, the Bank and the International Monetary Fund began looking for a new way to lighten the debt burden of the most heavily indebted poor countries. Declaring that "the fragmented approach followed thus far by the international financial community to address the debt problem of the poorest countries has reached its limit," an internal memo proposed setting up a new fund which would pay off some of the debts those countries owed to multilateral development institutions—that is, the Bank, the Fund, and the regional development banks. The memo named twenty-four countries—most of them in Africa—that have unsustainable debt burdens. Taken together, they owe more than $115 billion to their foreign creditors—$10 billion to the Bank alone.

The fund would be operated by the Bank and would be funded with about $8 billion, which would contribute $700 million to it; the IMF and the regional development banks would contribute $1.5 billion; and donor governments and commercial creditors would contribute $3.6 billion in the form of debt forgiveness.

The Bank envisions a two-stage process by which a severely indebted country could reduce its debt burdens. First, the country would implement a strict structural adjustment program for from three to six years, after which bilateral and commercial lenders would forgive 90 percent of the debts owed them. If after all this, the country's debt level is still judged to be unsustainable, the new fund would pay off an undefined portion, perhaps 40 percent, of the debts it owes multilateral institutions.

The proposed new fund, the memo explained, would "reduce the pressure on the Bank to lend [in order] to maintain positive net transfers" and would enable it "to regain the high ground on debt issues." The fund would also keep the write-off of multilateral debt at arm's length from the institutions themselves. The Bank's analysts expressed hope that this would convince financial markets that the Bank was not really forgiving its own debt because, as they said, "a [direct] write-down of IBRD loans [would] adversely affect its high credibility in financial markets."

Reaction to the plan was not what the Bank had hoped for. Oxfam criticized the three- to six-year delay before debt forgiveness could begin, and other critics called for the program to be extended to more countries. More worryingly, Japan expressed the view that debt forgiveness by the multilaterals would set a dangerous precedent, and Germany and France objected to the IMF's making its contribution to the debt relief fund with money raised by the sale of its gold reserves. The United States favored the plan, but said that funds for it should come from the multilateral institutions themselves, not the donor countries. None of the bilateral or commercial lenders were happy about the suggestion that they should forgive 90 percent of their debts before the multilateral institutions forgive any of theirs.

---

Wolfensohn raised expectations in the Bank—and for it, though in his first year he was not able to produce the dramatic changes that many had hoped for. Like so many of his predecessors, he began his efforts to "break the armlock that bureaucracy has placed on this institution," with a bureaucratic restructuring. He created a new layer of senior management—putting five managing directors between himself and his vice presidents—in the hope that this would reduce the autonomy of the powerful VPs and bring them more strictly under his control.

A steady stream of new ideas and new pledges came out of the Bank. More senior staff would be stationed in the countries for whose loan programs they were responsible. The Bank would cooperate with non-governmental organizations on a review of structural adjustment lending. The Bank would become more like the private sector by creating an "internal market" within the institution, in which its economists and technical experts would compete to sell their services to loan managers. Of the latter idea, the *Financial Times* remarked that Wolfensohn could better "achieve the entrepreneurial changes he claims to want . . . by sweeping privatization of bank functions."

With no experience in running a bureaucracy as large and entrenched as the Bank, Wolfensohn got mired down in that bureaucracy. His push for change was most noticeable, not on the ground, but in the Bank's many conference rooms, which were booked solid for committee meetings and discussion groups about how to achieve change. "It's as though someone had kicked a big termite mound," said one manager. "People are running around like crazy. I've never been to so many meetings in my life." A "change management" committee was established and charged with coming up with a plan for reorganizing the Bank. A task force on social development, with ten distinct "satellite groups," was set up to "analyze the social aspects of development." By the end of his first year, a new term—"change fatigue"—had entered the Bank's lexicon and Wolfensohn admitted that " 'Change Management' has been overmanaged. We've spent too much time on it."

Wolfensohn, who held regular meetings with staff in an effort to keep enthusiasm for change alive, often expressed dismay at "the lack of interpersonal generosity," the absence of a team spirit at the Bank. He often said that he wanted the Bank to be a family in which, as he put it, "we can say that we care, that we can cry about poverty, that we can laugh when people have a good time, that we can embrace our clients, that we can feel part of them, where we can tell our kids we made a difference." These are heartwarming sentiments, but they do not constitute a new vision for the Bank, or a new vision of development. "What he doesn't realize is that we've lost our role," said one long-serving official. "When we first started, developing countries didn't have bachelor degrees; now they have Nobel Prizes. Then we could bribe them; now they can get money from other sources. We're even losing our influence with the donors."

As the early impetus for change became bogged down in a bureaucratic morass, the enthusiasm and optimism with which the staff had greeted Wolfensohn began to erode, as did his own confidence in his ability to slay the dragon of Bank bureaucracy. The staff's deep-rooted mistrust of senior management in general—and many of those Wolfensohn chose as his top lieutenants in particular—reappeared. Three of the five managing directors he appointed are considered protégés of Ernest Stern. None had shown evidence of having radical new ideas about how the Bank should be run or about the nature of development. The same managers who rose to power under the existing system were overseeing the reform effort.

Few staffers trusted their superiors enough to risk voicing criticism openly, though they were invited to do so. The Economist reported that "some Bank staff also have doubts about their new boss's high profile. They say that he is egotistical and unwilling to share credit for success. Others say he is more concerned with public relations than with substance." "The cognitive dissonance between high-level pronouncements and daily practice is at an all-time high," one staffer remarked. Convinced that the Wolfensohn revolution would fail, that, as one employee put it, it would "become stuck in the bureaucratic cobweb," many decided, in time-honored Bank tradition, to concentrate on fighting proposed changes that might undermine their hard-won positions. Asked about the morale of his colleagues, one longtime staffer replied, "I don't ask; I just lock my door."

In a meeting on March 12, 1996, Wolfensohn tried to salvage his reform effort. He pleaded with the three hundred senior managers present to help him "break though this glass wall, this unseen glass wall, to get enthusiasm, change, and commitment. Unless you give the leadership and unless you have the belief . . . we cannot win. . . . I don't know what else we can do," he said, "to try and bring about change in the institution. I just don't know what else to do. . . . I just beg you to think about it." If nothing else, Wolfensohn's extraordinary speech, which was one of the few Bank documents to be leaked in the first nine months of his presidency, was, in part, intended to make it clear that if his efforts at reform failed it would not be his fault, but the fault of an entrenched and cynical bureaucracy.

Wolfensohn's determination to make the Bank efficient and responsive was not matched by a coherent vision of what the Bank should be doing to achieve the poverty reduction of which he so often spoke. He has not addressed, far less resolved, the internal contradictions in the Bank's mission, the contradictions that have resulted in many of its borrowers spiraling deeply into debt, that have exacerbated the gap between the rich and the poor, and that have required the poor to pay the greatest costs of development while receiving few of its benefits. Better management and an improved esprit de corps will not cure these problems.

"Wolfensohn's more likely than previous presidents to pull the Bank out of some of its big boondoggles," says Brent Blackwelder, president of Friends of the Earth, "but in terms of structural adjustment, he still accepts the conventional wisdom. He accepts the model of development that has failed all along. He won't change the Bank's basic philosophy on lending. With Wolfensohn, we're still up against a stone wall, but it's a much smarter stone wall."

# Epilogue

The Bank's purpose, as defined by its founders, is "to assist in the reconstruction and development of territories of members by facilitating the investment of capital for productive purposes." By the 1960s, however, it had developed broader ambitions. It had, in the jargon of a later decade, "reinvented itself" by adding to its other duties an explicit mandate to fight world poverty. Every president since McNamara has said that poverty reduction is the Bank's *chief* objective.

But despite the Bank's best efforts, that objective is, in many ways, farther away than ever. In 1972 the Bank said that 800 million people lived in absolute poverty—"a condition of life so degraded by disease, illiteracy, malnutrition, and squalor as to deny its victims basic human necessities." That number has since increased by 60 percent to 1.3 billion, out of a world population of 5.5 billion (80 percent of the world's population live in developing countries).

There are, however, some bright spots in this picture. One is that the growth in absolute poverty has not kept pace with population growth, thus the proportion of the developing world living in absolute poverty has declined from 40 to 25 percent. In addition, virtually all developing countries have experienced improvements in a number of important indicators of well-being, including life expectancy and adult literacy rates. Nonetheless, the Bank acknowledges that "many countries have done poorly, and in some living standards have actually fallen during the past thirty years." Bank figures show that of the 4.5 billion people in developing countries, 1 billion lack clean water, 2 billion do not have sanitation facilities, 100 million girls are kept out of school, and nearly 8 million children die every year from polluted air, dirty water, and easily preventable diseases.

There is, of course, no hard and fast definition of poverty. At present, the Bank defines poverty as a per capita income of no more than two dollars a day in terms of U.S. purchasing power, and absolute, or extreme, poverty as half that income. Thus, anyone whose annual income is equivalent to $730 or more is not considered poor. But wherever the poverty line is drawn, the developing world is getting poorer and poorer in relation to the rich countries.

In 1948 the United Nations estimated the average per capita annual income to be around $100 in the developing countries and roughly $1,600 in the United States. By 1993 per capita income in the developing world had risen, but only to $1,100, while in the United States it had soared to $25,000. Thus, the income ratio of the United States to the developing world increased from 16:1 to 23:1 during the past half-century.

That picture is overly rosy, however, because much of the developing world's economic growth has occurred in just a few countries. The most changed are South Korea and Singapore, where per capita GDP increased by more than 550 percent between 1960 and 1990. During the same period, per capita GDP in the forty-five poorest countries grew by only 27 percent. And at least seven countries, including Guinea, Somalia, Madagascar, and Zambia, had lower per capita incomes, in real terms, in 1990 than they had in 1960. By 1996, nineteen countries, including Ghana, Venezuela, and Nicaragua, were in that position.

By now, the rich countries are so far ahead of the poor that simple mathematics demonstrates that the poor are unlikely ever to catch up, and will be hard-pressed even to narrow the gulf between themselves and the rich. In the high-income economies with their per capita income of $23,000, an annual growth rate of 2 percent gives the average citizen an extra $460 per year. In the developing countries, where per capita income is $1,000, the same growth rate increases income by only $20 dollars a year. Thus, as a paper by two World Bank officials points out, an even rate of growth "will exacerbate inequality, while scarcely denting poverty." For the gap between rich and poor to shrink rather than widen, the poor countries would have to have many times the economic growth of their rich counterparts. But this has not happened: During the period from 1980 to 1993, per capita income in rich countries grew by an average 2.2 percent per year, while in the developing world it grew by less than 1 percent. A few countries—Mauritius, China, Indonesia, Thailand, Botswana, and South Korea—had average annual growth rates of between 4 and 8 percent.

In other respects, also, the gap between the rich and the poor is widening. Between 1960 and 1991, the developing world halved its infant death rate, but the industrial world reduced its rate even more dramatically. Thus, today the infant death rate in poor countries is no longer 4.25 times higher than in the rich countries, but 5 times higher. In sub-Saharan Africa, it is more than 7 times higher. Developing countries are also further behind industrial countries now than they were in 1980 in terms both of the average education level of adults and the percentage of children enrolled in school.

Even in those fields in which the gap between the rich and poor world is closing—such as per capita food supply—the developing world's advancement has been slow and uneven. Most developing countries have more food supplies per capita now than they did in 1965. However, at least thirteen, including Peru, Nicaragua, Kenya, Zaire, Cambodia, Ethiopia, Burundi, and Afghanistan, now have less food per capita than they did thirty years ago. Moreover, more than half the countries for which statistics are available do not have enough food to provide all their citizens with their minimum daily requirement of calories.

In any case, per capita figures—whether for GDP, food supplies, or anything else—are simply mathematical averages, reached by dividing national statistics by population. In reality, of course, neither food, nor money, nor anything else is distributed evenly in any country, rich or poor. McNamara tried to impress this fact on his board of governors in 1973: "We must recognize that a high degree of inequality exists not only between developed and developing nations but within the developing nations themselves. . . . The poorest 40 percent [of the population in developing countries] receive only 10 to 15 percent of the total national income." McNamara set as "a minimum objective that the distortion in income distribution within these nations should at least stop increasing by 1975, and begin to narrow with the last half of the decade."

Like most of McNamara's other objectives, however, this one was never met. In 1992, in half the developing countries for which the United Nations was able to obtain information on income distribution, the poorest 40 percent of the population still received 15 percent or less of national income. In Brazil, for example, the bottom 40 percent of the population has only 7 percent of the national income, and the top 20 percent has 32 times as much income as the bottom 20 percent.

It is not only income that is inequitably distributed in developing countries, but also health services, education, food, safe water, and sanitation. In all these categories, according to the United Nations, women are worse off than men, and the rural population is worse off than city dwellers. Overall, 88 percent of people in cities have access to safe water and 69 percent have sanitation facilities, while only 60 percent of people who live in the country have safe water and only 18 percent have sanitation facilities. Children in rural areas are only 80 percent as likely as children in cities to be well nourished. Women in developing countries receive, on average, only half as many years of schooling as men.

Though not as skewed as in many developing countries, income distribution in the rich countries is also distorted. In the group of industrialized democracies known as the Organization for Economic Cooperation and Development, the bottom 40 percent of the population receives only 18 percent of the national income. The top 20 percent gets 7 times as much of the national income as the bottom 20 percent.

Comparing incomes—not within a particular country or between countries, but globally—one discovers that the income of the richest 20 percent of the world's population is now 150 times greater than that of the poorest 20 percent. But, while admitting that "the processes driving economic development are by no means fully understood," the Bank insists that "rapid and sustained development is no hopeless dream, but an achievable reality." Meanwhile, the gap between rich and poor continues to widen.

————

The Bank's founders envisioned a rosy picture of a future in which its loans would bring economic growth to its borrowers, making their citizens prosperous and increasing world trade, thus reinforcing global prosperity, strengthening the bonds between nations, and creating the climate for a lasting peace. That this picture has not materialized is due both to the false assumptions on which the Bank was established and to the structure of the Bank itself.

Perhaps the key assumption underlying the Bank's creation was that there was a condition called underdevelopment and that virtually every country in Asia, Africa, and Latin America suffered from it. According to this view, scores of distinct nations, as well as thousands of regional cultures, are indistinguishable—and myriads of social, political, and economic problems are merely aspects of a single global crisis. Such a situation—if it existed—might indeed call for the creation of a centralized agency able to apply a uniform remedy: Development. That crude and inadequate analysis is still the central tenet of the Bank's philosophy. Still today, the Bank believes that "development is the most important challenge facing the human race."

According to *Webster's* dictionary, developed countries are those with "a relatively high level of industrialization and standard of living." The embodiment of development, the country with the highest standard of living—as measured by per capita GNP—is the United States. The price of attaining even a small portion of its success is abandonment of traditional values and ways of life and the adoption of a more modern—read "American"—approach to life. But many cultures are refusing to accept that their teachings, languages, and mores are obsolete. Indeed, the argument is often heard—from Americans and others—that the prime American values are greed and selfish individuality, that the American way of life is debased and debasing, and that it should be shunned, not imitated. On the other side, many—again, both in America and elsewhere—argue that the rest of the world would benefit from an injection of the enterprise, openness to change, and optimism that made the United States the richest country on earth.

In fact, this debate is wrongheaded. For, even in the unlikely event that it could be shown that one particular culture or way of life is superior to all others, it is dangerous to promote a human monoculture. Variety is as important to the survival of the human species as it is to that of crops. Monocultures lack depth and resilience. They lack the ability to adapt to and survive catastrophic changes in the physical, social, or psychological climate. In contrast, our fast-shrinking but still highly varied collection of thousands of cultures is a rich fund of human knowledge and experience. The human race will need to call on that fund to answer the unforeseen questions it will be asked in coming decades and centuries.

———

Another assumption on which the Bank was founded is that poor countries cannot modernize without money and advice from abroad. This assumption conveniently created a role for the industrialized nations, but it has never been universally accepted that a developing country's growth is linked directly to how much foreign currency it can obtain. Lauchlin Currie, one of the Bank's key advisors in its early days, cited a number of eminent economists who shared with him "a consensus that the dependence of growth on a greater abundance of foreign exchange has not been established." In 1969, the Pearson Commission, which had been established by the Bank to put the case for more development funding, admitted that the "correlation between the amounts of aid received in the past decades and the growth performance is very weak." The commission also acknowledged that "despite the impression that poor countries are too poor to save anything," they had in fact provided most of their own investment capital. During the 1960s, domestic savings financed 85 percent of investment in developing countries. And today the developing world saves and invests in their own economies at a higher rate than do the United States and Europe. In any case, the hundreds of billions of dollars developing countries borrow from abroad each year are more than canceled out by the hundreds of billions they send back each year in debt service. In 1994, for example, the developing world received $167.8 billion in foreign loans and paid out $169.5 billion in debt service—a net transfer from the poor to the rich nations of $1.7 billion.

The amount of money a country has is not as important a determinant of growth as is how efficiently it uses all its capital resources—not only money, but also land, equipment, and labor. A 1968 paper by the World Bank found that "an increase in the supply of capital . . . does not explain at a maximum more than one-half of the estimated growth of gross national product in the many countries studied." In most cases, the Bank concluded, growth is at least half due to improvements in the quality of the workforce and in the efficiency of management and resource use. As political scientist Kari Levitt has observed, "Development ultimately is not a matter of GNP, or money, or physical capital, or foreign exchange, but of the capacity of a society to tap the root of popular creativity, to free up and empower people to exercise their intelligence and their individual and collective efforts to achieve a better life."

The Bank was established to lend money, not to give it away. In particular, it is a lender of foreign currencies and it demands to be repaid in the same currencies it lends—chiefly those of the world's wealthiest countries. In order to obtain enough of the desired currencies to repay their Bank loans, borrowers must sell more to the rich countries than they buy from them. But the rich countries want to be net exporters, not importers. The impossibility of satisfying everyone on this scale has long been realized—economists refer to it as "the transfer problem." According to political scientist

Cheryl Payer, "The Marshall Plan aid was extended in grant form precisely because it was recognized that the United States did not want to receive the massive flow of goods from European factories which they would have been required to accept in repayment for the loans."

The transfer problem was at the heart of the collapse of the foreign bond market in the 1930s and of the world depression. In 1932, economist Allin Dakin, writing in the *Harvard Business Review*, warned that America's protectionist trade policies meant American holders of foreign bonds would not be repaid unless they continued to lend. "Payment through the use of exports is quite unlikely under our present high-tariff policy. . . . The only means [borrowers will have] of making repayments to us on past loans will be more financing and the flotation of additional borrowings. Refunding operations will probably become more and more of the total of foreign issues."

Thus it has been with the World Bank; refunding operations have become more and more of the total of its lending. The result has been an accumulation of debt by the Bank's borrowers—and a gradual loss of sovereignty as well. No creditor is willing to keep refunding forever without asserting some control over the way the debtor conducts business. In earlier times, the great powers did not hesitate to use military force to bend recalcitrant debtors to their will. In his classic essay, "Public Debts," published in 1887, the American economist Henry Carter Adams wrote that "the granting of foreign credits is the first step toward the establishment of an aggressive foreign policy, and under certain conditions, leads inevitably to conquest and occupation."

The Bank's approach to its debtors is not so crude. Instead of sending in the Marines, it offers advice on how countries should manage their finances, make their laws, provide services to their people, and conduct themselves in the international market. Its powers of persuasion are great, due to the universal conviction that, should it decide to ostracize a borrower, all other major national and international powers will follow its lead. Thus, by the excessive lending—born of an underlying inconsistency in its mission—the Bank has added to its own power and depleted that of its borrowers.

Many individuals and groups, from environmentalists and business leaders to economists and politicians, regard the Bank's increasing power as a positive thing—if it is used to further their agendas in the developing countries. Others, however, have expressed concern that massive lending is creating an international dependency problem, a permanent underclass of nations that have lost much of their self-reliance, self-confidence, and self-respect. Many respected figures in the developing world have condemned foreign aid as a habit-forming drug, one that offers a hard-to-resist vision of a better life while undermining the chances of actually obtaining that life. "Please don't lend us any more money," pleaded Adrian Lajous, formerly Mexico's executive director at the World Bank, in *The Wall Street Journal*. "Not even if we ask for another quick fix." In 1991 a task force headed by Muhammad Yunus, founder of Bangladesh's much-emulated Grameen Bank, blamed development aid for "a fast erosion of national self-respect [and] self-confidence in [the country's] ability to solve its own problems" and called for the country to wean itself from it.

The Bank agrees that "aid is no substitute for domestic programs that provide the incentives and create the efficient institutions required to increase domestic production more rapidly," and concedes that "external assistance can weaken the resolve of governments to tackle developmental problems." Aid, according to the eminent conservative British economist Peter Bauer, tends to strengthen the status quo, not to bring about change. "Aid increases the power, resources, and patronage of governments compared with the rest of society and therefore their power over it."

As bad as it is for a country to go into debt unnecessarily, and to lose sovereignty and a sense of self-reliance in the process, matters are made much worse when the money is invested fruitlessly or harmfully. Despite the Bank's self-confidence, it has provided its borrowers with some breathtakingly bad advice. In the early days, when it was preoccupied with physical infrastructure, its experts often failed to realize the full ecological, social, and even economic implications of the vast schemes it was promoting. But the Bank's real shortcomings as an advisor became apparent only when it expanded its lending beyond physical infrastructure to the "social infrastructure" of developing countries.

By the early 1960s, it was evident that economic growth does not automatically raise living standards. Although the upper classes were benefiting from economic growth, the poor were falling further and further behind. The Bank decided to try to reach the poor more directly, through loans for health and education projects, for small-scale agriculture, and for urban renewal. Though it had no expertise or experience in its newly chosen field of mass poverty reduction, the Bank was buoyed by its sense of superiority over all other interested parties—over other international institutions, over national governments, over voluntary organizations, and certainly over the people who were to benefit from its help. It was also resigned to the fact that its war on poverty would not be without casualties. As former Bank Vice President David Hopper explained, "You can't have development without somebody getting hurt." And indeed, the Bank's decades-long series of grand experiments in poverty reduction have cost many billions of dollars and millions of disrupted human lives, and required the sacrifice of vast areas of productive forests, soils, rivers, and coastlines.

The past half-century of development has not profited the poorest people, nor the poorest countries. Rather, they have paid dearly—and their descendants will continue to pay dearly—for the disproportionately small benefits they have received. On the other hand, there are many who *have* profited from development. Certainly the Bank as a bureaucracy has prospered, as have the bureaucracies—national and international—with which it has done business. Many heads of government, especially those who rule without the support of the populace, have relied on the Bank to supply the cash they could not otherwise obtain. Well-connected contractors, exporters, consultants, and middlemen—especially those in the rich countries— have also prospered from Bank-financed projects. Multinational corporations and international banks are benefiting from an improved business climate in countries following World Bank advice. Their relatively small investment in fifty years of development has left the rich countries—and especially their richest citizens—richer than ever before. Given all this, and given the fact that development funds, including the World Bank's, are ultimately supplied by the ordinary taxpayers in donor nations, there is much truth in the saying that development—at least in the monopolistic, formulaic, foreign-dominated, arrogant, and failed form that we have known—is largely a matter of poor people in rich countries giving money to rich people in poor countries.

# Notes

Sources are cited in the notes as follows:

• Items in the bibliography (p. 395) are cited by last name of the author(s) only. Some items will be found in the list of authored World Bank Publications.
• Short titles are used for some works that have been previously cited within the same chapter. These generally consist of the author's last name and a short form of the work's title; the facts of publication are omitted. In special cases, only the title is cited.

## Prologue

1 • more than 11 percent: World Bank; *World Debt Tables 1996*, vol. 1, p. 193.
2 • "virtually every dimension": Bretton Woods Commission, p. 73.

## Chapter 1

5 • the same effect: Paranjype (1991), p. 23.
6 • down payment on the land: Morse, p. 85.
8 • three days to complete: Paranjype (1991), p. 21.
• *Jungle Book*: Ibid., p. 28.
• Sardar Sarovar Dam: The name comes from Vallabh Patel (popularly known as Sardar), who was a hero of the Indian independence movement and the first minister of home affairs after independence. *Sarovar* is Hindi for "large lake."
• biggest water development scheme in India: Morse, p. 237.
• 4.8 million acres . . . and 30 million people: P. A. Raj, *Facts: Sardar Sarovar Project* (Gandhinagar, India: Sardar Sarovar Nigam Ltd., 1990), pp. 9–11.
• at least 320,000 people: McCully (1994).

10 • thirty-one different resettlement sites: Morse, p. 105.

• "how can we go": Author's interview with Kanti Bhoga, 16 April 1993.

11 • foundation stone: Raj, *Facts*, p. 8.

• at least eight hundred families: Morse, pp. 89–90.

• Gujarat, the driest of the three states: Under the tribunal's ruling Gujarat will have 70,000 oustees, but gain 4.3 million acres (1.8 million hectares) of irrigation, drinking water for 135 towns and 8,000 villages, and 230 MW of power. Rajasthan, to the north of Gujarat, will have no oustees and will get irrigation water for 180,000 acres (75,000 hectares) and drinking water for two districts. Maharashtra, with 13,500 oustees, will get irrigation for 90,000 acres (37,500) hectares and 400 MW of power. Madhya Pradesh will have 115,000 oustees—more than all the other states put together—but the only thing that the state will get is 800 megawatts of hydropower. Morse, p. 62.

• Narmada Sagar Projects: *Sagar* is Hindi for "ocean," a reference to the reservoir.

• another 200,000 people: Alvares and Billorey, p. 16.

• cost another $1.6 billion: Ibid., p. 52.

• recoup its cost: Morse, p. 250.

• "completed at the same time": A World Bank memo summarizing the tribunal's decision, quoted in Morse, p. 238.

12 • Three-quarters of these people: Maloney, p. 3.

• displaced millions of people: Morse, p. 53.

• at least their previous standard of living: World Bank, "Social Issues Associated with Involuntary Resettlement in Bank-Financed Projects," February 1980, cited in Morse, p. 23.

• "adequate safeguards are provided": World Bank, "Tribal People in Bank-Financed Projects," Operational Manual, Statement No. 2.34, February 1982.

• "would not be prepared to assist": Ibid.

• no national laws: Morse, p. 19.

• Ousted landowners: Ibid., pp. 20–21.

• "lands of quality": Ibid., p. 19.

13 • some villagers appealed: Author interview with Girish Patel, 4 May 1993.

• "invariably undervalues land": Morse, p. 95.

• "could be seen camping": Ibid., p. 96.

• No one even knew: Ibid., p. 44.

• the Bank dropped its insistence: Ibid., p. 45.

• already harmed thousands of people: Ibid., p. 47.

• refused to approve the dam: Ibid., pp. 302–3.

14 • Several hundred people: Ibid, p. 91.

• 60,000 people: "Multiple Impacts of the Sardar Sarovar Project," *Lokayan Bulletin* 9, no. 3/4 (1991): 42.

• forcing them to close: Narmada Ghari Navnirman Samiti, p. 77.

• prime minister's house: "Multiple Impacts of the Sardar Sarovar Project," *Lokayan Bulletin* 9, no. 3/4 (1991): 42.

• the Long March: "Multiple Impacts of the Sardar Sarovar Project," ibid.: 42; "The Jan Vikas Sanghgarsh Yatra: A First Hand Account," ibid.: 65–78.

16 • "The execution of Sardar Sarovar": B. D. Sharma. "Letter to Prime Minister V. P. Singh." April 1990, reproduced in ibid.: 126–33.

• "must be deemed to have lapsed": Narmada Control Authority Environmental Sub-Group, *Agenda Notes,* 7 September 1990, item no. IX-3(53), quoted in "Multiple Impacts of the Sardar Sarovar Project," ibid.: 37.

• the 105 legal covenants attached: World Bank, Mission Supervision Report, Form 590, 31 May 1990, cited in ibid.: 34.

• 1,500 large dams: The International Commission on Large Dams defines a large dam as one 15 meters or higher. According to Patel, p. 29, India has 1,652 such dams. Another definition of large dams is those having reservoirs of 60 square kilometers or more. According to Maloney, p. 3, India has 1,589 dams meeting that description.

• temples of Modern India: McCully (1996), p. 1.

• many more dams and irrigation projects are planned: *India Irrigation Sector Review:* Vol. 1, p. 1.

• almost no benefit: Morse, p. 300.

17 • Panam Dam: Estimates Committee of Gujarat Legislature, *Report on Dams*, 1987.

• "poorly operated and maintained": World Bank, *India Irrigation Sector Review*, Vol. 1, p. 9.

• leaving only a trickle: Ibid, p. 12.

• "economic viability [has] been poor all along": Ibid, p. 10.

• improving the performance of existing irrigation systems: Ibid, p. ii.

• "they have opposed it": Anil Sharma, "Funds Shortage Hits Narmada Projects," Times of India News Service, 1 February 1993.

18 • half the country's large dams: McCully (1996), Chapter 9.

• "it is impossible for Madhya Pradesh": Deo, p. 63.

• there is no guarantee: Morse, p. 244.

• without them: Ibid., p. 250.

19 • only 28 percent: Paranjype (1990), p. 143–45.

• "the hydro benefits": Author interview with anonymous World Bank employee, 3 December 1992.

• "reducing the amount of land to be irrigated": Author interview with anonymous World Bank official, 4 December 1992.

• The extra 19 feet: Morse, p. 244.

20 • "That's official": Author interview with Amar Gargesh, 4 May 1993.

• it includes several hundred: Morse, p. 297.

• "no corresponding increase": Ibid.

• "The argument in favor": "In Defense of Enslaving," *Lokayan Bulletin* 9, no. 3/4 (1991): 98.

21 • "so that others may live in happiness": Alvares and Billorey, p. 18.

• "living in the slums of Baroda": Interview with Balraj Maheshwari, 16 April 1993.

• "the sharing never comes": Interview with Father Joseph, 17 April 1993.

• "We are not enamored of the old way": Interview with Girish Patel, 5 April 1993.

22 • if they entered the submergence zone: Morse, p. 178.

• "vomiting, diarrhoea, and dehydration": Ibid., p. 112.

23 • "an increasingly repressive campaign": Asia Watch, *Before the Deluge: Human Rights Abuses at India's Narmada Dam* (Washington, DC: Asia Watch, 1992).

• led the Japanese government: "SSP Machinery Lying in Japan for Want of Forex," *Indian Express*, 16 March 1993.

• nothing of the sort: Morse, pp. 127–38.

24 • most important client: Mason and Asher, p. 678.

• "the Jewel in the Crown": Grenfell oral history, p. 7.

• "It was really becoming an embarrassment": Interview with member of Morse Commission, 24 June 1993.

26 • "In practice, it's another story": Ibid.

• no environmental impact assessment: Morse, p. xxi.

• the Bank's own experts had warned: Ibid., pp. 273, 280, and 308.

• "death traps": Ibid., p. 27.

• "People have died": Ibid., p. 329.

• A succession of deadlines: "Multiple Impacts of the Sardar Sarovar Project," *Lokayan Bulletin* 9, no. 3/4 (1991): 39–40.

• "there developed an eagerness": Morse, p. 354.

27 • "step back from the Project": Ibid., p. xxv.

• "a comprehensive set of actions": World Bank, *India: Sardar Sarovar (Narmada) Proj-*

_ects, Review of Current Status and Next Steps,_ memorandum to World Bank executive
`irectors from the vice president and secretary, 11 September 1992, p. 15.

`ey'll never suspend anything": Author interview 22 September 1992.

` World Bank Must Withdraw": Unsigned editorial, _Financial Times,_ 21 September

`ank may reject": Letter from Bradford Morse and Thomas Berger to Lewis
October 1992, p. 5.

28    `ow egregious the situation": Statement of E. Patrick Coady, U.S. executive
`ting of the World Bank Executive Board, 23 October 1992.

• `a fait accompli": _World Rivers Review,_ second quarter, 1993, p. 8.

• `n: Morse, p. xiii.

• th`ight new loans: World Bank, _Monthly Operational Summary_
(Wash`June 1993); Probe International, "World Bank Makes Up with
India, Pr`New Loans," _World Bank Backgrounder,_ no. 20, 25 June
1993.

29    • "They legitin`or years": Author interview with Smitu Kothari, 4 April
1993.

• "This is not the case`Bank, memorandum from Ibrahim Shihata to Joseph
Wood, 30 March 1993.

• "significant in anybody's language": Lewis Preston, World Bank press conference,
Washington, DC, 19 July 1994.

# Chapter 2

30    • Ivar Kreuger: Apart from those mentioned in the notes, the main sources for my ac-
count of Kreuger's career are Max Winkler, "Playing with Matches," _The Nation,_ 25
May 1932; "The Collapse of the Kreuger Legend," _The Literary Digest,_ 7 May 1932,
p. 36; "Ivar Kreuger," 3 parts, _Fortune,_ May, June, and July 1933; " 'Poor Kreuger,' "
_Time,_ 21 March 1932, pp. 15 and 45–50; T. G. Barman, "Ivar Kreuger: His Life and
Work," _Atlantic Monthly,_ August 1932.

• one of the world's wealthiest men: " 'Poor Kreuger,' " p. 48; "Ivar Kreuger," Part 1,
p. 80.

• the most powerful financier in the world: "Ivar Kreuger: His Life and Work," p. 243.

31    • the Legion of Honor: "Ivar Kreuger," Part 1, p. 56.

• financed the loan to France: " 'Poor Kreuger,' " p. 48.

• famously good investments: "Ivar Kreuger: His Life and Work," p. 242.

• used the money to build: Oliver (1975), p. 70.

• "a black record of embezzlement": Sampson, p. 60.

32    • "How such a man": Sampson, pp. 60–61.

• more than $17 billion worth of foreign bonds: Max Winkler, _New York Times,_ 31
December 1931, cited in Dakin, p. 227.

• from chain stores to religious institutions: Feis, pp. 42–43.

• they carried high interest rates: Up to 2 percent higher than high-yield domestic bonds,
according to Dakin, pp. 233–35.

• "outrageously high profits": U.S. Senate Committee on Finance, _Prohibit Financial
Transactions with any Foreign Government in Default on its Obligations to the United
States._ 73rd Cong., 1st sess., 1933, Report 20.

• "competing on almost a violent scale": Allen, p. 315.

• "a horde of American bankers": Ibid.

• trying to drum up business in Colombia: U.S. Senate Committee on Finance, _Sale of
Foreign Bonds or Securities in the United States,_ 72nd Cong., 1st sess., 1931, p. 845.

• "Colombia is going wild on borrowing": Cleona Lewis, p. 381.

● a loan to the city of Budapest: Ibid., p. 377.

● "finally persuaded to borrow three million dollars": Ibid., p. 377.

● "flat on its back and gasping for breath": *The Nation,* 15 March 1933, p. 274.

33  ● "default within five years": U.S. Senate Committee on Finance, op. cit., p. 1587.

● plead with them to offer less: Cleona Lewis, p. 380.

● Peru defaulted on those bonds: *The Nation,* 15 March 1933, p. 275.

● it was already in default: Cleona Lewis, p. 410.

● a survey by J. P. Morgan & Company: "Who Buys Foreign Bonds—and Why?" *Literary Digest,* 29 January 1927.

● "schoolteachers, army officers, country doctors, stenographers, clerks": Soule, p. 180.

● chief reason for investing: "Who Buys Foreign Bonds—and Why?"

● benefited only a small elite: Lawrence Dennis, " 'Sold' on Foreign Bonds," *The New Republic,* 19 November 1930, p. 10.

● right alongside an existing road: U.S. Senate Committee on Finance, op. cit., p. 1600.

● "hundreds of thousands of Indians": Ibid., p. 1601.

● Colombia borrowed $150 million: Makin, p. 50.

34  ● Bolivia, for example, borrowed $21 million: Ibid., pp. 1585–86.

● 38 percent . . . were in default: Cleona Lewis, p. 398.

● "We sought and rejoiced": Feis, p. 16.

● half the banks holding defaulted foreign bonds: Soule, p. 177.

● "numberless small country banks": Soule, p. 178.

● "no mere gambler": *The Economist* is quoted in Barman, "Ivar Kreuger," p. 238.

35  ● "Europe was starving for money": "Ivar Kreuger," Part 2, p. 88.

● hundreds of millions of dollars: Kreuger lent almost $400 million to Europe: Ibid.

● every country except Argentina was in default: Cleona Lewis, p. 400.

36  ● Fearing chaos when the news broke: "The Collapse of the Kreuger Legend," p. 36.

● "The man who was driven": "Ivar Kreuger," Part 1, p. 57.

● "worse than had been feared": "The Collapse of the Kreuger Legend," p. 36.

● "I speak of Mr. Ivar Kreuger": "Ivar Kreuger," Part 2, p. 63.

● "It seemed almost too good to be true": Barman, "Ivar Kreuger," p. 242.

● scores of fictitious businesses: "Ivar Kreuger," Part 2, p. 82.

37  ● "the manipulations were so childish": Ibid., Part 3, p. 72.

● "we had no doubt": Ibid., p. 71.

● his lenders didn't actually require him: "The Collapse of the Kreuger Legend," p. 37.

● pronounced them forgeries: "Ivar Kreuger," Part 2, pp. 59, 78.

● "a very Puritan of finance": Ibid., Part 1, p. 57.

● a forger and a swindler on a colossal scale: Barman, "Ivar Kreuger," p. 238.

● by taking bribes in return for loans: "Ivar Kreuger," Part 2, p. 78.

● This single loan: Ibid., p. 90.

● forced to move to more modest quarters: Ibid., p. 80.

38  ● "innumerable widows and orphans": Winkler, "Playing with Matches," p. 590.

● "the suicides were coming in": "Ivar Kreuger," Part 2, p. 78.

● a fatal blow to the trade in foreign bonds: Cleona Lewis, p. 400.


# Chapter 3

39  ● deepened the global depression: "It was felt [by the U.S. Treasury], for example, that the sudden cessation in 1928, and particularly in 1931, of long-term capital exports by the United States has contributed to the intensity of the depression and the breakdown of the international gold standard." Oliver (1971), p. 23.

● country after country: Horsefield, pp. 4–5.

40  • a two-pronged plan: Oliver (1971), p. 25.
    • draw up a more formal paper: Eckes, p. 46.
    • "were quite inseparable": Maffry oral history, p. 6.
41  • the central bank for the nations of the world: Horsefield, p. 18.
    • "new-fangled international monetary unit": John Maynard Keynes, address to House of Lords on the IMF, 23 May 1944.
    • "the future economic government of the world": Ibid.
    • responsibility of both the debtor and the creditor nations: Oliver (1975), p. 78, citing John Maynard Keynes, *A Revision of the Treaty* (London: Macmillan, 1922), pp. 161–62.
    • "a permanent institution for international monetary cooperation": United Nations, *Bretton Woods Proceedings,* p. 98.
    • the public would not accept two: Oliver (1975), p. 150.
42  • the bank idea surfaced aboard the *Queen Mary:* Oliver (1971), p. 49.
    • "the most monstrous monkey-house": The countries were "namely, Colombia, Costa Rica, Dominica, Ecuador, Salvador, Guatemala, Haiti, Honduras, Liberia, Nicaragua, Panama, Paraguay, Philippines, Venezuela, Peru, Uruguay, Ethiopia, Iceland, Iran, Iraq, Luxembourg. . . . To these might perhaps be added: Egypt, Chile, and (in present circumstances) Yugoslavia." Donald Moggridge, ed. *The Collected Writings of John Maynard Keynes,* vol. 26 (London: Macmillan and Cambridge University Press), 1980, p. 42.
    • dancing lessons with Arthur Murray: Eckes, p. 139.
    • "the Bank probably didn't take more than a day and a half": Knapp oral history, 1975, p. 41.
    • International Trade Organization: Horsefield, pp. 171–75.
    • As for the World Bank, the Bank's organization and financing is explained in its Articles of Agreement.
43  • most private lenders were reluctant: Howard et al., pp. 28, 70.
    • "only for proper purposes and in proper ways": United Nations, op. cit., p. 87.
    • the top five shareholders: Initially these were the United States, Britain, China, France, and—after Russia declined to join—India.
44  • "seeks to create an economic strait-jacket": Neylan's critique is bound with Keynes's address to the House of Lords, 23 May 1944, in a booklet in the library of the University of California at Berkeley (call no. HG 3881 N45), p. 46.
    • "in which we have only a minority interest": Eckes, p. 167.
    • "thoroughly respected": Allan Drury, quoted in ibid., p. 201.
    • "a nation that comes to rely on gifts and loans": "Taft Starts Fight to Bar World Bank," *New York Times,* 13 July 1945.
    • fewer than a quarter of the population: Eckes, p. 182.
    • "playing 'Santa Claus' to the world": Ibid., p. 167.
    • "one of the most elaborate and sophisticated campaigns": Ibid., p. 168.
45  • "everybody began rattling their GUNS": Ibid., pp. 195–96.
    • "pledges of a better postwar world": Ibid., p. 201.
    • rewrote the Bretton Woods treaty: Ibid., p. 182.
    • only the United States, South Africa, and Venezuela: Ibid., p. 202.
46  • "I knew more about Bretton Woods than anybody": Lieftinck oral history (I), pp. 1–2.
    • "children with little flags": Lieftinck oral history (II), p. 2.
    • Keynes condemned Bank salaries as "scandalous": Mason and Asher, p. 39.
47  • "little more than schemes of the United States": Oliver (1975), p. 227.
    • his friends blamed the meeting: Ibid., p. 226.
    • felled by a fatal heart attack: Ibid., pp. 81–83.
48  • "a bold new program": Truman, pp. 227–29.
    • "help them realize their aspirations": Ibid., p. 226.
49  • "a world half prosperous and half starving": United Nations, *Money and the Postwar World* (New York: UN Information Office), 1945, p. 4.

- "just another device for channeling hard-earned U.S. savings": Mason and Asher, p. 126.
50 • a succession of influential financiers: Ibid., p. 41; Oliver (1975) p. 226.; Collado oral history, p. 61.
- "Our only market was the United States": Machado oral history, p. 8.
- "a whoop in hell": Oliver (1975), p. 233.
- "that was an excruciating job": Machado oral history, p. 9.
- "I did all sorts of strange things": Collado oral history, pp. 60–61.
- "a certain degree of desperation": Ibid., pp. 62–63.
51 • "specific projects": World Bank Articles of Agreement, Article III, Section 4(v).
- "productive purposes": Ibid., Article I(ii).
- Meyer held out against the pressure: Mason and Asher, p. 46.
- "more of an idea about a project": Ibid., p. 155.
- "was good for $40 million": Ibid., p. 47.
52 • the country was still in default: Ibid., p. 156.
- demoralized the Bank's staff: Garner oral history (I), p. 5.
- for a time even lived together: Black oral history, p. 5.
- the Bank's achievements in its first year: Mason and Asher, p. 36.
- "split by dissension, sadly lacking in prestige": E. Lockett, *The New York Times Magazine,* 29 May 1949.
- "there wasn't a Wall Street man": Oliver (1975), p. 249.
53 • "more concerned with protecting the interests of their former clients": Ibid., p. 238.
- "create markets for U.S. trade": Isaacson and Thomas, p. 429.
- more than twice the normal rate: Oliver (1975), p. 246.
- "bending over backwards to accommodate [small] dealers": "World Bank Bonds Quickly Marketed," *New York Times,* 16 July 1947.
- until the French government gave evidence of its economic soundness: Isaacson and Thomas, p. 429.
- its lendable capital: Members deposited only 20 percent of their subscriptions to the Bank in cash, and most of the cash was in currencies that were unacceptable in international commerce. Only about $700 million of the Bank's capital was in the form of U.S. dollars and gold, and nearly $600 million of that was the U.S. contribution. Mason and Asher, p. 105.
- a rowboat compared to the Marshall Plan's *Queen Elizabeth:* Oliver (1975), p. 239.
54 • "we were Wall Street bill collectors": Garner oral history (I), pp. 13–14.
- the day after Chile reached a settlement with its foreign creditors: Mason and Asher, p. 157.
- "little understanding of or interest in the Third World": Isaacson and Thomas, p. 732.

## Chapter 4

55 • "I wanted to make a career in the Chase Bank": Black oral history, pp. 51–52.
- "the happiest years of my life": Ibid.
56 • friendly and approachable: Boskey oral history, p. 3; Waterston oral history, p. 16.
- "go out of business in due course": Oliver (1975), p. 239.
- "a sort of bridge between war and peace": Black oral history, p. 20.
- only three loan applications: Mason and Asher, p. 53.
- "they should borrow money from us": Machado oral history, p. 14.
- offered no details about specific projects: Mason and Asher, p. 162.
- no accompanying documentation: Machado oral history, p. 17.
- "lack of well-prepared and well-planned projects": Quoted in Acheson et al., p. 73.
57 • "Well, it doesn't appeal to me": Garner oral history (I), p. 29.

• "not only in special circumstances but generally": Report by a group of experts to the Secretary-General of the UN: *National and International Measures for Full Employment*, Lake Success, NY, 1949, p. 92, quoted in Mason and Asher, p. 261.

58 • "a loan for a purpose or purposes unknown": Ibid.
• "we sometimes refuse to lend": Ibid., p. 233.
• only developing country to receive a program loan: Ibid., p. 264.
• Colombia became the first country: Ibid., pp. 299–301.
• first comprehensive analysis of the Colombian economy: Hartwig, p. 111.
• a five-year, $2.5 billion (equivalent to $20 billion in 1993): Currie (1950), p. 593, set the program's cost at 5 billion Colombian pesos. In 1950, 1.95 Colombian pesos = $1.00 (IMF, *International Financial Statistics*, vol. 3, Part 3, July–Dec. 1950, p. 18).

59 • "translate a foreign report into a national program": Currie (1981), p. 60.
• aided in its deliberations by Currie himself: World Bank, *Bank Operations in Colombia*, p. 22; Mason and Asher, p. 301.
• the committee endorsed the Currie report: Howard et al., p. 84.
• hired Currie and American economist Albert Hirschman: Meier and Seers, p. 90; Currie (1981), p. 70.
• "the expectation of bountiful loans": Ibid., pp. 62–63.
• the Bank lent Colombia more than $300 million: Howard et al., p. 132.
• more money per capita than any of its other borrowers: Currie (1981), p. 60.
• "too many Bank missions": Lilienthal, vol. 5, pp. 294–96.
• autonomous public agencies . . . [which] the Bank helped establish: World Bank, *Bank Operations in Colombia*, p. 23; Howard et al., p. 3, 113–14 (Table 4).

60 • two dozen other countries: Mason and Asher, p. 302.
• more than half of all its loans: 87 out of 150 loans. Howard et al., p. 52.
• "You can dislike us all you want to": Black oral history, pp. 355–56.
• "It is most dangerous": Quoted in Adams (1991), pp. 66–67.
• "The apostles of a new life": E. R. Black, *The Diplomacy of Economic Development* (New York: Atheneum), 1963, pp. 11–12.

61 • "it was a wonderful feeling": Waterston oral history, p. 8.
• "an ambitious economic development plan": Meiers and Seers, p. 90.
• "without close study of local surroundings": Ibid.
• "knowledge was held only by a few foreign experts": Ibid., pp. 90–91.
• "unlimited latent capacity of the average man": David Lilienthal, "The Road to Change," *International Development Review*, December 1964, p. 10.

62 • "an adequate supply of power, communications and transportation facilities": Annual Report, 1951, p. 14.
• "It was the availability of financing": Mason and Asher, p. 152.

63 • "ideas that were more congenial to the Bank": Cairncross oral history, p. 6.
• "the EDI mafia": Waterston oral history, p. 13.
• "a steel works, an airline, a six-lane highway": Meiers and Seers, p. 64.
• "pure water had many valuable side effects": Morris, p. 227.

64 • the Bank rejected Colombia's request: Currie (1981), p. 64.
• " 'We can't go messing around with education and health' ": Ibid., pp. 61–62.
• more than 50 percent of Colombia's public spending . . . went to transportation, whereas education received only a few percent: Hartwig, p. 116; World Bank, *Bank Operations in Colombia*, p. 53.
• "too much on transportation projects": Hartwig, p. 116.
• "Garner was in a lecturing mood": Lilienthal, vol. 4, p. 15.

65 • "We cannot and will not lend more": Eugene R. Black, "The World Bank at Work," *Foreign Affairs Quarterly*, April 1952, p. 411.
• "the altitude of its standards": Morris, pp. 227–28.
• consider ways of making money available: Mason and Asher, p. 382.
• "showed extraordinary ingenuity": Ibid., p. 383.

• "the Bank is . . . an independent organization": Ibid., p. 563. The Bank does have to pay "due regard" to decisions of the Security Council taken under Articles 41 and 42 of the UN Charter. Under those articles the Security Council can take measures to maintain international peace and security. Lawyers Committee for Human Rights, p. 26.
• "busybody empire-builders or do-gooders": Mason and Asher, p. 561.
• "competing official lending institutions": Ibid., p. 462.

66 • "an idea to offset the urge for SUNFED": Weaver, p. 28.
• "IDA had to be invented": Mason and Asher, p. 380.
• per capita income below a certain level: The formal guideline is $1,395, but in practice the cutoff point has been lower—$865 in 1995, for example. World Bank Annual Report 1995, pp. 205–6.

67 • a subsidiary international finance corporation: Mason and Asher, pp. 346–47.
• "private capital is not available": International Finance Corporation, *Articles of Agreement*, Article I(i).
• It has its own chief executive: The IFC's organization and finances are explained in its Articles of Agreement.
• paid-in capital of $80 million: Mason and Asher, p. 350.
• the United States contributed $35 million: IFC Annual Report, FY63, p. 37.
• "so repugnant to conservative secretaries of the U.S. Treasury": Mason and Asher, p. 347.

68 • it lent or invested $18 million: IFC and World Bank Annual Reports, FY63.
• Twenty years later: Ibid., FY83.
• a dispute between Britain and Iran: Mason and Asher, pp. 595–610.
• "concentrate on other important issues": Lilienthal, vol. 3, p. 199.
• an Indus Basin Development Fund: Australia, Canada, Germany, New Zealand, Pakistan, the U.K., the U.S., and the World Bank were parties to the Indus Basin Development Fund, which totaled $895 million, including $9 million from the Bank (for Pakistan's Mangla Dam) and $174 from India. Mason and Asher, p. 626; World Bank annual reports, 1961, p. 22, and 1968, p. 21.

69 • "international civil service": Morris, p. 232.


Chapter 5

70 • 370 loans worth more than $7 billion: Loans from 1947 to 1962 totaled $7.2 billion. World Bank, *Commitments Detail Report*.
• the Bank's net income was $83 million: World Bank Annual Report, FY63.
• "The Bank was piling up profits": Mason and Asher, p. 407.
• "a heavy charge for the peoples that receive them": Miguel Aleman, 3 September 1952, quoted in World Bank, *As Others See Us . . . Testimonials*, fiftieth anniversary press release, 1994.
• admiring articles about its work: *Reader's Guide to Periodical Literature* (Minneapolis: H. H. Wilson), March 1961–February 1963.

71 • "Black made a point, a brilliant point": McKitterick oral history, pp. 16–17.
• "by development is meant to the Bank Group an increase in GNP": Mason and Asher, p. 480.
• "by fostering more rapid growth": Ibid., p. 655.
• an average rate of 4.8 percent a year: Pearson, p. 27. The Bank's overall growth target was a 5.5 percent annual increase in gross national product and a 2.5 percent annual rise in per capita GNP. Currie (1981), p. 4.

72 • "Relatively poor countries will always be with us": Acheson et al., p. 78.
• "and if not, why not?": International Bank for Reconstruction and Development, *Report on End-Use Policies and Procedures of the Bank*, 8 July 1964, cited by Mason and Asher, pp. 255, 259.

• the Bank begin to evaluate completed projects: The first performance audit report is dated October 1972. World Bank, *Directory of OED Reports,* September 1992.

• To this day, the Bank has only examined nine: Compare reports listed in *Directory of OED Reports,* September 1992, with loans and credits as listed in World Bank, *Statement of Development Credits and Statement of Loans,* 30 November 1992.

• "the old pastoral ways": Morris, p. 119.

73   • "Yanhee stands like a very talisman of change": Ibid., p. 112.

• "was not unanimously acclaimed": Ibid., p. 186.

• "Whether or not it succeeds": Ibid., p. 186.

• "transform the destinies of a nation": Ibid., p. 113.

• The list comprises seven dams, five railways: This list is derived from World Bank, *Statement of Development Credits,* 30 November 1992.

• $1.9 billion, more than a third of the Bank's development lending: IBRD and IDA lending during Black's reign (1949–1962) totaled $6.9 billion, of which $1.7 billion went to rich countries and $5.2 billion to developing countries. World Bank, *Commitments Detail Report.*

• Black devoted $2 billion: Sklar and McCully, p. 67–70.

• Black's Bank built dams in Ghana, Zambia: Ibid.

74   • By 1994, the Bank had spent $28 billion: Ibid., pp. 5, 10.

• "bring an end to the increasingly acute shortage of electricity": World Bank, press release No. 495, 21 August 1957. In addition to those cited, my sources for the Yanhee story include Organization for Economic Cooperation and Development, *Development Assistance: Efforts and Policies of the Members of the Development Assistance Committee,* 1968 review (Paris: OECD), December 1968, pp. 199–207; James Fahn, "Thirsting for Dam Efficiency," *The Nation* (Bangkok), 8 February 1993; "Dam Threatens Mae Yom Park," *Bangkok Sunday,* 10 May 1992; Electricity Generating Authority of Thailand, *EGAT 1991–1992* (Public Relations Department, February 1992); Tennessee Valley Authority, *TVA—Symbol of Valley Resource Development* (TVA Technical Library), June 1961.

• "in these rich rice lands of Siam": Morris, pp. 119–21.

• "They said we must sacrifice for all": Suda Kanjanawanawan, "A Time of Reckoning," *The Nation* (Bangkok), 10 June 1990.

75   • "Nobody wants to go to Bangkok": Author interview, 20 April 1993.

76   • more than 1.4 million acres in the Basin: *Perspectives on the Water Crisis* (Bangkok: Project for Ecological Recovery, February 1993), pp. 3, 13.

• government-commissioned study warned that there was not enough water: Ibid., p. 13.

• only enough water to irrigate half a million acres: Ibid., p. 13.

• the Agriculture Ministry ordered the area: "Panel Backs Crop Reduction," *Bangkok Post,* 13 February 1993.

• "we can't eat teardrops": Kanjanawanawan, op cit.

77   • "we oppose the project": Probe International, "World Bank Consultants Attacked and Beaten," World Bank Backgrounder No. 35, 28 July 1994.

• "they would have been unable to comprehend the problem": King, p. 254.

78   • "turned out to be even more attractive": Ibid., p. 355.

• "not itself carried out any studies": World Bank, *Response to Statements of Environmental Organizations,* 19 June 1984, p. 16.

• "far outweigh its potential adverse effects": Ibid.

• "now definitely worse off": Thayer Scudder, transcript of recorded interview with Patrick McCully, 11 March 1994, p. 7.

• "disastrous" for farming and fisheries: Ibid., p. 8.

• "contained in one small booklet": Morris, p. 217.

• "We had to go back to the contributing governments": Aldewereld oral history (II), p. 18.

79   • The dam displaced ninety thousand people: Michael Cernea, "Bridging the Research

Divide: Studying Refugees and Development Oustees," in T. Allen, ed., *In Search of Cool Ground: Displacement and Homecoming in Northeast Africa* (New York: James Curry Publishers, 1995).

• "the people were better off": Author interview with Wapenhans, 7 December 1992.

• the British set up a preparatory commission: Hart, pp. 21–22. Hart gives the most complete account of the building of the dam.

• "the Queen of Development": McKitterick oral history, p. 23.

• "She influenced me more than anyone": Shapley, p. 507.

• "That, basically, is the justification": Hart, pp. 40–41.

• 8,500-square-kilometer reservoir: Ibid., p. 76.

80  • "It will be a feather in Ghana's cap": Ibid., p. 28.

• "economical only for the general public": Ibid., p. 49.

• "the sheer size of the project is itself a problem": International Bank for Reconstruction and Development, *Economic Report on Ghana*, October 1957, p. 50.

• "not necessarily bring outstanding benefits to Ghana": Ibid., p. 53.

• "the Volta Project is not very attractive": *The Economy of Ghana*, 29 June 1960, p. 20.

• "they said we had to get the World Bank Ghana loan all buttoned up": Lilienthal, vol. 5, p. 232.

• as soon as the Bank approved the loan: Hart, p. 77.

• the eighty thousand villagers, mostly subsistence farmers and fishermen, whom the dam displaced: Much of my account of the relocation of the oustees is from Ronald Graham, "Ghana's Volta Resettlement Scheme," in Goldsmith and Hildyard, pp. 131–39.

• Resettlement was left until the last moment: "Because the flooding started before schedule, the relocation program became more of an emergency measure." World Bank, *Response to Statement of Environmental Organizations*, 11 January 1984, p. 17.

81  • the United Nations had to intervene: Hart, p. 85.

• causing serious harm to the downstream environment: Butcher, p. 11.

• "massive dosing of the river with DDT": Ibid.

• the abandonment of 40 percent of the land area of northeastern Ghana: Melinda S. Meade, ed., *Conceptual and Methodological Issues in Medical Geography*, Studies in Geography, no. 15. (Chapel Hill: University of North Carolina, 1980), p. 39, cited in Goldsmith and Hildyard, vol. 1, pp. 85–86.

• easing the problem in certain areas: Butcher, p. 11.

82  • "the people of the country won't accept or understand that": Lilienthal, vol. 6, p. 236.

• takes 45 percent of all Ghana's hydroelectricity: Yao Graham, "Drought Dims Ghana's Hydroelectric Power," *World Rivers Review*, November 1995, p. 7.

• irrigation would be at least as profitable: C. K. Annan, "Was Ghana's Akosombo Dam the Best Option?" *World Water*, September 1989, p. 36. Annan is the former head of the Ghana Water Supply Industry.

83  • Akosombo was ranked thirty-seventh: Robert Goodland, "The 'Big Dams' Debate," The John R. Freeman Lecture, Massachusetts Institute of Technology, Cambridge, Mass., 16 April 1990, p. 23.

• "a short-sighted and prodigiously narrow-minded project": Yao Graham, "Drought Dims Ghana's Hydroelectric Power," *World Rivers Review*, November 1995, p. 36.

• brought Akosombo power production to a near halt: Ibid., p. 36.

• a smaller irrigation project would be more economical: Lilienthal, vol. 5, p. 3.

• "there was something here that went beyond engineering": Ibid., vol. 4, p. 214.

• "The trouble with Iran": Ibid., p. 341.

84  • "the Bank's freedom of choice had been considerably reduced": King, p. 218.

• "crime against the nation": Tendler, p. 112.

• "despite the large cost overruns": World Bank, *Bank Operations in Colombia*, p. 89.

85  • "substantial economic benefits were lost": Aldewereld oral history (II), p. 5.

• "the Bank considered its lending to the Indian Railways as very successful": Ibid., p. 5.

• "the expansion of gold mining operations": World Bank Annual Report, FY53–54, p. 20.
• "one of the most spectacularly interesting projects": Morris, p. 187.
• "It is the only route of easy construction": Hartwig, p. 117.
• cost not $58, but $98 million: World Bank, *Bank Operations in Colombia*, p. 63.
• "reduced the quality of their work": Hartwig, p. 117.
• "he would have omitted the railroad": Lilienthal, vol. 5, p. 43.

86    • "a most painful and lengthy process": World Bank, *Bank Operations in Colombia*, p. 64.
• "a widespread misuse of the region's natural resources": Ibid., p. 67.
• "even under the most favorable assumptions": Ibid., p. 66.
• a national highway network that largely duplicated the railroad: Hartwig, p. 121.
• "has had dubious results": World Bank, *Bank Operations in Colombia*, p. 72.
• three times the original estimate: Ibid., pp. 35, 56.
• on the recommendation of a mission led by George Woods: World Bank Annual Report, 1953, p. 16.
• a mission led by George Woods: Oliver (1995), pp. 26, 47.
• "Kaiser interests took more of Woods' time than any other one enterprise": Ibid., p. 26.

87    • made that small country the fifth-largest recipient: Mason and Asher, p. 199.
• "foreign enclave, developed with foreign capital": Richard Westebbe, *The Economy of Mauritania* (New York: Praeger, 1971), p. 11.
• "to bring the age of industrialization to Mauritania": Ibid., p. 51.
• used to deepen and widen the canal: World Bank Annual Report 1960, p. 29.
• "be returned to private ownership": World Bank Annual Report, 1962, p. 28.

Chapter 6

88    • "his quarter in the telephone": Grenfell oral history, p. 33.
• "Now you listen to me": Benjenk oral history, pp. 23–24.
• Egypt's expropriation of the Suez Canal Company in 1956: Mason and Asher, p. 641; Woods also helped establish DFCs in India, Pakistan, and the Philippines: Ibid., p. 360.

89    • "the most solvent and profitable of international organizations": "The World's Banker," *New York Times,* 16 October 1962.
• half of that was going right back: George Woods, "Development—the Need for New Directions," Address to the Swedish Banker's Association, Stockholm, 27 October 1967, p. 9.
• 4.8 percent a year: Pearson, p. 358.
• foreign debts were growing three times as fast: Between 1955 and 1962 they increased by an average of 15 percent a year. Avramovic et al., p. 99.
• "constitute a serious obstacle": Avramovic and Gulhati, p. 59.
• "The fact is": Lilienthal, vol. 6, p. 237.
• "explosive": World Bank Annual Report, 1971, p. 50.
• using a huge proportion of their foreign loans simply to pay the interest: Pearson, p. 74.
• if borrowing continued at existing levels: Ibid.

90    • "the bank is rich in prestige and accomplishments": "The World's Banker," *New York Times,* 16 October 1962.
• per capita growth was only about half that: Average per capita growth of GDP for developing countries from 1950 to 1967 was about 2 to 2.5 percent. Pearson, p. 27.
• In 1947, average per capita income: Statistics on per capita incomes are from the World Bank Annual Report, 1947, p. 7.
• By 1966, average per capita income had risen: World Bank, *Social Indicators of Development, 1991–92;* p. 323.
• $120 in the forty poorest developing countries: Oliver (1995), p. 185.

• In the United States . . . five times greater than that of the poorest: "Income Gap in Poor Countries," *Des Moines Register*, 3 October 1972.

• fifteen or thirty times richer: Ibid.

• had left the poor of the developing world poorer: McNamara, pp. 5, 104.

91  • "I never saw a more rigid institution": Lilienthal, vol. 5, p. 480.

• "I'm not sure that is anything to be proud of": Friedman oral history (I), p. 42.

• "Little people only think in terms of rates of return": Oliver (1995), p. 157.

• he expanded the Bank's economic staff from twenty to more than two hundred: Ibid., pp. 98, 104.

• "more and more what we find ourselves talking about": World Bank Annual Report, 1966–67, preface.

• an overall economic policy of which it approved: "The performance by a country in the promoting of its economic development is an important criterion for financial assistance from the Bank or IDA." World Bank Annual Report, 1968, p. 7.

92  • far less than 1 percent of the Bank's lending: Between 1947 and 1966, IBRD lent $9.7 billion; Mason and Asher, p. 832. During that period, loans for education and water supply totaled $51 million. World Bank, *Commitments Detail Report*.

• "creditworthiness was essentially a function of growth": Mason and Asher, p. 471.

• heavy indebtedness was "a serious obstacle": Avramovic and Gulhati, p. 59.

93  • "any increases in debt service obligations": World Bank Annual Report, 1965–66, p. 35.

• went "to each loan officer": Friedman oral history (I), p. 51.

• "There is no future in the World Bank Group": Ibid., p. 62.

• "this flow can be expected to increase": World Bank Annual Report, 1964–65, p. 62.

• "lighten the [debt] service burden": World Bank Annual Report, 1963–64, p. 8. Another example is in the Bank's Annual Report, 1965–66, p. 45: "The increasing burden of debt servicing of developing countries points to the need for funds on easier terms."

• carried out twenty-one reschedulings: Mason and Asher, p. 224, Table 7-10.

94  • "likely to encounter serious and protracted debt service difficulties": Mason and Asher, p. 224.

• "the Bank ought to do more": Friedman oral history (III), p. 38.

• "the same effect as a balance-of-payments loan": Grenfell oral history, pp. 17–19.

• for a total of nearly $1.5 billion: World Bank, *Statement of Development Credits*.

95  • Keynes had anticipated: Mason and Asher, p. 212.

• "Do we expect this country to pay back the loans": Author interview, 3 December 1992.

• turned rapidly to disappointment and cynicism: In his address to the Swedish Bankers' Association, Woods bemoaned the "discouragement and skepticism about the general effectiveness of aid." Woods, op. cit., p. 12.

• "would simply send good money after bad": Ibid., p. 4.

• increasing the proportion of GNP they gave to development: Ibid.

• "waste, inefficiency and even dishonesty": Ibid., p. 12.

• "reduced to a sort of delinquent despair": Ibid., p. 10.

96  • "the inadequacy of the Bank's efforts": Knapp oral history (I), pp. 10–11.

• "For God's sake, listen": Grenfell oral history, pp. 25–26.

• "an IBM machine with legs": Shapley, p. 102.

• "I think Bob is going to jump out the window": McKitterick oral history, p. 7.

• impressed by a speech he gave: Shapley, p. 416.

97  • talking on the phone to his New York stockbroker: Grenfell oral history, p. 22.

• "to help the largest number of people": Shapley, p. 18.

• "freely develop their own highest potential": McNamara, p. 108.

• "the rich and the powerful": McNamara, p. 240.

• "gorged himself on statistics": Clark, p. 168.

98  • "He kept talking in billions": Shapley, p. 471.

- "filed out in a state of shock": Clark, p. 168.
- "bringing out of bottom drawers": Ibid.
- $11.6 billion in the next five years: McNamara, p. 6.
- the Bank raised a record sum: "In the past 90 days the World Bank has raised more funds by borrowing than in the whole of any single calendar years in its history." Ibid., p. 8.
- "has increased, is increasing and ought to be diminished": Ibid., p. 5.

99
- "growth was not trickling down": Ul Haq oral history, p. 3.
- "have received disproportionate shares": Ibid., p. 154.
- "has been of little or no benefit": Chenery et al.
- "more equitable income distribution is absolutely imperative": McNamara, p. 165.
- survive on 30 cents a day: In terms of U.S. purchasing power. Ibid., p. 242.
- "degraded by disease, illiteracy, malnutrition, and squalor": Ibid., pp. 238–39.
- Mere economic growth, he asserted, would not end this destitution: Ibid., p. 151.
- "highjacked by the privileged": Ul Haq oral history, pp. 3–4.
- "disparities in income will simply widen": McNamara, pp. 245–46.
- "finance for productive purposes": World Bank Articles of Agreement, Article I (ii).
- "saw poverty alleviation as a sop": Feinberg (1986), p. 90.

100
- "certain narrow and highly privileged sectors": Clark, p. 173.
- "reasonable redistribution of land": McNamara, pp. 154–55.
- "primary emphasis not on the redistribution of income and wealth": Robert McNamara, "Address to the World Band Board of Governors," Nairobi, 1973, quoted in Lappé and Collins, p. 393.
- no conflict between social justice and economic growth: According to Feinberg and Kallab (1984, I), p. 88, Hollis Chenery et al. in *Redistribution with Growth* "argued that income redistribution could take place without slowing developing nations' rates of growth. This idea became, in a sense, the Bank's intellectual centerpiece and its marching order through the 1970s."
- dramatically increase their exports: McNamara, p. 165.
- "refus[ing] to lend to manufacturing enterprises in the public sector": Mason and Asher, p. 27.
- "to be turned over to private control": Ibid., p. 466.

101
- even state-controlled agricultural enterprises: Naim, p. 13.
- "tremendous pressure within the institution to reach lending targets": Baum oral history, p. 13.
- "whether you kept to your lending targets": Benjamin King interview, 12 March 1992.
- "There is little doubt": Howard et al., p. 27.
- "There was tension": Baum oral history, p. 13.
- "The brownie points were earned": King oral history, p. 42.

102
- "overriding concern with forms and procedures, not with substance": Hughey.
- "it's very hard to say the project works": Ibid.
- "the main object was to go out and make loans": Benjamin King interview, 12 March 1992.
- "based less on intimate knowledge of and experience with Senegal": World Bank, *Annual Review of Evaluation Results,* for 1989, p. 73.
- "We're like a Soviet factory": Hughey.
- "their customary rather leisurely perfectionism": Clark, p. 174.
- pushed through in the last two months of the fiscal year: World Bank, *Commitments Detail Report.*

103
- " 'Otherwise you're out of a job' ": King oral history, p. 42.
- "we'd hold out for 100 percent": Hughey.
- the true rate of erosion: Ibid.
- "We must keep on lending": King oral history, p. 50.
- enormous and fast-growing indebtedness: In the short period between 1970 and 1973,

a number of countries, including Ghana, Chile, Pakistan, Indian, Indonesia, and Sri Lanka, rescheduled their debts or simply defaulted. McNamara, p. 241.

• "far from relaxing the momentum": Ibid., pp. 240–41.
• "the foremost world center": Clark, p. 170.
• "development goes far beyond a mastery of techniques": *New York Times,* 29 November 1967.

104  • "You know I have a weakness for numbers": Oliver (1995), p. 230.
• "statistical approach to reality": Hughey.
• "What can't be counted, doesn't count": Baum oral history, p. 18.
• "obsessive concern for details and statistics": Hughey.
• "surrounded himself with fancy mathematical economists": Lilienthal, vol. 7, p. 391.
• "People who antagonize him or contradict him": Hughey.
• "ruled the place through fear": Shapley, p. 87.
• "uncomfortable if dissenting voices were raised": Ul Haq oral history, p. 6.
• "very good at manipulating statistics": Shapley, p. 568.
• McNamara took the Bank's annual lending: World Bank Annual Reports, 1968, 1981.
• more than $77 billion: World Bank, *Commitments Detail Report.*
• he doubled the size of the staff in a year and tripled it in three: Grenfell oral history, p. 21.

105  • "That does not make for a happy ship": Maddux, p. 17.
• "We will have failed": Ibid., p. 13.

# Chapter 7

106  • Less than 10 percent: Between 1969 and 1981 the Bank made $3.7 billion worth of loans for education, $525 million worth of loans for health and family planning; $2 billion worth of loans for water supply. The total, $6.2 billion, is 8 percent of $77 billion.
• one-third of the Bank's financing was for agriculture: Feinberg et al., p. 89.

107  • "the best way to reduce the level of default": *Assault on World Poverty,* p. 143.
• It invested billions of dollars: Bruce Rich, "Multi-Lateral Development Banks: Their Role in Destroying the Global Environment," *The Ecologist* 15, no. 1/2 (1985): 61.
• pesticides accounted for 10 percent: Ibid.
• large and medium-sized farming operations: "Approximately one-fourth of all credit financed by the Bank was intended for small-scale producers." *Assault,* p. 106.
• holdings of 12 acres or less: Ibid., pp. 118, 124.
• only the top 20 percent of Third World farmers: Ibid., p. 244.
• those with less than 112 acres: Lappé and Collins, p. 394.
• three-quarters of the farmers in the targeted areas: *Assault,* p. 159.

108  • "made to comparatively affluent farmers": Mason and Asher, p. 477.
• "the purpose of the Bank was to promote economic development": Ibid.
• creating undesirable employment effects: Ibid.
• if the Bank didn't lend India the money, someone else would: Ibid., p. 250.
• "three companies would benefit from the project": Central Agricultural Division, Eastern Africa Projects Department, *Zaire: Appraisal of the Oil Palm Project,* Report No. 1592-ZR, 29 March 1978, p. 1.
• the Bank helping private monopolies: Interview with World Bank employee, 14 June 1995.
• The loan was classified as agricultural: The following description of the loan is taken from the Bank's 1978 Annual Report, p. 79.

109  • "improvement of both social conditions on the plantations and the earnings of the worker": Central Agricultural Division, Eastern Africa Projects Department, op. cit., Annex 3, p. 3, and Annex 2, p. 6.

• "the local population would probably be better off if it grows its own cash crops": Ibid., Annex 2, p. 6.

• the project was a failure: This description is taken from Agriculture Operations, Africa Regional Office, *Project Completion Report, Zaire Oil Palm Project,* 24 May 1991, pp. 5, 10.

• "contributed substantially to policy formulatıon": Ibid., p. v̇.

• one-third of all its agricultural loans were for livestock operations: *Assault,* p. 125.

• "the relatively well-to-do ranchers in Latin America": Mason and Asher, p. 712.

• a single cow requires 10 or more acres of grazing land: Caufield, p. 111.

• "the tax revenues generated from these ranches": Lappé and Collins, p. 398, citing Uma Lele, *The Design of Rural Development* (Baltimore: The Johns Hopkins University Press, for the World Bank, 1976).

• the biggest ranches were the least efficient producers: World Bank, *Project Audit Report: Honduras First Livestock Development Project.* Operations Evaluation Department Report 1920, February 1978, p. 5.

110   • "help large farmers take evasive action": World Bank, *Agricultural Credit Programs,* Operations Evaluation Department Report 1357, November 1976, p. 66.

• "work to the disadvantage of the small farmer": World Bank, *Bank Operations in Colombia: An Evaluation,* p. 128.

• "loans contributed to the displacement of tenants": *Assault,* p. 122.

• the Bank evaluated fourteen representative irrigation projects: World Bank, *Annual Review of Evaluation Results for 1989,* Operations Evaluation Department, p. 49.

• only three of the fourteen: Ibid., p. 118.

• "water shortages, flooding, soil waterlogging or salinization, incomplete construction": Ibid., p. 51.

• "the term of their expected useful life": Ibid.

• "some degree of adverse impact on the environment": Ibid., p. 52.

• it was so waterlogged and saline: Ibid., p. 52.

• "Large farmers were found to have captured the bulk": Ibid., p. 52; Table 3-5, p. 119.

111   • "increased demands on family labor": Ibid., p. 52.

• In presenting the projects to the board: Ibid., p. 118.

• In actuality, only six projects reached 10 percent: Ibid.

• "a tribute to sensible government policies": Jose Botafogo, "Development and Environment: A Reply to 'The Ecologist,' " *The Ecologist,* no. 5/6 (1985).

• "a decline in crops grown for local consumption": Canada, House of Commons, *Hearings before the Subcommittee on International Financial Institutions of the Standing Committee on Finance,* p. 50.

• more than 85 percent of Indian children under five: Bharat Dogra, "Forcing the Starving to Export their Food," *The Ecologist* 15, no. 1/2 (1985): 42.

• "a state of destitution, semi-starvation and chronic malnutrition": D. L. Sheth, quoted in John Madeley, "Does Economic Development Feed People?" *The Ecologist* 15, no. 1/2 (1985): 39.

112   • two independent scientists credit the Green Revolution: Uma Lele and Balu Bumb, *South Asia's Food Crisis* (Washington, DC: World Bank, 1994), p. 2.

• Lele and Bumb also list the problems: Ibid.

• "In fact, some decline has been noted": Rajagopalan oral history, p. 23.

• "there's no reason to apply the insecticide": Interview with Ken Fisher by Daniel Zwerdling, *All Things Considered,* National Public Radio, 31 July 1994.

113   • "contribute to the development process": *Assault,* p. 105.

• "the modernization and monetization of rural society": Ibid., p. 3.

• "instruments to draw farmers from subsistence to commercial agriculture": Ibid., p. 120.

• a 1976 report on Papua New Guinea: World Bank, *Papua New Guinea: Economic Situation and Development Prospects,* 14 July 1976.

- local circumstances: For an enumeration of some circumstances of farming in some African societies, see George Ayittey, "Economic Atrophy in Black Africa," *Cato Journal*, no. 1 (Spring/Summer 1987): 218.

114
- "A characteristic of PNGs": World Bank, *Papua New Guinea*, p. 18.
- an extra crop of rice in the dry season: Hartmann and Boyce, p. 6.
- The average cooperative had forty-three members: Arne Stroberg, *Organizational Aspects of a Tubewell Project in Bangladesh* (Dacca: Bangladesh, March 1977).
- not aware of the fact that they have been included in the scheme: Ibid.

115
- "no more than a few signatures he had collected": Hartmann and Boyce, p. 6.
- "I no longer ask who is getting the well": Ibid., p. 7.
- squatters, sharecroppers, or day laborers: *Assault*, p. 250.
- "may well be a necessary condition": Ibid., p. 226.
- "egalitarian distribution of land": World Bank, *World Development Report, 1990*, p. 53.
- the Bank will not fund land-reform projects: *Assault*, pp. 199, 229–30.
- its own programs and policies have worsened the problem of landlessness: Ibid., p. 122.
- "affect the power base of the traditional elite groups": Ibid., p. vi.

116
- "Avoiding opposition from powerful and influential sections of the rural community is essential": Ibid., p. 40.
- "an important measure to instill investor confidence": World Bank, "Peru: Public Investment Program, 1981–85," Consultative Group Presentation, 27 April 1981, p. 6, quoted in Theresa Hayter and Catherine Watson, "The World Bank's Agricultural Policies: Rhetoric and Reality," *The Ecologist* 15, no. 5/6 (1985): 222.
- "likely to be more popular": World Bank, *World Development Report, 1990*, p. 53.
- the largest international investor in land colonization projects: Cernea, p. 148.
- "we are still feeling our way": McNamara, p. 155.
- "We will have to improvise and experiment": Ibid., p. 249.
- "began to reconsider its resettlement strategy": World Bank, *Project Performance Audit Report, Nepal Settlement Project*, Operations Evaluation Department, report no. 4567, 20 June 1983, p. 4.
- "also serious damage to the environment": Ibid., p. 5.

117
- "Areas were completely clearfelled": Ibid., p. 8.
- it turned out to be only 7 percent: Ibid., p. 60.
- the Bura Irrigation Project: Rosenblum and Williamson, pp. 266–67; Barbara Gunnell, "The Great Bura Irrigation Scheme Disaster," *African Business*, April 1986.
- more than $20,000 per family: Cernea, p. 151.
- things were so bad at the Bura site: Gunnell, op. cit., p. 20.
- poorly prepared feasibility study: Ibid.
- half of Kenya's entire rural development budget: Author interview with Thayer Scudder, 26 July 1993.

118
- The Transmigration Project: This section draws heavily on Caufield, pp. 188–208; World Bank, *Indonesian Transmigration Sector Review*, 24 October 1986, pp. xiv–xv; and Rich, pp. 34–38.
- "McNamara wanted to work with Suharto": Author interview with anonymous World Bank employee, 13 January 1983.
- "McNamara knew that Suharto's resettlement program was politically inspired": Shapley, p. 537.
- more than $1 billion for Transmigration: Rich, pp. 35–36.
- By 1990, about 7 million people had moved: Ibid., p. 35.

119
- "It doesn't mean undoing the damage you did": Author interview with anonymous World Bank employee, 18 September 1995.
- the most successful Bank-financed colonization schemes: Author interview with Thayer Scudder.

- "FELDA is undoubtedly one of the most important and efficient settlement agencies in the world.": World Bank, *Project Audit Report, Johore Land Settlement Project,* Operation Evaluation Department Report No. 4221, December 1982, p. 7.
- Jengka Triangle Land Settlement: World Bank, *The Jengka Triangle: Projects in Malaysia,* Impact Evaluation Report, Operations Evaluation Department, 1987.
- "could be better used for helping the remaining poor": Ibid., p. 48, viii.
- twenty years to reimburse FELDA: Ibid., p. 5.
- the settlers receive some form of title: Ibid., pp. 5, 23.
- "significant improvement of settler's incomes": Ibid., p. vii.

120
- Settler families earn approximately twice as much: Ibid., pp. 33, 83.
- 85 percent are satisfied with their new situation: Ibid., pp. 27, 65.
- The aspect of the project that pleased them most: Ibid., p. 88.
- They most disliked the lack of roads: Ibid., p. 86.
- "largely undisturbed forest and swamp land": Ibid., p. 49.
- The freshwater fish population has also dwindled: Ibid., p. 51.
- there has been no environmental monitoring: Ibid., p. 53.
- hundred indigenous tribal people were later found to live in the forest: Ibid., p. 52.
- "striking degree of planning and control": Ibid., p. 26.
- "stifling the settlers' sense of initiative": Ibid., p. viii.
- 51 percent want their children to be civil servants: Ibid., p. 30.
- Women receive technical assistance only by special prior arrangement: Ibid., pp. 28–29.
- less than three-quarters of the settlers: Ibid., pp. 24, 83.
- "are the most expensive rainfed settlement projects in the Bank's portfolio": Ibid., p. 49.
- $15,000 ($24,000 in 1993 dollars) to resettle each family: Ibid., p. 10; and World Bank, Planning Assumptions Committee, *Standard World Bank Deflators,* Table 1, "U.S.$, Calendar Year Basis."

121
- to review twenty-seven of its resettlement projects: World Bank, *The Experience of the World Bank with Government-Sponsored Land Settlement,* Operations Evaluation Department, report no. 5625, 1 May 1985.
- "major inadequacies": Ibid., pp. 94–96.
- major ecological damage had occurred or was likely to have occurred: Ibid., p. ix. Scudder did not look at damage caused downstream outside the project area.
- the Bank to cancel or stop a loan: Ibid., p. 95.
- "probably exceeds average rural income": Ibid., p. 88.
- "a lack of understanding within the Bank": Ibid., p. ix.
- half of the sixty-four area development and settlement projects approved: World Bank, *Rural Development: World Bank Experience, 1965–86,* 1988, Annex 6, p. 126.

122
- more than half the population of the developing world: Vicki Allen, "World Bank Sees Crisis in Urban Growth and Decay," *Washington Post,* 18 September 1994.
- half the population lives in shantytowns: Cohen, p. 38.
- 190 million people living in "absolute poverty": Ayres, p. 92, 153.
- "concentration on large infrastructure and industrial projects": Ibid., p. 153.
- a staggering $40,000: Ibid., p. 39.
- "previously unproductive assets, such as jewelry": Ibid., p. 20.

123
- the poor should have security of tenure: Ibid., p. 17; Ayres, p. 177.
- "our housing projects have been successful and beneficial": Author interview with anonymous Bank employee, 28 September 1993.
- the average rate of return was almost 50 percent: Cohen, p. 45.
- the Bank has rarely been able to meet its dual goal: Ayres, p. 163.
- "excluded entirely the majority of low-income families": Campbell, p. 11.
- there were not enough takers for all the loans available: Ibid., p. 12.
- "Problems developed after the start-up period": Cohen, p. 26.

124
- "many of the plots have been unofficially transferred": World Bank, *Project Comple-*

*tion Report: Tanzania—First National Sites and Services Project*, Operations Evaluation Department, report no. 4941, February 1984, p. 26.
- "the poor were selling out to richer people": Newman.
- "a rapid deterioration of project housing stock": Campbell, p. 15.
- "Why should Mexico borrow dollars": Author interview, 28 September 1993.

125
- "zero data on whether housing": Ibid.
- "has remained largely outside the scope of our projects": Jonathan Katzenellobogen, "World Bank 'Stagnant, Confused,' Says Former Director," *Africa Now* (London), no. 13, May 1982, p. 89.
- for only 4 percent of the Bank's annual lending: Cohen, p. 2.
- 80 percent of its projects satisfactory: The Bank's *Annual Reports on Evaluation Results* for the years 1987 (pp. 99–102 and 111), 1988 (Annex 2, Table 2-7, p. 94, and Table 2-1, pp. 85–88), and 1989 (Table 2-1) reported on 380 projects that were approved during McNamara's time in office. Fifty-nine percent of the 189 agriculture and rural development projects were judged satisfactory. Sixty-seven percent of the 57 urban (shelter and water supply) projects were satisfactory. Seventy-nine percent of the 134 industry and energy projects were satisfactory.

# Chapter 8

126
- "the size of a country's external debt": World Bank Annual Report, 1971, p. 52.
- "even more confident today than we were a year ago": McNamara, p. 456.
- "stimulate external flows of capital to developing countries": World Bank Annual Report, 1982, p. 12.
- they had supplanted the World Bank: In 1960, private loans to developing countries amounted to $440 million, while the World Bank lent nearly three times that much, $1.2 billion. In 1970, private banks lent $3 billion, and the World Bank lent only $2.5 billion. Lomax, pp. 5–7; World Bank, *Commitment Details Report*.

127
- Russian-owned Banque Commerciale pour L'Europe du Nord, whose cable address, Eurobank: Sampson, p. 109.
- "a remarkable conspiracy of silence": Paul Einzig, *Foreign Dollar Loans in Europe*, (New York: St. Martins, 1965), p. vi. Cited in Sampson, p. 139.
- in 1960, only eight American banks had branches abroad. By 1978, 140 did: Gwynne, p. 53; Mayer (1974), p. 436.
- they accounted for at least half the profits: Makin, p. 134.
- "debts past the possibility of repayment": *Banking*, November 1969, p. 45.
- "repaid out of the proceeds of additional loans": Ibid., January 1970, p. 52.
- flocked to Europe since the mid-sixties to feast on the trade in Eurodollars: Ulman.

128
- "giving loans to second- and third-rate borrowers": *Wall Street Journal*, 24 November 1972.
- "derived at least half their earnings": Ibid., 24 November 1972.
- "for productive purposes": World Bank Articles of Agreement, Article I (ii).

129
- "preferably based on firsthand experience": Friedman, p. 79.
- a government could never "go bankrupt": Wriston.
- the collapse of the Bardi and Peruzzi banks: Makin, p. 37.
- "The active and working elements in no community": John Maynard Keynes, *A Tract on Monetary Reform* (London: Macmillan), 1923.
- Citibank's loans to just five of its Latin American clients: Makin, p. 15. In August 1982, Citibank's net corporate assets were $4.9 billion. It had $9.8 billion in outstanding loans to just five Latin American countries, Mexico, Brazil, Venezuela, Argentina, and Chile.

130
- "very few performed any type of credit analysis": Gwynne, p. 107.
- "It was the easiest money going": Sampson, p. 141.

131

132

133

134

135

136

• small American banks had entered the overseas loan market: Mayer (1984), p. 243.

• Gwynne entered the banking world in the late 1970s: Gwynne, p. 27.

• "and three months of banking experience": Ibid., p. 56.

• "one 32-year-old vice-president with a halting fluency in Spanish": Ibid., p. 54.

• "They hate to be left out": Sampson, p. 115.

• "no accurate idea of the total extent of their debt": World Bank Annual Report, 1971, p. 50.

• Venezuela's declaration: Gwynne, p. 152.

• "a virtual compendium of bad or questionable information": Ibid., p. 74.

• "If you had connections, you told the central bank": Ibid., p. 151.

• "phony intermediary companies that recontract with foreign suppliers": Henry.

• Zaire had accumulated a foreign debt of $5 billion: World Bank, World Debt Tables 1992, p. 659.

• he had stashed away in banks and property throughout Europe: Adams (1991), p. 130.

• claims to be the seventh-richest man in the world: Cooke, Stephanie. "Redistributing the Blame in Africa," Institutional Investor, September 1990.

• "What is that, after twenty-two years as head of state": Adams (1991), p. 131.

• de la Madrid deposited at least $162 million: Henry.

• capital flight from Latin America equaled the increase in its external debt: "Third World Finance Survey," The Economist, 25 September 1993, p. 11.

• "This was no coincidence": Morgan Guaranty Trust, p. 5.

• capital flight from just eighteen developing countries: Ibid., pp. 2–3.

• Mexico alone lost at least $35 billion: World Bank, Country Economics Department, 1990, p. 101.

• A new specialty, "international private banking": Henry.

• American banks had $31 billion: Morgan Guaranty Trust, p. 4.

• "cooperation among the world's powerful": Raymond Baker, "Riding the Rivers of Dirty Money," Washington Post, 4 June 1995.

• "The problem is, they're all in Miami": Henry.

• Half of all the money lent to Latin America in 1976: Payer (1991), p. 84, citing figures from Inter-American Development Bank, External Debt and Economic Development in Latin America (1984), p. 19.

• "defaults are inevitable": David Levine, "Developing Countries and the $150 Billion Euromarket Financing Problem," Euromoney, December 1975, p. 14.

• more than $600 billion in 1981: "Third World Finance Survey," The Economist, 25 September 1993, p. 8.

• "the willingness of the banks to keep on lending": Quek Pek Lim, "Hectic Year of Borrowing," Euromoney, January 1978, p. 14.

• "the Fund can't be giving danger signals": Cary Reich, "Why the IMF Shuns a 'Super' Role," Institutional Investor, September 1977, p. 185.

• "would have raised inconvenient doubts about the Bank's own lending program": Feinberg et al., p. 7.

• Zaire stopped making payments: Delamaide, p. 57.

• "If we can do it for Zaire, we can do it for anybody": "Heading off Zaire's Default," Institutional Investor, March 1977, p. 28.

• to cover Zaire's outstanding loan payments: Delamaide, p. 58.

• "no (repeat: no) prospect for Zaire's creditors to get their money back": Ibid., p. 60.

• Its foreign debt was $4.4 billion: Gwynne, p. 50.

• a new infusion of cash, $386 million: Delamaide, p. 63.

• nearly a quarter of a billion dollars: $242 million, according to figures in World Bank, Statement of Development Credits and Statement of Loans, vol. 2, 30 November 1992, pp. 414–16.

• in return for a loan of $200 million: Gwynne, p. 51.

• its members contributed another $10 billion: Ibid.

- Loans to non-oil-producing developing countries tripled: Lissakers, p. 163.
137 - " 'I think they'll be able to take your money' ": Sampson, p. 12.
- a *New York Times* Op-Ed piece: Wriston.
- one-quarter of all the money borrowed: Gwynne, p. 53.
- 70 percent of new loans went to pay interest on old debt: Schumer and Watkins.
- "new borrowing has been used to service outstanding debt": World Bank Annual Report, 1982, pp. 25–26.
- keeping up payments on its past debts: Payer (1991), p. 84, citing figures from Inter-American Development Bank, *External Debt and Economic Development in Latin America*, 1984, p. 19.
- downgraded the bonds of nine top U.S. banks: Makin, p. 17.
- "probably one of the most dynamic economies in the world today": *Byline*, newsletter of Manufacturers Hanover Trust, December 1981, quoted in Benjamin Weiner, "The Banks Should Have Known Better," *New York Times*, 19 December 1982, sec. 3, p. 2.
138 - "considerable scope for sustained additional borrowing": "Why the Major Players Allowed It to Happen," *International Currency Review*, May 1984, p. 25.
- explained that Mexico could not repay the $81 billion: Eighty-three percent of Mexico's debt was held by commercial banks. Makin, pp. 14–15.
- more than two-thirds of Citibank's net corporate assets: Ibid., p. 15.
- 80 percent of its net assets at risk in Mexico: Ibid., p. 136.
- more than twice their net worth: Ibid., pp. 15, 138.
- "200 million sullen South Americans sweating away in the hot sun": *Fortune*, 25 July 1983, p. 6.
- the six largest banks in the United States would be bankrupt: Makin, p. 136.
139 - "The IMF is acting as enforcer": Lissakers, p. 160.
- The deadline was met: Makin, p. 15.
- " 'like Butch Cassidy and the Sundance Kid' ": Lissakers, p. 170.
- allowed to charge hefty fees: Makin, p. 166.
- "We hope they never repay!": Lissakers, p. 168.
- The United States also did much to encourage banks: Makin, p. 135; Gall, p. 186.
- "The examiners would not question these loans": Mayer (1984), p. 249.
140 - "insistent appeals from the U.S. government": Mosley et al., vol. 0, pp. 302–3.
- it announced a "special action program": Delamaide, p. 150.
141 - "the Bank alone is fit for such a task": Feinberg et al., p. 3.
- "We need billion-dollar pipelines now": author interview with Bank employee, 23 May 1985.
- "to avoid an impending balance-of-payments crisis": "Lending for Structural Adjustment," Memorandum to the World Bank board, R80-17, IDA/R80-22, 5 February 1980.
141 - "failed to insist on any reasonable standards of efficiency": Thomas et al., p. 3.
- "except in special circumstances": World Bank Articles of Agreement, Article III, Section 4 (vii).
- "nonproject loans" to 10 percent of its annual: Stanley Please, quoted in Feinberg and Kallab (1984, II), p. 85.
- "They felt that they were not being given the full systematic presentation": Please oral history, pp. 15, 18.
- Many of the executive directors argued: Mosley et al., vol. 1, pp. 35–36, summarizes the board's concerns about structural adjustment when it was first proposed.

# Chapter 9

143 - pumping out money faster than it ever had before: In 1980 The Bank disbursed $5.7 billion. By 1986 that figure had doubled to $11.4 billion and adjustment lending ac-

counted for $3.2 billion, more than half the increase. World Bank Annual Report, 1986, p. 8; World Bank, Country Economics Department, 1990, p. 69.

• convert short- and medium-term developing country debt: In 1980, the Bank's share of the developing world's total external debt was 5.8 percent; by 1990, it was 10 percent. World Debt Tables 1992–93, p. 160.

• The Bank "earned its keep": Sweeney, p. 113.

• "it wants to keep pumping the money out": Wall Street Journal, 22 February 1983.

• "enough cash to continue paying interest on their old loans": Schumer and Watkins, p. 14.

144   • had worked closely with the Bank: Delamaide, p. 149.

• "It pains me to say this": Ul Haq oral history, p. 16.

• "She cut off anybody who ever had any relationship with Hollis Chenery": King oral history, p. 58.

• "Dissent was little tolerated": Mosley et al., vol. 1, p. 24.

145   • has changed more than twenty major pieces of legislation: Public Interest Research Group, The World Bank and India (New Delhi: Public Interest Research Group), 1994, p. 60.

• "We will have to approach them with humility": Crittenden.

• "Let me declare myself as being skeptical": Knapp oral history (II), p. 74.

• would solve the debt problems of most developing countries: Feinberg et al., p. 7.

146   • no more than five loans and be completed within three to five years: Thomas et al., p. v.

• annual inflation exceeding 100 percent: Taylor, p. 110.

• a former World Bank official named Turkut Ozal: Mosley et al., vol. 2, p. 13.

• a total of $1.5 billion: There was a loan a year: 1980, $275 million; 1981, $300 million; 1982, $305 million; 1983, $300 million; 1984, $376 million. World Bank, Statement of Development Credits, 30 November 1992.

147   • summary of the goals for the first SAL: World Bank, Ninth Annual Review of Project Performance Audit Results, 1983, p. 220.

• in general they were remarkably vague: Thomas et al., p. 456.

• a growth in exports: Taylor, p. 112.

• 25 and 30 percent export subsidies: Ibid.

• an inflation rate that hovered around 50 percent: Ibid., p. 110.

• real wages fell substantially: Thomas et al., p. 455.

• $1.4 billion worth of SECALs: By 1988 Turkey had received eight sectoral adjustment loans (of which four are "B loans"). In 1985, $300 million; in 1986, two totaling $333 million; in 1987, three totaling $375 million; in 1988, two totaling $430 million. World Bank, Statement of Development Credits, 30 November 1992.

148   • "a decisive shift in income distribution away from wage-earners": Mosley et al., vol. 2, p. 27.

• "the military regime . . . was able to implement its adjustment program": Thomas et al., p. 460.

• "despite Turkey's substantial adherence to World Bank policy advice": Ibid., pp. 460–61.

• "achieved most, if not all, of the original objectives": World Bank, Annual Review of Project Performance Audit Results, 1987, p. 82.

• "no major shortcomings": Ibid., p. 155.

• huge debt takes almost a third of its export earnings: World Development Report, 1995, p. 207.

• "by depressing wages and draining productive resources from industry": Servet Yildirim, "Turkish Business Dismisses Ciller's Rosy Talk," Reuters, 20 October 1994.

149   • a 15 percent cut in real wages, a real devaluation of the lira, and half a million people losing their jobs: Ibid., "OECD Warns Turkey of Crisis Unless Measures Taken," Reuters, 20 December 1994; and "Turkish Business Dismisses Ciller's Rosy Talk," Reuters, 20 October 1994.

• adjustment loans constituted between 25 and 30 percent: "Structural adjustment and other forms of policy-based lending such as sector lending now account for probably 25 to 30 percent, if not more, of Bank lending." Please oral history, p. 24.

• raise the 10 percent ceiling to 25 percent: World Bank Annual Report, 1989, p. 80.

• adjustment lending exceeded 25 percent: In 1987, sector and structural adjustment lending was 23 percent of the Bank's total. In 1988, it was 25 percent; in 1989, 30 percent; in 1990, 26 percent; in 1991, 26 percent; in 1992, 27 percent; in 1993, 17 percent; in 1994, 12 percent; and in 1995, 24 percent. World Bank Annual Reports, 1987, p. 21; 1988, p. 65; 1989, p. 39; 1991, p. 13; 1992, p. 19; 1993, p. 15; 1994, p. 15; 1995, p. 36; Ludlow, p. 245.

• eighty-eight countries had embarked: this statistic was supplied by the World Bank's press office, 1 November 1995.

• a single one had kept to the Bank's original timetable: Barber Conable in Thomas et al., p. v.

• "instead of disappearing, adjustment lending intensified": Ibid.

• In 1989 Senegal's per capita income was lower: World Bank, *Annual Review of Evaluation Results*, 1989, p. 73.

• countries that began adjusting in the early 1980s and are still doing so: World Bank, *Statement of Development Loans*, 30 June 1995.

150 • "to supplement the [$100 million] education sector–adjustment loan": World Bank Annual Report, 1993, p. 150, and 1992, p. 163.

• "just how popular structural adjustment lending was going to become": Thomas et al., p. 2.

• "People often ask, 'Why bribe governments' ": Ibid., p. 4.

• sixteen countries had eased or eliminated controls on farm prices: Nossiter, p. 134.

• remarkably inventive in finding ways to do so: Jamaican and Philippino examples given in Mosley et al., vol. 1, p. 139.

• The Bank claims a fairly high level of compliance: World Bank, *Adjustment Lending: An Evaluation of Ten Years of Experience* claimed that 60 percent of the conditions attached to the Bank's adjustment loans were fully implemented and that "substantial progress" was made on another 20 percent. Mosley et al., vol. 1, p. 136, points out that compliance is judged by "junior person[s] with little knowledge of the country or of the specific lending operation." Working from documents supplied by the borrower, these staffers rate compliance with each condition on a scale of 1 to 5. "Evidently, the entire process is an exercise of judgement, much of it not at all expert."

151 • "The World Bank's capacity to supervise all this": Thomas et al., p. 218.

• "overly optimistic": World Bank, *Effectiveness of SAL Supervision and Monitoring*, p. 34.

• loan to Bolivia "was unsuccessful": World Bank, *Structural Adjustment Lending: A First Review of Experience*, pp. 24, 33, cited in Bovard, p. 14.

• "complied with the spirit of the Loan Agreement": Ibid.

• "Bolivia was a disaster": Please oral history, p. 17.

• delaying the release of the second installment: Mosley et al., vol. 1, p. 166.

• it has only ever canceled one SAL: Ibid.

• "the darling of the [World] Bank's economists": Fraser (1992).

• star pupil of free-market economic development: Chandler (1995).

• thirteen adjustment loans totaling $6 billion: *Adjustment Lending and Mobilization of Private and Public Resources for Growth*, p. 76.

• "graduates of the same U.S. universities": Fraser (1992).

152 • "they will tell you how to do it better": Ibid.

• "a constitutional amendment was drawn up": Ibid.

• "It has substantially opened its economy": Hanke and Walters, p. 161.

• Mexico's inflation rate fell: Fraser (1994).

• "anchor in [the government's] anti-inflationary program": Thomas et al., p. 512.

- half its government bonds were in foreign hands: Swardson and Hamilton.
153  • barely enough to keep pace with its population growth: Heredia and Purcell, p. 3.
- half what they had been ten years earlier: Development Group for Alternative Policies, *Structural Adjustment Programs: Questions and Answers* (Washington, DC: Development Group for Alternative Policies, 1992).
- drastically reduced or eliminated: Heredia and Purcell, pp. 24–25.
- infant deaths due to malnutrition almost tripled: Ibid., p. 4.
- "skewed and concentrated pattern of ownership distribution": World Bank, *Public Enterprise Reform Loan, Program Performance Audit Report*. Operation's Evaluation Department, report no. 10849, June 1992.
- the top one-fifth of the population received 48 percent: Statistics on income distribution are from Heredia and Purcell, p. 10.
- The country's wealthiest man, Carlos Slim: Ibid.
- lost access to the land on which they had traditionally farmed: Jerome I. Levinson, "Mexico's Failed Strategy," *Washington Post*, 15 February 1995.
- the number of billionaires in Mexico rose: "The Billionaires," *Forbes*, 18 July 1994.
154  • "Mexican poverty," said Finance Minister Aspe in 1993, "is a genial myth": Chris Aspin, "Poverty Hampers Mexico's First-World Status Push," Reuters, 1 November 1993.
- "The Zapatistas are only saying what many Mexicans want": Fraser (1994).
- 61 percent of Mexicans sympathized: Ibid.
- "ordinary Latin Americans want more of the cake": "More for More: Latin America," *The Economist*, 16 April 1994, p. 48.
- "a type of Ponzi scheme": Swardson and Hamilton.
- This borrowing helped drive Mexico's foreign debt: Heredia and Purcell, p. 6.
155  • "The Mexicans wanted to avoid depreciating their currency": Patrick Low interview, 29 September 1993.
- In a matter of weeks, Mexico's foreign reserves fell: Swardson and Hamilton; "Mexico Crisis Ambushed," Dow Jones News Service, 6 July 1995.
- "to start preparing new operations": "IMF, World Bank—Mexico," Dow Jones News Service, 11 January 1995.
156  • effects of the government's austerity program were dramatic: these examples from Isaac Levi, "Peso Crisis," *Associated Press*, 18 June 1995.
- "sets a dangerous precedent": "Economist Survey: Mexico Starts Again," *The Economist*, 26 August 1995, p. 11.
- the Bank lent Mexico $500 million: World Bank Annual Report, 1995, p. 119.
- "a bailout of a foreign country": Tim Carrington and Dianne Solis, "Mexico Currency Falls Nearly 10% Amid Rescue Plan Doubt," *Wall Street Journal*, 31 January 1995.
- "We marvel at the ability of all you guys": Clay Chandler, "Lawmakers Seek Say in Mexico Aid Plan," *Washington Post*, 15 February 1995.
- "We're going to [put] . . . conditions on their budget": Clay Chandler and Kevin Merida, "New Concerns Rise Over Mexico Loan Deal," *Washington Post*, 24 January 1995.
157  • "The country keeps going into debt to pay its debts": Jorge Banalies, "Clinton, Zedillo accused of 'Coverup,'" United Press International, 10 October 1995.
- Mexico had requested that repayment of the remaining $1.3 billion: Ibid.
- "the cycle of hype and bust": Lance Taylor and Jonathan Schlefer, "Mexico's Made-in-USA Mess," *Washington Post*, 7 October 1995.
- "repudiate the liberal approach": Chandler (1995).
- It attributed the peso crisis to bad timing: "World Bank Says Decisions on Mexico Package Were Made Too Late," Dow Jones News Service, 10 March 1995; "Mexico Crisis Looks Deeper Than It Is—World Bank," Reuters, 12 January 1995.
- "how brisk the recovery will be": "World Bank's Edwards Sees Mexico Recovery Through 1996," Dow Jones News Service, 9 October 1995.

- a study by Goldman, Sachs & Co.: Tim Carrington, "Private-Capital Flows Can Hurt Poor Nations," *Wall Street Journal*, 30 January 1995.
- "the free-market economic model all it was cracked up to be": Swardson and Hamilton.
- "many of the intellectual or analytical underpinnings": Thomas et al., p. 217.

158
- Jeffrey Sachs of Harvard University: Jeffrey Sachs and Andrew Warner, *Natural Resources Abundance and Economic Growth* (Cambridge, Mass.: Harvard University, Institute for International Development), October 1995.
- "the most protracted and deepest depression": Oxfam (UK), *Embracing the Future . . . Avoiding the Challenge of World Poverty*, July 1994, p. 3.
- resource exploitation diverts capital and labor from manufacturing and industry: Alan Gelb, *Oil Windfalls: Blessing or Curse?* (New York: Oxford University Press, 1988).
- "even an extra 1 or 2 percent": "Trade Deficit Still Looms Large," Dow Jones News Service, 10 October 1995.
- the terms of trade for developing countries: Martin Khor, *Our Planet* (journal of United Nations Environment Program) 7, no. 1, p. 20.
- "If they keep their economy pretty well aligned": Author interview with Patrick Low, 29 September 1993.

159
- "[We] need structural adjustment": "UK Report Criticizes IMF and World Bank," United Press International, 28 June 1994.
- "it's a corporate strategy": Author interview with Doug Hellinger, 2 December 1992.
- "Those who have the money": Mahbub ul Haq, *The Third World and the International Economic Order* (Washington, DC: Overseas Development Council), 1976.

160
- "systematically and through multiple channels": World Bank, *The East Asian Miracle*, p. 5.
- "the Bank cooked the study": Michael Lewis, "Where Credit Is Due," *The New Republic*, 13 February 1995, p. 34.
- assume that everyone would benefit: World Bank, *Adjustment Lending: An Evaluation of Ten Years of Experience*, p. 12; and Mosley et al., vol. 1, p. 11.

161
- real wages were half what they had been in 1982: *Development Group for Alternative Policies, Structural Adjustment Programs: Questions and Answers*. Washington, DC: Development Group for Alternative Policies, 1992.
- "a favorable effect on the poor": World Bank, *Adjustment Lending: An Evaluation of Ten Years of Experience*, p. 12.
- "the number of people in poverty": Jolly et al., p. 67.
- availability of food per person declined: Ibid., Table 1.7.

162
- "have been an important contributory element": Ibid., pp. 287–88.
- "the decade of despair": Quoted in Adams (1991), p. 159.
- Among the reverses cited by the report: UNICEF, pp. 16–17.
- "It is hardly too brutal an oversimplification": quoted in Adams (1991), p. 160.
- "in the short run, some of the poor may lose out": *World Development Report, 1990*, p. 120.
- "the cost of making no adjustment is also great": "Bank: Poverty May Undermine Latin Reforms," *Emerging Markets*, 27 September 1993, p. 13.
- the proportion of people in poverty: *Latin America and the Caribbean: A Decade After the Debt Crisis*, p. 123.
- Other Bank studies acknowledged: World Bank, *Adjustment Lending: An Evaluation of Ten Years of Experience*, p. 6; *Adjustment Lending: Policies for Sustainable Growth*, pp. 2, 5, and 31.

163
- "the social costs of adjustment": Ibid., pp. 2–3.
- "increase social sector expenditures": Ibid., pp. 2, 5.
- "the opposition of those who are adversely affected": World Bank, *Towards Sustainable Development in Sub-Saharan Africa* (Washington, DC: World Bank), 1984, p. 44, cited in Hancock, p. 129.

- "adjustment lending that addresses social issues": World Bank Annual Reports, 1993, p. 38; 1995, p. 20.
- "It will not be possible for any member": United Nations Information Office, *Money and the Postwar World* (New York: United Nations, 1945), p. 26.
- "This book should be called *Catch 22.*": Andrew Meldrum, "Investing in Health," *Africa Report,* Nov.–Dec. 1993, p. 34.
- "simply 'bolting-on' social welfare provisions": Oxfam (UK), p. 8.
- "We're saying we have failed": "World Bank Checks Impact of SAPs," Inter-Press, 2 July 1996.
- may need *more* state investment in infrastructure: Mosley et al., vol. 1, p. 303.

164   • "little evidence of strong results from adjustment programmes": Tony Killick, *Improving the Effectiveness of Financial Assistance for Policy Reforms,* report for World Bank Development Committee, 1994.
- "disorderly adjustment without Bank support": World Bank, *Adjustment Lending: Policies for Sustainable Growth,* p. 4.
- "a consequent reduction in poverty": World Bank, *Adjustment Lending and Mobilization of Private and Public Resources for Growth,* p. 14.
- "excessive external borrowing": This is one of "the targets for policy change" under SALs, according to World Bank, *Adjustment Lending: An Evaluation of Ten Years of Experience,* p. 12.
- "The Bank and the Fund set out to influence policy": "Fine Art of Persuasion," *The Economist,* 12 October 1991, p. 34.
- It does not, however, appear to reduce inflation: Mohsin Khan, *The Macroeconomic Effects of Fund-Supported Adjustment Programs,* IMF Staff Papers 37(2) (Washington, DC: International Monetary Fund, June 1990). The countries studied also receive adjustment support from the Bank.
- "statistically significant drop": A 1992 World Bank study on sub-Saharan Africa cited in *Global Finance,* September 1993, p. 113. In addition, World Bank, *Adjustment Lending: Policies for Sustainable Growth,* p. 11, states that "only rarely did they [adjusting countries] experience an increase in investment, either public or private."

165   • increased by 23 times: Swardson and Hamilton.
- Third World debt more than doubled: *World Debt Tables, 1992–3,* p. 160.
- less than 20 percent of the GDP: Examples taken from *World Debt Tables 1994.*
- "It is not even clear": Mosley et al., vol. 1, p. 302. The World Bank agrees that "economic returns to adjustment loans have been hard to quantify." World Bank, *Adjustment Lending: An Evaluation of Ten Years of Experience,* p. 14.
- "It isn't working": "Biting the Hand That Squeezed Them," *The Economist,* 21 October 1995, p. 48.
- "the theory is right": Rex Nutting, "Congress Urged to Reform IMF, Bank," United Press International, 19 April 1995.

# Chapter 10

167   • "the reverence in which the World Bank was held": Canada, House of Commons, *Hearings Before the Sub-committee on International Financial Institutions of the Standing Committee on Finance,* p. 33.
- "These activists didn't have a history with the Bank": Ibid.
- "undeveloped frontier region": Denis Mahar, "Development of the Brazilian Amazon: Prospects for the 1980s" in Moran.

168   • "turn the Bank into a real swamp": George C. Lodge, "The World Bank: Mission Uncertain," Harvard Business School, case study N9-792-100, 4 May 1992, p. 3.
- "reviewed by a special environmental unit": A. W. Clausen, "Sustainable Development:

The Global Imperative," Fairfield Osborn Memorial Lecture in Environmental Science, Washington, DC, 12 November 1981, in World Bank, *The Development Challenge of the Eighties: A. W. Clausen at the World Bank, Major Policy Addresses 1981–86* (Washington, DC: World Bank, 1986), pp. 29–30.

169  • "careful in-house studies": Robert McNamara, address to the United Nations Conference on the Human Environment, Stockholm, June 1972, p. 7.
• 150 loans: World Bank Annual Report, 1972, pp. 53–60.
• "make sure that every project was looked at": Lee oral history, p. 5.
• "Jim Lee was a bloody nuisance": Rajagopalan oral history, p. 25.
• Prince Bernhard of the Netherlands: Lee oral history, pp. 3–4.

170  • agreed to hold hearings: U.S. Congress.
• "the misleading impression that past trends continue": World Bank, *Response to Statements of Environmental Organizations, Sent by the U.S. Executive Director* (unpublished, 11 January 1984), p. 1.
• "the human and ecological costs of *not* going ahead with projects": Ibid., p. 8.
• "What they're really saying": Rich, p. 119.

171  • "environmental effects of the project are avoided or kept to a minimum": World Bank, *Response to Statements of Environmental Organizations*, p. 1.
• "as a matter of routine, environmental issues are not considered": World Bank memo, "From Louis de Azcarate to Files," 30 March 1984, cited in Rich, p. 118.
• "not finance projects that displace people": World Bank, *Comprehensive Environmental Policy*, 1984.
• "The Bank slammed the door in our faces": Author interview with Patricia Adams, 11 June 1993.
• "Think about poor people": Rich, p. 125.
• "the developing world will have to make do with dung": World Bank, External Affairs Department, *Setting the Record Straight: Energy Efficiency in Developing Countries*, March 1994.

172  • Senate subcommittee responsible for appropriations: Senate Appropriations Committee, Subcommittee on Foreign Operations.
• House subcommittee in charge of World Bank appropriations: House Appropriations Committee, Subcommittee on Foreign Operations.
• at least twenty hearings: Rich, p. 138.
• "In appearing before you in June 1983": U.S. Congress, House Committee on Banking, Finance and Urban Affairs, Subcommittee on International Development Institutions and Finance, *Draft Recommendations on the Multilateral Development Banks and the Environment*. 98th Cong., 2d sess., 1984, pp. 11–12.
• "When people find out what's been going on": Nicholas Claxton (producer), *The Price of Progress*, Central Television (London), 1987.
• "the notorious Balbina dam": Hugh Foster, U.S. alternate executive director, Statement to the Board of Directors of the World Bank, 19 June 1986, quoting from the World Bank's unpublished *Appraisal Report for the Balbina Dam*.

173  • "it was a stupid mistake to build Balbina": Catherine Caufield, "The World Bank vs. the World," *Joint Annual Meeting News*, 24–25 September 1988.
• Northwest Region Integrated Development Program, or Polonoroeste: My account of Polonoroeste owes much to Bruce Rich's book, *Mortgaging the Earth*. Rich and his colleague Stephen Schwartzman played an important role in bringing the problems of Polonoroeste to light in the United States.
• the Bank lent more than half a billion dollars: There were "six closely interlinked World Bank loans for a total of US $434.4 million." World Bank, Operations Evaluation Department, *Environmental Aspects and Consequences of the Polonoroeste Program* (confidential), 26 November 1990, p. viii. In 1989 the Bank made a seventh loan, for $99 million, for mosquito control.

174  • not proceeding in line with the Bank's plans: U.S. Congress, Senate Committee on

Appropriations, Subcommittee on Foreign Assistance and Related Programs, *International Concerns for Environmental Implications of Multilateral Development Bank Projects,* 99th Cong., 2d sess., 1986, p. 2.

• the largest man-made change to the earth's surface: Rich, p. 28.

• had died through violence or disease: Brazilian Catholic church's Indigenous Missionary Council (CIMI), cited in *National Geographic* 174, no. 6 (1990): p. 792.

• an epidemic of malaria: World Bank, Operations Evaluation Department, *Environmental Aspects and Consequences,* pp. xiv, 120.

• "increasing the security of the large landowners": Lutzenberger's testimony is reprinted in Jose Lutzenberger, "The World Bank's Polonoroeste Project," *The Ecologist* 15, no. 1/2 (1985): 69–70.

• "an opportunity to develop sustainable agriculture": World Bank, *Response to Statements of Environmental Organizations,* pp. 8–9.

175    • "continued shifting cultivation and land degradation": Ibid., p. 9.

• "your concerns will be considered": Roberto Gonzalez Cofino, letter to Bruce Rich, 7 November 1984.

• summarize the Polonoroeste story: The memos that follow are taken from Rich, pp. 141–45.

176    • "infrastructure, agriculture, health and even ecology and Amerindian welfare": "Summary of Discussions at the Meeting of the Executive Directors of the Bank and IDA, and the Board of Directors of IFC, December 1, 1981," 15 December 1981, p. 2, quoted in Rich, p. 144.

• "little progress has been made": N. O. Tcheyan, telex to Brazil's Mario Andreazza, minister of the interior, "Subject: Amerindians—Polonoroeste," 17 March 1983, quoted in Rich, p. 145.

• "the current international economic crisis": World Bank, "World Bank Loan of 465.2 Million to Assist Settlements in the Amazon Region of Brazil," press release, 27 October 1983.

• "As you know better than anyone else": Robert W. Kasten, Jr., letter to A. W. Clausen, 24 January 1985.

177    • emergency measures to protect the environment and Indian lands: Rich, p. 126.

• "the Bank misread": Barber Conable, address to the World Resources Institute, Washington, DC, 5 May 1987.

• "contributed both directly and indirectly to the acceleration of environmental degradation": World Bank, Operations Evaluation Department, *Environmental Aspects and Consequences,* p. xv.

• "the distorting influence of powerful economic and political interests": Ibid., p. xix.

• "at a considerably earlier date": Ibid., p. xxi.

• "In the absence of the Bank's support": Ibid.

• "preserve the Amazon's remaining natural resources": World Bank, *The World Bank Group and the Environment, Fiscal 1990* (Washington, DC: World Bank, 1990).


## Chapter 11

178    • adjustment loans to thirty-eight countries: World Bank, *Adjustment Lending and Mobilization of Private and Public Resources for Growth,* Table A1.5.

• He dismissed the hard-liners: Mosley et al., vol. 1, p. 24.

179    • "the best way to achieve . . . growth": Quoted in Cavanagh et al., p. 3.

• "dampen the criticism": Rotberg oral history, p. 37.

• cut the staff of six thousand: World Bank Annual Report, 1988, p. 46.

• asking every employee to resign: Kaletsky.

• "he needed Ernie": Rotberg oral history, p. 37.

- no experience of China: Friedland, "Unrest at the World Bank," *Institutional Investor,* September 1987, p. 336.
- spoke no Portuguese: Ibid., p. 349.

180
- "whispers at the water cooler": Ibid., p. 333.
- "riddled with faction and distrust": Kaletsky.
- "hardly a match": Friedland op. cit., p. 336.
- "I was the average congressman": Ibid., p. 335.
- "a 'hands-off' leader": Kaletsky.
- "What they call bureaucracy": Ibid.
- the workforce was back up to six thousand: At the end of fiscal 1986, the Bank had 6,002 full-time staff; that number dropped to 5,657 by the end of fiscal year 1988; four years later, at the end of fiscal year 1992, the number was up to 6,046. World Bank Annual Reports, 1987, p. 26; 1988, p. 47; and 1992, p. 103.
- The regional divisions were supposed to review each loan proposal: Robert Goodland, "Environmental Priorities for Financing Institutions," *Environmental Conservation* 19, no. 1 (Spring 1992): 10.

181
- only six were trained ecologists: World Bank Annual Report, 1991, p. 60; David Wirth, *Environmental Reform of the Multilateral Development Banks* (New York: Mott Foundation, 1992), p. 9.
- "the absence of skills": Rajagopalan oral history, pp. 26–27.
- "has gone totally technocratic": Author interview with anonymous Bank employee, 23 August 1995.
- "They know we're rocking the boat": Author interview with anonymous Bank employee, 22 September 1992.

182
- environmental impact studies: World Bank, *Operational Directive on Environmental Assessment,* 1989 (updated in October 1991).
- likely to have a significant impact on the environment: World Bank, *Mainstreaming the Environment,* Table 4.1. I have included in the total 117 projects that were not screened because they were adjustment loans.
- "Sound ecology is good economics": Barber Conable, address to the World Resources Institute, Washington, DC, 5 May 1987.
- quadruple the Bank's lending for forestry: World Bank Annual Report, 1991, Box 3-3, p. 54.
- "synonymous with environment": Author interview with anonymous Bank employee, 28 February 1996.
- logging equipment, sawmills, and papermills: Ninety-six percent of all bank forestry lending between 1949 and 1978 was for industrial forestry. World Bank, *Forestry Development: A Review of Bank Experience,* Table 1.3.
- pay more attention to "afforestation": Ibid., pp. 6–7.
- from $10 million to $75 million: Ibid., Table 1.3.
- "this resource provides valuable foreign exchange": Quoted in Bharat Dogra, "The World Bank vs. the People of Bastar," *The Ecologist* 15, no. 1/2 (1985): 45.
- "social forestry": World Bank, *Forestry Development,* Table 1.3.

183
- "completion reports have cast doubts": Ibid., p. 12.
- "these projects are beset with financial problems": Ibid., p. 16.
- The main recipient of the Bank's social forestry funds: World Bank, *Forestry Development,* Table 1.1.
- villagers in the Indian state of Karnataka: Pandurang Ummayya and Bharat Dogra, "Planting Trees—Indian villagers Take the Decision into Their Own Hands," *The Ecologist* 13, no. 5 (1983): 186.

184
- Africa's biggest timber exporter by the year 2000: Korinna Horta, "The Last Big Rush for the Green Gold," *The Ecologist* 21, no. 3 (May–June 1991).
- logging of 30 million acres of intact rainforest: Ibid.
- "shifted its focus entirely to forest protection": Korinna Horta, *Report on the World*

*Bank's Forestry and Fisheries Management Project for Guinea* (Washington, DC: Environmental Defense Fund, 1992), p. 6.

• "following the SAR to the letter": Ibid., p. 6.

• a $13 million follow-up loan: World Bank, *World Bank Monthly Operational Summary* (Washington, DC: World Bank, April 1996), p. 8.

185 • one of the largest dislocations ever financed by the Bank: Keith Bradsher, "Rain Forest Project in Africa Stirs Debate at World Bank," *New York Times,* 12 October 1991. Later the number of people to be resettled was reduced to 40,000.

• "the needs and welfare of forest-dwelling people": World Bank, *The Forest Sector* (Washington, DC: World Bank, 1990).

• "commercial logging in primary tropical moist forests": World Bank Annual Report, 1992, p. 57.

• "not available on reasonable terms": World Bank Articles of Agreement, Article I (ii).

• "sufficiently profitable to attract capital": World Bank, *Forest Policy Implementation Review* (Washington, DC: World Bank, April 1994), p. 25.

• "primarily environmental": World Bank, *The World Bank Group and the Environment, Fiscal 1992,* p. 128.

• Conable's last year, it made fourteen: World Bank Annual Report, 1991, p. 60.

186 • Other "environmental projects": these examples are taken from World Bank, *Making Development Sustainable: The World Bank Group and the Environment, Fiscal 1994,* pp. 231–32.

• not extractive reserves, but colonization settlements: Chico Mendes, letter to Barber Conable, 13 October 1988, quoted in *Forum das ONGs e Movimentos Sociais Que Atuam em Rondonia. (Request for Inspection Submitted to the World Bank Inspection Panel on the Rondonia Natural Resources Management Project),* July 1995, pp. 24–25.

• letters detailing the actions of the Brazilian government: Ibid.

187 • $730 million worth of grants to 115 projects: World Bank Annual Report, 1994, p. 47.

• These included: These examples come from the GEF's Quarterly Operations Report, August 1995.

188 • "foreign loafers with tax-free salaries": Friedland, *Institutional Investor,* p. 335.

• "post-mission travel-induced strokes": Letter from Grant Sinclair (advisor in the Population and Human Resources Division of the Bank's regional office for Asia), dated February 9, 1990, quoted in "Memos of the Month: Let Them Eat Honey-Roasted Peanuts," *Washington Monthly,* June 1990, p. 35.

189 • "They also tend to lose your luggage": Tim Cullen, quoted in Ringle.

• "No one can imagine why in the world": Ibid.

• paid 30 percent more than UN employees: "Affluent Apparatchicks," *The Economist,* April 24, 1993, pp. 75–76; and Michael Irwin, "Why I've Had It with the World Bank," *Wall Street Journal,* 30 March 1990.

• the average salary for Bank professionals: Nelson, pp. 2, 4; World Bank Annual Report, 1995, p. 127 and Appendix 6, p. 207.

• "exceed [those] in the public sector in all surveyed markets": Nelson, p. 2.

190 • "more generous than those available in the United States": Ibid., p. 4.

• "make a hell of a lot more money:" Chandler (1994).

• the best house in town: Ringle.

• the Bank provides lavish benefits: Information provided by the Bank's Benefits Service Division.

191 • keep them in conditions of slavery: For more details on this problem see Martha Honey, "Abused Domestics Escape World Bank, IMF Employees," Inter Press Service, 27 June 1995.

• the Bank's high running costs: "Affluent Apparatchicks," op. cit., p. 75.

• Spiritual Unfoldment Society: Michael McAteer, "Banking on Spirituality," *Toronto Star,* 15 April 1995.

192  • "similar facilities in the Washington area were racially exclusive": World Bank, *Questions and Answers,* p. 115.


## Chapter 12

193  • "the Bank does not interfere": World Bank, Information and Public Affairs Division, *Current Questions and Answers* (Washington, DC: World Bank, 1993), p. 13.
  • "only economic considerations": World Bank Articles of Agreement, Article IV, Section 10.
  • "too much politics, too little finance": Issacson and Thomas, p. 428.
  • "influence the politics and strategies of aid recipient countries": Acheson et al, p. 83.
  • borrowers should not be "hypersensitive": World Bank, *Study on Supplementary Financial Measures: Report to UNCTAD,* December 1965, p. 46.
194  • "In the typical case": Mason and Ahser, p. 434.
  • supposedly internal contests: The three following examples are taken from ibid., p. 433.
  • Julian Grenfell . . . vividly recalled an instance: Grenfell oral history, pp. 2–3.
195  • "tends to become more politicized": World Bank, *Adjustment Lending Policies for Sustainable Growth,* p. 62.
  • "They are like Tweedledee and Tweedledum": Author interview with Deepak Nayyar, 3 April 1993.
  • before sending it to Parliament: Cavanagh, p. 41.
  • "a crisis of governance": World Bank, *Managing Development: The Governance Dimension,* p. 6.
196  • "direct economic effects": I. Shihata, "Issues of 'Governance' in Borrowing Members," memorandum of the vice president and general counsel (December 21, 1990), p. 2. Cited in Lawyers Committee for Human Rights, p. 44.
  • "In Korea the old school tie": Cairncross oral history, p. 19.
197  • "infiltrated with strategically placed EDI alumni": Mason and Asher, pp. 329–30.
  • quarter of its borrowings are in dollars: World Bank Annual Report, 1994, p. 181.
  • the single country with a veto over amendments: In 1988, when the American share in the Bank dropped below 20 percent, the board amended the Articles so that future amendments would require an 85 percent rather than an 80 percent vote. Gwin, p. 48.
  • Poland . . . resigned shortly thereafter: "Unable to obtain a loan and unable to participate constructively in the work of the Bank, Poland withdrew from the institution in 1950." Mason and Asher, p. 171.
  • "The Bank is fully cognizant": World Bank Annual Report, 1947–48, p. 14.
198  • "There was that childish criticism": Lieftinck oral history, p. 14.
  • "unseemly compensation for their service": Quoted in Gwin, p. 30.
  • dependent on the cash contributions of its rich members: IDA also gets some funding from IBRD. For example, in FY 1994, IBRD transferred SDR (Special Drawing Rights) 333 million to IDA, whose resources that year totaled SDR 5,223. World Bank Annual Report, 1994, p. 172.
  • George Woods sought a commitment of $3 billion: Oliver (1995), pp. 112, 205–7.
199  • "he wished to show who was master": Clark, p. 179.
  • "harebrained schemes": Robert Ayres, "Breaking the Bank," *Foreign Policy* 43 (Summer 1981): 105.
  • its officials were overpaid: Clyde Farnsworth, "Treasury Official Defends World Bank," *New York Times,* 28 March 1979,
  • "paying his own people less": Shapley, pp. 571–72.
  • The loan outraged American conservatives: Bovard, p. 4; Shirley Scheibla, "Asian Sink-

ing Fund: The World Bank Is Helping to Finance Vietnam," *Barron's,* 3 September 1979, p. 7.

200  • five other countries: The other countries were Cambodia, Laos, Cuba, Angola, and the Central African Empire.

• lack of a "rational development policy": Brown, pp. 188–90; "House Passes Foreign Aid Bill, Slashing Funds for World Bank", *New York Times,* 7 September 1979; Clyde Farnsworth, "Foreign Aid Threatened" *New York Times,* 10 December 1979, p. D1.

• "organs of international aid": David Stockman, *The Triumph of Politics: How the Reagan Revolution Failed* (New York: Harper and Row, 1986), p. 119.

• "a unique coalition of liberals": Makin, p. 17.

• report was generally favorable to the Bank: U.S. Treasury Department, *United States Participation in Multilateral Development Banks in the 1980s* (Washington, DC: Treasury Department, February 1982).

201  • the U.S. Treasury and the Fed "directed" the Bank's lending: Gwin, p. 45.

• the CIA's desire to have "early warning": "U.S. Spy Agency May Be Tapping Foreign Banks' Computer Data," *International Banking Regulator,* January 17, 1994; author interview with Stephen Pizo, June 24, 1994.

• "for security tracking purposes": "U.S. Spy Agency May Be Tapping Foreign Banks' Computer Data," op. cit.

• "suddenly showed up": Ibid.

• "to look again more carefully": Ibid.

• Shihata declined to comment: He did so through the World Bank press officer, Peter Riddleberger, 25 September 1995.

202  • these directives instruct the U.S. ED: Brown, pp. 195–216, enumerates laws that links the behavior of the U.S. ED to American political considerations.

• "no one even bothers to ask why": Author interview with Eveline Herfkens, 7 June 1995.

• members did not have to put in any additional cash: Mason and Asher, p. 97.

• "I don't think we'll ever have to do it again": Black oral history, pp. 38–39.

• will not ask for another capital increase before 2005: Personal communication by Peter Riddleberger of the Bank's Press Office, 25 September 1995.

• at least five years earlier: Bretton Woods Commission, p. C-206.

• "make the economy scream": Stephen Volk, *NACLA Report on the Americas,* Sept.–Oct. 1993. See also N. Davis, *The Last Two Years of Salvador Allende* (London: Tauris and Co., 1985), pp. 20–22.

• Conable stopped or cut back on loans: Friedland, *South,* pp. 9–10.

• the case of the Aswan High Dam: Mason and Asher, pp. 627–41.

204  • $1.25 billion loan to Argentina in October 1988: This was actually composed of four separate loans for housing, trade policy, electric power, and the banking sector. The episode is described in Mosley et al., vol. 1, p. 48, and Polak, p. 31.

• the Bank put together a $918 billion package of loans: This consisted of $368 million for a Northern Border Environment Project, $350 million for water and sanitation services, and $200 million to modernize solid-waste services in medium-sized cities.

• "in the North American Free Trade Agreement": Gary Lee, "World Bank, Mexico Agree on Pollution Cleanup Loan," *Washington Post,* 28 September 1993.

205  • "linked to the debate on the North American Free Trade Agreement": World Bank, *Executive Project Summary, Northern Border Environmental Project,* quoted in "Border Groups Question World Bank Environmental Loan Package," *BorderLines* 2, no. 3 (September 1994): 6.

• "successive American presidents have found the World Bank . . . extremely useful": "And Jamaica's Urgent Need," *Washington Post,* 26 January 1981.

• "than for the U.S. to dictate to foreign governments": "Foreign Aid Irony," *The Baltimore Sun,* 18 June 1981.

• "an international outlaw": Elaine Sciolino, "Christopher Signals a Tougher U.S. Line Toward Iran," *New York Times,* 31 March 1993.

• its charter prohibited such politically motivated actions: World Bank, *Comments of the Legal Department of the Bank,* May 4, 1967, quoted in Mason and Asher, p. 588–89.

206  • "internal World Bank documents indicate": Economist Intelligence Unit, *EIU Country Report (Malawi),* no. 4, 1992.

• "designed to help the poor": Personal communication, press office, 1 November 1995.

• "the undesirable regimes would come and go": Knapp oral history (II), p. 57.

207  • "They just take the money and laugh": Malcolm Gladwell, "Harnessing the World Bank to the West," *Insight,* 9 February 1987, p. 8.

• a hydrodam on the Chixoy River: Key sources for the events concerning the Chixoy dam include Alecio, Wilkinson, and Bryson.

• "did not want the example of resistance by Rio Negro to spread": Alecio, pp. 31–32.

• "the inhabitants of Rio Negro": Ibid., p. 26.

208  • "The turmoil surrounding resettlement": Michael Cernea, "Socio-Economic and Cultural Approaches to Involuntary Population Resettlement," in World Bank, International Lake Environment Committee, *Guidelines on Lake Management,* vol. 2, World Bank Reprint Series, no. 468 (1991), p. 181.

• "were seriously flawed": Memorandum to the executive directors and the president, in World Bank, *Project Completion Report on Guatemala Chixoy Hydroelectric Power Project,* 31 December 1991, p. 40.

• "the World Bank did not consider it to be appropriate": Ibid., p. 50.

• "the damned thing wouldn't work": Author interview with Bank employee, 8 August 1995.

• in an area known for its active seismic faults: McCully (1996), Chapter 4.

• from the original estimate of $340 million to $1 billion: Bryson.

• "Providing a tyrant with fifty-year interest free loans": James Bovard, "Inside the World Bank: What They're Doing with Your Money Is a Crime," *Reason,* Spring 1989, p. 28.

• "We must make our government realize": Joe Cuomo, "Chinese Dissident Advocates Divestment," *Wall Street Journal,* 26 April 1989.

• "can rely on outside sources of financing": Isabel Letelier, and Michael Moffitt, *Human Rights, Economic Aid and Private Banks* (Washington, DC: Institute of Policy Studies, 1979).

• "If a regime became so unpopular": Knapp oral history (II), p. 58.

209  • "economic development should come first": Shahid Javed Burki, head of the World Bank's China-Mongolia directorate, quoted in "WB Official Tells World Not to Pick on China," *Bangkok Post,* 21 October 1991.

• "I personally had the unhappy duty": Knapp oral history (II), pp. 58–59.

• "a courageous, ruthless and perhaps undemocratic government": Deepak Lal, *The Poverty of Development Economics* (London: Institute of Economic Affairs, 1983), cited in Mosley et al., vol. 1, p. 145.

• "authoritarian regimes are not necessary": Lawrence Summers, "Research Challenges for Development Economists," *Finance and Development,* September 1991, p. 5.

210  • "The Bank knew about the corruption under Ershad": Author interview with Tasneem Siddiqui, 15 March 1993.

• "to study the Government's economic development program": World Bank Annual Report, FY65, p. 81.

• "with one-party rule": World Bank, *Annual Review of Evaluation Results,* 1989, p. 78.

211  • "The villagers knew what Nyerere did not": Nossiter, pp. 130–31.

• "downplayed or ignored": World Bank, *Annual Review of Evaluation Results,* 1989, p. 78.

• "when aid can be ineffective": World Bank, *World Development Report,* 1991, p. 48.

212  • "a sympathetic review of a Communist economy": "Resurrection of the Dead," *Wall Street Journal,* 10 August 1979.

# Chapter 13

213 • "You don't last at the World Bank": Sweeney, p. 111.
• "They are the best and the brightest": Author interview with Thayer Scudder, 26 July 1993.
• "tendencies toward the stuffy": Morris, p. 61.
• "arrogant sons of bitches": Author interview of Bank consultant, 1 September 1993.
214 • "supremely self-confident": Author interview with Benjamin King, 3 December 1992.
• "a deterioration in the skills of Bank staff": Irwin, p. 8.
• "more skilled than Bank staff": Ibid.
• "a reduced proportion of staff with hands-on implementation experience": World Bank, *Bank Experience in Project Supervision*, p. 48.
• "managing business functions in developing countries": World Bank, *Effective Implementation: Key to Development Impact* ("The Wapenhans Report"), p. 18.
• nine months each year: Memo of staff meeting with James Wolfensohn, March 1995. "He pointed out that the average age of staff in the Bank increases by 9 months every year."
• "deficient skills": "The Wapenhans Report," p. 17.
• "in the areas of procurement, private-sector development": World Bank Annual Report, 1993, p. 64.
• it lacks skilled staff: Ibid.
• the Bank's staff is ever-expanding: 1990 figures from *Annual Report*, 1991, p. 104. 1995 figures from Questions and Answers.
• the administrative budget increased: From $900 million in 1990 to $1.4 billion in 1995.
• loans and amount of money lent stayed roughly level: In 1990 = $20.8 billion, 222 loans; in 1991 = $22.7 billion, 229 loans; in 1992 = $21.7 billion, 222 loans; in 1993 = $23.7 billion, 245 loans; in 1994 = $20.8 billion, 222 loans; in 1995 = $22.5 billion, 242 loans.
• "we can't find a connection": *Euromoney*, September 1993, p. 88.
• "could do twice as much": Irwin, p. 2.
215 • In 1981 there were twenty-one staff members: Toru Kusukawa, "Funds Procurement and the World Bank," paper prepared for the Bretton Woods Commission, April 1993, p. 2.
• "difficult to remove deadwood": Retirement aside, annual turnover is only about 2.5 percent. Irwin, p. 6.
• "crucial element of the Bank's culture": Bretton Woods Commission, p. 282.
• "you don't know where it goes": Author interview with Bank employee, 5 June 1995.
216 • "*decreased* their feeling of commitment to the Bank": Ned Rosen, Staff Survey Report, submitted to WB/IFC Staff Association, 10 July 1988.
• job satisfaction at the Bank was 2.8: Ibid.
• "the achievement of project quality": World Bank, *Report of the Task Force on the Relationship of Loan Processing to Project Quality* (Washington, DC: World Bank, 1992), cited in "The Wapenhans Report," p. 16.
• "overwhelmed by responsibilities": Ibid., p. 19.
• Division chiefs spend 52 percent of their time: Bretton Woods Commission, p. 283.
• "intense rivalry with other clans": Bretton Woods Commission, p. 282.
• "dukes, running their departments": Irwin, p. 3.
• If a project crosses this hurdle: personal communication, World Bank press office, 1 March 995; World Bank figures on IBRD/IDA dropped projects for FY 1989–94, from Program and Budget Review Division.

217  • reverse public discontent: "Bangladeshis Decry Plans to Build Flood Embankment," Reuters, 27 November 1995.

• enough projects to meet its five-year lending targets: "Experience has shown that we do not get enough good projects to appraise unless we are involved intimately in their identification and preparation." Baum, quoted in Mason and Asher, p. 235.

• "threatens the institution's ability to assess": Bretton Woods Commission, p. 296.

218  • by 1995, the figure was up to $64 million: World Bank Annual Report, 1995, p. 42.

• "policies the Bank currently favors instead of the country's felt needs": "The Wapenhans Report," Annex B, p. 13.

• only 20 percent were well prepared: World Bank, *Annual Review of Project Performance Audit Results*, 1987, pp. 106, 123.

• "I visited Mexico several times": The loan was approved in January 1949. Report by M. J. Madigan, quoted in Spottswood, p. 5.

219  • the Bank failed to recognize such subsidies: Mason and Asher, p. 237.

• "palace revolution": King oral history, p. 31.

• "The top people were not economists": Haralz oral history, pp. 9–10.

• "Whatever is used, it's quite arbitrary": Author interview with bank staffer, 3 December 1992.

• "Though they are cited as measurements": Feinberg et al., p. 109.

220  • In the case of India's Narmada Dam: Canada, House of Commons, *Hearings Before the Subcommittee on International Financial Institutions of the Standing Committee on Finance*, p. 49.

• Agronomist David Hopper: This story was told by David Hopper in "The World Bank's Challenge: Balancing Economic Need with Environmental Protection," World Wildlife Fund's World Conservation Lecture, London, 3 March 1988.

221  • "sidewalks and parks into middle class neighborhoods": Tova Solo. "Understanding the Constraints of Urban Formal Sectors," unpublished paper, 1993, p. 5.

• "the old dog of a question": Weiner oral history, p. 13.

• "the fungibility argument is a red herring": Baum oral history, p. 37.

• Robert Kennedy spoke about it: Address to students at the University of Kansas, 1968.

222  • devised by the economists Herman Daly and John Cobb: Herman Daly and John Cobb, *For the Common Good* (Boston: Beacon Press, 1990).

• Genuine Progress Indicator: Clifford Cobb, Ted Halstead, and Jonathan Rowe, "If the GDP Is Up, Why Is American Down?" *Atlantic Monthly,* October 1995.

• "it's not working": Author interview with Herman Daly, 3 December 1992.

• "It was kind of like pornography": Author interview with Herman Daly, 22 October 1995.

223  • In 1995 the World Bank unveiled its own system: World Bank, *Monitoring Environmental Progress: A Report on Work in Progress* (Washington, DC: World Bank, 1995).

• "If anything the method is too businesslike": Letter from John O'Connor to the editor of *The Economist,* 14 October 1995, p. 8.

• "if you've run out of oil": Author interview with Herman Daly, 22 October 1995.

• "working both sides of the street": Mason and Asher, p. 234.

• "achieving personal recognition": "The Wapenhans Report," p. 12.

• "you just have to be rather biased": Author interview with Benjamin King, 3 December 1992.

• "usually over-optimistic, sometimes strikingly so": World Bank, *Rural Development: World Bank Experience, 1965–86*, p. 51.

224  • Martin Karcher: The following remarks are taken from an interview Karcher gave Korinna Horta of the Environmental Defense Fund, 9 September 1995.

• "When I worked on Bangladesh": Robert Wade, "Unpacking the World Bank: Lending versus Leverage," unpublished paper, 1989, quoted in Mosley et. al., vol. 1, p. 72.

• "a lot of incentives not to be tough": Author interview with Patrick Coady, 29 September 1993.

225 • "a pervasive part of the Bank's culture": World Bank, Operations Evaluation Department, *Colombia, the Power Sector and the World Bank* (Washington, DC: 1990).
   • "One of the things that drove me crazy": Author interview with Patrick Coady, 29 September 1993.
   • "parachutings in": Klitgaard, p. 74.
   • "But that's not how the Bank works": Sweeney, p. 112.
   • "more than $500,000 per cabinet minister": Klitgaard, p. 21.
   • Equatorial Guinea had no such strategy: Ibid., pp. 15, 21.
   • "the reports of the team members were assimilated": Ibid., p. 52.

226 • 38 percent of its professional staff are citizens of developing countries: Information supplied by Richard Gregory, 7 June 1995. In 1980, according to Van der Laar, p. 107, "Over 95 percent of the Young Professionals [the Bank's intern program for professionals] from Part II [i.e., developing] countries have done part or all of their academic studies overseas." Van der Laar also states that 45 percent of YPs were graduates of just ten American universities.
   • "They were horrible": Ferrer oral history, p. 23.
   • "these were urbanites who took Ph.D.s": Author interview with consultant, 24 July 1993.

227 • "through the eyes of the underprivileged": Address by Barber Conable to the board of governors of the World Bank and IFC, Washington, DC, 30 September 1986.
   • "The team has to stay together": Author interview with consultant, 24 July 1993.
   • "We met every morning at the hotel": Author interview with consultant, 2 November 1993.

228 • "We used to refer to the 'World Bank farmers' ": Author interview with consultant, 24 July 1993.
   • "There's a perceptible shift": Author interview with Bank employee, 30 October 1995.
   • "the importance of literacy and numeracy skills": Salmen (1992), pp. 7–8.
   • beneficiary assessment was the single most important element: World Bank Annual Report, 1994, p. 34.
   • "many Bank staff and borrower-government personnel feel": Salmen (1995), p. 14.
   • "what refinements the beneficiaries would like": Author interview with Bank employee, 2 November 1995.
   • "slaughterhouses to increase municipal income": Solo, *Understanding the Constraints*, p. 2.
   • "When I go with a task manager": Author interview with Bank employee, 30 October 1995.

229 • "Nowhere does the Bank tell governments": Author interview with Bank employee, 24 August 1995.
   • "bother with World Bank–style resettlement": Author interview with Christopher Willoughby, 14 March 1993.
   • "clear people out before": Author interview with Bank staffer, 4 December 1992.
   • "The Bank was very good about this project": Author interview with Bank staffer, 25 September 1993.
   • "They figure—rightly": Author interview with staffer, 4 December 1992.

230 • "only health, population, nutrition projects": Author interview with Kraske, 29 September 1993.
   • "environmental guidelines in every project": Oxfam (UK), p. 16.
   • $50 million loan to rejuvenate Indonesia's once-vibrant sugar cane industry: Newman.
   • "in most SARs, references to the type of land": Butcher, p. 10.
   • 40 percent of the appraisals for hydro projects: Ibid., p. 9.

231 • expensive emergency power from diesel generators: Patrick McCully, "Drought Brings Energy Crisis in Honduras," *World Rivers Review,* 2nd Quarter, 1994, p. 8.
   • "a much better designed system": Author interview with Bank employee, 29 June 1995.
   • "none of us, I must confess, really understood": Oliver (1995), p. 189.

233 • "highly inadequate in a very inaccessible region": World Bank, *Environmental Impact of Multilateral Development Bank-Funded Projects*, p. 477.
• "The World Bank would have us believe": Daniel Southerland, "Wu Says World Bank Funds Forced Labor," *Washington Post*, 23 October 1995.
• "China does not tell us about its military installations": Ibid.
• "responsible for administering some prisons": "Forced Labor Allegations Unfounded, World Bank Says." *World Bank News*, 22 December 1995, p. 2.

234 • "finds an excuse to leave the table": Leonard Frank, "The Development Game," *Granta* 20, Winter 1986, p. 240.
• "best to take the government figures": Ibid., pp. 140–41.

235 • "guys who don't give a damn": Author interview with Thayer Scudder, 26 July 1993.
• "They listen to the people": Author interview with Majibul Huq Dulu, 12 March 1993.
• "Consultants are generally supposed to agree": Lilienthal, vol. 7, May 1971, p. 213.
• the board may not propose loans: "A very basic principle which was established by Jack McCloy when he came in . . . namely, that no loan proposal can be initiated by the Board": Knapp oral history (II), p. 59.

236 • "that was a real shortcoming of the board": Author interview with Patrick Coady, 29 September 1993.
• "If I vote against today's project": Kandell, p. 109.
• "I represent borrowers": Author interview with Eveline Herfkens, 7 June 1995.
• "I think there's a serious conflict": Author interview with Eveline Herfkens, 7 June 1995.
• "something of a bon vivant": Pound and du Bois, 29 December 1990.
• "given to no one": Ibid.
• two leading opposition figures in Zaire: Ibid., 29 and 31 December 1990.
• the Bank's Operational Memos . . . were denied to them: Spottswood, p. 42.
• "too many comments": Irwin, p. 3.
• "has always puzzled me": Herman Daly, farewell lecture to World Bank, 14 January 1994.
• "The overriding principle": Author interview with Patrick Coady, 29 September 1993.

238 • "Nowadays, executive directors have come from the second and third tiers": Rajagopalan oral history, p. 31.
• "the caliber of the board has tended to decline": Bretton Woods Commission, p. 281.
• another worthy candidate: In 1995, the two senior EDs had held that title for only five years.
• "It is impossible": Bretton Woods Commission, p. 280.
• "decades of experience at the Bank": Ibid., p. 281.
• "It's a pretty good system": Author interview with Bimal Jalan, 6 June 1995.
• "Directors never spoke to each other": Baum oral history, p. 19.

239 • "They were more than ever dependent on the Bank": Author interview with Willi Wapenhans, 7 December 1992.
• "poor-country directors hesitate": "Not There Yet," *The Economist*, 16 May 1992, p. 112.
• fastest-growing item in the Bank's administrative budget: Bretton Woods Commission, p. 304.
• "the skills of the Executive Directors' advisors": Irwin, p. 8.
• "The Board is ill-equipped": Bretton Woods Commission, p. 299.
• "The projects were just too complex": Haralz oral history, p. 24.
• "Projects get approved that shouldn't be": Kandell, p. 110.

240 • "involve complex issues or innovative features": World Bank Operational Manual, BP 10.00—Annex K, October 1994.

241 • "Lofty indeed was the condescension": Morris, pp. 62–63.
• "his hearty congratulations": Ibid.

## Chapter 14

242   • several thousand multi-million-dollar contracts: Ludlow, p. 7.
      • it disbursed $17 billion: World Bank Annual Report, 1995, p. 37.
      • Local bids are discounted by 10 to 15 percent: Sanford (1991), p. 42.
      • about 44 percent of the Bank's funds: World Bank Annual Report, 1995, pp. 208–9.
      • "Most of our money doesn't go to the South": Author interview with Bank staffer, 22 September 1992.

243   • "Major subscribers of Bank capital": Mason and Asher, p. 187.
      • in proportion to their shareholdings in the Bank: World Bank Annual Report, 1995, pp. 176, 195, 209–10.
      • they receive half the money: Ibid., pp. 209–10.
      • American firms alone have received $24 billion: Ibid., pp. 153, 176, 210.
      • "As the loan is disbursed": "Survey: The IMF and The World Bank," *The Economist,* 12 October 1991, p. 10.
      • "the promotion and reward system": World Bank, *Bank Experience in Project Supervision,* p. 36.
      • "the least glamorous part": Warren C. Baum, *The Project Cycle* (Washington, DC: World Bank, 1993), p. 19.
      • The way time is allocated: World Bank, *Bank Experience in Project Supervision,* p. 57.

244   • "due attention to considerations of economy and efficiency": Articles of Agreement, Article III, Section 5 (b).
      • a study carried out in 1993 by the Bank's accounting division: World Bank, Central and Operations Accounting Division, *Financial Reporting and Auditing Task Force,* 8 October 1993.
      • "inconsequential for project management purposes": Ibid., p. 1.
      • "it is even impossible to make reconciliations": Ibid., p. 4.
      • "many of whom lack independent and skilled staff": Ibid., p. 5.
      • "a severe shortage of financial specialists": Ibid., p. 1.
      • "a lack of sufficient interest and understanding": Ibid., p. 5.
      • "project management itself is not under control": Ibid., p. 2.
      • "a car means a lot": Author interview with Bank consultant, 4 April 1994.

245   • "no inspector would ever have discovered this": Author interview with Bank official, 3 December 1992.
      • "Saying, 'Well, it's really up to the government' ": Author interview with engineering firm official, 29 April 1993.
      • "become almost universal": Robert Keatley, "New Agency Girds to Fight Corruption, Widespread in International Contracts," *Wall Street Journal,* 21 May 1993.
      • rough guide to the hierarchy of graft: Michael McNickle, "Group Set to Combat Third-World Graft," *International Herald Tribune,* 2–3 October 1993, p. 15.
      • "the amounts will vary from country to country": Peter Eigen, *Transparency International: The Coalition against Corruption* (Washington, DC: Transparency International, 1993).

246   • 10 to 15 percent in Indonesia: Barry Newman, "In Indonesia, Attempts by World Bank to Aid Poor Often Go Astray," *Wall Street Journal,* 19 November 1977, p. 26.
      • "If waste and corruption is soon tackled": "Indonesia Warned State Funds Being Wasted," Reuters, 23 November 1993.
      • the most corrupt countries in Asia: "Indonesia Most Corrupt in Asia—Consultancy," *Bangkok Post,* 20 April 1993.
      • recipients of World Bank loans to East Asia: World Bank Annual Report, 1993, p. 166.
      • "the most efficient and economical manner": Baum, *Project Cycle,* p. 21.

- "getting away with much misprocurement": World Bank, *Bank Experience in Project Supervision*, p. 36.
- infamous $640 toilet seat: Colman McCarthy, "Educating the Admirals," *Washington Post*, 24 March 1985.
- "Sounds more like a Harvard graduate course": Lappé and Collins, p. 403.
- "World Bank officials were apparently told": "Letter from London," *Far Eastern Economic Review*, 7 February 1975.
- "premature deterioration of civil works": World Bank, *Annual Review of Evaluation Results*, 1989, p. 54.

247
- "the only thing keeping the project alive": Judith Evans, "The Yacyreta Cauldron Boils," *Joint Annual Meeting News*, 15 October 1991, p. 37.
- "World Bank raised questions": Shirley Christian, "Billion Flow to Dam (and Billions Down Drain?)," *New York Times*, 29 April 1991.
- "suspicions have been raised": Judith Evans, "The Price of Instability," *Joint Annual Meeting News*, 16 October 1991, p. 37.
- "financed the Falklands war": Author interview with Bank employee, 25 Sept. 1993.
- an inspection team visiting the dam: Glenn Switkes, "Yacyreta: Government Officials Join Chorus of Disapproval," *World Rivers Review*, August 1995, p. 12.

248
- The Bank is the single largest source of work: Willi Wapenhans, quoted in Pratap Chatterjee, "IDA Not Impressive," *Bankcheck*, September 1994.
- It pays out more than a billion a year: Ludlow, p. 268.
- "that's fine with them": Author interview with Bank consultant, 4 April 1994.
- local "conditions, procedures, and customs": Baum and Tolbert, p. 560.
- "The borrowing country insists that they want local consultants": "The Wapenhans Report," Annex B, p. 7.

249
- primarily the United States, Britain and France: World Bank Annual Report, 1995, Appendices 9 and 10.
- "a World Bank money-pistol put to his head": Lilienthal, vol. 5, p. 373.
- Bangladesh's Ministry of Finance commissioned a study: Bangladesh Project Management Institute, *Utilization of Expatriate Consultancies in Bangladesh*, (Dacce: External Resources Division, Bangladesh Ministry of Finance, 1990).
- average monthly cost of $9,500 per consultant: Ibid., p. 6.

250
- "The foreign experts come": Klitgaard, p. 101.
- "a tiny portion of the salary of an expert": Association of Friends of Nature and the Environment (ASSOANE), *Problems of the World Bank's Forestry Sector Loan . . . in the Conservation of the Dense Tropical Forests of Diecke and Ziama* (Conakry, Guinea: ASSOANE, 1992), p. 4.
- "It is foreign personnel that controls": Ibid.
- "the most visible of project results": Korinna Horta, *The World Bank's Forestry and Fisheries Management Project for Guinea: A Failed Approach to Natural Resource Management* (Washington, DC: Environmental Defense Fund, 1992), p. 5.
- six is also the number of guards: Ibid.

251
- Forty-two percent of the experts: Bangladesh Project Management Institute, *Utilization of Expatriate*, p. 5.
- "the orange tint in his hair": Klitgaard, p. 101.
- elicit only one interested response: Ibid., p. 178.
- "cannot even add and divide": Ibid., p. 179.
- "could be solved by professional integrity": Author interview with Upendra Gautam, 27 February 1993.

252
- because Nepal has never been colonized: Author interview with Joseph Manickavasagam, 9 March 1993.
- "consultantization is the next step": Author interview with Mohinddin Farooque, 11 March 1993.
- "could be in Iceland": Author interview with Atiq Rahman, 11 March 1993.

• West Bengal refused a World Bank loan: "Indian State Spurns World Bank Terms," United Press International, 8 July 1994.

• "is a systematical destructive force": Edward Jayco, "African Capacity Building," address to African-American Conference, Reston, Virginia, May 19–21, 1993.

• "blame staff for poor project performance": World Bank, *Bank Experience in Project Supervision*, p. 38.

• "an unloved chore": Willi Wapenhans, *Oral Briefing of the Joint Audit Committee at Its Meeting on June 22, 1993*, pp. 6–7.

253 • the project completion report: World Bank, Infrastructure and Energy Operations Division, Latin America and the Caribbean Regional Office, *Ecuador: Emergency Petroleum Reconstruction Project, Project Completion Report* (Washington, DC: World Bank, 1993).

• "an unusually comprehensive program of data collection and analysis": Harbison and Hanushek, p. 36.

• "do not provide very strong support for its efficacy": Ibid., p. 176.

• "Nowhere . . . did [the project] achieve its objective": Ibid., p. 183.

• lower than was predicted at appraisal: Pohl and Mihaljek, p. 6; see also World Bank, *Annual Review of Evaluation Results*, 1993, p. 112.

• 8 percent have a negative rate of return: Pohl and Mihaljek, p. 25.

• "has increased considerably over time": Ibid., p. 29.

254 • "you know something's wrong when you don't get paid back": Author interview with Willi Wapenhans, 7 December 1992.

• about forty-five professionals and twenty-five support staff: World Bank, *Annual Report on Operations Evaluation (FY93)*, p. 26.

• a year or two after the project is completed: Baum and Tolbert, p. 384.

• OED investigator bases his evaluation on the completion report: Author interview with OED official, 3 December 1992.

• A project is judged satisfactory if: World Bank, *Annual Review of Evaluation Results*, 1992, p. 62.

• "The two main questions to be answered": Author interview with OED official, 3 December 1992.

• Fewer than two-thirds satisfactory: World Bank, *Annual Review of Evaluation Results*, 1993, p. 122.

• a more or less steady decline: Ibid., p. 150.

255 • 44 percent were judged likely to be sustainable: Ibid., p. 120.

• both satisfactory and sustainable: Ibid., pp. 120, 135.

• "I don't attach much credence": Author interview with OED official, 3 December 1992.

• 90 loans had been the subject of Impact Evaluation Studies: World Bank, *Directory of OED Reports;* author telephone interview with Rachel Weaving, of the Bank's Social and Economic Data Division, 2 November 1995.

• no one outside the OED asked for the full text: World Bank, *Bank Experience in Project Supervision*, p. 17.

• "focuses on what is intended": Ibid.

256 • "not as good as we would like": Author interview with Rachel Weaving, 2 November 1995.

• "they might be doing it": Author interview with Bank staffer, 3 May 1996.


# Chapter 15


257 • "the most influential behind-the-scenes banker": Robert Teitelman, "The Man Behind the Morgan Mask," *Institutional Investor*, October 1991, p. 212.

- "We tend to be a bit arrogant": Rowen, Hobart, "Lewis Preston Aims to Ax World Bank's Arrogance," *Washington Post,* 24 May 1992.

258
- "to ensure that [the Bank's] loans actually produced the benefits": World Bank Annual Report, 1993, p. 60.
- The memo contained Summer's thoughts: Lawrence Summers, World Bank office memorandum, 12 December 1991, reprinted in "Let Them Eat Pollution," *The Economist,* 8 February 1992.
- "perfectly logical, but totally insane": Jose Lutzenberger, letter to Lawrence Summers, February 1992.

259
- the arguments for more pollution are wrong: In a letter to *The Economist* after his memo was published, Summers said, "It is not my view . . . or that of any sane person . . . that the dumping of untreated toxic wastes near the homes of poor people is morally or economically defensible." *The Economist,* 15 February 1992.
- "seriously misrepresented the main thrust": Author interview with Morse Commission member, 23 June 1993.
- "There is reason to be concerned!": Wapenhans, p. 1.
- the proportion of completed projects that were judged unsuccessful: 15 percent in 1981; 37.5 percent in 1991. "The Wapenhans Report," p. ii.
- "the evidence of gross non-compliance is overwhelming": Ibid., p. 9.
- "gradual, but steady deterioration": Ibid., p. ii.
- "systematic and growing bias": Wapenhans, p. 1.
- "approval culture": "The Wapenhans Report," p. iii.
- "staff perceive appraisals as marketing devices": Ibid., p. 14.
- "nearly exclusive focus on new commitments": Wapenhans, p. 4.
- "something is not quite right": Wapenhans, p. 1.

260
- "nobody is then held accountable for anything": "Chairman's Farewell Blasts World Bank," *Bankcheck,* January 1994, p. 5.
- "Bank staff can't be individually accountable": Author interview with Jochen Kraske, 29 September 1993.
- "in the horse racing game": Canada, House of Commons, *Hearings before the Subcommittee on International Financial Institutions of the Standing Committee on Finance,* p. 72.
- too weak and too vague: U.S. Government Accounting Office, *Multilateral Development: Status of World Bank Reforms,* Briefing Report to Congressional Requesters, June 1994, p. 2.
- "Ernie's fingerprints all over it": "H Street Blues," *The Economist,* 1 May 1993, p. 91.

261
- the largest tenant in Washington, D.C.: Maryann Haggerty, "For the World Bank, Cost-Cutting Begins with a New Lease," *Washington Post,* 18 December 1994.
- "mismanagement and misconduct": Ibid.
- decision to build in central Washington "insane": Al Kamen, "World Bank Building—and Cost—Going Up," *Washington Post,* 22 September 1993.
- the Bank had learned from its mistakes: "World Bank Discloses Results of Inquiry into New Building Project," WB news release no. 93/S5, 14 July 1993.
- risen to $314 million: Chandler (1994).
- "200,000 child immunizations in the third world": "Smoked Out," *The Economist,* 29 May 1993, p. 108.

262
- fifty-seven five-star hotels: Cindy Skrzycki, "For the World Bank's Travelers, a First-Class Ejection," *Washington Post,* 3 January 1994.
- reduce annual costs by $12.5 million: World Bank, *Questions and Answers,* p. 114.
- cut its administrative budget by at least 10 percent: World Bank Annual Report, 1995, p. 16.
- savings of $16 million could be had: Pratap Chatterjee, "World Bank Staff 'Outraged' by Budget Cut Proposal," Inter Press Service, 26 September 1994.

• dislocate two and a half million people: World Bank, *Resettlement and Development*, pp. 2–2, 2–7.

• "Forced resettlement is about the worst thing": Nicholas Claxton (producer), *The Price of Progress*, Central Television (London), 1987.

• a policy on involuntary resettlement: World Bank, *Resettlement and Development*, p. v.

• the "fundamental goal of the Bank's policy": Ibid., p. vi.

• the projects reviewed had no resettlement plan: Ibid., Table 5.3.

263   • a gross underestimate of the number of people affected: Ibid., Tables 5.1 and 5.2.

• doing better than those who agreed to move: World Bank, *Kedung Ombo Multipurpose Dam and Irrigation Project, Project Completion Report* (Washington, DC: World Bank, 1994), p. 7.

• "neglect of the unfolding resettlement disaster": Ibid., Annex 3, paragraph 18.

• Kenya's Kiambere Hydropower Dam: Impact on the oustees described in World Bank, *Resettlement and Development*, pp. 4/9; Butcher, p. 15.

264   • "My understanding is that the Bank is involved in only three percent": Keith Grant, "Preston Defends World Bank's Social Record," Reuters, 1 October 1994.

• "involuntary resettlement is an inevitable result": John Gittings, "Bank Aids People Its Work Uproots," *The Guardian*, 11 April 1994.

• will displace more than half a million people: Personal communication, World Bank Press Office, 1 November 1995.

• a memo about a survey of dam safety: William Price, "India Dam Safety Project," World Bank office memorandum to Shawki Barghouti, 1 February 1995.

• "only the tip of the iceberg": Ibid., p. 2.

• In "Ghandi Sagar the consequences of a dam failure": Ibid., p. 3.

265   • "mere data cannot be used": Nelson Ridley of the Bank's New Delhi field office, quoted in Neelam Jain, "World Bank Report Condemns India's Dams," United Press International, 6 April 1995.

• "the orderly conduct of its operations": Mason and Asher, p. 58.

• an appeal to World Bank and IMF staff: *Bankcheck*, September 1994, p. 23.

• "it leaks like a sieve": Please oral history, p. 5.

• "the World Bank is one of the most transparent institutions": Canada, House of Commons, *Hearings*, p. 25.

266   • each recommending a different policy: Cavanagh, p. 145.

• "even more power under Mr. Preston": Kris Herbst, "Ernie Stern's Legend Reaches New Heights," *Emerging Markets*, 1 September 1993, p. 21.

• "a genuine attempt": "H-Street Blues," *The Economist*, 1 May 1993, p. 109.

• "there is supposed to be a presumption": Author interview with Chad Dobson, 30 April 1996.

• the Bank's violations "may materially harm their rights": "World Bank Inspection Panel news release no. 1," 7 September 1994.

• "The panel has been very, very constrained": Author interview with Bank official, 3 May 1996.

• it must first ask the board for permission: World Bank, *The Inspection Panel: An Overview* (Washington, DC: World Bank, 1994).

• It was, they said, the Pokomo, who had alerted scientists: Pratap Chatterjee, "Activists, World Bank Clash," Inter Press, 27 May 1993; Korinna Horta, *Statement by Korinna Horta, Staff Economist, Environmental Defense Fund, Concerning FY 1994 Authorization for the GEF* (Washington, DC: Environmental Defense Fund), 5 May 1993.

• "The so-called voluntary resettlement": Chatterjee "Activists, World Bank Clash."

• "a blatant attempt to buy environmental respectability": Friends of the Earth, *Testimony before Congress on World Bank Appropriations*, 1 March 1993, p. 14.

269   • "the lake ecosystem is delicate": World Bank, *Malawi Fisheries Development Project, Staff Appraisal Report* (Washington, DC: World Bank, 1991), p. 7.

• helped Ecuador adopt legal reforms that will attract foreign oil companies: On 7 October 1993, the Ecuadorian newspaper *Hoy* reported that "the new hydrocarbon law is not ready . . . with the objective of opening the oil sector to private companies. . . . Francisco Roldan, lawyer for Maxus company, wrote the law with the direct guidance of the World Bank." Quoted in Kay Treakle (Bank Information Center), *Ecuador: Structural Adjustment and Indigenous and Environmental Resistance* (Washington, DC: World Bank, 1995), p. 13.

• "The World Bank has paid for the rewriting of Ecuador's laws": Author interview with Glen Switkes, 30 April 1996.

• six projects worth $60 million: World Bank, *Making Development Sustainable: The World Bank Group and the Environment*, p. 137.

• increased use of carbon dioxide–emitting fossil fuels: World Bank Annual Report, 1995, p. 36.

• "It has some very good people": Author interview with Bank employee, 13 September 1995.

• "After a long battle": Author interview with Bank employee, 22 September 1992.

270 • "committed to working with non-governmental organizations": "Global Environmental Facility," World Bank Information Brief no. E.01.8-92.

• "a consistent, biased exaggeration": World Bank, *Interim Report of the Independent Evaluation of the Global Environmental Facility—Pilot Phase*, 26 August 1993, pp. 63–64.

• "lack of agreement among industrial and developing countries": Ibid., p. 50.

• "the many instances of unsatisfactory practices": Ibid., p. 70.

• the most important source of external financing for energy development: World Bank Energy Series Paper No. 7, October 1989.

271 • more money for it than for any other sector: Sanford (1991), p. 53.

• "developing countries have made some progress": World Bank, "Energy and Development," World Bank Information Brief, no. H.01.8-92.

• Less than 2 percent of the Bank's planned energy loans: Greenpeace, *Energy Wasted: The World Bank, Climate Change and Unsustainable Energy Lending* (Washington, DC: Greenpeace, 1994), p. 3.

• "about 60 percent of the net flow of resources out of developing countries": World Bank Energy Sector Management Assistance Program, "Implementing Energy Efficiency Activities in Developing Countries," activity initiation brief, April 1990, pp. 3–4.

• "commonly greater than 20 percent": World Bank, "Energy and Development," and "Energy Efficiency," World Bank Information Brief no. H.03-6-92. A 1991 study carried out for the Bank: USAID *Opportunities for Improving End-Use Electricity Efficiency in India* (Washington, DC: USAID), November 1991.

272 • devoted less than 1 percent of its energy lending to such measures: Michael Phillips, *The Least-Cost Energy Path for Developing Countries* (Washington, DC: International Institute for Energy Conservation, 1991).

• "small amounts of energy are used": World Bank, "Energy and Development."

• announced a new policy on energy efficiency: World Bank, "Energy Efficiency and Conservation in the Developing World," World Bank Policy Paper, January 1993, pp. 11–12.

• less than 1 percent of the projects the Bank was preparing: Greenpeace, *Energy Wasted* p. 3.

• only two of forty-six energy loans the Bank was preparing: EDF, *Power Failure* (Washington, D.C.: Environmental Defense Fund and Natural Resources Defense Council, 1994), p. 19.

• "biggest new source of greenhouse gas emissions on earth": EDF, "IBRD NTPC Loan: Global Warming Implications," Memo, June 1993.

• "the right of people to live in pristine poverty": Tim Cullen, "Personal View: Sleepless and Irritable in Suburbia," *Financial Times,* 10 October 1994.

273 • "Steve Schwartzman knows Polonoroeste better than anyone": Author interview with Bank employee, 22 September 1992.

• "they broke through the Bank's self-image": Author interview with Bank employee, 24 August 1995.

• "well-organized environmental and human rights groups": "Highlights from the President's February 22 Meeting with VPs," World Bank office memorandum, 23 February 1993.

• "become a virtual parallel institution": "Bank, Fund Face Closer Scrutiny," *Emerging Markets*, 1 September 1993.

• responding aggressively to criticism: "If you engage in confrontation when the situation calls for it you'll not only feel better, but you'll also be more effective in your job." Herb Schmertz and William Novak, *Goodbye to the Low Profile: The Art of Creative Confrontation* (Boston: Little Brown, 1986), quoted in "Bank Hires PR Maestro," *Bankcheck*, January 1994, p. 1.

• "we want to be your partner": Herb Schmertz, *Report to the World Bank on Public Affairs Activities* (Washington, DC: The Schmertz Company).

274   • "The President's Office places a high priority": Alexander Shakow, "Mortgaging the Earth—Request for Help," internal World Bank memo, 15 February 1994, p. 1.

• "tell success stories from the field": Brown, p. 5.

• a list of one hundred Bank projects: World Bank, *Five Decades of Development: 100 Examples of the World Bank in Action*.

• The Bank initially refused to supply the loan numbers: David Wigg, "100 Projects etc.," World Bank memorandum to Bill Brannigan, 8 November 1994.

• no documentation for the other sixty-four: Jane Monahan, office memorandum to William Brannigan, 19 December 1994.

• "the first reliable form of transportation": World Bank, *Five Decades of Development: 100 Examples of the World Bank in Action.*

• the Bank had described the railroad: World Bank, *Bank Operations in Colombia: An Evaluation*, pp. 67, 72.

• "A very impressive piece of climbing": Richard Murphy, "Greenpeace Protest Angers World Bank," Reuters, 4 October 1994.

275   • "piece of cheap theatrics": Ibid.

• "NGOs whose business involves theatrics": Richard Murphy, "World Bank Dismisses Environmentalist Attacks," Reuters, 6 October 1994.

• "My message is simply this": Luke Hill, "World Bank Said Needed More Than Ever," United Press International, 6 October 1994.

• "I would certainly agree that in the past": Andrew Steer, interviewed in *The World Bank at Fifty*, Part 2: "Interview with Andrew Steer," aired on 13 December 1994. Transcript (No. 9450) prepared by Common Ground.

# Chapter 16

276   • $10 billion less than its optimistic projections: Ludlow, p. 400.

• "a striking feature of the Preston Bank": World Bank press conference, 23 April 1995, p. 4.

• a billion dollars more than five years earlier: IFC Annual Report, 1992, p. 5; 1994, p. 6.

• In 1984, the Bank lent forty times as much as the IFC: In 1984, the IFC lent $396 million, 2.5 percent of the World Bank's $15.5 billion. In 1994, it lent $2.5 billion, 12 percent of the World Bank's $20.8 billion.

• expected to cost a quarter of a billion dollars: World Bank, *Questions and Answers*, p. 114.

• "IFC's presence in a project provides comfort": World Bank, *Contributing to Development*, p. 11.

277   • nearly six dollars from other sources: IFC Annual Report, 1995, p. 8.

- "to straighten out the public sector": Author interview with Eveline Herfkens, 7 June 1995.
- in China, for example, most of its projects are large-scale joint ventures: "IFC Announces $158.7 Million in Loans for China," Reuters, 26 October 1995.
- One-third of its financing now supports such projects: IFC Annual Report, 1994, p. 5.

278
- "a shift away from lending to governments": Bretton Woods Commission, p. 110.
- "It is a reflection of the changed economic environment": Ibid.
- recommendation that the World Bank be abolished: "Ex-Thatcher Advisor Would Like to Abolish IMF, Bank," Reuters, 24 October 1994.
- "almost the only game in town": "World Bank Unit Sees Continued Strong Growth," Reuters, 27 September 1995.
- "a reduction in state activity": Bretton Woods Commission, p. 108.
- "more likely to be efficiently used": World Bank, Contributing to Development, p. 2.

279
- "large loans to governments": Bretton Woods Commission, p. 108.
- "We are prepared to lend": David Briscoe, "World Bank," Associated Press, 26 September 1994.
- "a climate conducive to private enterprise": Lewis Preston, "The Future Role of the World Bank Group: Challenges and Guiding Principles," address to Bretton Woods Commission Conference, Washington, DC, 21 July 1994, p. 2.
- "the changes in these countries were in the main generated in the countries": Bretton Woods Commission, p. 107.
- Sixty percent of its investments: Argentina, India, Brazil, Mexico, Pakistan, Turkey, Indonesia, Thailand, Chile, and Philippines. IFC Annual Report, 1995, pp. 123–57.
- Argentina alone has received almost 10 percent: Ibid., pp. 11, 28–31.
- "They're salesmen": Author interview with Chevron executive, 4 June 1995.

280
- "a systematic bias to optimism in project evaluation": Guy Pfeffermann and Gary Bond, "IFC and Development," Finance and Development, December 1989, p. 42.
- net income of $188 million in 1995: IFC Annual Report, 1995, p. 14.
- "The problem is this": Edwin Finn, "A Shot in the Foot," Forbes, 14 July 1986.

281
- the other members took up its share of the investment: James Jukwey, "Shell Stays in Nigeria Despite Pressure on Hangings," Reuters, 14 November 1995.
- "our partners in the financial community": "New IFC Guidelines Forge Closer Ties with Private Sector," World Bank News, 14 December 1995.
- "the stormtroopers of privatization": "Bankers Seek Further Reform of World Bank's IFC," Reuters, 10 January 1996.
- "IFC has graduated a few countries": Ibid.
- "one of the largest and finest remaining forests": Ancient Forests International, "World Bank/Chilean Forest," press release, 5 August 1993.

282
- invest another $2.8 million in the company: IFC Annual Report, 1994, p. 87.
- "waged a systematic campaign of terror": Pastoral Lands Commission et al., Letter to IFC, 5 May 1993, p. 2.
- "the Government was acting responsibly": Ian J. Bridge, (IFC), Letter to Steve Schwartzman, 4 June 1993, p. 2.
- Six months later, the local public prosecutor filed charges: Steve Schwartzman (Environmental Defense Fund) and Jeronimo Nunes (Pastoral Lands Commission), Letter to William Ryrie, 5 May 1993, pp. 1–2.
- dump pesticides, gasoline, and oil into local streams: Ibid., p. 3.
- "climate of tension and insecurity": Ibid.
- "it would be inappropriate for IFC to interfere": Bridge, Letter to Steve Schwartzman, p. 3.

283
- "The project suffered large losses": IFC, Annual Portfolio Evaluation Report—FY92, Annex B.
- force about three thousand people from their homes: IFC, Technical and Environment

Department, *IFC Review of Projects Involving Resettlement, 1989–1994,* October 1994, p. 3.
- "projects must comply with applicable World Bank environmental policies": Ibid., p. 1.
- the environmental unit reviewed 290 projects: IFC Annual Report, 1995, p. 84.
- only 14 out of 213 projects: Ibid.

284  • The Multilateral Investment Guarantee Agency: MIGA's financing and powers are described in World Bank, *MIGA: The First Five Years and Future Challenges* (Washington, DC: World Bank, 1994), p. 9.
- "played a catalytic role": World Bank, "The Multilateral Investment Guarantee Agency," World Bank Information Brief no. A.07.8-92.
- dumps more than 100,000 tons of tailings: Lori Udall, "Irian Jaya's Heart of Gold," *World Rivers Review,* August 1995, pp. 10–11.

285  • "The dumping of tailings into the river": Pratap Chatterjee, "U.S. Mine in Indonesia Loses Insurance Cover for Environment Abuses," Inter Press Service, 3 November 1995.
- eleven people . . . were slaughtered: The murders and subsequent investigations are addressed in "UT Tie to Mine Firm Prompts Resignation," United Press International, 19 September 1995; Lewa Pardomuan, "Indonesian Rights Mission Accuses Army over Deaths," Reuters, 22 September 1995; "Indonesian Rights Group Returns to Irian Jaya," Reuters, 13 September 1995; and Udall, "Irian Jaya's Heart of Gold," pp. 10–11.
- "It is not really our problem": Pratap Chatterjee, "World Bank Arm Insures Destructive Mining," Inter Press Service, 14 August 1995.
- "Freeport's implementation of the Project": Associate Counsel General, OPIC, Letter to Freeport McMoran, 31 October 1995.
- personal appeal to President Clinton by Indonesia's President Suharto: Chatterjee, "World Bank Arm Insures Destructive Mining."

286  • almost all of which were from the former Soviet Union: The five not from the FSU or the former eastern bloc are Namibia, Mongolia, the Marshall Islands, Switzerland, and Micronesia.
- "the Bank and the Fund have usually had a clear idea": *The Economist,* 12 October 1991, p. 47.
- added 140 staff to its Europe and Central Asia office: World Bank Annual Report, 1992, p. 105.
- Between 1993 and 1995, 16 percent of the Bank's lending: Total IBRD and IDA lending, 1993–95, was $66.8 billion, of which loans to countries of the former Soviet Union and eastern bloc totaled $11.1 billion.
- the proportion increases to 32 percent: 1993–95 lending to China, Cambodia, Laos, and Vietnam totaled $10.1 billion (of which loans to China account for $9.2 billion).
- increased by 80 percent: From $59 billion to $106 billion. *World Debt Tables,* 1996, p. 390; Barbara Crosby (World Bank Press Office), personal communication, 2 May 1996.
- spirited an estimated $50 million": Raymond Baker. "Riding the Rivers of Dirty Money," *Washington Post,* 4 June 1995.
- not subject to taxes or tariffs: World Bank Articles of Agreement, Article VII, Section 9 (a).

288  • "proposed a market-based reform": World Bank, *Annual Review of Evaluation Results 1993,* p. 65.
- "all four projects failed": Ibid.
- "improving the efficiency of the urban transport system": World Bank Annual Report, 1988, p. 129.
- "This town, Madurai, had an excellent network of private buses": Taken from an 21 August 1991, letter to economist Judy Shelton by the owner of a private company who saw her discussing foreign aid on the CNN program *Crossfire* and wrote her about the effects of the loan; quoted in Bandow and Vasquez, pp. 221–22.

289 • two-thirds of its industrial lending: World Bank, *World Bank Support for Industrialization in Korea, India, and Indonesia*, p. 1.

• so it helped to establish: Howard et al., p. 54.

• "it is an open question": Mason and Asher, p. 363.

• wealthy individuals and state-run enterprises: Ibid., p. 374; Gordon, p. 10; World Bank, *Financial Intermediation Policy Paper*, pp. iv and 12, and *Annual Review of Project Performance Audit Results*, 1986, p. 45.

• "borrowers willingly defaulted": World Bank, *World Development Report*, 1989, pp. 58–60.

• almost half had 25 percent of their loans in arrears: World Bank, *Financial Intermediation Policy Paper*.

• half their loans in arrears: World Bank, *World Development Report*, 1989, pp. 58–60.

• "Almost all big politicians": "Bhutto Protests at Being Listed as Loan Defaulter," Reuters, 28 August 1993.

• the amount of the national deficit: Ibid.

290 • lend money at artificially low interest rates: World Bank, *Financial Intermediation Policy Paper*, p. 12.

• minus 10 or 20 percent: World Bank, Country Operations Department IV, *Yugoslavia Financial Sector Restructuring: Policies and Priorities*, vol. 2, 30 November 1989, annexes, pp. 46–108 ("1987 Financial Results of the Nine Commercial Bank Groups"), cited in Bandow and Vasquez, p. 114.

• liabilities of from $300 million to $1.2 billion: Ibid.

• "few [Bank-funded DFIs] have become financially viable": World Bank, *Financial Intermediation Policy Paper*, Industry Department, 8 July 1985, p. iv.

• roughly $20,000 to $30,000—and has run as high as $540,000: World Bank, *Annual Review of Project Performance Audit Results*, p. 171.

• 40 percent of the Bank's DFI loans: Ludlow, p. 222.

• "The subsidies received by DFIs have often far exceeded the profit": Yaron, p. 1.

• "key instrument for transmitting support": World Bank, *Evaluation Results*, 1993, p. 86.

• "the Bank now limits its DFI operations": World Bank, Operations Evaluation Department, *DFCs in Three Latin American Countries*. OED Precis No. 23, January 1992, p. 1.

• the Bank channeled $1.8 billion: World Bank Annual Report, 1995, p. 31.

• "they will have no nasty surprises": Paul Lewis, "World Bank Chief Backs Public Projects," *New York Times*, 11 October 1995.

• By 1994 more than a third of all its lending: World Bank, *Questions and Answers*, p. 98.

291 • lend money to infrastructure projects in developing countries: Because of the Bank's Articles of Agreement, it must first obtain a counterguarantee from the government concerned.

• until the reforms it has been promoting since 1980 "take root": World Bank Annual Report, 1995, p. 31.

• "to get commercial banks back into the project-lending": "Banks Should Get Back to Project Loans—Preston," Reuters, 6 October 1994.

• "Many big banks are falling over themselves to lend": "Dam Good Business This, Chaps," *The Economist*, 26 August 1995, p. 61.

• $167 billion of private capital: *World Debt Tables 1996*, vol. 1, p. 11.

• Africa got less than 3 percent: Ibid.

• "tend to move on interest movements": "World Bank's Preston Warns on 3rd World Capital Flows," Reuters, 1 October 1994.

• "private capital is available on reasonable terms": World Bank Articles of Agreement, Article I (ii).

292 • "no one [at the bank] had taken this article very seriously": Bandow and Vasquez, p. 80.

• "a marvelous document of high bureaucratese": Ibid., p. 81.

- Twenty-five countries have graduated from IDA: World Bank Annual Report, 1995, p. 14.
- "We are prepared to lend": David Briscoe, "World Bank," Associated Press, 26 September 1994.
- $3 per capita on health services: Paul Lewis, "World Bank Moves to Cut Poorest Nations Debts," New York Times, 16 March 1996.
- becoming so poor that they could only borrow from IDA: World Debt Tables 1994–95, vol. 1, p. 42.
- "more aggressive policy of graduation": Bretton Woods Commission, p. 9.

293
- Between 1990 and 1993, the Bank gave a rating of unsatisfactory: World Bank, Annual Review of Evaluation Results, 1990, p. 113; 1991, p. 74; 1992, p. 240; 1993, p. 155.
- twice what it was during the previous two decades: World Bank Annual Reports, 1946–95.
- what developing countries spend on education in total: Rajagopalan oral history, p. 20.
- "main contribution must be advice": World Bank, Priorities and Strategies for Education: A World Bank Review (Washington, DC: World Bank, 1995).
- secondary schools and colleges are much more heavily subsidized: Ibid.
- "The Bank's basic economic premise": Cavanagh, pp. 167, 170.

294
- "means taking away the subsidies from the rich": Pratap Chatterjee, "Education: World Bank Wants to Know Why Its Projects Are Getting Worse," Inter Press Service, 17 May 1995.
- About 40 percent of its education loans: "IMF-Girls Count," Associated Press, 5 October 1994.
- for every one thousand girls in India that receive an additional year: Nicholas Burnett, Priorities and Strategies for Education (Washington, DC: World Bank, 1995).
- purchase of equipment, materials, and books: Ludlow, p. 141.
- a higher proportion of advisors: Ibid.
- have met their goals in this regard: World Bank, Annual Review of Evaluation Results, 1993, pp. 119, 121.
- "not in the education ministry": Pratap Chatterjee, "Education."
- about $1.2 billion a year: World Bank Annual Reports, 1985, p. 125; 1988, p. 156; 1989, p. 182; 1992, p. 193; 1994, p. 147; 1995, p. 36.
- AIDS prevention and treatment programs: David Brown, "World Bank to Emphasize AIDS as Economic Threat," Washington Post, 27 November 1994.

295
- "where benefits to the poor are maximized": Oxfam (UK), p. 8.
- "It is regularly pointed out": Salmen (1992), p. 8.
- "uncaring government bureaucrats": Author interview with Christopher Willoughby, 14 March 1993.
- lacked status in the eyes of the villagers: Salmen (1995), p. 12.
- "it was considered weak and improper": Ibid., p. 9.

296
- limited its education loans to vocational and technical: Mason and Asher, pp. 204–5.
- to triple its education lending: In 1974 it was $153 million; in 1979, $440 million.
- "Now it is part of the new orthodoxy": World Bank press conference, 23 April 1995, p. 4.
- "large public investment schemes become vehicles for the interests": Briscoe, p. 17.
- "Poor people want and are willing to pay for": Ibid.
- latrines would cost a three-member family almost $16 a month: "Defending a Basic Right," Earth Island Journal, Summer 1995, p. 10.
- annual income per capita is $300: World Bank, World Development Report, 1995, p. 162.
- "Once government paternalism ceases": Briscoe, "World Bank," p. 17.
- "The poor have skills": quoted in Adams (1991), p. 187.
- now owned by its two million borrowers: Syed Ahmeduzzaman, "Bangladesh Plans New Strategy to Fight Poverty," Reuters, 28 April 1994.

• In 1995 it made half a billion dollars worth of loans: "Lender to Poor Says Banks Must Do More," *San Francisco Chronicle,* 2 September 1995.

• repayment rate for Bangladesh's private banks averages 27 percent: Syed Ahmeduzzaman, "Bangladesh Plans New Strategy to Fight Poverty."

• per capita income among Grameen borrowers increased 35 percent: Salmen (1992), p. 10.

• 4 percent of women who did not borrow: David Gibbons, "Grameen Bank Female Loanees, 10 Years Later," *The Daily Star Weekend Magazine* (Dhaka), 19 March 1993, p. 1.

• "to poor people of working age": Jorge A. Banales, "World Bank Program to Support World's Poorest," United Press International, 14 July 1995.

• "really peanuts compared to the need": Edith M. Lederer, "Women-Money," Associated Press, 7 September 1995.

• "purveyor of capital": World Bank Annual Report, 1995, p. 125.

• "a knowledge-based institution": World Bank Annual Report, 1994, p. 55.

• "We need to find a way to become an advisor": World Bank press conference, 23 April 1995, p. 9.

• "lubricated by lending operations": Mason and Asher, p. 426.

• "the largest 'development research university' in the world": Bretton Woods Commission, p. 297.

299  • "busy gutting it now for public release": Author interview with Bank employee, 21 October 1995.

• "deteriorated in relevance and readability": Mark Malloch Brown, p. 10.

• "failed, for example, to anticipate the oil price rises": Feinberg et al., p. 92.

• 23 percent higher than the United Nations' estimate, 44 percent higher than the IMF's: Klitgaard, p. 59.

• the actual 1988 figure of 15 million CFAs: *World Debt Tables,* 1992, p. 245.

• "quality of its agricultural price forecasting": World Bank, *Report of the Joint Audit Committee,* 14 November 1989, para. 94, quoted in George and Sabelli, p. 87.

• by 2010 the world price of wheat and rice will be double: "World Bank, FAO Grain Harvest Estimates Too Rosy": Dow Jones News Service, 1 May 1996.

• Lester Brown of the Washington-based think tank the Worldwatch Institute: Ibid.

• forecasts were off by between 33 percent and 75 percent: Feinberg et al., p. 7.

300  • "too hopeful": World Bank, *World Development Report,* 1991, p. 28.

• Ibid., p. 29.

• the Bank's economic department forecast that the Latin America and the Caribbean would grow at 3.5 percent: World Bank, Economic Department, *Global Economic Prospects and the Developing Countries,* April 1995.

• "it is quite possible": "World Bank Upbeat on Latam Growth, Despite Mexico," Reuters, 8 October 1995.

301  • "There is a surprisingly large volatile element": Carl Hartman, "World Bank—Luck," Agence France-Presse, 28 December 1993.

• "This whole desire to build a research empire": Ul Huq oral history, pp. 26–27.

• "exclusive, self-serving, and of insufficient objectivity": Bretton Woods Commission, p. 297.

• "politically inspired shifts in policy direction": Ibid.

• "the Bank is inhabited by a large number of highly talented professionals": Ranis, p. 4.

• "virtually untouched by modern economic development": World Bank, *Country Report on Lesotho* (1975), p. 1, quoted in Ferguson, p. 25.

302  • claims that the poorest 40 percent of the population own 31 percent of the cattle: Ferguson, p. 45.

• "It is almost inconceivable": Ibid., p. 27.

• "not some sort of staggeringly bad scholarship": Ibid.

• "planners regarded the paralyzing bureaucracy of the government": Ibid., p. 225.

- "it must make Lesotho out to be an enormously promising candidate": Ibid., p. 69.
303    • "If Lesotho is poor": Ibid., p. 37.


Chapter 17

304    • "had virtually run the Bank": Kris Herbst, "Ernie Stern's Legend Reaches New Heights," *Emerging Markets,* 1 September 1993, p. 21.
305    • "Look, it's my favourite groupie!": Finn.
- "meeting heads of state on an equal footing": Blustein.
- "the Man with the Golden Rolodex": Ullmann.
- identified him as "a possible candidate": James Wolfensohn, keynote address, World Resources Institute dinner honoring him, Washington, DC, 2 October 1995, p. 2.
- "their own taxpayers would not foot the bill": Speech by George Shultz to the American Economic Association, Washington, DC, 5 January 1995, quoted in Gene Kramer, "Shultz-IMF-Russia," Associated Press, 7 January 1995.
- "reached a decent old age": Quoted in "After 50 Years, World Bank More Unpopular Than Ever," Probe International press release, 4 October 1994, p. 2.
306    • "brillant ideas of the 1940s": Sweeney, p. 114.
- "The World Bank is a case in point": Bretton Woods Commission, p. 83.
- "no one can reform international organizations": McKitterick oral history, p. 25.
- "not as a lender of money to governments": Bretton Woods Commission, pp. 1–2.
- "The Bank has perhaps lagged slightly": World Bank press conference, 23 April 1995, p. 3.
- Ryrie's advice that the Bank practice "self-restraint": Bretton Woods Commission, p. 110.
- one-third of its loans were targeted to the poor: World Bank Annual Report, 1995, p. 21.
- one-third "included influential forms of participation by directly affected stakeholders": Ibid., p. 22.
- one-third were "primarily environmental": World Bank, *Mainstreaming the Environment,* Annexes C and D.
307    • "devoted to improving women's status": World Bank Annual Report, 1995, pp. 20–21, 27; World Bank news release no. 95/01, "Human Capital Operations."
- one-quarter of the Bank's lending was for adjustment: In 1988, sector and structural adjustment lending was 25 percent of the Bank's total. In 1989, it was 30 percent; in 1990, 26 percent; in 1991, 26 percent; in 1992, 27 percent; in 1993, 17 percent; in 1994, 12 percent; in 1995, 24 percent. World Bank Annual Reports, 1988, p. 65; 1989, p. 39; 1991, p. 13; 1992, p. 19; 1993, p. 15; 1994, p. 15; 1995, p. 36; Ludlow, p. 245.
- "Adjustment, as it now operates": World Bank press conference, 23 April 1995, p. 6.
- "If you look at our portfolio in India": Author interview with Eveline Herfkèns, 7 June 1995.
- in 1995 India received thirteen loans, worth more than $2 billion: The information on India's education loans is from World Bank Annual Reports for 1995, pp. 77; 1994, pp. 144, 149; and 1993, pp. 150, 166.
- "Larry is being a bit naughty there": *Washington Post,* 26 June 1993.
- loans in these three categories totaled $56 billion: Agriculture loans totaled $21 billion, energy $19 billion, and transportation $15.5 billion. World Bank Annual Reports, 1992, p. 193; 1995, p. 36.
- The fastest-growing categories of Bank lending: Ibid. World Bank Annual Report, 1995, p. 36, gives World Bank financial loans as $2.5 billion. On p. 31, however, it puts the figure at $3 billion.
- "identify those values and beliefs": *Conference on Ethics and Spiritual Values,* bro-

chure for conference sponsored jointly by the World Bank, the Center for Respect of Life and Environment, and the World Bank Spiritual Unfoldment Society, Washington, DC, 2–3 October 1995.

308    • attracted support from dozens of celebrities: "Celebrities Join Fast to Protest Hunger," *San Francisco Chronicle,* 24 April 1993.

• "the growing scourge of hunger": World Bank Annual Report, 1994, p. 49.

• "the conference was not simply a public relations exercise": "Highlights from Mr. Preston's Meeting with the VPs on 13 December 1993," unpublished World Bank memo, p. 2.

• "wants to be everything": Author interview with Bank staffer, 28 September 1993.

• "we will probably emerge in that role": "World Pours Out Relief, Joy at Bosnia Peace," Reuters, 21 November 1995.

• "connections between people": Quoted in Peter Sisler, "World Bank Investing in Peace," United Press International, 5 March 1996.

309    • "used as a dumping ground": James Orr, executive director of the Bretton Woods Committee, quoted in *Euromoney,* September 1993, p. 88.

• it made an unsuccessful bid to take control: Deborah McKenzie, "Battle for the World's Seed Banks," *New Scientist,* 2 July 1994, p. 4.

• "pushed into a new role": Jessica Matthews, "The Changing Nature of National Sovereignty: Some Implications for the World Bank," a paper prepared for the World Bank president's retreat, 12 March 1993.

• "ever-changing fads-du-jour": Ranis, p. 10.

• "We tried to do everything under the sun": Rajagopalan oral history, pp. 16–17.

• "everybody agreed that there were too many goals": Haralz oral history, p. 22.

• "resist the temptation to take on tasks which they cannot solve": "Tietmayer Says IMF, Bank Should Stick to Mandate," Reuters, 4 October 1994.

310    • "the World Bank is a relationship bank": Malloch Brown, p. 2.

• "lots of staff can make this claim": Alexander, Nancy. "News & Notices," Alexandria, VA: *Breed for the World,* January 1996.

• "They only cooperate with the respectable NGOs": author interview with Sunil Roy, 23 March 1993.

• "I am not one of those who believe that the World Bank has changed": Rotberg oral history, p. 39.

• the poor perception of the Bank: This is U.S. executive director's paraphrasing, in a letter to Wolfensohn, dated 7 May 1995, of a remark Wolfensohn had made to her.

311    • "will have an extensive impact on living conditions": Rich Miller, "World Bank Criticized over $1 Billion Nepal dam Plan," Reuters, 19 December 1994.

• "the Bank can no longer support infrastructure projects": Eduardo Lachica, "Environmentalists Are Opposing Plans of World Bank to Build Dam in Nepal," *Wall Street Journal,* 12 September 1994,

• "quick to go on the offensive": Memo of staff meeting with James Wolfensohn, March 1995.

• "I expect from you loyalty to the institution": Letter from James Wolfensohn to World Bank staff, 1 June 1995.

312    • "the World Bank has got things wrong": Joel Joffe and Dianna Melrose, "Report on Meeting with Jim Wolfensohn," Oxfam (UK) internal memo, 19 May 1995, p. 2.

• "an institution that we can be proud of": James Wolfensohn, keynote address, World Resources Institute dinner honoring James D. Wolfensohn," Washington, DC, 2 October 1995, p. 12.

• "I haven't come with any magic insight": Blustein.

313    • "it has really started to affect their behavior": Ibid.

• "All of a sudden, we have a leader": Ibid.

• "We all work here because we care about the world": Letter from James Wolfensohn to World Bank staff, 1 June 1995.

• "putting a smile on a child's face": Rex Nutting, "Rich Must Aid Poor, Wolfensohn Says," United Press International, 10 October 1995.

• "savior mentality": Richard Richardson of the Overseas Development Council, quoted in Blustein.

• "tendency to humiliate his subordinates": Suzanna Andrews, "Why Doesn't Anyone Believe Me When I Say I Just Love the Arts?" GO, May 1991, p. 222.

• "Jim's a screamer": Ibid.

• "defensive, thin-skinned and insecure": Patti Waldmeir, "Wolfensohn's Search for Global Relevance," Financial Times, 30 May 1996.

314    • an open letter to Preston in the Financial Times: "The World Bank Must Withdraw Immediately from Sardar Sarovar," 21 September 1992, p. 6.

• "We'll just have to start cutting off the money": Chandler (1994).

315    • force IDA to cut its 1996 lending program: Joint World Bank–NGO press conference, p. 12.

• "the United States would remain a major continuing player in IDA": World Bank, Multilateral Development Banks: Issues for Congress, p. 14.

• "We cannot assume in the current negotiations": William Boston, "Germany Fails to Assure World Bank on Funding," Reuters, 21 November 1995.

• "We and most of the other donors": Ibid.

• "We may be seeing the end of IDA": Author telephone interview with Jonathan Sanford, 25 September 1995.

• "reposition the Bank": This, according to Mark Malloch Brown, is "the principal goal" of the Bank's new communications strategy. Malloch Brown, p. 1.

• "unveiled a major campaign": World Bank press release no. 1995/S93, 16 May 1995.

316    • "there are no plans at present": "Raised Eyebrows on Hill Quash World Bank's Ads," Wall Street Journal, 22 June 1995.

• "a self-interest Bank": World Bank press briefing, 23 April 1995, p. 8.

• "cultivating new allies": World Bank office memorandum from Mark Malloch Brown, 3 May 1995, p. 5.

• "developing the long term relationships": Ibid., p. 6.

• "higher volume than ever before:": Ibid., pp. 5–6.

317    • "play into the hands of the right-wing": Joffe and Melrose, "Report on Meeting with Jim Wolfensohn," p. 2.

• "I want to know right now who will work with me": Lori Udall, notes on meeting with Wolfensohn, 4 April 1995.

• "We see that change is coming": Joint World Bank–NGO press conference, 11 October 1995, pp. 19, 33.

• "everybody with a commitment to poverty reduction": Ibid., p. 10.

• "the world's 3 billion poorest people": James D. Wolfensohn, "1.3 Billion People Living on a Dollar a Day," Washington Post, 12 October 1995.

• "The poorest people in the world": "House Cuts World Bank," Dow Jones News Service, 25 May 1995.

• "We are really alarmed": Jane Holligan, "Bolivia Alarmed by Cheap Loan Cuts," United Press International, 19 October 1995.

• "reckless cuts": Martin Crutsinger, "Clinton—World Economy," Associated Press, 11 October 1995.

318    • .15 percent: World Bank, World Development Report, 1995, p. 196.

• The Bank's total reserves: World Bank Annual Report, 1995, p. 142.

• "We're going to have great difficulty": "Lawmaker Attacks World Bank for Blocking U.S. Bids," Reuters, 18 April 1996.

• more than one-third of them are severely indebted: World Bank Annual Report, 1995, pp. 205–6; World Debt Tables 1995, vol. 1, pp. 50–51.

• 220 percent of the value of its exports: Ibid., p. 49.

• ratio of debt to exports much higher than 220 percent: Ibid., pp. 55–57.

319  • more than $188 million worth of IBRD loans was in arrears: World Bank, *Questions and Answers,* p. 9. This does not include those countries that are in nonaccrual with the Bank, that is, have not made payments for six months or more.
• succeeded in reducing arrears substantially: Ibid., p. 12.
• several hundred million dollars a year: $245 million in 1995. "World Bank Allocates FY95 Income," World Bank news release no. 96/FOS, 1 August 1995.
• no payments for at least eighteen months on Bank loans totaling $6 billion: World Bank Annual Report, 1995, pp. 157, 185.
• 3 percent of the Bank's outstanding loans: As of 1995, the Bank had set aside $3.7 million, less than 2 percent of its outstanding loans, against possible loan losses. World Bank Annual Report, 1995, p. 157.
• "they can stay there as long as they want": Author interview with Jessica Einhorn, 4 December 1992.
• give more than 40 percent of their annual debt service payments to the Bank: World Bank, *The Multilateral Debt Facility,* pp. 4–5.
• reduced or forgave $10 billion worth of debt: World Bank, *World Debt Tables 1993–94.*
• The Debt Crisis Network estimates: Joint World Bank–NGO press conference, p. 19.
320  • paid Guyana's World Bank and IMF arrears: Adams (1994), p. 11.
• so that Nicaragua could pay off its arrears: World Bank, "Informal Board Seminar," p. 2.
• France paid off Cameroon's arrears to the Bank, and the United States and Japan gave Peru a "bridging" loan: Adams (1994), p. 11.
• $65 million to clear Haiti's arrears: "Nations to Help Clear Haitian Debt," United Press International, 14 October 1994.
• By 1995, it had made $300 million: Malvina Pollock (World Bank Debt and Finance Unit), personal communication to author, 24 April 1996.
• nineteen in number as of 1995: World Bank, *World Debt Tables 1994–95,* p. 42.
• "to help them service their IBRD debt": World Bank, *Questions and Answers,* p. 25.
• converted $1.3 billion of IBRD debt to IDA debt: Ibid.
• "The yields on Brady bonds are just enormous": "For One Expert, U.S. Stocks Are Far Too Expensive," *Washington Post,* 12 August 1995.
• reduced by one-third of $190 billion: World Bank, *Questions and Answers,* p. 27, and personal communication, Malvina Pollock (World Bank Debt and Finance Unit), 24 April 1996.
321  • "making specific loans that are explicitly for the purpose of debt and debt-service reduction": World Bank internal memorandum, 2 May 1990, quoted in Gwin, p. 45.
• "This is a two-way street": Rosemary Werret, "Nobrega Explains Arrears and Seeks IMF Accord," *Joint Annual Meeting News,* 25 September 1989.
• Three-quarters of the 70 IBRD countries: *World Debt Tables 1994–95* (on computer disc) extract DT NTR MIBR CD (net transfer to IBRD), 1987.
• gave IBRD $1.5 billion more than they got from it: *World Debt Tables 1994–95,* vol. 1, p. 194.
• in 1995 the figure was $2.1 billion: Ibid., and World Bank Annual Report, 1995, pp. 142, 143, 171.
• "take care that there is a positive net transfer": Author interview with Eveline Herfkens, 7 June 1995.
322  • "new lending to pay old interest": Tom Cox, "World Bank: Development's Foe," *Wall Street Journal,* 29 July 1988.
• "funds to service their external debts": Knapp oral history (III), pp. 20–21.
• "just fakes": Kamarck oral history (II), p. 4.
• only with loans that are economically sound investments: "The World Bank does not make loans which, in its opinion, cannot be justified on economic grounds." International Bank for Reconstruction and Development, Information Statement, 16 September 1992, p. 10.
• "I'd fire anyone who said that": Author interview with Uwe Bott, 9 September 1992.

323  • "Money is fungible": Author interview with Jessica Einhorn, 4 December 1992.
     • the largest borrower: Ibid., p. 196.
     • admitted that more than a third of its completed projects were unsuccessful: "The Wapenhans Report," pp. ii, 4.
     • "It's not for us to judge": Author interview with Uwe Bott, 9 September 1992.
     • "its preferred creditor status": Moody's Investor Services, *Moody's Sovereign Credit Report, International Bank for Reconstruction and Development,* September 1991, p. 1.
     • "There is no specific commitment to preferred creditor treatment": Letter from Hugh N. Scott to Patricia Adams, 27 June 1991.
     • "whether these flows can be sustained indefinitely": Canada, *Report of the Auditor-General of Canada to the House of Commons,* Toronto, 1992, p. 286.
324  • "Now, suddenly, it's yes": Author interview with Eveline Herfkens, 7 June 1995.
     • "It shouldn't make a lot of difference": Author interview with David Beers, 18 July 1994.
     • Interest payments made by just five countries: 1993 IBRD income was $9.4 billion (World Bank Annual Report, 1993, p. 192). Interest payments by the five countries in 1993 totaled $3.5 billion (*World Debt Tables, 1994–95,* vol. 2). Debt service payments by the same five countries totaled $8 billion, 44 percent of all the debt service payments received by the Bank in 1993.
     • paid-in, usable capital and reserves of about $23 billion in 1995: Bretton Woods Commission, p. 187, World Bank Annual Report, 1995, p. 142.
     • "S&L crisis sitting out there": "Senate Budget Panel Chief Wants World Bank Loan Report," Dow Jones News Service, 15 February 1995.
     • "It is sitting in a shoebox": Author telephone interview with Jonathan Sanford, 25 September 1995.
325  • "asking for 20 or 30 billion dollars?": Author interview with Bank employee, 29 June 1995.
     • "it is approving a potential financial commitment": Canada, *Report of the Auditor-General,* p. 314.
     • the Organization of African Unity called on the Bank and the Fund: Solomon Gomes, special political affairs officer at OAU, quoted in Peter Alan Harper, "US–Africa Trade," Associated Press, 17 September 1993.
     • "cancel or substantially reduce": "Church Leaders Call for World Bank, IMF Reform," Reuters, 24 September 1994.
326  • "alleviate the crushing debts of the African nations": "Key Quotes from Pope's Blueprint for Africa," Reuters, 15 September 1995.
     • "part of the solution": World Bank, *Questions and Answers,* p. 25.
     • its $19 billion in reserves: This is the Bank's $15 billion in retained earnings, and the $3.7 billion it has set aside against possible loan losses. World Bank Annual Report, 1995, p. 157.
     • "writing off World Bank loans would hurt": World Bank, *Questions and Answers,* p. 25.
     • "the fragmented approach followed thus far": World Bank, *The Multilateral Debt Facility,* p. 2.
     • owe more than $115 billion: Ibid., p. 24.
     • an undefined portion—perhaps forty percent: Ibid., p. 25.
     • "regain the high ground on debt issues": Ibid., p. 8.
     • "affect its high credibility in financial markets": Ibid., p. 8, 15.
     • "break the armlock": Alver Carlson, "World Bank's Wolfensohn Calls for a New Compact," Reuters, 10 October 1995.
     • "sweeping privatization": Michael Prowse, "Wolfensohn's Task," *Financial Times,* 22 April 1996.
     • "kicked a big termite mound": Author interview with Bank staffer, 22 March 1996.

- "change management has been overmanaged": Patti Waldmeir, "Wolfensohn's Search for Global Relevance," *Financial Times,* 30 May 1996.
- "the lack of interpersonal generosity": Michael Holman and Patti Waldmeir, "World Bank Chief's Cry from the Heart," *Financial Times,* 29 March, 1996.
- "we can say that we care": Ibid.
- "we've lost our role": Author interview with Bank official, 16 April 1996.

327
- "some Bank staff also have doubts": "Mr. Wolfensohn's New Clients," *The Economist,* 20 April 1996.
- "The cognitive dissonance": Author interview with Bank employee, 6 May 1996.
- "become stuck in the bureaucratic cobweb": Author interview with Bank employee, 23 November 1995.
- "I just lock my door": Author interview with Bank official, 30 January 1996.
- "break though this glass wall": Michael Holman and Patti Waldmeir. "World Bank Chief Accuses Staff of Blocking Reforms," *Financial Times,* 29 March 1996.
- "Wolfensohn's more likely than previous presidents": Author interview with Brent Blackwelder, 30 January 1996.

# Epilogue

- 1.3 billion in absolute poverty: Rex Nutting, "Rich must aid poor, Wolfensohn says," United Press International, 10 October 1995.
- 80 percent of whom live in developing countries: *World Development Report 1995,* pp. 162–63.

330
- "many countries have done poorly": *World Development Report 1991,* p. 1.

331
- Bank figures show: Wolfensohn, James, Keynote Address to World Resources Institute, 2 October 1995, p. 4; and Murphy, Richard, "World Bank Dismisses Environmentalist Attacks," Reuters, 6 October 1994.
- The Bank defines poverty: *Latin America and the Caribbean,* p. 123.
- In 1948, the United Nations estimated: These figures have not been corrected to reflect purchasing power. United Nations, *Statistical Yearbook* (Lake Success, New York: United Nations Statistical Office), 1949, p. 21, 372; *World Bank Annual Report, 1947–1948,* p. 9.
- per capita income in the developing world: *World Development Report 1995,* p. 163.
- statistics on per capita income in rich and poor countries 1980–1990: United Nations Development Program, *Human Development Report,* 1993, pp. 142–43, 193, 213.
- By 1996, nineteen countries: "Rich and Poor Further Apart," *San Francisco Chronicle,* 15 July 1996.
- "will exacerbate inequality, while scarcely denting poverty": Goodland, Robert, and Herman Daly, *Ten Reasons Why Northern Income Growth Is Not the Solution to Southern Poverty,* internal paper, World Bank 17 July 1992, p. 7.
- statistics on average annual growth rates in rich and poor countries, 1980–1993: *World Development Report 1995,* pp. 162–63.

332
- infant death rate: United Nations Development Program, *Human Development Report* (New York: Oxford University Press), 1993, p. 213.
- the education gap: *Human Development Report 1993,* pp. 148, 214. The table from which these figures are taken, "Widening South-North Gaps," is omitted from the 1995 *Human Development Report.*
- per capita food supply figures: Ibid., pp. 142–43.
- more than half the countries: 49 out of 78 countries. Ibid., pp. 142–43.
- "a high degree of inequality": Robert McNamara, Speech to the Board of Governors, Nairobi, Kenya, 24 September 1973, p. 259.

- income distribution in developing countries: *Human Development Report 1995*, pp. 178–79.

333  • figures on safe water and sanitation: Ibid., pp. 166–67.
- Children in rural areas are only 80 percent as likely: *Human Development Report 1993*, p. 155.
- only half as many years of schooling as men: Ibid., p. 153.
- per capita income in OECD countries: Ibid., p. 202.
- 150 times greater: Korten, David, *Sustainability and the Global Economy*, presentation to The Environmental Grantmakers Association, 13 October 1994, pp. 6–7, citing *Human Development Report 1992*.
- "an achievable reality": *World Development Report 1991*, p. 1.

334  • "the most important challenge facing the human race": *World Development Report 1991*, p. 1.

335  • "the dependence of growth on a greater abundance of foreign exchange": Currie (1981), p. 15.
- "correlation between the amounts of aid received in the past": Quoted in Nossiter, p. 128.
- "poor countries are too poor to save anything": Pearson, p. 30.
- domestic savings financed 85 percent of investment: Pearson, pp. 30–31.
- the developing world saves and invests . . . at a higher rate: developing countries: savings, 22 percent; investment, 24 percent; U.S.: 15 percent and 16 percent, respectively; EEC: 22 percent and 19 percent. *Human Development Report 1995*, p. 212.
- received $167.8 billion in foreign loans: *World Debt Tables, 1996*, vol. 1, pp. 193–4.
- A 1968 paper by the World Bank: *Some Aspects of the Economic Philosophy of the World Bank*, Washington, DC: World Bank. 1968, p. 7.

336  • "the Marshall Plan aid was extended in grant form": Payer, Cheryl, *Lent and Lost* (London: Zed Books, 1991), p. 21.
- "Payment through the use of exports is quite unlikely": Dakin, pp. 234–36.

337  • "Please don't lend us any more money": Lajous, Adrian, "A Note to Mexico's Creditors: No More Loans Please," *Wall Street Journal*, 2 October 1987.
- "fast erosion of national self-respect": Mohammad Yunus, et al., *Report of the Task Force on Self-Reliance*, Dacca, Bangladesh, 10 February 1991, p. 1.
- "External assistance can weaken the resolve of governments": World Bank, *Towards Sustained Development in Subsaharan Africa*, Washington, DC: World Bank, 1984, p. 45, quoted in Nossiter, p. 111.
- "Aid increases the power": P. T. Bauer, *Equality, the Third World, and Economic Delusion* (London: Weidenfeld and Nicolson, 1981), p. 103.

338  • "you can't have development without somebody getting hurt": Adrian Cowell, producer, *The Price of Progress*. Central Television (London), 1986.

# Bibliography

The Bibliography is arranged as follows:
- General Bibliography
- World Bank Publications
  - Publications with no listed author (listed alphabetically by title)
  - Authored publications (listed alphabetically by author's last name)
  - Oral histories of members of the World Bank staff

Acheson, A. L. K., et al., eds. *Bretton Woods Revisited*. Toronto: University of Toronto Press, 1969.

Adams, Patricia. *Odious Debts*. London: Earthscan, 1991.

———. *The World Bank's Finances: An International S&L Crisis*. Washington, DC: Cato Institute, 1994.

Alecio, Rolando. "Uncovering the Truth: Political Violence and Indigenous Organizations." In *The New Politics of Survival*, edited by Minor Sinclair. New York: Monthly Review Press, 1995.

Allen, Frederick Lewis. *The Lords of Creation*. New York: Harper and Bros., 1935.

Alvares, Claude, and Ramesh Billorey. *Damming the Narmada*. Penang, Malaysia: Third World Network and Asia-Pacific People's Environmental Network, 1988.

Arenson, Karen. "World Bank Seen Increasing Its Capital." *New York Times*, 28 March 1979.

Arndt, H. W. *Economic Development: The History of an Idea*. Chicago: University of Chicago Press, 1987.

*Assault on World Poverty*. Baltimore: Johns Hopkins University Press, 1975.

Avramovic, Dragoslav, and Ravi Gulhati. *Debt Servicing Problems of Low-Income Countries 1956–58*. Baltimore: Johns Hopkins University Press (for the World Bank), 1960.

Avramovic, Dragoslav, et al. *Economic Growth and External Debt*. Baltimore: Johns Hopkins University Press (for the World Bank), 1964.

Ayres, Robert. *Banking on the Poor: The World Bank and the World's Poor*. Cambridge, MA: Massachusetts Institute of Technology, 1983.

Ball, Nicole. *Pressing for Peace: Can Aid Induce Reform?* Policy Essay No. 6. Washington, DC: Overseas Development Council, 1992.

Bandow, Doug, and Ian Vasquez. *Perpetuating Poverty.* Washington, DC: Cato Institute, 1994.

Barman, T. G. "Ivar Kreuger: His Life and Work," *Atlantic Monthly,* August 1932.

Baum, Warren C., and Stokes Tolbert. *Investing in Development.* New York: Oxford University Press (for the World Bank), 1985.

Black, Jan Knippers. *Development in Theory and Practice.* Boulder: Westview Press, 1991.

Blustein, Paul. "The World Bank Personified." *Washington Post,* 9 October 1995.

Bovard, James. *The World Bank vs. the World's Poor.* Washington, DC: Cato Institute, 1987.

Bretton Woods Commission. *Bretton Woods: Looking to the Future.* Washington: Bretton Woods Commission, July 1994.

Brown, Bartram S. *The United States and the Politicization of the World Bank.* London: Kegan Paul International, 1992.

Bryson, Christopher. "Guatemala: A Development Dream Turns into Repayment Nightmare." *Christian Science Monitor,* 1 May 1987.

Campbell, Horace. "Tanzania and the World Bank's Urban Shelter Project: Ideology and International Finance." *Review of African Political Economy* 42 (1988): pp. 5–18.

Canada. House of Commons. *Hearings Before the Sub-Committee on International Financial Institutions of the Standing Committee on Finance,* 11 May 1992.

Carosso, Vincent. *Investment Banking in America: A History.* Cambridge, MA: Harvard University Press, 1970.

Caufield, Catherine. *In the Rainforest.* New York: Alfred A. Knopf, 1984.

Cavanagh, John, et al., eds. *Beyond Bretton Woods.* London: Pluto Press, 1994.

Cernea, Michael, ed. *Putting People First.* New York: Oxford University Press (for the World Bank), 1991.

Chandler, Clay. "A Chorus of Critics Say the World Bank Has Hurt the Poor and the Environment." *Washington Post,* 18 June 1994.

———. "Peso Crisis Causes Global Financial Jitters." *Washington Post,* 1 February 1995.

Chenery, Hollis, et al. *Redistribution with Growth.* Oxford, UK: Oxford University Press, 1974.

Clark, Colin. *Conditions of Economic Progress.* London: Macmillan, 1940.

Clark, William. "Robert McNamara at the World Bank." *Foreign Affairs* 60, no. 1 (1981): 00–00.

"The Collapse of the Kreuger Legend." *The Literary Digest,* 7 May 1932.

Crittenden, Ann. "World Bank, in Shift, Lending for Trade Debts." *New York Times,* 26 May 1980.

Currie, Lauchlin. *The Basis of a Development Program for Columbia.* Baltimore: Johns Hopkins University Press, 1950.

———. *The Role of Economic Advisers in Developing Countries.* Westport, CT: Greenwood Press, 1981.

Dakin, Allin. "Foreign Securities in the American Money Market, 1914–1930." *Harvard Business Review,* January 1932.

Daly, Herman. *Steady-State Economics.* Washington, DC: Island Press, 1991.

Delamaide, Darrell. *Debt Shock.* New York: Doubleday, 1984.

Dennis, Lawrence. " 'Sold' on Foreign Bonds." *The New Republic.* Five-part series, 19 November–17 December 1930.

———. "What Overthrew Leguia." *The New Republic,* 17 September 1930.

Deo, R. C. Singh. "Venting Ire upon the Narmada." *Lokayan Bulletin* 9, no. 3/4 (1991): p. 60–64.

Eckes, Alfred E. *A Search for Solvency.* Austin: University of Texas Press, 1975.

Farnsworth, Clyde H. "Legislative Snags Peril Foreign Aid." *New York Times,* 10 December 1979.

———. "Treasury Official Defends World Bank." *New York Times,* 28 March 1979.

Farvar, M. T., and J. P. Milton, eds. *The Careless Technology.* Garden City, NY: Natural History Press, 1973.

Feinberg, Richard E., and Valeriana Kallab, eds. *Adjustment Crisis in the Third World.* New Brunswick, NJ: Transaction Books, 1984.

———. *Uncertain Future: Commercial Banks and the Third World.* New Brunswick, NJ: Transaction Books, 1984.

Feinberg, Richard E., et al. *Between Two Worlds: The World Bank's Next Decade.* New Brunswick, NJ: Transaction Books, 1986.

Feis, Herbert. *The Diplomacy of the Dollar.* New York: Norton, 1966.

Ferguson, James. *The Anti-politics Machine.* Minneapolis: University of Minnesota Press, 1994.

Finn, Edwin A. "When Wolfensohn Talks, Big Business Listens—Carefully." *Forbes,* 26 December 1988.

Fisher, William F., ed. *Toward Sustainable Development: Struggling over India's Narmada River.* Armonk, NY: M. E. Sharpe, Inc., 1995.

Fraser, Damian. "Mexico's Growing Intimacy with World Bank." *Financial Times,* 3 March 1992.

———. "The Poor Make Their Presence Felt." *Financial Times,* 17 and 19 February 1994.

Friedland, Jonathan. "Inside Job at the World Bank." *South,* September 1987.

———. "Unrest at the World Bank." *Institutional Investor,* September 1987.

Friedman, Irving. *The Emerging Role of Private Banks in the Developing World.* New York: Citicorp, 1977.

Gall, Norman. "Games Bankers Play." *Forbes,* 5 December 1983.

George, Susan, and Fabrizio Sabelli. *Faith and Credit.* Boulder: Westview Press, 1994.

Goldsmith, Edward, and Nicholas Hildyard. *The Social and Environmental Effects of Large Dams.* Camelford, UK: Wadebridge Ecological Centre, 1984.

Gwin, Catherine. *U.S. Relations with the World Bank 1945–1992.* Washington, DC: The Brookings Institution, 1994.

Gwynne, S. C. *Selling Money.* New York: Weidenfeld and Nicolson, 1986.

Hancock, Graham. *Lords of Poverty.* London: Macmillan, 1989.

Hanke, Steve, and Alan Walters. "The Wobbly Peso." *Forbes,* 4 July 1994.

Hart, David. *The Volta River Project.* Edinburgh: Edinburgh University Press, 1980.

Hartmann, Betsey, and James Boyce. "Bangladesh: Aid to the Needy?" *International Policy Report,* 4, no. 1 (1978).

Hartwig, Richard. *Roads to Reason: Transportation, Administration and Rationality in Colombia.* Pittsburgh: University of Pittsburgh Press, 1983.

Hayter, Theresa. *Aid As Imperialism.* London: Penguin Books, 1971.

Henry, James. "Where the Money Went." *The New Republic,* 14 April 1986.

Heredia, Carlos, and Mary E. Purcell. *The Polarization of Mexican Society.* Washington, DC: Development Group for Alternatives Policies, 1994.

Hirschman, Albert. *Development Projects Observed.* Washington, DC: The Brookings Institution, 1967.

Horsefield, J. Keith. *The International Monetary Fund 1945–1965.* Vol. 1. Washington, DC: International Monetary Fund, 1969.

"House Passes Foreign Aid Bill, Slashing Funds for World Bank." *New York Times.* 7 September 1979.

Howard, J. B., et al. *The Impact of International Organizations on Legal and Institutional Change in Developing Countries.* New York: International Legal Center, 1977.

Hughey, Ann. "Is the World Bank Biting Off More Than It Can chew?" *Forbes,* 26 May 1980.

*Human Development Report.* New York: Oxford University Press (for the United Nations Development Program), 1993, 1995.

"In Defense of Enslaving." *Lokayan Bulletin* 9, no. 3/4 (1991): pp. 98–103.

"Inside the World Bank: What They're Doing with Your Money Is a Crime." *Reason,* Spring 1989.

Isaacson, Walter, and Evan Thomas. *The Wise Men.* New York: Simon and Schuster, 1986.

Irwin, Michael. *Banking on Poverty: An Insider's Look at the World Bank.* Washington, DC: Cato Institute, 1990.

Ives, Jack. *Himalayan Dilemma*. London: Routledge and Kegan Paul, 1989.

"The Jan Vikas Sanghgarsh Yatra: A First Hand Account." *Lokayan Bulletin* 9, no. 3/4 (1991): pp. 65–78.

Jolly, Richard, et al. *Adjustment with a Human Face*. Oxford, UK: Clarendon Press, 1987.

Jorgensen, Erika, and Jeffrey Sachs. *Default and Renegotiation of Latin American Foreign Bonds in the Interwar Period*. Cambridge, MA: National Bureau of Economic Research, 1988.

Kaletsky, Anatole. "When a Shake-out Fails to Shape Up." *Financial Times,* 4 August 1987.

Kandell, Jonathan. "Undamming the World Bank." *Audubon Magazine,* May–June 1993.

King, John A. *Economic Development Projects and Their Appraisal*. Baltimore: John Hopkins University Press, 1967.

Klitgaard, Robert. *Tropical Gangsters*. New York: Basic Books, 1990.

Lappé, Frances Moore, and Joseph Collins. *Food First*. New York: Ballantine Books, 1978.

Lawyers Committee for Human Rights. *The World Bank: Governance and Human Rights*. New York: Lawyers Committee for Human Rights, 1993.

Lewis, Cleona. *America's Stake in International Investments*. Washington, DC: The Brookings Institution, 1938.

Lewis, John, et al. *Strengthening the Poor: What Have We Learned?* U.S. Third World Policy Perspectives, no. 10. Overseas Development Council. New Brunswick, NJ: Transaction Books, 1988.

Lilienthal, David. *The Journals of David Lilienthal*. New York: Harper and Row, 1964–1983.

Lilienthal, David E. "The Road to Change." *International Development Review,* December 1964.

Lissakers, Karin. "Dateline Wall Street: Faustian Finance." *Foreign Policy,* Fall 1983.

Lomax, David. *The Developing Country Debt Crisis*. New York: St. Martin's Press, 1986.

Loxley, John. "Structural Adjustment Programmes in Africa: Ghana and Zambia." *Review of African Political Economy,* (Spring, 1990).

Ludlow, Nicholas H. *The Development Bank Business Market*. Washington, DC: Development Bank Associates, 1993.

Maddux, John L. *The Development Philosophy of Robert S. McNamara*. Washington, DC: The World Bank, 1981.

Magdoff, Harry. "Third World Debt: Past and Present." *Monthly Review* 37, no. 9 (February 1986): pp. 1–10.

Makin, John H. *The Global Debt Crisis*. New York: Basic Books, 1984.

Maloney, Clarence. *Environmental and Project Displacement of Population in India*. Indianapolis: Universities Field Staff International, 1990–91.

Mason, Edward S., and Robert E. Asher. *The World Bank Since Bretton Woods*. Washington, DC: The Brookings Institution, 1973.

Mayer, Martin. *The Bankers*. New York: Weybright and Talley, 1974.

———. *The Money Bazaars*. New York: Dutton, 1984.

McCully, Patrick. *Sardar Sarovar Project: An Overview*. Berkeley, CA: International Rivers Network, 1994.

———. *Silenced Rivers*. London: Zed Press, 1996.

McKibben, Bill. *Hope, Human and Wild*. Boston: Little, Brown, 1995.

McNamara, Robert S. *The McNamara Years at the World Bank*. Baltimore: Johns Hopkins University Press, 1981.

Meiers, Gerald, and Dudley Seers, eds. *Pioneers in Development*. New York: Oxford University Press, 1984.

Moran, Emilio, ed. *Dilemma of Amazonian Development*. Boulder: Westview Press, 1983.

Morgan Guaranty Trust. "LDC Capital Flight." *World Financial Markets* (New York), March 1986.

Morris, James. *The Road to Huddersfield*. New York: Pantheon Books, 1963.

Morse, Bradford, et al. *Sardar Sarovar: The Report of the Independent Review*. Ottawa: Resource Futures International, 1992.

Mosley, Paul, et al. *Aid and Power*. 2 vols. London: Routledge, 1991.

"Multiple Impacts of the Sardar Sarovar Project." *Lokayan Bulletin* 9, no. 3/4 (1991): pp. 32–46.

Murphy, Kathleen. *Macroproject Development in the Third World*. Boulder: Westview Press, 1982, pp. 6, 13–17.

Narmada Ghati Navnirman Samiti. "News from the Narmada Valley." *Lokayan Bulletin* 8, no. 1 (1990): 00–00.

Nelson, Benjamin. *World Bank and IMF*. Washington, DC: Government Accounting Office. National Security and International Affairs Division, July 17, 1995.

Newman, Barry. "Missing the Mark." *Wall Street Journal*, 10 November 1977.

Nolan, Janne E., ed. *Global Engagement: Cooperation and Security in the 21st Century*. Washington, DC: The Brookings Institution, 1994.

Nossiter, Bernard. *The Global Struggle for More*. New York: Harper and Row, 1987.

Oliver, Robert. *Early Plans for a World Bank*. Princeton Studies in International Finance 29, 1971.

———. *George Woods and the World Bank*. Boulder: Lynne Rienner, 1995.

———. *International Economic Cooperation and the World Bank*. London: Macmillan, 1975.

Oppenheimer, Franz. "Don't Bank on the World Bank." *American Spectator*, October 1987.

Oxfam (UK). *Embracing the Future . . . Avoiding the Challenge of World Poverty*. London: Oxfam, July 1994.

Pal, Mahendra. *The World Bank and the Third World Countries of Asia*. New Delhi, 1985.

Paranjype, Vijay. "The Cultural Ethos." *Lokayan Bulletin* 9, no. 3/4 (1991): pp. 21–31.

———. *High Dams on the Narmada*. New Delhi: Indian National Trust for Art and Cultural Heritage, 1990.

Pastora, Manuel. "Latin American Debt Crisis and the IMF." *Latin American Perspectives*, Winter 1987.

Patel, C. C. *Sardar Sarovar Project: What It Is and What It Is Not*. Gujarat, India: Sardar Sarovar Narmada Nigam Ltd., 1991.

Payer, Cheryl. *Lent and Lost*. London: Zed Books, 1991.

———. *The World Bank*. New York: Monthly Review Press, 1982.

Pearce, David, and Jeremy Warford. *World Without End*. New York: Oxford University Press, 1993.

Pearson, Lester B., et al. *Partners in Development: Report of the Commission on International Development*. New York: Praeger, 1969.

Please, Stanley. *The Hobbled Giant*. Boulder: Westview Press, 1984.

Polak, Jacques. *The World Bank and the IMF*. Washington, DC: The Brookings Institution, 1994.

"Poor Kreuger." *Time*, 21 March 1932.

Pound, Edward, and Martin du Bois. "Cozy Ties: IMF, World Bank Aide Has Dealings Hinting at Conflict of Interest." *Wall Street Journal*, 29 December 1990.

———"Two Foes of Mobutu Demand Inquiry into de Groote's Ties to Zaire Regime." *Wall Street Journal*, 31 December 1990.

Ranis, Gustav. *Defining the Mission of the World Bank Group*. Paper prepared for Bretton Woods Commission, 1993.

Rattner, Steven. "Washington Watch: Cutting I.M.F.-World Bank Pay." *New York Times*, 19 May 1979.

Reed, David. *Structural Adjustment and the Environment*. Boulder: Westview Press, 1992.

Repetto, Robert. *Wasting Assets*. Washington, DC: World Research Institute, 1990.

Rich, Bruce. *Mortgaging the Earth*. Boston: Beacon Press, 1994.

Ringle, Ken. "Breaking Open the World Bank." *Washington Post*, 25 September 1990.

Rosenblum, Mort, and Doug Williamson. *Squandering Eden: Africa at the Edge*. New York: Harcourt Brace Jovanovitch, 1987.

Sachs, Wolfgang. "On the Archeology of the Development Idea." *Lokayan Bulletin* 8, no. 1 (1990).

Sampson, Anthony. *The Money Lenders*. New York: Viking Press, 1981.

Sanford, Jonathan E. *World Bank: Answers to 26 Frequent Questions*. Congressional Research Service, 1991.

———. *Multilateral Development Banks: Issues for Congress*. Congressional Research Service, 1995.

Schumer, Charles, and Alfred Watkins, "Faustian Finance." *The New Republic*, 11 March 1985.

Shapley, Deborah. *Promise and Power: The Life and Times of Robert McNamara*. Boston: Little, Brown, 1993.

Sklar, Leonard, and Patrick McCully. *Damming the Rivers: The World Bank's Lending for Large Dams*. Berkeley, CA: International Rivers Network, 1994.

Soule, George. *Prosperity Decade*. New York: Rinehart, 1947.

Stein, Howard, and Nafziger, E. Wayne. "Structural Adjustment, Human Needs, and the World Bank Agenda." *Journal of Modern African Studies* 29, no. 1 (1991).

Summers, Lawrence. "Research Challenges for Development Economists." *Finance and Development*, September 1991.

Swardson, Anne, and Martha M. Hamilton. "Investment Funds Link Economies." *Washington Post*, 20 August 1995.

Sweeney, Paul. "Who's in Charge at the World Bank?" *Global Finance*, September 1993.

Taylor, Lance. *Varieties of Stabilization Experience*. Oxford, UK: Clarendon Press, 1988.

Tendler, Judith. *Electric Power in Brazil: Entrepreneurship in the Public Sector*. Cambridge, MA: Harvard University Press, 1968.

Thomas, Vinod, et al., eds. *Restructuring Economies in Distress*. New York: Oxford University Press, 1991.

"Three Multinational Banks Criticized." *New York Times*, 22 March 1979.

Trainer, Ted. *Developed to Death*. London: Green Print, 1989.

Truman, Harry S *Memoirs*. Vol. 2, *Years of Trial and Hope*. New York: Doubleday, 1956.

Ullmann, Owen. "Breaking the Bank." *Washingtonian*, October 1995.

Ulman, Neil. "Eager Lenders." *Wall Street Journal*, 24 November 1972.

UNICEF. *The State of the World's Children*. Oxford, UK: Oxford University Press, 1989.

United Nations. *Proceedings and Documents: UN Monetary and Financial Conference, Bretton Woods, New Hampshire*. New York: UN Information Office, 1945.

———. *Money and the Postwar World*. New York: UN Information Office, 1945.

United States Treasury. *The Bretton Woods Proposals*. Washington, DC: US Treasury, 1945.

U.S. Congress. Subcommittee on International Development Institutions and Finance, of the House Committee on Banking, Finance and Urban Affairs. *Environmental Impact of Multilateral Development Bank-Funded Projects*. 98th Cong., 1st sess., 1983.

———. Senate Committee on Finance. *Sale of Foreign Bonds or Securities in the U.S.* 4 parts.

Van der Laar, Art. *The World Bank and the Poor*. Boston: M. Nijhoff, 1980.

*Wall Street Journal.* "Foreign Aid's Industrialized Poverty," 8 November 1989.

Weaver, James H. *The International Development Association*. New York: Praeger, 1965.

Wilkinson, Tracy. "In Still-Violent Guatemala, a Brave Search for Justice." *Los Angeles Times*, 2 January 1995.

Winkler, Max. "Playing with Matches." *The Nation*, 25 May 1932.

"World Bank and IMF Loans Going to Bail Out Big Banks." *New York Times*, 1 March 1981.

Wriston, Walter. "Banking Against Disaster." *New York Times*, 14 September 1982.


## World Bank Documents (No Author Listed)


*Adjustment in Africa*. World Bank Policy Research Report, 1993.

*Adjustment Lending: An Evaluation of Ten Years of Experience*. Country Economics Department, Policy and Research Series, no. 1, 1988.

*Adjustment Lending and Mobilization of Private and Public Resources for Growth.* Country Economics Department, Policy and Research Series, no. 22, 1992.

*Adjustment Lending: Policies for Sustainable Growth.* Country Economics Department, Policy and Research Series, no. 14, 1990.

Annual Reports for the years 1944–94. Washington, DC: World Bank. 1946–96.

*Annual Report on Operations Evaluation (FY91).* Operations Evaluation Department, Report No. 9925 (restricted distribution), 18 September 1991.

*Annual Report on Operations Evaluation (FY93).* Operations Evaluation Department, Report No. 12389 (restricted distribution), 8 October 1993.

*Annual Report on Portfolio Performance (FY94).* Washington, DC: World Bank, 1995.

*Annual Review of Evaluation Results.* For the years 1988–93. Washington, DC: Operations Evaluation Department, 1990–95.

*Annual Review of Project Performance Audit Results.* For the years 1973–87. Washington, DC: Operations Evaluation Department, 1975–89.

*Bank Experience in Project Supervision.* Washington, DC: Operations Evaluation Department, 30 April 1992.

*Bank Operations in Colombia: An Evaluation.* Operations Evaluation Department, Report no. Z-18 (confidential), 25 May 1972.

*Commitments Detail Report—IBRD and IDA Lending, July 1946–March 1994.* Computer disc. Washington, DC: World Bank, 1994.

*Contributing to Development.* Washington, DC: International Finance Corporation, 1992.

*The East Asian Miracle: Economic Growth and Public Policy.* A World Bank Policy Research Paper. New York: Oxford University Press, 1993.

*Effective Implementation: Key to Development Impact* ("The Wapenhans Report"). Report of the World Bank's Portfolio Management Task Force. Washington, DC: World Bank, 1992.

*Effectiveness of SAL Supervision and Monitoring.* Operations Evaluation Department Report No. 9711 (restricted distribution), 24 June 1991.

*Factors Affecting IBRD Lending in the Eighties and Implications for the Nineties.* Financial Policy and Risk Management Department, August 1992.

*Financial Intermediation Policy Paper.* World Bank Industry Department, 8 July 1985.

*Forestry Development: A Review of Bank Experience.* Washington, DC: Operations Evaluation Department, 22 April 1991.

*IDA in Retrospect.* Oxford, UK: Oxford University Press (for the World Bank), 1982.

*IFC and the Environment, Annual Review 1992.* Washington, DC: International Finance Corporation, 1992.

*India Irrigation Sector Review.* Vol. 1. Agriculture Operations Division, India Country Department, Report No. 9518-N (restricted distribution), 27 June 1991.

*Latin America and the Caribbean: A Decade After the Debt Crisis.* Washington, DC: World Bank, September 1993.

*Mainstreaming the Environment.* Washington, DC: World Bank, 1995.

*Making Development Sustainable.* Washington, DC: World Bank, 1994.

*Managing Development: The Governance Dimension.* A World Bank Discussion Paper. Washington, DC: World Bank (restricted distribution), 26 June 1991, p. 6.

*The Multilaterial Debt Facility for Heavily Indebted Poor Countries.* Unpublished paper, 25 July 1995.

*Nepal Settlement Project, Project Performance Audit Report.* Operations Evaluation Department, Report No. 4567 (restricted distribution), 20 June 1983.

*Project Performance Audit Report.* South Bassein (India) Offshore Gas Development Project. Operations Evaluation Department, Report No. 10839 (restricted distribution), 29 June 1992.

*Process Review of the FY93 Annual Report on Portfolio Performance.* Operations Evaluation Department, Report No. 12858 (restricted distribution), 18 March 1994.

*Process Review of the FY94 Annual Report on Portfolio Performance.* Operations Evaluation Department, Report No. 14068 (restricted distribution), 22 March 1995.

*Questions and Answers.* Washington, DC: External Affairs Department, April 1995.
*Resettlement and Development.* Washington, DC: Environment Department, 8 April 1994.
*Response to Statements of Environmental Organizations sent by the U.S. Executive Director.* Unpublished. 11 January 1984.
*Rural Development: World Bank Experience, 1965–86.* Washington, DC: Operations Evaluation Department, 1988.
*Statement of Development Credits and Statement of Loans.*
*Structural Adjustment Lending: A First Review of Experience.* Washington, DC: Operations Evaluation Department, Report No. 6409, 24 September 1986.
*Trade Policy Reforms Under Adjustment Programs.* Operations Evaluation Department, 1992.
"The Wapenhans Report." See *Effective Implementation: Key to Development Impact.*
*The World Bank Group and the Environment, Fiscal 1992.* Washington, DC: World Bank, 1992.
*The World Bank Group and the Environment, Fiscal 1993.* Washington, DC: World Bank, 1993.
*World Bank Structural and Sectoral Adjustment Operations.* Operations Evaluation Department, Report No. 10870 (restricted distribution), 30 June 1992.
*World Bank Support for Industrialization in Korea, India, and Indonesia.* Washington, DC: Operations Evaluation Department, February 1991.
*World Debt Tables.* For the years 1968–94. Washington, DC: World Bank, 1970–96.
*World Debt Tables.* Data on diskette. For the fiscal years 1991–92 to 1993–94. Washington, DC: World Bank.
*World Development Report.* For the years 1976–94. New York: Oxford University Press (for the World Bank), 1978–96.
*Zaire: Appraisal of the Oil Palm Project.* Eastern Africa Projects Department, Report No. 1592-ZR (restricted distribution), 29 March 1978.
*Zaire Oil Palm Project: Project Completion Report.* Agriculture Operations, Africa Regional Office, Report No. 9598 (restricted distribution), 24 May 1991.


## World Bank Publications with Authors

Briscoe, John. "*Poverty and Water Supply: How to Move Forward.*" Finance and Development Department, December 1992.
Butcher, David. *A Review of the Treatment of Environmental Aspects of Bank Energy Projects.* Energy Series, Industry and Energy Department Working Paper No. 24, March 1990.
Cohen, Michael. *Learning by Doing: World Bank Lending for Urban Development, 1972–82.* Washington, DC: World Bank, 1983.
Gordon, David. *Development Finance Companies, State and Privately Owned.* World Bank Staff Working Paper No. 578, 1983.
Harbison, Ralph, and Eric Hanushek. *Educational Performance of the Poor.* New York: Oxford University Press (for the World Bank), 1992.
International Bank for Reconstruction and Development. Articles of Agreement (as amended, effective 16 February 1989). Washington, DC: World Bank.
Malloch Brown, Mark. *Communications Strategy Update.* World Bank Office Memorandum, 3 May 1995.
Marsden, Keith, and Therese Belot. *Private Enterprises in Africa.* World Bank Discussion Paper 17, 1987.
Nellis, John. *Public Enterprises in Sub-Saharan Africa.* World Bank Discussion Paper 1, 1986.
Pohl, Gerhard, and Dubravko Mihaljek. *Project Evaluation in Practice: A Statistical Analysis of Rate of Return Divergences of 1,015 World Bank Projects.* Washington, DC: World Bank, December 1989.
Salmen, Lawrence F. *Beneficiary Assessment.* Environment Department, Social Assessment Series, no. 23, July 1995.
———. *Reducing Poverty.* Poverty and Social Policy Series, no. 1, 1992.

Spottswood, A. D. *The Evolution of Project Appraisals and the Projects Department* (typescript). World Bank/IFC Archives, January 1970.

Wapenhans, Willi. "Oral Briefing of the JAC [Joint Audit Commission] at Its Meeting on 22 June 1992 on the Portfolio Management Task Force."

Yaron, Jacob. *Assessing Development Finance Institutions: A Public Interest Analysis.* World Bank Discussion Paper No. 174, 1992.

## Oral Histories

These oral histories are available in the office of the World Bank Archives. Some are also in the Oral History Collection of Columbia University.

Aldewereld, Simon. (Interview I) Interviewer: Robert Oliver, 2 November 1985.

Aldewereld, Simon. (II) Interviewer: Robert Oliver, 6 November 1985.

Baum, Warren. Interviewer: Robert Oliver, 23 July 1986.

Benjenk, Munir. Interviewer: Robert Oliver, 18 November 1985.

Black, Eugene. Interviewer: Robert Oliver, 1961.

Boskey, Shirley. Interviewer: Robert Oliver, 14 July 1986.

Cairncross, Sir Alexander, and William Diamond. Interviewer: Charles Ziegler, 10 January 1985.

Chenery, Hollis. Interviewer: Robert Asher, 27 January 1983.

Collado, Emilio. (I) Interviewers: T. Wilson and R. McKinzie, 7 July 1971.

Collado, Emilio. (II) Interviewer: Richard McKinzie, 11 July 1974.

Ferrer, Jose Figueres. Interviewers: D. R. McCoy and Richard McKinzie, 8 July 1970.

Friedman, Irving. (I) Interviewer: Robert Oliver, March 1974.

Friedman, Irving. (II) Interviewer: Robert Oliver, 15 July 1985.

Friedman, Irving. (III) Interviewer: Robert Oliver, 21 June 1986.

Garner, Robert L. Interviewer: Robert Oliver, 19 July 1961.

Grenfell, Julian. Interviewer: Robert Oliver, 15 July 1986.

Haralz, Jonas. Interviewers: William Becker and David Milobsky, 11 November 1993.

Kamarck, Andrew. Interviewer: Robert Oliver, 2 November 1985.

King, Benjamin. Interviewer: Robert Oliver, 24 and 25 July 1986.

Knapp, J. Burke. (I) Interviewer: Richard D. McKinzie, 24 and 30 July 1975.

Knapp, J. Burke. (II) Interviewer: Robert Asher, 6 and 29 October 1981.

Knapp, J. Burke. (III) Interviewer: Robert Oliver, 5 September 1986.

Lee, James. Interviewer: Bogomir Chokel, 1985.

Lieftinck, Peter. (I) Interviewer: Robert Oliver, 19 November 1985.

Lieftinck, Peter. (II) Interviewer: Charles Zeigler, 5 February 1987.

Machado, Luis. Interviewer: Robert Oliver, 18 July 1961.

Maehlum, Jorunn. Interviewers: William Becker and Jochen Kraske, 22 June 1994.

Maffry, August. Interviewer: Richard D. McKinzie, 19 January 1973.

McKitterick, Nathaniel M. Interviewer: Robert Oliver, 24 July 1985.

Please, Stanley. Interviewer: Charles Ziegler, 26 August 1986.

Rajagopalan, Visvanathan. Interviewers: William Becker and David Milobsky, 10 June 1993.

Rosenstein-Rodan, Paul. Interviewer: Robert Oliver, 1961.

Rotberg, Eugene. Interviewers: William Becker and David Milobsky, 22 April 1994.

Stanton, William. Interviewer: Robert Oliver, 16 July 1986.

Ul Haq, Mahbub. Interviewer: Robert Asher, 3 December 1982.

Waterston, Albert. Interviewer: Bogomir Chokel, 14 May 1985.

Weiner, Mervyn L. Interviewer: Robert Oliver, 16 and 17 July 1986.

Westebbe, Richard. Interviewer: Robert Oliver, 25 January 1988.

# Index

and Clausen policy, 144
consultant contracts, 249
contracts vs. contributions to Bank, 243
foreign aid, and GNP, 318–19
and debt forgiveness, 330
early debts and state defaults, 31–32
early foreign bond sales, 31–32, 34, 38, 39
and Eurodollar market, 127
IDA contribution agreement of 1996, 319–20
and IFC creation and contributions, 67–68
Mexican loan guarantees, 155–57
as model of development, 335
and Narmada project, 23, 28
per capita income, 90
and Peru's arrears, 322
political influence on Bank, 197–205
and private lending, 139
pushes for Akosombo Dam, 80
trade deficit, 158
voting share, 43
U. S. Agency for International Development, 271
U. S. Congress, 158, 178, 197, 198–205, 366n
and capital appropriations, 327–28
and complaint review, 267
and environment and social policy, 170–72
IDA funding debate, 315–20
and information policy, 265–66
and project audits, 254
U. S. House of Representatives, 23, 47, 170–71, 174, 198, 200, 233, 315, 316, 319
U. S. Senate, 32, 44, 45, 172, 198, 315, 316
Urban Department, 229
Urban poor
and economic reforms, 161–62
ERR in projects for, 220–21
McNamara projects for, 121–25
and resettlement standards, 229, 263
Urban renewal projects, 122, 263, 338
Urban transport loans, 288
Uruguay, 74
Uzbekistan, 277, 327

Varma, S. C., 20–21
Venezuela, 45, 215
adjustment programs protests, 161
blockade, 138
dam projects, 74
foreign debt estimates, 131
IFC loans, 277

and private capital, 291
urban poor projects, 220–21
Venture capital funds, 278
Victoria, Lake, 186
Vietnam, 286, 385n
embargo on loans, 200
loan of 1978, 199–99
War, 96, 97, 104, 198
"Villagization," 206–7, 210–11
Vinson, Fred, 47
Volcker, Paul, 201, 306
Volta Aluminum company (Valco), 82
Volta River Project, 79–83

Wages
and adjustment programs, 161, 162
Mexican, and 1995 crisis, 155, 156, 161
Turkish, 147, 148, 149
Waigel, Theo, 316
WALHI (environmental group), 285
Wallis, Stewart, 318
Wall Street, 51, 52–53, 54, 70, 98
Wall Street Journal, 124, 127, 143, 156, 199, 212, 240, 245–46, 338
Walters, Sir Alan, 152, 278
Wapenhans, Willi, 79, 179, 214, 217–18, 239, 252, 254, 298, 301, 324
report on failing projects, 257–61, 312
Ward, Barbara, 79, 305
War reparations, 40–41
Washington Post, 154, 157, 189, 205, 305, 311
Water and Sanitation Policy Unit, 296
Water projects
charging poor for, 296
discouraged by Bank, 63–65
evaluations, 293
McNamara and, 106
need for, 19–20, 332, 334
Woods and, 92
Waters, Maxine, 156
Waterston, Albert, 61
"Wealth index," 223
Webb, Richard, 168
Weiner, Mervyn, 219
West, Gerald, 285
West Bengal, India, 252
Westebbe, Richard, 87
West Indies, 167
Westinghouse, 319
Weyerhaeuser, 319
Wheat, 21
White, Harry Dexter, 39–40, 41, 42, 47, 49
Wilde, Oscar, 131

~ author of *In the Rainforest* and
~ionment correspondent for Britain's *New*
~er work has appeared in *The New Yorker* and
~ves in northern California.